THE

LIFE AND CHARACTER

OF

JOHN PAUL JONES,

The Chev PAUL-JONES

THE

LIFE AND CHARACTER

OF

JOHN PAUL JONES,

A CAPTAIN IN THE UNITED STATES NAVY.

DURING THE

REVOLUTIONARY WAR.

BY JOHN HENRY SHERBURNE,

Author of "The European Tourist's Guide;" "Naval Sketches;" "Erratic Poems;" "Etiquette," "Osceola, a Tragedy;" "John Adams's Administration, from 1797 to 1801," &c., &c.

"*Spectemur agendo.*"—Let us be tried by our actions.

SECOND EDITION.

NEW YORK:
ADRIANCE, SHERMAN & CO., PUBLISHERS,
NO. 2 ASTOR HOUSE.
MDCCCLI.

R. Craighead, Printer and Stereotyper,
112 *Fulton street, New York.*

TO THE

Honorable William A. Graham,

SECRETARY OF THE UNITED STATES NAVY,

THIS HISTORICAL NAVAL WORK,

FROM THE

ORIGINAL MANUSCRIPTS,

IS MOST RESPECTFULLY INSCRIBED,

AS A SLIGHT TRIBUTE TO HIS TALENTS AS A STATESMAN, AS WELL AS THE ESTEEM AND HIGH REGARDS OF

THE AUTHOR.

LETTERS

From the late President Thomas Jefferson, President James Madison, Judge Story, of the U. S. Supreme Court, the late Mathew Carey, Esq., of Philadelphia, and the Hon. William A. Graham, Secretary of the Navy, to the Author, relative to Paul Jones.

Monticello, February 14, 1825.

DEAR SIR,

During my residence in Paris, I was much acquainted with Commodore John Paul Jones, whose life you propose to write, and had much to do with him ; yet my memory is so decayed that from that source I can furnish you nothing worth a place in his history. I believe I cannot better comply with your request than by sending you ***all*** the papers relating to him in my possession. His letters to me, ***which are many,*** will probably throw some lights, which you may not possess, on his occupation during that period. His death happened after I left Paris, and I presume you know that the National Assembly, then sitting, expressed ***their respect*** for him by ***wearing mourning.*** I shall be glad if what I furnish may add anything to the establishment of that ***fame*** which ***he truly merited.***

Be pleased to accept for yourself the assurance of my great respect,

THOMAS JEFFERSON.

Montpelier, April 28, 1825.

DEAR SIR,

I have received your letter of the 23d instant, inclosing a copy of your prospectus of a biography of *John Paul Jones.* The subject you have chosen for your pen, gives you an opportunity of doing *justice* to an *individual* whose *heroism* will fill a brilliant page in the history of the American Revolution.

I am sorry it is not in my power to add to the materials you have derived from other sources. I must regret, also, that my personal acquaintance with Captain Jones was so slight and transient, that I ought not to attempt a view of his character. His bust, by Houdon, is an exact likeness ; pourtraying well the characteristic features stamped on the countenance of the original.

Whenever you may find it convenient to make the visit to Mrs. Madison and myself, as recommended by your father and your uncle, Governor John Langdon, our welcome of you will be the more cordial, as it will at the same time manifest our friendly recollections of both of them.

With our respects and good wishes,

JAMES MADISON.

COL. JOHN H. SHERBURNE,
Washington City.

Washington City, February 17, 1825.

DEAR SIR,

General La Fayette not having your address, has sent me the papers herewith inclosed, relative to Captain John Paul Jones, requesting them to be delivered to you.

Yours, very respectfully,

JOSEPH STORY.

LETTER from the late Mathew Carey, Esq., to the Author, expressing his great astonishment and agreeable surprise in reading the "Life of Paul Jones," whom he always thought to be a *freebooter* in the American Revolution, until reading the documentary history of the hero's life.

Philadelphia, November 25, 1825.

MY DEAR SIR,

I have read with intense interest your "*Life of John Paul Jones,*" and it must be regarded as a valuable *national* object, placing, as it does, in strong relief, the shining qualities of this hero, not only as a *naval commander*, but as a *profound politician*. The latter quality appears clearly and distinctly in various parts of his correspondence, wherein are developed views of the proper policy of this country, which are worthy of the first statesmen that sat in the Congress of 1774 and 1775, men *never* exceeded in the annals of the world for *sagacity, patriotism,* and *public spirit*.

No man has been the subject of more gross and shocking abuse, and none of those who have distinguished themselves in the Revolution were so little known as *he* has been to the nation to whose service he devoted all the energies of his magnanimous soul. I confess, for one, I always regarded *Paul Jones* as very few degrees above a *freebooter,* who, in the prospect of plunder, was reckless of his life. I am now thoroughly *undeceived,* and consider him as deserving a conspicuous rank among the most *illustrious* of those heroes and statesmen who not only formed a wreath around the brow of this country, but secured her a prouder destiny than ever fell to the lot of any other portion of mankind. The lion-like courage of *Paul Jones* was by no means the first of his qualities. Candor obliges me to say that the *mechanical execution* of the work is far from being worthy of the subject, which I presume you will remedy in a *second edition,* which, for the honor of the country, I hope will meet with encouragement.

Yours very truly, &c.,

MATHEW CAREY.

COL. JOHN H. SHERBURNE,
Register of the Navy Department,
Washington City.

Navy Department, March 27, 1851.

SIR,

I have the pleasure to acknowledge the receipt of your letter of the 26th instant, accompanying the steel engraving of the head of that model of naval heroes, *John Paul Jones.*

The accessories with which it is embellished are highly appropriate and instructive; and I doubt not the whole picture will be esteemed a valuable addition to the work it is intended to illustrate.

I am, sir, with high respect,

Your ob't servant,

WILLIAM A. GRAHAM,

Secretary of the Navy.

COL. JOHN H. SHERBURNE,
2 *Astor House, New York.*

INTRODUCTION.

It is in the revolutions of empires that truly great men make themselves known. In the tranquil scenes of peace the human intellect, with little excitement, and without a grand object, is inert, exhausted in common pursuits, or wastes itself in placid contemplation, or in the pleasures of life. When powerful sentiments animate the heart, and enlightened views direct us to the attainment of benefits calculated to secure the freedom, happiness, and prosperity of the human race, the soul expands, the mental faculties assume their natural proportion and energy, and, in defiance of the artificial distinctions of society, genius and talents, however originally obscure, burst from concealment, shine with resplendent lustre, and manifest themselves in actions which command the esteem and admiration of the world. The history of all nations, ancient as well as modern, attests the truth of this assertion; and France, in particular, within the last thirty-five years, furnishes proof in abundance, that whatever distinctions are created by systems of social order, in behalf of birth and fortune, nature distributes her favors without regard to wealth or rank.

Of all the political revolutions, the incidents of which are recorded in the annals of nations, that of the British American Colonies was the most daring and manly. In other instances, the poverty of an exchequer, the feebleness of a sovereign or ministry, or the derangement of public affairs, has been seized upon as affording a favorable opportunity for emancipation and independence. But in that of the British American Colonies, the people vindicated their rights, and contended for their liberties, when Great Britain was the preponderating power of Europe; when she had men of the first capacity in the cabinet, illustrious warriors in the field, a navy which defied the fleets of all other powers, and pecuniary resources over which her treasury had unlimited control. Notwithstanding these prodigious advantages, the people of the Colonies did not hesitate to remonstrate, to resist encroachments, and finally to appeal to arms. They did not disguise from themselves the fearful odds of such an encounter, but relying on the justice of their cause, on the Divine protection, and on the intelligence of their community, they firmly supported their claims, triumphed over the formidable armaments of Great Britain, and established their title to unrestricted sovereignty, with a courage and a constancy which have been acknowledged and applauded in every quarter of the globe.

The generous devotion which the people of the colonies exhibited in the cause of freedom, attracted the sympathy of patriotic and liberal minds in France, in Germany, and even in Scotland, England, and Ireland, from which the united Colonies derived a vast moral force. Individuals from each of those counties resorted to the standard of America, previously, as well as subsequently to the declaration of independence. The Marquis de la Fayette, the Barons Steuben and De Kalb, General Montgomery, and Lord Stirling, are names familiar to the ears of the Fathers of the Revolution and their descendants. To these may be added that of John Paul Jones, whose chivalric spirit and undaunted valor, whose active disposition and nautical skill were themes of eulogy at the court of Versailles, matter of astonishment and jealousy to that of

London, and whose reputation and renown spread terror on the seas, and along the shores of Great Britain and Ireland.

The naval strength of the British Empire being pre-eminent, the efforts to be made by America on the ocean, were proportionally more difficult and dangerous than those on the land, which, nevertheless, were sufficiently arduous. The services of John Paul Jones, consequently, were highly valuable; and it will be found, in the succeeding pages, that Congress duly appreciated them. He was an experienced navigator, and had an exactness of penetration which enabled him, almost instinctively, to discriminate between what was merely of doubtful execution, and what was wholly impracticable. Hence he was generally successful in his enterprises, scarcely ever failing in an undertaking or expedition, unless through the jealousy or disobedience of others, or the inclemency of the weather.

The labors of John Paul Jones for the furtherance of the American cause, were incessant. Whether in port or at sea, he was indefatigable. He had a genius prone to adventure, and of all the naval commanders of that day, he planned and executed, both in America and in Europe, the most annoying expeditions against the enemy. Such was his intrepidity that he was appalled by no peril, however great, and his presence of mind never forsook him, even in the most sudden and extraordinary emergencies. No one was more deeply embued with a conviction of the vital consequences of the contest to mankind, and no person felt a more honest zeal for its successful issue. His correspondence evinces that he foresaw the glorious destinies of the new American nation, even whilst it was struggling into existence. He was not in the least tainted with the vice of avarice; and, with him, money was uniformly a consideration secondary to the promotion of the public welfare. Tenacious of the rights of those under his command, and as just as he was generous, he enjoyed the friendship and favor of men of probity and honor everywhere. He was not merely countenanced, but caressed at the French court, and kings, nobles, ministers, and ladies of fashion and influence did not hesitate to reward and sustain him for his brilliant exertions against the marine of England, and her commerce.

The character of John Paul Jones has been much misrepresented by those who have heretofore undertaken to write his life. They have, for the most part, depicted him as a plunderer, a pirate, cruel and unprincipled. The venal British press and British antipathies have been the source of his defamation. The present work, written from authentic documents, will redeem his name from the odium hitherto cast upon it. An attentive perusal will satisfy the reader that he was a man of close observation, of profound reflection, and that his style is that of an individual of good ordinary English education, which, indeed, is common to the youth of all classes in Scotland. His correspondence indicates plain sense, without affectation; and, in some passages, it will be discovered that he was not altogether deficient in the sentimental and more refined species of writing. His character, in truth, had a cast of the romantic in it, which gives to the history of his life a most interesting and agreeable complexion. As one of our earliest naval heroes, he merits the respect and veneration of every citizen of the United States; and the statesman and politician, as well as the officers and seamen of our gallant navy, will discover in the incidents of his eventful career, illustrations of occurrences in our revolutionary war, which may enlighten their judgments, and furnish an example worthy of imitation.

THE

LIFE AND CHARACTER

OF

JOHN PAUL JONES.

JOHN PAUL JONES was the son of Mr. John Paul, a respectable gardener. He was born at Arbigland, in the parish of Kirbean, and stewartry of Kirkcudbright, in the month of July, 1747, and received the rudiments of his education at the parochial school. The contiguity of his residence to the shore of the Solway Firth, inspired him with an early predilection for a seafaring life; and while yet a mere child, he hoisted his flag on board his mimic ship, and issued audible mandates to his imaginary officers and crew, with all the consequence of a legitimate commander. Nor was he content with this. As his skill in manœuvring improved, he ventured to criticise the nautical knowledge of practical sailors; and in the eager and confident tone with which, from the eminence on which he took his station, he thundered forth his orders to the vessels which were entering the port at Carse-thorn, might be remarked the ardent and enterprising mind of one who felt that he was born to future command.

His partiality to a sailor's life was so determined that his friends resolved to indulge it; and accordingly, at the age of twelve, he was sent across the Firth to Whitehaven, where he was bound apprentice to Mr. Younger, a respectable merchant in the American trade. His first voyage was made on board the Friendship, Captain Benson. His course was steered for the Rappahannoc, and before he had completed his thirteenth year, he landed on the shores of that country which he was destined to adopt as his own. His home, while the ship was in port, was the house of an elder brother, who, having married a native of Virginia, had previously settled there. Here his early prepossessions in favor of America were confirmed, and from that period it had become the country of his fond election.

Our adventurer, being at length freed from the trammels of apprenticeship, made several voyages to foreign ports, and in the year 1773, again went to Virginia to arrange the affairs of his brother, who had died there without leaving any family; and about this time, in addition to his original surname, he assumed the *patronymic* of Jones, his father's christian-name having been John. This custom, which is of classical authority, has long been prevalent in Wales, and in various other countries, although it is not practised in that part of the island in which he was born.

This visit revived and riveted the attachment which young Paul Jones had conceived for America; and in spite of the native ardor and restless activity of his mind, he resolved to withdraw from the vicissitudes of a sea-faring life, to fix his residence in the country, and to devote the remainder of his days to retirement and study. He was little aware of the turbulent scenes in which he was soon to perform a part, nor of the conspicuous figure he was to make in them.

The discontents of the colonists had by this time occasioned much commotion, and their murmurs became daily deeper and more frequent, till at last they broke off all connexion with the parent country. Towards the latter part of the year 1775, it was determined by Congress to fit out a naval force to assist in the defence of American independence, and an anxious search was made for friends to the cause who should be at once able and willing to act as officers on board their vessels. It now appeared that Jones had, in his romantic schemes of tranquil enjoyment, falsely estimated the natural bent of his genius. With deep interest he had watched the progress of those political events which were to decide the fate of his adopted country; and, when an open resistance was made to the dominion of Britain, he could no longer remain an inactive spectator. Having only just completed his twenty-eighth year, he was full of bodily vigor and of mental energy, and he conceived that his nautical skill would qualify him to be a distinguished assertor of the rights of the colonists. He was appointed, on the 22d of December, 1775, first lieutenant of the Alfred, and on board that vessel, before Philadelphia, he hoisted the flag of independent America with his own hands, *the first time it was ever displayed.**

The following resolution, taken from the Journals of Congress, verifies the fact of his having been one among the first of those who were selected to vindicate the rights of the country at sea:

In Congress, 22d Dec. 1775.

Resolved, That the following naval officers be appointed:

Ezek. Hopkins, Esq., Commander-in-Chief of the fleet.

Dudley Saltonstall, Captain of the Alfred.

Abraham Whipple, " Columbus.

Nicholas Biddle, " Andrew Doria.

John B. Hopkins, " Cabot.

1*st Lieutenants*,—John Paul Jones, Rhodes Arnold, —— Stansbury, Hersted Hacker, Jonathan Pitcher.

2*d Lieutenants*,—Benjamin Seabury, Joseph Olney, Elisha Warner, Thomas Weaver, —— McDougall.

* The account of Jones, thus far, has been taken from the Edinburgh Encyclopedia, and as the author learned from the late Mr. Lowden, the nephew of Jones, was written from the lips of Mr. Lowden's mother for that work by Dr. Duncan, of Dumfries, Scotland.

3d Lieutenants,—John Fanning, Ezekiel Burroughs, Daniel Vaughan.

Resolved, That the pay of the commander-in-chief of the fleet be one hundred and twenty-five dollars per month.

Some time was necessary to the equipment of the fleet, but the subjoined extract of a letter written by Lieut. Jones to the Hon. Mr. Hewes, then an influential member of Congress from North Carolina, demonstrates that the newly appointed officers were not idle. They received their commissions the latter part of December, 1775, and on the 17th of the succeeding February they put to sea:

"When I undertook to write you an account of our proceedings in the fleet, I did not imagine that I should have been so stinted in point of time: I owed you a much earlier account; but since our arrival here, the repairs and business of the ship have required my constant attention. I will endeavor to be more punctual hereafter; in the meanwhile, hope you will excuse this omission till I can account for it personally. I pass over what was prior to our arrival at the Capes of Delaware—where we were met by the Hornet sloop, and Wasp schooner, from Maryland.

"On the 17th of February, the fleet put to sea with a smart northeast wind. In the night of the 19th (the gale having increased), we lost company with the Hornet and Fly, tender. We steered to the southward, without seeing a single sail or meeting with anything remarkable, till the 1st of March, when we anchored at Abaco, one of the Bahama Islands, having previously brought to a couple of New Providence sloops to take pilots out of them. By these people we were informed that there was a large quantity of powder, with a number of cannon, in the two forts of New Providence. In consequence of this intelligence the marines and landsmen, to the number of 300 and upwards, under the command of Captain Nicholas, were embarked in the two sloops. It was determined that they should keep below deck until the sloops were got in close to the fort, and they were then to land instantly and take possession before the island could be alarmed. This, however, was rendered abortive, as the forts fired an alarm on the approach of our fleet. We then ran in, and anchored at a small key three leagues to windward of the town, and from thence the Commodore despatched the marines, with the sloop Providence and schooner Wasp to cover their landing. They landed without opposition, and soon took possession of the eastern garrison, which, after firing a few shot, the islanders abandoned. The next morning the marines marched for the town, and were met by a messenger from the governor, who told Captain Nicholas, that 'the western garrison (Fort Nassau) was ready for his reception, and that he might march his force in as soon as he pleased.' This was effected without firing a gun on our side—but the governor had sent off 150 barrels of powder the night before. Enclosed you have an inventory of the cannon, stores, &c., which we brought off in the fleet. We continued at New Providence till the 17th ult., and then brought off the governor and two more gentlemen prisoners. Our course was now directed back for the continent, and, after meeting with much bad weather, on the 5th inst., off Block Island, we took the Hawke schooner, of six guns, one of Capt. Wallace's tenders, and the bomb brig Bolton, of eight guns and two howitzers. The next morning we fell in with the Glasgow man-of-war, and a hot engagement ensued, the particulars of which I cannot communicate better than by extracting the minutes which I entered on the Alfred's log-book. I have the pleasure of assuring you that the commander-in-chief is respected through the fleet, and I verily believe that the officers and men, in general, would go any length to execute his orders."

The same letter contains some excellent observations on the courtesy which ought to prevail among the officers of the navy. Lieutenant Jones remarks :—

"It is certainly for the interest of the service that a cordial interchange of civilities should subsist between superior and inferior officers ; and, therefore, it is bad policy in superiors to behave towards their inferiors indiscriminately, as though they were of a lower species. Men of liberal minds, who have been long accustomed to command, can ill brook being thus set at nought by others who pretend to claim the monopoly of sense. The rude, ungentle treatment which they experience, creates such heartburnings as are nowise consonant with that cheerful ardor and spirit which ought ever to be the characteristic of an officer ; and, therefore, whoever thinks himself hearty in the service, is widely mistaken when he adopts such a line of conduct in order to prove it, for to be well obeyed, it is necessary to be esteemed."

He then adds :—

"The fleet having been reinforced with two hundred men lent from the army, is now in condition for another enterprise, and we expect to embrace the first wind for Rhode Island, where I hope we shall meet with better success, as we understand that the Scarborough is now there. It is proposed to clean the ships at Providence, Rhode Island, so that our detention there will admit of a return of letters from Philadelphia."

The annexed is the memorandum of the engagement with the Glasgow, referred to in a preceding extract.

"At 2 A.M. cleared ship for action. At half past two, the Cabot, being between us and the enemy, began to engage, and soon after we did the same. At the third glass the enemy bore away, and, by crowding sail, at length got a considerable way ahead, made signals for the rest of the English fleet at Rhode Island to come to her assistance, and steered directly for the harbor. The Commodore then thought it imprudent to risk our prizes, &c. by pursuing farther; therefore, to prevent our being decoyed into their hands, at half past six made the signal to leave off chase and haul by the wind to join our prizes. The Cabot was disabled at the second broadside. The captain being dangerously wounded, the master and several men killed. The enemy's whole fire was then directed at us, and an unlucky shot having carried away our wheel-block and ropes, the ship broached to, and gave the enemy an opportunity of raking us with several broadsides before we were again in condition to steer the ship and return the fire. In the action we received several shot under water, which made the ship very leaky; we had besides the mainmast shot through, and the upper works and rigging very considerably damaged; yet it is surprising that we only lost the second lieutenant of marines and four men, one of whom (Martin Gillingwater), a midshipman, prisoner, who was in the cockpit, and had been taken in the bomb brig Bolton yesterday; we had no more than three men dangerously and four slightly wounded."

Notwithstanding the success of the enterprise against New Providence, and the alacrity expressed in the letter of Lieut. Jones, of the 14th of April, 1776, for a new expedition, the squadron was not in a condition to put to sea again immediately. The seamen were afflicted with sickness, after their return to the continent. Nearly a month had elapsed before the Andrew Doria and Cabot could be prepared for another cruize, which they were to undertake in company, for four weeks, from Rhode Island. The Alfred and Columbus could not be fully manned for want of men. It became necessary to enlist seamen, and this was difficult, as numbers of them had been enrolled for the army. In a letter from Lieut. Jones to the Honorable Mr. Hewes, dated at New York, the 19th of May, 1776, he represents that "the seamen, almost to a man, had entered into the army before the fleet was set on foot; and I am well informed that there are four or five thousand seamen now in the land service." This class of persons, always amongst the most patriotic, had been thrown out of employment at the commencement of general hostilities with Great Britain, and promptly resorted to the standard of their country under General Washington, until arrangements could be made by Congress for giving more scope to their energies on the element to which they had been accustomed.

The difficulty of procuring seamen was not the only one which the infant American navy had to encounter. The unfortunate engagement with the Glasgow produced considerable dissatisfaction, and occasioned unfavorable reflections to be cast on the officers of the fleet. Although the behavior of Lieut. Jones was not particularly called in question, he evidently felt very sensibly the severity of the common animadversions, as every man of spirit and honor necessarily would have felt in a similar situation. Writing on this topic to the Honorable Mr. Hewes, he remarked that his "feelings as an individual were hurt by the censures that had been indiscriminately thrown out. My station," he observes, "confined me to the Alfred's lower gun-deck, where I commanded during the action; yet, though the commander's letter, which has been published, says, 'all the officers in the Alfred behaved well,' still the public blames me among others for not taking the enemy. But a little consideration will place the matter in a true light; for no officer, under a superior, who does not stand charged, by that superior, for cowardice or misconduct, can be blamed on any occasion whatever." He wrote to Mr. Hewes, "I wish a general inquiry might be made respecting the abilities of officers in all stations, and then the country would not be cheated." Whilst it must be admitted that the expression of these sentiments does credit to Lieut. Jones, it may be noted that the dissatisfaction manifested by the public at the failure of our squadron to capture the Glasgow, was, perhaps, nothing more than the effect of that disappointment, which, in every community, is experienced on the want of success in any combat, military or naval. Victory, whether the result of skill or accident, is sure to be applauded, whilst discomfiture or defeat, let it proceed from what cause it may, is uniformly regarded with coldness, if not with condemnation. Lieut. Jones, being a subordinate officer, and having no imputation cast upon him by the Commodore, was in no manner responsible for the operations of the squadron, and, under all the circumstances incident to the action with the Glasgow, her escape is to be ascribed more to the necessity of preserving the young colonial navy for future and greater services than to any want of capacity or valor in the officers. Two Courts Martial were held on board the Alfred. The consequence of the second one, as far as it affected Lieut. Jones, was an order for him to take command of the sloop Providence, on the 10th of May, 1776. In this armed vessel he arrived at New York, on the 18th of that month, after a passage of thirty-six hours from Rhode Island, with a return of upwards of one hundred men, besides officers, which General Washington had lent to the fleet at New London. At New York he applied himself to the shipping of mariners.

The navy of America had just been brought into existence. Rank, and relative duties, both superior and inferior, were to be established; and these are not, in the freshness of any institution, easily regulated. Naval and military officers are justly tenacious of their rights in this respect. The possession of these rights constitutes their reward for past exertion, and the hope of obtaining and exercising them is an excitement to further efforts. Until precise lines of distinction could be drawn, until the newly appointed officers could be habituated to urbanity in command, and submission in obedience, so essential to the maintenance of order and harmony, something of an acrimonious temper would creep in to impair the force of authority, and weaken the ties of social and official intercourse. At the beginning of the revolution Congress were obliged to act with much wisdom and address in this particular, in relation to the station and advancement of officers in the army as well as in the navy. In the former, the controlling influence and equity of General Washington smothered and conciliated many unpleasant differences. In the navy there was no individual of such unrivalled ascendancy. Not but that all were willing to fight for their country; but rank is an affair of personal honor, in which every one believes himself bound to sustain his claims. Lieut. Jones had an aspiring mind, which impelled him to seek promotion as a means of signalizing himself. His opinion of the qualifications requisite in a naval commander, however, was not extravagant, and evinces nothing of an arbitrary disposition. Writing to the Honorable Mr. Hewes, he tells him, "in my opinion, a commander in the navy ought to be a man of strong and well connected sense, with a tolerable education, a gentleman as well as a seaman, both in theory and practice: for want of learning, and rude, ungentle manners are by no means characteristic of an officer." There is no officer of the navy of the present day, it is presumed, who will not concur in the propriety of this delineation of what is required in an accomplished naval commander.

Lieut. Jones had been offered the command of the Fly, at Reedy Island, in the Delaware, previously to the sailing of the expedition against the Bahamas, but declined it, considering her only as a paltry message boat, suitable for a midshipman. The command was then given to the lieutenant of the Cabot; and upon this circumstance was founded a claim to priority unfavorable to Jones. The naval service, moreover, began to attract attention, and new applicants presented themselves for appointment. To the Honorable Mr. Hewes, Lieut. Jones unbosomed himself on this delicate subject. "There is little confidence to be placed in reports," said he in his letter of the 19th of May, 1776, to that gentleman, "otherwise the lieutenants of the fleet might have reason to be uneasy when they are told that the several committees have orders to appoint all the officers for the new ships, except only the captains. I cannot think that they will be so far overlooked, who have at first stept forth, and shown at least a willingness: nor can I suppose that my own conduct in the service will, in the esteem of the Congress, subject me to be superseded in favor of a younger officer, especially one who is said not to understand navigation." He then adverts to the proffered command of the Fly, and his refusal of it, and proceeds,—"On my appointment to the Providence I was indeed astonished to find my seniority questioned. The Commodore told me he must refer to the Congress. I have received no new commission. I wish the matter in dispute may be first cleared up. I will cheerfully abide by whatever you think is right. At the same time I am ready to have my pretensions inquired into by men who are judges. When I applied for a lieutenancy, I hoped, in that rank, to gain much useful knowledge from those of more experience than myself. I was, however, mistaken: for, instead of gaining information, I was obliged to inform others. I formed an exercise, and trained the men so well to the use of the great guns in the Alfred, that they went through the motions of broadsides and rounds as exactly as soldiers generally perform the manual exercise." This can scarcely be called egotism. Lieut. Jones was unsupported by family connexions in this country, and had to rely on his own merit and the disinterested patronage of members of Congress, and other eminent patriots, for promotion. It was, therefore, but simple justice to himself, whilst he submitted his pretensions to the test of inquiry, to speak of what he had already done of a useful nature to the service.

On the 13th of December, 1775, Congress had directed that thirteen frigates should be built, which, by a resolution of the 6th of June, 1776, were denominated the Congress, Randolph, Hancock, Washington, Trumbull, Raleigh, Effingham, Montgomery, Warren, Boston, Virginia, Providence, and Delaware. They were ordered to be constructed in different ports of the colonies, and Lieut. Jones was anxious to obtain the command of one of them. "I should esteem myself happy," said he, in a letter to Mr. Hewes, "in being sent for to Philadelphia, to act under the more immediate direction of the Congress, especially in one of the new ships. The largest, and I think by far the best, of the frigates was launched the day after I left Providence; but, from what I can learn, neither of them will equal the Philadelphia ships." His wishes, it appears, were not gratified. He was continued in the command of the Providence, which required heaving down, repairing and refitting, before she could proceed on another cruize. After he had procured as many men as were to be enlisted at New York, he was ordered back to Rhode Island for instructions.

At what precise time Lieut. Jones sailed from thence in search of the enemy, is unknown. He was employed for some time in escorting vessels from Rhode Island into the sound. He was then ordered to Boston, to take under convoy certain vessels laden with coal for Philadelphia. According to a letter which he wrote to the Honorable Robert Morris, dated on board the

Providence, at sea, on the 4th of September, 1776, it is manifest that he had been previously to that time, actively engaged in annoying the British trade, and it is believed that, at this time, he acted with unlimited instructions. That letter is remarkable on account of two passages in it; one of which refers to some misfortune which had deeply afflicted him, but which he forbears to explain; the other to the qualifications of the officers of the navy, and the relative rank of officers in the land and naval service. The former proves that he was a person of much sensibility and of correct feeling. The rank of the officers in the navy was still unsettled; and Lieut. Jones, fearful that he might be superseded by his juniors, was anxious to remove every pretext for giving to another the precedence which he considered as due to himself. This motive, it is to be presumed, induced him to write to the Honorable Mr. Morris, in the following manner: "I conclude that Mr. Hewes has acquainted you with a very great misfortune which befel me some years ago, and which brought me into North America. I am under no concern whatever, that this, or any past circmstance of my life, will sink me in your opinion. Since human wisdom cannot secure us from accidents, it is the greatest effort of reason to bear them well." This is a judicious and philosophical reflection, and the effusion of no ordinary mind. The misfortune of which he speaks would not have implicated his moral character, or he would not have enjoyed the confidence and friendship of the Honorable Mr. Hewes, to whom, as Jones informed Mr. Morris, the particulars were known.

On the other topic, concerning the capacity and relative rank of officers, Lieut. Jones displayed a laudable zeal for the improvement of the navy. His plan of a previous examination of officers is now actually in practice with the investigation of the proficiency of young midshipmen, which annually takes place. This passage of his letter to Mr. Morris is brief and to the purpose :—

"As the regulations of the navy," he says, "are of the utmost consequence, you will not think it presumption, if, with the utmost diffidence, I venture to communicate to you such hints as, in my judgment, will promote its honor and good government. I could heartily wish that every commission officer was to be previously examined; for, to my certain knowledge, there are persons who have already crept into commission without abilities or fit qualification: I am myself far from desiring to be excused. From experience in ours, as well as from my former intimacy with many officers of note in the British navy, I am convinced that the parity of rank between sea and land or marine officers, is of more consequence to the harmony of the service, than has generally been imagined. In the British establishment, an admiral ranks with a general, a vice-admiral with a lieutenant-general, a rear-admiral with a major-general, a commodore with a brigadier-general, a captain with a colonel, a master and commander with a lieutenant-colonel, a lieutenant commanding with a major, and a lieutenant in the navy ranks with a captain of horse, foot, or marines. I propose not our enemies as an example for our general imitation, yet, as their navy is the best regulated of any in the world, we must in some degree imitate them, and aim at such farther improvement as may one day make ours vie with, and exceed theirs. Were this regulation to take place in our navy it would prevent numberless disputes and duellings, which otherwise will be unavoidable."

From the cruize in which he was engaged, on the 4th of September, 1776, he returned to Newport, Rhode Island, on the 7th of October following, and on the 17th again wrote to the Honorable Robert Morris, who had cordially permitted his confidential correspondence. This letter of the 17th of October, exhibits the character of Lieut. Jones in so just a light, and in a short compass shows his past success, his diligence, his sympathy, his liberality, his anxiety for the growth of the navy, and ardent wishes to prosecute the war to a speedy and triumphant issue, that it is but justice to his memory to insert it here entire.

"*Providence Sloop of War at Newport,*
Rhode Island, 17*th Oct.* 1776.

"HONORED SIR,

"I wrote to you at sea 4th ult. by the Brigantine Sea Nymph, my second prize. I have taken sixteen sail—manned and sent in eight prizes, and sunk, burnt, or destroyed the rest. The list of prizes is as follows:

1.	The Brigantine Britannia, whaler,	manned and sent in.
2.	" Brigantine Sea Nymph, West Indies,	
3.	" Brigantine Favorite, "	
4.	" Ship Alexander, Newfoundland,	
5.	" Brigantine Success, "	
6.	" Brigantine Kingston Packet, Jam.,	
7.	" Brigantine Defiance, Jersey,	
8.	" Sloop Portland, whaler,	

1.	The Ship Adventure, Jersey,	burnt, or otherwise destroyed.
2.	" Brigantine Friendship, do.,	
3.	" Schooner John, London,	
4.	" Schooner Betsey, Jersey.	
5.	" Schooner Betsey, Halifax.	
6.	" Schooner Sea Flower, Canso,	
7.	" Schooner Ebenezer, "	
8.	" Schooner Hope, Jersey,	

"I have written from time to time to the Marine Board, and furnished them with particular accounts of all my proceedings, and I now send copies of my former letters. I arrived here 7th inst. I would not have lost a day without writing to you and to the board, had not the commodore proposed to me to take command of an expedition, with the Alfred, Providence, and Hampden, to destroy the fishery of Newfoundland, but principally to relieve a hundred of our fellow citizens, who are detained as prisoners and slaves in the coal pits of Cape Breton. All my humanity was awakened, and called up to action by this laudable proposal; and I have been successfully employed in refitting and getting the Providence in readiness, but am under the greatest apprehension that the expedition will fall to nothing, as the Alfred is greatly short of men. I found her with only about thirty men, and we have with much ado enlisted thirty more; but it seems the privateers entice them away as fast as they receive their month's pay. It is to the last degree distressing to contemplate the state and establishment of our navy. The common class of mankind are actuated by no nobler principle than that of self-interest; this, and this alone determines all adventurers in privateers; the owners, as well as those whom they employ. And while this is the case, unless the private emolument of individuals in our navy is made superior to that in privateers, it never can become respectable; it never will become formidable. And without a respectable navy—alas! America! In the present critical situation of affairs, human wisdom can suggest no more than one infallible expedient: enlist the seamen during pleasure, and give them all the prizes. What is the paltry emolument of two thirds of prizes to the finances of this vast continent!* If so poor a resource is essential to its independency, in sober sadness we are involved in a woful predicament, and our ruin is fast approaching. The situation of America is new in the annals of mankind, her affairs cry haste, and speed must answer them. Trifles, therefore, ought to be wholly disregarded, as being in the old vulgar proverb 'penny wise, and pound foolish.' If our enemies, with the best established and most formidable navy in the universe, have found it expedient to assign all prizes to the captors, how much more is such policy essential to our infant fleet; but I need use no arguments to convince you of the necessity of making the emoluments of our navy equal, if not superior, to theirs. We have had proof that a navy may be officered almost on any terms, but we are not so sure that these officers are equal to their commissions; nor will the Congress ever obtain such certainty, until they, in their wisdom, see proper to appoint a board of admiralty, competent to determine impartially the respective merits and abilities of their officers, and to superintend, regulate, and point out, all the motions and operations of the navy.

"Governor Hopkins tells me, that he apprehends I am appointed to the Andrew Doria; she is a good cruizer, and would, in my judgment, answer much better, were she mounted with 12 six-pounders, than as she is at present, with 14 fours. An expedition of importance may be effected this winter, on the coast of Africa, with part of the original fleet. Either the Alfred or Columbus, with the Andrew Doria and Providence, would, I am persuaded, carry all before them; and give a blow to the English African trade, which would not soon be recovered, by not leaving them a

* It will be seen, in the sequel, that, by certain resolutions of Congress, of the 25th of November, 1775, Congress assigned two thirds of the value of all captures made by public ships of war to the use of the United Colonies. These are the "two thirds" to which Lieut. Jones alludes. The remaining one third was divided into twenty parts, and ordered to be distributed among the captors in the proportions mentioned in a resolution of the 6th of January, 1776.

mast standing on that coast. This expedition would be attended with no great expense; besides, the ship and vessels mentioned are unfit for service on a winter coast, which is not the case with the new frigates. The small squadron for this service ought to sail early, that the prizes may reach our ports in March or April. If I do not succeed in manning the Alfred, so as to proceed to the eastward, in the course of this week, the season will be lost; the coal fleet will be gone to Halifax and the fishermen to Europe. I will not, however, remain inactive, but proceed to cruise in the sloop near Sandy Hook. Three of my prizes have arrived here, and one or two more to the eastward.

"I am," &c.

During the time he was at sea, he fell in with the frigate Solebay of 28 guns, near the Island of Bermuda, and had a sharp action with her, which lasted several hours. The Providence carried but 12 guns, six-pounders, and Jones was exceedingly fortunate in making his escape from an adversary so decidedly superior in force. Proceeding thence in the direction of Nova-Scotia, he had an encounter near Cape-Sables, with the Milford, of 32 guns at long-shot. Being unable to cope with her, he ran into a small harbor and destroyed some fishing vessels. He next went to Isle-Madame, destroyed the fishing establishments there, and set on fire every vessel he could not take away. In effecting all this destruction of property and loss to the enemy, he was absent not more than six weeks and five days.

Some estimate may be formed of the individual profits accruing from the cruize in which Lieut. Jones had been occupied, from the number of his captures, and the following regulations of Congress for the distribution of prize-money:—

"In Congress, Jan. 6th, 1776.

"*Resolved*, That the commander in chief have one-twentieth part of prize-money, taken by any ship or ships, armed vessel or vessels, under his orders and command.

"That the captain of any single armed ship or vessel have two-twentieth parts for his share; but if more ships or armed vessels be in company when a prize is taken, then the two-twentieth parts be divided amongst all the said captains.

"That the captain of marines, lieutenants of the ships or armed vessels, and masters thereof, share together, and have three twentieth parts divided among them equally of all prizes taken when they are in company.

"That the lieutenants of marines, surgeons, chaplains, pursers, boatswains, gunners, carpenters, the masters' mates, and the secretary of the fleet, share together, and have two-twentieth parts and one half of one twentieth part divided among them equally, of all prizes taken when they are in company.

"That the following warrant and petty officers, viz. (allowing for each ship six midshipmen, for each brig four midshipmen, and each sloop two midshipmen, one captain's clerk, one surgeon's mate, one steward, one sailmaker, two carpenter's mates, one cook, one cockswain, two sergeants of marines for each ship, and one sergeant for each brig and sloop), have three-twentieth parts divided among them equally; and when a prize is taken by any ship or vessel on board or in company in which the commander-in-chief is, then the commander-in-chief's cook or cockswain to be added to this allotment, and have their shares with these last mentioned.

"That the remaining eight-twentieth parts and one half of the twentieth part be divided amongst the rest of the ship or ships' companies, as it may happen, share and share alike.

"That no officer or man have any share but such as are actually on board their several vessels when any prize or prizes are taken, excepting only such as may have been ordered on board any other prizes before taken, or sent away by his or their commanding officers."

Congress subsequently altered this regulation, as appears by the subjoined resolution, and probably upon the suggestion of Lieut. Jones, as the alteration took place so soon after he had written to Mr. Morris:

"In Congress, Oct. 30th, 1776.

"*Resolved*, That the rank of the officers of marines be the same as officers of similar commissions in the land service.

"That the commanders, officers, seamen, and marines, in the continental navy, be entitled to one half of merchantmen, transports, and store-ships, by them taken, from and after the first day of November, 1776, to be divided amongst them in the shares and proportions fixed by former resolutions of Congress.

"That the commanders, officers, seamen, and marines, in the continental navy, be entitled to the whole value of all ships and vessels of war belonging to the crown of Great Britain by them made prize of, and all privateers authorised by his Britannic Majesty to war against these States, to be divided as aforesaid."

Lieut. Jones took command of a squadron in Rhode Island on the 22d of October, 1776, but finding that he could not man the ship and two small vessels of which it consisted without losing too much time, he determined to leave the Providence and proceed with the Alfred and Hampden. He took the men out of the Providence and her prizes, by which means he made up a muster-roll of upward of 140. When, on the 27th, he was ready to proceed, the Hampden was run upon a sunken ledge, which knocked off her false keel, in consequence of which she became so leaky that she was condemned as not being sea-worthy, and the men were immediately shifted to the Providence. His expectations from the expedition were not sanguine, having been delayed in his arrangements a fortnight longer than he had contemplated. He finally put to sea, with the Alfred and Providence, in the month of November. In this adventure he took a vessel from Liverpool, and the armed ship Mellish, having on board a company of soldiers and 10,000 suits of uniform. This capture was very opportune. The American army was much in want of clothing, and so valuable a prize tended to reanimate the spirits of the soldiers. He also took a third vessel on the 16th of November, and on the 18th following, the Providence parted company in the night. He proceeded, nevertheless, to Isle Royale, destroyed a valuable transport there, and burnt the buildings appropriated to the whale and cod-fisheries. Not far from that island he took another vessel, which was laden with ling and furs, and on the following day captured a privateer mounting sixteen guns. On his return to the continent, he once more fell in with the Milford frigate, but eluded her, and, with his prizes, arrived at Boston, on the 10th of December, 1776.

The main object of the enterprise against Isle-Royale was not effected. The intention of Lieut. Jones was to liberate the Americans who were confined in the coal-mines there. He attributes the failure to the behavior of the officer who commanded the Providence. In a letter to the Hon. Mr. Hewes, dated at Boston, on the 12th of January, 1777, he remarks: "the captain of the Providence thought proper to dispense with his orders and give me the slip in the night, which entirely overset the expedition." In like manner he complains of a prize-master, who violated his instructions by going into Dartmouth, Mass., instead of a port in North Carolina, whither he had been ordered.

These irregularities arose altogether, it is believed, from the omission of Congress to establish a due gradation of rank among the officers of the navy. That body had been so incessantly employed in business of vital importance, both foreign and domestic; and there were so many objects to attend to in the organization of a new government that they had little time to devote to minor details. It was not until three months after the Declaration of Independence that the relative rank of officers in the naval service was established. On the 10th of October, 1776, it was settled in the following manner, and a vessel assigned to each:

Rank of Captains in the Navy, established by Congress, October 10th, 1776, viz.:

	Commanders.	Vessels.	Guns.
No. 1.	James Nicholson, . . .	Virginia,	28
2.	John Manly, ...	Hancock,	32
3.	Hector M'Neil, . . .	Boston,	24

	Commanders.	Vessels.	Guns.
4.	Dudley Saltonstall,	Trumbull,	28
5.	Nicholas Biddle,	Randolph,	32
6.	Thomas Thompson,	Raleigh,	32
7.	John Barry,	Effingham,	28
8.	Thomas Read,	Washington,	32
9.	Thomas Grinnell,	Congress,	28
10.	Charles Alexander,	Delaware,	24
11.	Lambert Wickes,	Reprisal,	16
12.	Abraham Whipple,	Providence,	28
13.	John B. Hopkins,	Warren,	32
14.	John Hodge,	Montgomery,	24
15.	William Hallock,	Lexington,	16
16.	Hoysted Hacker,	Hampden,	—
17.	Isaiah Robinson,	Andrew Doria,	14
18.	John Paul Jones,	Providence,	12
19.	James Josiah,	———,	—
20.	Elisha Hinman,	Alfred,	28
21.	Joseph Olney,	Cabot,	16
22.	James Robinson,	Sachem,	10
23.	John Young,	Independence,	10
24.	Elisha Warner,	Fly,	—
	Lieut. John Baldwin,	Wasp,	8
	Lieut. Thomas Albertson,	Musquito,	4

Jones was by no means satisfied with this regulation; and, with the exception of Captains Saltonstall, Biddle, Whipple, and Hopkins, considered himself as having been superseded by the first seventeen on the list. It was probably for the purpose of soothing him, that Congress, on March the 15th, 1777, passed the subjoined resolution:

"In Congress, *March* 15, 1777.

"*Resolved*, That Daniel Waters, and Samuel Tucker, be appointed Captains in the Navy of the United States, and that they have the command of two of the three ships ordered to be purchased. And that the command of the other ship be given to Captain John Paul Jones, until better provision can be made for him."

On the same day that the relative rank of the captains was

IN CONGRESS.

The DELEGATES of the UNITED STATES of *New Hampſhire, Maſſachuſetts-Bay, Rhode-Iſland, Connecticut, New-York, New-Jerſey, Pennſylvania, Delaware, Maryland, Virginia, North-Carolina, South-Carolina,* and *Georgia*, TO

John Paul Jones, Esquire,

WE, repoſing eſpecial Truſt and Confidence in your Patriotiſm, Valour, Conduct, and Fidelity, DO, by theſe Preſents, conſtitute and appoint you to be *Captain* ~~of the armed~~ ~~called the~~ in the ~~Service~~ *Navy* of the United States of North-America, fitted out for the Defence of American Liberty, and for repelling every hoſtile Invaſion thereof. You are therefore carefully and diligently to diſcharge the Duty of *Captain* by doing and performing all manner of Things thereunto belonging. And we do ſtrictly charge and require all Officers, Marines and Seamen under your Command, to be obedient to your Orders as *Captain* And you are to obſerve and follow ſuch Orders and Directions from Time to Time as you ſhall receive from this or a future Congreſs of the United States, or Committee of Congreſs for that Purpoſe appointed, or Commander in Chief for the Time being of the Navy of the United States, or any other your ſuperior Officer, according to the Rules and Diſcipline of War, the Uſage of the Sea, and the Inſtructions herewith given you, in Purſuance of the Truſt repoſed in you. This Commiſſion to continue in Force until revoked by this or a future Congreſs:

DATED at *Philadelphia October 10th 1776.*

By Order of the CONGRESS,

John Hancock PRESIDENT.

T. *Chas Thomson secy*

From the Original in possesion of Col. John H. Sherburne, Author of "The Life and Character of John Paul Jones."

fixed, a commission was made out for Captain Jones, which, as a revolutionary document, may gratify curiosity. It is expressed in these terms:—

"IN CONGRESS.

"*The Delegates of the United States of New Hampshire, Massachusetts Bay, Rhode Island, Connecticut, New York, New Jersey, Pennsylvania, Delaware, Maryland, Virginia, North Carolina, South Carolina, and Georgia, To*

"JOHN PAUL JONES, ESQ.

"We, reposing especial trust and confidence in your patriotism, valor, conduct, and fidelity, DO, by these Presents, constitute and appoint you to be Captain in the Navy of the United States of North America, fitted out for the Defence of American Liberty, and for repelling every hostile invasion thereof. You are therefore carefully and diligently to discharge the duty of Captain by doing and performing all manner of things thereunto belonging. And we do strictly charge and require all Officers, Marines, and Seamen under your command, to be obedient to your orders as Captain. And you are to observe and follow such orders and directions from time to time, as you shall receive from this or a future Congress of the United States, or Committee of Congress for that purpose appointed, or Commander-in-Chief for the time being of the Navy of the United States, or any other your superior Officer, according to the Rules and Discipline of War, the usage of the sea, and the instructions herewith given you, in pursuance of the trust reposed in you. This commission to continue in force until revoked by this or a future Congress.

"*Dated at Philadelphia, October* 10*th*, 1776.

"*By Order of the Congress*,

"John Hancock, *President.*

"*Attest.* Charles Thomson, *Secretary.*

The uniform of the Officers of the Navy had been regulated by the Marine Committee on the 5th of September, 1776. It may be gratifying to those of the present day to be informed what it was. It is thus described in a resolution of the Committee:—

"IN MARINE COMMITTEE,

"*Philadelphia, September* 5, 1776.

"*Resolved*, That the uniform of the Officers in the Navy of the United States be as follows:—

Captains . . Blue cloth with red lappels, slash cuff, stand up collor, flat yellow buttons, blue britches, red waistcoat with narrow lace.

Lieutenants Blue with red lappels, a round cuff faced, stand up collor, yellow buttons, blue britches, red waistcoat plain.

Masters. . . Blue with lappels, round cuff, blue britches, and red waistcoat.

Midshipmen Blue lappeled coat, a round cuff, faced with red, stand up collor, with red at the button and button hole, blue britches, and red waistcoat.

"*Extract from the Minutes*,
JOHN BROWN, *Secretary*."

"*Uniform of the Marine Officers.*

"A green coat faced with white, round cuff, slashed sleeves, and pockets, with buttons round the cuff, silver epaulett on the right shoulder, skirts turned back, buttons to suit the facings.

"White waistcoat and britches edged with green, black gaiters and garters, green shirts for the men if they can be procured."

The respect to be paid to the pendant and to continental ships of war, was enjoined by Congress on the 29th of October, 1776, in the resolution which follows. The national flag was not definitively established until June of the succeeding year:—

"IN CONGRESS, *October* 29, 1776.

"*Resolved*, That no private ships or vessels of war, merchant ships, or other vessels, belonging to the subjects of these States, be permitted to wear pendants when in company with continental ships or vessels of war, without leave from the commanding officer thereof:

"That if any merchant ship or vessel shall wear pendants in company with continental ships or vessels of war, without leave from the commander thereof, such commander be authorised to take away the pendant from the offender:

"That if private ships or vessels of war refuse to pay the respect due to the commanders of ships or vessels of war, the captain or commander so refusing shall lose his commission."

On the 15th of November, 1776, the Congress granted a bounty to the officers and men for the capture of enemy vessels, established the relative rank of the officers in the navy and army, and fixed the pay of the officers and men in the navy, as specified in the annexed resolution. To the rate of pay in 1776, is added the pay in 1825, from a comparison of which the increase of compensation in the course of the last forty-nine years may be discerned:

"IN CONGRESS, *November* 15, 1776.

"*Resolved*, That a bounty of twenty dollars be paid to the commanders, officers, and men of such continental ships or vessels of war as shall make a prize of any British ships or vessels of war, for every cannon mounted on board such prize at the time of such capture; and eight dollars per head, for every man then on board, and belonging to such prize:

"That the rank of the naval officers be to the rank of officers in the land service as follows:

Admiral	as a	General,
Vice Admiral	"	Lieut. General,
Rear Admiral	"	Major General,
Commodore	"	Brig. General,
Captain of a ship of 40 guns and upwards,	"	Colonel,
" " " 20 to 40 guns .	"	Lieut. Colonel,
" " " 10 " 20 " .	"	Major,
Lieutenant in the navy . . .	"	Captain.

"That the pay of all officers and men in the American navy, from the date of the new commissions under the free and independent States of America, be as follows:

Of Ships of 20 guns.	Per Calendar Month.		Of 10 to 20 guns.
	IN 1776.	IN 1825.	IN 1776.
Captain	$60	$100	$48
Lieutenant	30	40	24

Of Ships of 20 guns.	Per Calendar Month. In 1776.	In 1825.	Of 10 to 20 guns. In 1776.
Master	30	40	24
" Mate	15	20	15
Boatswain	15	20	13
" Mate	9½	19	9
Gunner	15	20	13
" Mate	9½		9
Surgeon	25	50	21⅔
" Mate	15	30	13⅓
Carpenter	15	20	13
" Mate	9½	19	9
Cooper	9	18	9
Midshipman	12	19	12
Armorer	9	18	9
Sail Maker	10	20	10
" Mate	8⅓		8⅓
Yeoman	8½		8½
Quarter Master	9	18	8½
Cook	9	18	8½
Cockswain	9	18	9
Captain's Clerk	15	25	12
Steward	10	18	10
Chaplain	20	40	
Yeoman of powder room	9½		9
Master-at-Arms	10	18	9
Seaman	8	12	8

" That vessels under ten guns be commanded by lieutenants :
" That the pay of the officers in such vessels be :

Lieutenant Commanding	$30	$50
Mate	15	40
Boatswain	12	20
Gunner	12	20
Carpenter	12	20

" That the other officers and men, the same as in vessels from ten to twenty guns.

Marine officers—Captain,	$30	$40
Lieutenant	20	30

"Non-commissioned officers and soldiers, the same as in the land service."

Allowances for subsistence were made on the 21st of July, 1777. The following is the resolution for that object:—

"In Congress, *July* 21*st*, 1777.

"*Resolved*, That commanders of continental vessels of war of ten guns and upwards, be allowed five and one third dollars per week for subsistence, while in domestic or foreign ports:

"That commanders of vessels under ten guns, be allowed four dollars per week for subsistence, while in domestic or foreign ports:

"That commanders of continental vessels of war of ten guns and upwards, be allowed whilst at sea two dollars and two thirds per week, for cabin expenses:

"That lieutenants, surgeons, captains of marines, and chaplains, be allowed four dollars per week subsistence in domestic ports, during such times as the ships they respectively belong to are not in condition to receive them on board:

"That the marine committee be empowered to allow such cabin furniture for continental vessels of war, as they shall judge proper."

Jones was now acting under the commission of captain from the independent authorities of the United States of America. He had, indeed, performed all the duties of a captain in virtue of his previous appointment. That appointment, together with all those which were made on the 22d of December, 1775, before the Colonies had proclaimed their separation from Great Britain, was produced by British maritime aggressions, which the Congress determined to resist and punish. Resolutions were adopted assigning the reasons which impelled the United Colonies to reprisal; and as they may be viewed as the origin of the American naval establishment, it may not be displeasing to the reader to be furnished with an opportunity of perusing them in this volume. They are as follow:—

"In Congress, *November* 25*th*, 1775.

"Whereas, it appears from undoubted information, that many vessels which had cleared at the respective custom-houses in these Colonies, agreeably to the regulations established by acts of the British Parliament, have, in a lawless manner, without even the semblance of just authority, been seized by his majesty's ships of war, and carried into the harbor of Boston and other ports, where they have been rifled of their cargoes, by orders of his majesty's naval and military officers there commanding, without the said vessels having been proceeded against by any form of trial, and without the charge of having offended against any law.

"And whereas, orders have been issued in his majesty's name to commanders of his ships of war, 'to proceed as in the case of actual rebellion against such of the seaport towns and places being accessible to the king's ships, in which any troops shall be raised or military works erected,' under color of which said orders, the commanders of his majesty's said ships of war have already burned and destroyed the flourishing and populous town of Falmouth, and have fired upon and much injured several other towns within the United Colonies, and dispersed at a late season of the year, hundreds of helpless women and children, with a savage hope that those may perish under the approaching rigors of the season who may chance to escape destruction from fire and sword, a mode of warfare long exploded amongst civilized nations.

"And whereas, the good people of these Colonies, sensibly affected by the destruction of their property, and other unprovoked injuries, have at last determined to prevent, as much as possible, a repetition thereof, by fitting out armed vessels and ships of force: in the execution of which commendable designs, it is possible that those who have not been instrumental in the unwarrantable violences above mentioned may suffer, unless some laws be made to regulate, and tribunals erected competent to determine, the propriety of captures: Therefore,

"*Resolved*, That all ships of war, frigates, sloops, cutters, and armed vessels, as are or shall be employed in the present cruel and unjust war against the United Colonies, and shall fall into the hands of, or be taken by the inhabitants thereof, be seized and forfeited to and for the purposes hereinafter mentioned:

"That all transport vessels in the same service having on board any troops, arms, ammunition, clothing, provisions, or military or naval stores, of what kind soever, and all vessels, to whomsoever belonging, that shall be employed in carrying provisions or other necessaries to the British army or armies, or navy, that now are or shall hereafter be within any of the United Colonies, or any goods, wares, or merchandise, for the use of such fleet or army, shall be liable to seizure, and, with their cargoes, shall be confiscated:

"That no master or commander of any vessel shall be entitled to cruize for, or make prize of any vessel or cargo, before he shall have obtained a commission from the Congress, or from such person or persons as shall be for that purpose appointed in some one of the United Colonies:

"That when any vessel or vessels shall be fitted out at the expense of any private person or persons, then the captures shall be to the use of the owner or owners of the said vessel or vessels: that where the vessels employed in the capture shall be fitted out at the expense of any of the United Colonies, then one third of the prize taken shall be to the use of the captors, and the remaining two thirds to the use of the said Colony; and where the vessels so employed shall be fitted out at the continental charge, then one third shall go to the captors, and the remaining two thirds to the use of the United Colonies: provided, nevertheless, that if the capture be a vessel of war, then the captors shall be entitled to one half of the value, and the remainder shall go to the Colony or Continent as the case may be, the necessary charges of condemnation of all prizes being deducted before distribution made:

"That the captures heretofore made by vessels fitted out at the continental charge were justifiable, and that the distribution of the captor's share of the prizes by Gen. Washington be confirmed, which is as follows:—

	Shares.		Shares.
A Captain or Commander,	6	A Mate, ...	1½
First Lieutenant, .	5	Gunner, ...	1½
Second Lieutenant, .	4	Gunner's Mate, .	1½
Surgeon, ...	4	Boatswain, . .	1½
Master, ...	3	Sergeant, . .	1½
Steward, ...	2	Private, . . .	1

After receiving his commission of the 10th of October, 1776, Capt. Jones was more intent than ever on devising the means of advancing the condition of the navy. He looked forward to its augmentation and perfection, and continued to present his reflections as to the course that should be pursued to attain those objects. Many of his ideas were valuable, and some of them have, in substance, been carried into effect by the present government upon a large scale. Writing to his friend, the Honorable Robert Morris, on the 10th of February, 1777, he said,—

"There are no officers more immediately wanted in the marine department, than commissioners of dock yards, to superintend the building, and outfit of all ships of war; with power to appoint deputies to provide and have in constant readiness, sufficient quantities of provision, stores, slops, &c., so that the small number of ships we have may be constantly employed, and not continue idle as they do at present: besides all the advantages that would arise from such appointments, the saving which would accrue to the continent is worth attending to; had such men been appointed at the first, the new ships might have been at sea long ago. The difficulty now lays in finding men who are deserving, and who are fitly qualified for an office of such importance.

"I must repeat what I asserted formerly, that unless some happy expedient can be fallen upon to induce the seamen to enter into the service for a longer term than twelve months, it will never be possible to bring them under proper subordination; and subordination is as necessary, nay, far more so in the fleet, than in the army. *Present* advantages, though small, will operate far more on the minds of seamen, than *future* prospects, though great. They ought at least to enter during the war, if not during pleasure."

In fulfilment of the resolution of Congress of the 17th of March, 1777, the Marine Committee addressed a letter to Capt. Jones, in the following terms:—

"In Marine Committee.

"*Philadelphia, March 25th*, 1777.

"The Congress, by a resolve of the 17th inst., having ordered that the agent at Boston should purchase, arm, and fit out, for the service of the United States, three fast sailing good ships, that will conveniently mount 18 six-pounders on one deck; and that Capt. John Paul Jones shall command one of said ships, until better provision can be made for him: Therefore,

"*Resolved*, That Capt. Jones shall have his choice of those three ships, and that he superintend the fitting of her out.

"*Extract from the minutes.*

"John Brown, *Secretary*."

"In Marine Committee.

"*Philadelphia, March 25th*, 1777.

"Sir,

"The agent, Mr. Bradford, has orders from this committee to purchase and fit out three armed vessels, pursuant to a resolve of Congress, which is transmitted to him, one of which you are to command, and the committee have directed that you should have your choice. Therefore you are desired to make your election as soon as the purchase shall be made, and to superintend and hasten the fitting her out for sea, with all possible expedition.

"We are, Sir,

"Your very humble servants,

"JOHN HANCOCK,
"WILLIAM WHIPPLE,
"WILLIAM ELLERY,
"ABRAHAM CLARKE,
"OLIVER WOLCOTT,
"THOMAS BANKE,
"ROBERT MORRIS.

"To Capt. JOHN PAUL JONES."

Before this plan was carried into execution, Jones received a new and honorable proof of the good opinion of Congress, by being ordered to proceed to France from Portsmouth in the French ship Amphitrite, with a positive order to the American commissioners at Paris to invest him with the command of a fine ship, as a reward for the zeal he had shown, and for the signal services which he had performed in vessels of little force. By the annexed letter to Mr. John Dobie it would seem that he was making preparations to embark in the Amphitrite; but, on account of difficulties made by her commander, he abandoned the design:

"*Boston, May 23d*, 1777.

"MR. JOHN DOBIE,

"You are hereby authorized to engage any prime seamen who may present themselves to serve under my command in the navy on board the ship Amphitrite, at Portsmouth, in New Hampshire, bound to France.—On arrival there they are to be turned over to one of the finest frigates of the French Navy, she having been purchased for the United States by their commissioners at the court of Paris, and to be put under my command.—You are directed to repair on board the ship at Portsmouth without loss of time, and your reasonable expenses will be allowed, as also the reasonable expenses of as many prime seamen as you may bring with you in proper time. If a passage can be procured from hence to Portsmouth by water, it will be the cheapest and best conveyance, especially for baggage.

"John P. Jones."

Capt. Jones had before, in one of his letters to a member of Congress, recommended that one of his prizes, the Mellish, should be converted into a ship of war. This had been determined upon by the Marine Committee, but, upon the receipt of a letter from him in May, 1777, the determination was abandoned, and he was appointed to the command of the Ranger. That committee wrote the following letter to him, from which it may be inferred that he was growing in the esteem of Congress, and in favor with the public in general:

"In Marine Committee.

"*Philadelphia, June* 18*th*, 1777.

"John Paul Jones, Esq.,

"Sir,

"Your letter of the 26th May to the Secret Committee was laid before Congress, and, in consequence thereof, the design of fitting the Mellish is laid aside; and you are appointed to command the Ranger ship of war lately built at Portsmouth. Col. Whipple, the bearer of this, carries with him the resolves of Congress appointing you to this command, and authorizing him, Col. Langdon, and you, to appoint the other commissioned as well as the warrant officers necessary for this ship, and he has with him blank commissions and warrants for this purpose.

"It is our desire that you get the Ranger equipped, officered, and manned as well and as soon as possible, and probably we may send you other instructions, before you are ready to sail. However, the design of the present is to prevent your waiting for such after you are ready for service in every other respect, and if that happens before the receipt of farther orders from us, you must then proceed on a cruize against the enemies of those United States conforming to the orders and regulations of Congress made for the government of the navy; and in conformity thereto take, sink, burn, or destroy all such of the enemies' ships, vessels, goods, and effects as you may be able.

"We shall not limit you to any particular cruizing station, but leave you at large to search for yourself where the greatest chance of success presents. Your prizes you will send into such safe ports in these United States as they can reach, your prisoners must also be sent in, and we recommend them to kind treatment.

"Any useful intelligence that comes to your knowledge must be communicated to us whenever you have opportunity.

"You are to preserve good order and discipline, but use your people well. The ship, her materials, and stores must be taken good care of, and every officer to answer to any embezzlements that happen in his department. You are to make monthly returns of your officers, men, &c. to the Navy Board, you are to be exceedingly attentive to the cleanliness of your ship and preservation of the people's healths.

"You are to afford assistance and protection to the American commerce whenever in your power; and on your return from this cruize, lay copies of your journal and log book before the Navy Board, and inform us the events of your voyage.

"We are, Sir,

"Your friends and servants,

"JOHN HANCOCK,
"ROBERT MORRIS,
"PHILIP LIVINGSTON,
"BENJAMIN HARRISON,
"A. MIDDLETON,
"NICHOLAS VAN DYKE,
"GEORGE WALTON."

The resolutions referred to are as follow: The designation of the flag, and the appointment of Captain Jones to the command of the Ranger on the same day, would seem to imply some connexion between the two circumstances. The Ranger was probably the first ship that bore the national flag to Europe.

"IN CONGRESS, *June 14th*, 1777.

"*Resolved*, That the flag of the thirteen United States be thirteen stripes, alternate red and white: that the Union be thirteen stars, white in a blue field, representing a new constellation.

"*Resolved*, That Captain John Paul Jones be appointed to command the ship Ranger.

"*Resolved*, That William Whipple, Esq., member of Congress, and of the Marine Committee, John Langdon, Esq., continental agent, and the said John Paul Jones, be authorised to appoint lieutenants and other commissioned, and warrant officers, necessary for the said ship; and that blank commissions and warrants be sent them, to be filled up with the names of the persons they appoint, returns whereof to be made to the Navy Board in the eastern department."

The subjoined letter to Lieutenant Elijah Hall shows that Captain Jones dealt frankly and honorably with his seamen. This was as wise as it was just, for the surest method of securing cheerful obedience, and preserving harmony among a ship's crew, is to inspire them at the outset with confidence in the integrity and equity of the commander:

"*Portsmouth, N. H., July 29th*, 1777.

"Lieut. ELIJAH HALL, U. S. Navy.

"SIR,

"As I learn from you that the seamen who have entered for the Ranger, for one cruize, expect to receive an advance of forty dollars, and that the landsmen expect to receive an advance of twenty dollars, as mentioned in the hand bills, and as I would by no means deceive any man who has entered, or who may enter, to serve under my command, it is proper that you should inform them, that at the time when Congress agreed to that advance, there was no intention of entering men except for three years, during the war, or for one year at least; yet, as I consider myself under an obligation to those men, who have so cheerfully entered, it being a proof of their good opinion of me, I would, at my own risk, give them orders on the agent here for the above advance, or for such part of it as they may find really necessary, but, upon inquiry, I am convinced that this would be contrary to the rules of Congress, and therefore hurtful to the service. I will, however, besides the bounty, give an order on the agent or paymaster of the navy, for the punctual payment of half the monthly wages, to every person under my command, who may leave wives or attorneys behind them, to receive it in their absence, as it afterwards becomes due, provided they enter for the term of twelve months, otherwise I am authorized to advance no more than one month's pay, besides slops to persons who enter only for one cruize. I wish to see every person about me happy and contented, and will do everything in my power to make them so. The conditions of the hand bills will be strictly complied with, and

"I am, Sir,
"Your very obedient
"and most humble servant,
"JOHN PAUL JONES."

"The above is a true copy from the original in my possession.
"ELIJAH HALL.
"*Portsmouth, Sept. 29th*, 1824."

Captain Jones was now on the eve of his departure for France. During his stay at Boston in the month of May, he wrote a letter to Stuart Mawey, Esq. which places his character in a new light. It would seem from that letter that he had once been a merchant in Tobago, and that he had pecuniary resources in that island as well as in England, from which, by untoward circumstances, he had been cut off; what these were he does not reveal. They probably arose from that misfortune at which he hinted in a letter to the Hon. Mr. Morris, as being known to the Hon. Mr. Hewes. According to his own account, he was in extreme distress when he joined the standard of America. But the letter to Mr. Mawey contains no expressions of regret for the part he had taken in the revolution. On the contrary, he declares his unshaken determination to adhere to the fortunes of America. The letter does infinite credit to the heart of Capt. Jones; and, after reading it, no impartial mind will venture to denounce him as illiterate, vulgar, unfeeling, or unprincipled. The sentiments which he expresses for his mother are true to nature, tender, and touching, and show that the profession of arms had not estranged his bosom from the more refined and affectionate sensations.

"*Boston, May* 4, 1777.

"STEWART MAWEY, Esq. Tobago.

"DEAR SIR,

"After an unprofitable suspense of twenty months, (having subsisted on *fifty pounds only* during that time,) when my hopes of relief were entirely cut off, and there remained no possibility of my receiving wherewithal to subsist upon from my effects in your island, or in England, I at last had recourse to strangers for that aid and comfort which was denied me by those friends whom I had entrusted with my all. The good offices which are rendered to persons in their extreme need, ought to make deep impressions on grateful minds. In my case, I feel the truth of that sentiment, and am bound by gratitude as well as honor to follow the fortunes of my late benefactors.

"I have lately seen Mr. Secaton (late manager on the estate of Archibald Stuart, Esq.), who informed me that Mr. Ferguson had quitted Orange Valley, on being charged with the unjust application of the property of his employers. I have been, and am extremely concerned at this accouut; I wish to disbelieve it, although it seems too much of a piece with the unfair advantage which, *to all appearance*, he took of me, when he left me in exile for twenty months, a prey to melancholy and want, and withheld my property without writing a word in excuse of his conduct.

"Thus circumstanced, I have taken the liberty of sending you a letter of attorney by Capt. Cleaveland, who undertakes to deliver it himself, as he goes for Tobago via Martinico. You have enclosed a copy of a list of debts acknowledged, which I received from Mr. Ferguson when I saw you last at Orange Valley. You have also, a list of debts contracted with me, together with Ferguson's receipt,* and there remained a considerable property unsold, besides some best Madeira wine, which he had shipped for London. By the state of accounts which I sent to England on my arrival on this continent, there was a balance due to me from the ship Betsey, of 909*l.* 15*s.* 3*d.* sterling; and in my account with Robert Young, Esq. of the 29th of January, 1773, there appeared a balance in my favor of 281*l.* 1*s.* 8*d.* sterling. These sums exceed my drafts and just debts together, so that, if I am fairly dealt with, I ought to receive a considerable remittance from that quarter.

"You will please to observe that there were nine pieces of coarse camlet shipped at Cork, *over and above the quantity expressed in the bill of lading.* It seems the shippers, finding their mistake, applied for the goods, and, as I have been informed from Grenada, Mr. Ferguson laid hold of this opportunity to propagate a report that all the goods which I put into his hands was the property of that house in Cork. If

* Copies of these lists are enclosed in the copy which Capt. Jones retained of this letter, and are now in the possession of the author of this volume. They are written in a fair hand, and the sums put down in counting-house order.

this base suggestion has gained belief, it accounts for all the neglect which I have experienced. But, however my connexions are changed, my principles as a man of candor and integrity are the same: therefore, should there not be a sufficiency of my property in England to answer my just debts, I declare that it is my first wish to make up such deficiency from my property in Tobago; and were even that also to fall short, I am ready and willing to make full and ample remittances from hence, upon hearing from you the true state of my affairs. As I hope my dear mother is still alive, I must inform you that I wish my property in Tobago or in England, after paying my just debts, to be applied for her support. Your own feelings, my dear Sir, make it unnecessary for me to use arguments to prevail with you on this tender point. Any remittances which you may be enabled to make through the hands of my good friend, Capt. John Palmer, of Cork, will be faithfully put into her hands. She has several orphan grand-children to provide for. I have made no apology for giving you this trouble: my situation will, I trust, obtain your free pardon.

"You can, if you please, correspond with me via any of the French or Dutch islands, by addressing your letters to John P. Jones, and care of the Hon. Robert Morris, Esq. Philadelphia, or I can hear from you through the hands of my friend, Capt. Plainer; he is frequently at Grenada, and perhaps may be there when this reaches your hands

"I am always, with perfect esteem, &c."

The Ranger at length put to sea, and, on the 2d of December, 1777, arrived at Nantes in France. From that port Capt. Jones proceeded, on the 13th of February, 1778, to Quiberon Bay and Brest, where he saluted the French Admiral, Count D'Orvilliers, with thirteen guns, which was returned with nine. This was the first salute of honor that the American flag had received from a foreign man-of-war. Jones delayed his salute, until assured from authority, that the compliment would be reciprocated.

Whilst at Nantes, Capt. Jones was favored by the American Commissioners with a letter of credit for 500 louis d'ors, which proves that he acted in concert with the public authorities of the United States, both at home and abroad. As a document establishing this fact, it is deemed proper to embody it in this account of his life.

"*Passy, January* 10, 1778.

"JONATHAN WILLIAMS, ESQ. *Nantes.*

"SIR,

"We desire you would advance to Capt. Paul Jones, of the Ranger, five hundred louis d'ors, for which your draft upon us will be paid.

"We are, Sir,
"Your most obedient servants,
"B. FRANKLIN,
"SILAS DEAN,
"ARTHUR LEE."

After considerable delay and many obstacles, most of which he attributed to the want of cordiality in the first lieutenant of the Ranger, and a spirit of mutiny among the crew, he sailed from Brest on the 13th of April, on a cruize in the Irish Channel, entered upon a very hazardous enterprise against Whitehaven, and spread great terror along the shores of Great Britain and Ireland.

On the same day of the descent at Whitehaven, another memorable occurrence took place, which contributed, for a time, to add greatly to the odium which the first had brought on his character, but which, in the end, enabled him to prove that he was possessed of the most disinterested and heroic qualities. In cruising off the coast of Galloway, it occurred to him, that, if he could get into his power a man of high rank and influence in the state, he should be able, by retaining him as a hostage, to insure to the American prisoners of war more lenient treatment from the British government. Knowing that the Earl of Selkirk possessed a seat in St. Mary's Isle, a beautiful peninsula at the mouth of the Dee, and being ill informed with regard to the political connexions of that nobleman, he destined him for the subject of his experiment.

It was in this adventure that he permitted the seizure of the plate of Lord Selkirk, at St. Mary's Isle, which he afterwards purchased and restored.

National prejudice has misrepresented this transaction; and, in order to heighten the popular indignation against Jones, it has been common to state, that his attempt on the person, and as it was supposed, the property of Lord Selkirk, was aggravated by ingratitude, his father having eaten of that nobleman's bread. Nothing can be more false. Neither Mr. Paul, nor any of his kindred ever was in the earl's employ, or had even the most distant connexion with his lordship, or his family; and in a correspondence which took place betwixt Jones and Lady Selkirk, relative to the restitution of the plate, a most honorable testimony was gratefully paid by Lord Selkirk to the Captain's character.

In connexion with the attempt upon Whitehaven, was the capture of the British ship-of-war Drake, of 20 guns. Captain Jones has given so particular an account of these exploits in a letter to the commissioners of the United States at Paris, that it will be preferred to any narrative of them that could be framed by another hand:—

"LETTER TO THE AMERICAN COMMISSIONERS AT PARIS.

"*Brest, May* 27, 1778.

"GENTLEMEN,

"I now fulfil the promise made in my last, by giving you an account of my late expedition.

"I sailed from Brest 10th of April. My plan was extensive. I therefore did not, at the beginning, wish to encumber myself with prisoners. On the 14th I took a brigantine between Scylla and Cape Clear, bound from Ostend with a cargo of flaxseed for Ireland, sunk her, and proceeded into St. George's Channel. On the 17th I took the ship Lord Chatham, bound from London to Dublin, with a cargo consisting of porter and a variety of merchandize, and almost within sight of her port; the ship I manned and ordered for Brest. Towards the evening of the day following, the weather had a promising appearance, and the winds being favorable, I stood over from the Isle of Man, with an intention to make a descent at Whitehaven. At 10 o'clock, I was off the harbor with a party of volunteers, and had everything in readiness to land, but, before eleven, the wind greatly increased, and shifted so as to blow directly upon the shore; the sea increased of course, and it became impossible to effect a landing. This obliged me to carry all possible sail, so as to clear the land, and to await a more favorable opportunity. On the 18th, in Glenbue Bay, on the south coast of Scotland, I met with a revenue wherry; it being the common practice of these vessels to board merchant ships, and the Ranger then having no external appearance of war, it was expected that this rover would have come alongside. I was, however, mistaken, for, though the men were at their quarters, yet this vessel outsailed the Ranger, and got clear, in spite of a severe cannonade.

"The next morning, off the Mull of Galloway, I found myself so near a Scotch coasting schooner, loaded with barley, that I could not avoid sinking her. Understanding that 10 or 12 sail of merchant ships, besides a tender brigantine with a number of impressed seamen on board, were at anchor in Loughryan in Scotland, I thought this an enterprise worthy attention, but the wind, which at the first would have served equally well to sail in or out of the Lough, shifted in a hard squall so as to blow almost directly in, with an appearance of bad weather; I was therefore obliged to abandon my project.

"Seeing a cutter off the lee-bow steering for the Clyde, I gave chase in hopes of cutting her off; but finding my endeavors ineffectual, I pursued no farther than the rock of Ailsa. In the evening I fell in with a sloop from Dublin, which I sunk to prevent intelligence.

"The next day, the 21st, being near Carrickfergus, a fishing boat came off, which I detained. I saw a ship at anchor in the road, which I was informed by the fisherman, was the British ship-of-war Drake, of 20 guns. I determined to attack her in the night. My plan was to overlay her cable, and to fall upon her bow, so as to have all her decks open, and exposed to our musketry, &c.; at the same time it was my intention to have secured the enemy by graplings, so that, had they cut their cables, they would not thereby have attained an advantage. The wind was high, and unfortunately the anchor was not let go so soon as the order was given; so that the Ranger was brought up on the enemy's quarter, at the distance of half a cable's length. We had made no warlike appearance, of course had given no alarm; this determined me to cut immediately, which might appear as if the cable had parted, and at the same time enabling me, after making a tack out of the Lough, to return with the same prospect of advantage which I had at the first. I was, however, prevented from returning; as I with difficulty weathered the lighthouse on the lee side of the Lough, and as the gale increased.

"The weather now became so very stormy and severe, and the sea so high, that I was obliged to take shelter under the south shore of Scotland.

The 22d introduced fair weather; though the three kingdoms as far as the eye could reach were covered with snow. I now resolved once more to attempt Whitehaven; but the wind became very light, so that the ship could not in proper time approach so near as I had intended. At midnight I left the ship, with two boats and thirty-one volunteers. When we reached the outer pier, the day began to dawn. I would not, however, abandon my enterprise; but despatched one boat under the direction of Mr. Hill and Lieutenant Wallingsford, with the necessary combustibles, to set fire to the shipping on the north side of the harbor, while I went with the other party to attempt the south side. I was successful in scaling the walls, and spiking up all the cannon in the first fort. Finding the sentinels shut up in the guard house, they were secured without being hurt. Having fixed sentinels, I now took with me one man only (Mr. Green), and spiked up all the cannon on the southern fort; distant from the other a quarter of a mile.

"On my return from this business, I naturally expected to see the fire of the ships on the north side, as well as to find my own party with everything in readiness to set fire to the shipping in the south. Instead of this, I found the boat under the direction of Mr. Hill and Mr. Wallingsford returned, and the party in some confusion, their light having burnt out at the instant when it became necessary. By the strangest fatality my own party were in the same situation, the candles being all burnt out. The day too came on apace; yet I would by no means retreat while any hopes of success remained. Having again placed sentinels, a light was obtained at a house disjoined from the town; and fire was kindled in the steerage of a large ship, which was surrounded by at least an hundred and fifty others, chiefly from two to four hundred tons burthen, and laying side by side aground, unsurrounded by the water. There were, besides, from seventy to an hundred large ships in the north arm of the harbor, aground, clear of the water, and divided from the rest only by a stone pier of a ship's height. I should have kindled fires in other places if the time had permitted. As it did not, our care was to prevent the one kindled from being easily extinguished. After some search a barrel of tar was found, and poured into the flames, which now ascended from all the hatchways. The inhabitants began to appear in thousands; and individuals ran hastily towards us. I stood between them and the ship on fire, with a pistol in my hand, and ordered them to retire, which they did with precipitation. The flames had already caught the rigging, and began to ascend the mainmast:—the sun was a full hour's march above the horizon; and as sleep no longer ruled the world, it was time to retire. We re-embarked without opposition, having released a number of prisoners, as our boats could not carry them. After all my people had embarked, I stood upon the pier for a considerable time, yet no persons advanced. I saw all the eminences around the town covered with the amazed inhabitants.

"When we had rowed to a considerable distance from the shore, the English began to run in vast numbers to their forts. Their disappointment may easily be imagined, when they found at least thirty heavy cannon, the instruments of their vengeance, rendered useless. At length, however, they began to fire; having, as I apprehend, either brought down ship guns, or used one or two cannon which lay on the beach at the foot of the walls dismounted, and which had not been spiked. They fired with no direction; and the shot falling short of the boats, instead of doing us any damage, afforded some diversion, which my people could not help showing, by discharging their pistols, &c., in return of the salute. Had it been possible to have landed a few hours sooner, my success would have been complete. Not a single ship, out of more than two hundred, could possibly have escaped, and all the world would not have been able to save the town. What was done, however, is sufficient to show that not all their boasted navy can protect their own coasts; and that the scenes of distress which they have occasioned in America may be soon brought home to their own door. One of my people was missing, and must, I fear, have fallen into the enemies' hands after our departure. I was pleased that in this business we neither killed nor wounded any person. I brought off three prisoners as *a sample.*

"We now stood over for the Scotch shore; and I landed at noon at St. Mary's Isle, with one boat only, and a very small party. The motives which induced me to land there are explained in the within copy of a letter which I have addressed to the Countess of Selkirk, dated the 8th instant.

"On the morning of the 24th I was again off Carrickfergus, and would have gone in had I not seen the Drake preparing to come out. It was very moderate, and the Drake's boat was sent out to reconnoitre the Ranger. As the boat advanced I kept the ship's stern directly towards her; and though they had a spy glass in the boat, they came on within hail, and alongside. When the officer came on the quarter-deck, he was greatly surprised to find himself a prisoner; although an express had arrived from Whitehaven the night before. I now understood, what I had before imagined, that the Drake came out in consequence of this information, with volunteers, against the Ranger. The officer told me, also, that they had taken up the Ranger's anchor. The Drake was attended by five small vessels full of people, who were led by curiosity to see an engagement. But when they saw the Drake's boat at the Ranger's stern they wisely put back.

"Alarm smokes now appeared in great abundance, extending along on both sides of the channel. The tide was unfavorable, so that the Drake worked out but slowly. This obliged me to run down several times, and to lay with courses up and main-topsail to the mast. At length the Drake weathered the point, and having led her out to about mid-channel, I suffered her to come within hail. The Drake hoisted English colors, and, at the same instant, the American stars were displayed on board the Ranger. I expected that preface had been now at an end, but the enemy soon after hailed, demanding what ship it was? I directed the master to answer, 'the American Continental ship Ranger; that we waited for them, and desired that they would come on; the sun was now little more than an hour from setting, it was therefore time to begin.' The Drake being astern of the Ranger, I ordered the helm up and gave her the first broadside. The action was warm, close, and obstinate. It lasted an hour and four minutes, when the enemy called for quarters; her fore and main-topsail yards being both cut away, and down on the cap; the top-gallant yard and mizen-gaff both hanging up and down along the mast; the second ensign which they had hoisted shot away, and hanging on the quarter-gallery in the water; the jib shot away, and hanging in the water; her sails and rigging entirely cut to pieces; her masts and yards all wounded, and her hull also very much galled. I lost only Lieutenant Wallingsford and one seaman, John Dougall, killed, and six wounded; among whom are the gunner, Mr. Falls, and Mr. Powers, a midshipman, who lost his arm. One of the wounded, Nathaniel Wills, is since dead: the rest will recover. The loss of the enemy in killed and wounded was far greater. All the prisoners allow that they came out with a number not less than a hundred and sixty men: and many of them affirm that they amounted to an hundred and ninety. The medium may, perhaps, be the most exact account; and by that it will appear that they lost in killed and wounded forty-two men. The captain and lieutenant were among the wounded. The former, having received a musket ball in the head the minute before they called for quarters; lived, and was sensible some time after my people boarded the prize. The lieutenant survived two days. They were buried with the honors due to their rank, and with the respect due to their memory.

"The night and almost the whole day after the action being moderate, greatly facilitated the refitting of both ships. A large brigantine was so near the Drake in the afternoon that I was obliged to bring her to. She belonged to Whitehaven, and was bound for Norway.

"I had thought of returning by the south channel; but, the wind shifting, I determined to pass by the north, and round the west coast of Ireland. This brought me once more off Belfast Lough, on the evening after the engagement. It was now time to release the honest fishermen, whom I took up here on the 21st. And as the poor fellows had lost their boat, she having sunk in the late stormy weather, I was happy in having it in my power to give them the necessary sum to purchase everything new which they had lost. I gave them also a good boat to transport themselves ashore; and sent with them two infirm men, on whom I bestowed the last guinea in my possession, to defray their travelling expenses to their proper home in Dublin. They took with them one of the Drake's sails, which would sufficiently explain what had happened to the volunteers. The grateful fishermen were in raptures; and expressed their joy in three huzzas as they passed the Ranger's quarter.

"I again met with contrary winds in the mouth of the North Channel, but nothing remarkable happened, till on the morning of the 5th current, Ushant then bearing S.E. by S., distance fifteen leagues, when seeing a sail to leeward steering for the Channel, the wind being favorable for Brest and the distance trifling, I resolved to give chase, having the Drake in tow. I informed them of my intentions, and ordered them to cast off. They cut the hawser. The Ranger in the chase went lasking between N.N.E. and N.N.W. It lasted an hour and ten minutes, when the chase was hailed and proved a Swede. I immediately hauled by the wind to the southward.

"After cutting the hawser, the Drake went from the wind for some time, then hauled close by the wind, steering from S.S.E. to S.S.W. as the wind permitted, so that when the Ranger spoke the chase the Drake was scarcely perceptible. In the course of the day many large ships appeared, steering into the Channel, but the extraordinary evolutions of the Drake made it impossible for me to avail myself of these favorable circumstances. Towards noon it became very squally, the wind backed from the S.W. to the W. The Ranger had come up with the Drake, and was nearly abreast of her, though considerably to the leeward when the wind shifted. The Drake was however kept by the wind, though, as I afterwards understood, they knew the Ranger, and saw the signal which she had hoisted. After various evolutions and signals in the night, I gave chase to a sail which appeared bearing S.S.W. the next morning at a great distance. The chase discovered no intention to speak with the Ranger; she was, however, at length brought to, and proved to be the Drake. I immediately put Lieut. Simpson under suspension and arrest, for disobedience of my orders, dated the 26th ult., a copy whereof is here inclosed. On the 8th, both ships anchored safe in this Road, the Ranger having been absent only twenty-eight days. Could I suppose that my letters of the 9th and 16th current, (the first advising you of my arrival, and giving reference to the events of my expedition; the last advising you of my draft in favor of Monsieur Bersolle, for 24,000 livres, and assigning reasons for that demand), had not made due appearance, I would hereafter, as I do now, inclose copies. Three posts have already arrived here from Paris, since Compte d'Orvilliers showed me the answer which he received from the minister, to the letter which inclosed mine to you. Yet you remain silent. M. Bersolle has this moment informed me of the fate of my bills; the more extraordinary, as I have not yet made use of your letter of credit of the 10th of January last, whereby I then seemed entitled to call for half the amount of my last draft, and I did not expect to be thought extravagant, when, on the 16th current, I doubled that demand. Could this indignity be kept secret I should disregard it; and, though it is already public in Brest and in the fleet, as it affects only my private credit, I will not complain. I cannot, however, be silent when I find the public credit involved in the same disgrace. I conceive this might have been prevented. To make me completely wretched, Monsieur Bersolle has told me that he now stops his hand, not only of the necessary articles to refit the ship, but also of the *daily provisions*. I know not where to find to-morrow's dinner for the great number of mouths that depend on me for food. Are then the continental ships-of-war to depend on the sale of their prizes for a daily dinner for their men? 'Publish it not in Gath!'

"My officers as well as men want clothes, and the prizes are precluded from being sold before farther orders arrive from the minister. I will ask you, gentlemen, if I have deserved all this? Whoever calls himself an American ought to be protected here. I am unwilling to think that you have intentionally involved me in this sad dilemma, at a time when I ought to expect some enjoyment. Therefore I have, as formerly, the honor to be, with due esteem and respect, gentlemen, yours, &c."

The copy of the letter to Lady Selkirk, to which Capt. Jones alludes, is in the words following. It is couched in terms as politic as gallant:

"*Ranger*, *Brest*, *May* 8, 1778.

"The Right Hon. the Countess of SELKIRK.

"MADAM,

"It cannot be too much lamented that in the profession of arms, the officer of fine feeling and of real sensibility should be under the necessity of winking at any action of persons under his command which his heart cannot approve; but the reflection is doubly severe, when he finds himself obliged, in appearance, to countenance such actions by his authority.

"This hard case was mine when, on the 23d of April last, I landed on St. Mary's Isle. Knowing Lord Selkirk's interest with his king, and esteeming as I do his private character, I wished to make him the happy instrument of alleviating the horrors of hopeless captivity, when the brave are overpowered and made prisoners of war.

"It was, perhaps, fortunate for you, Madam, that he was from home; for it was my intention to have taken him on board the Ranger, and to have detained him until, through his means, a general and fair exchange of prisoners, as well in Europe as in America, had been effected.

"When I was informed by some men whom I met at landing, that his lordship was absent, I walked back to my boat, determined to leave the island. By the way, however, some officers, who were with me, could not forbear expressing their discontent; observing that, in America, no delicacy was shown by the English, who took away all sorts of moveable property—setting fire not only to towns and to the houses of the rich without distinction, but not even sparing the wretched hamlets and milch-cows of the poor and helpless at the approach of an inclement winter. That party had been with me, the same morning, at Whitehaven; some complaisance therefore was their due. I had but a moment to think how I might gratify them, and at the same time do your ladyship the least injury. I charged the two officers to permit none of the seamen to enter the house, or to hurt anything about it,—to treat you, Madam, with the utmost respect,—to accept of the plate which was offered,—and to come away without making a search, or demanding anything else.

"I am induced to believe that I was punctually obeyed; since I am informed that the plate which they brought away is far short of the quantity expressed in the inventory which accompanied it. I have gratified my men; and when the plate is sold, I shall become the purchaser, and will gratify my own feelings by restoring it to you by such conveyance as you shall please to direct.

"Had the earl been on board the Ranger the following evening, he would have seen the awful pomp and dreadful carnage of a sea engagement; both affording ample subject for the pencil, as well as melancholy reflection to the contemplative mind. Humanity starts back from such scenes of horror, and cannot sufficiently execrate the vile promoters of this detestable war.

'For *they*, 'twas *they* unsheathed the ruthless blade,
And Heaven shall ask the havoc it has made.'

"The British ship-of-war Drake, mounting twenty guns, with more than her full complement of officers and men. * * * * * The ships met, and the advantage was disputed with great fortitude on each side for an hour and four minutes when the gallant commander of the Drake fell, and victory declared in favor of the Ranger. The amiable lieutenant lay mortally wounded, besides near forty of the inferior officers and crew killed and wounded. A melancholy demonstration of the uncertainty of human prospects, and of the sad reverse of fortune which an hour can produce. I buried them in a spacious grave, with the honors due to the memory of the brave.

"Though I have drawn my sword in the present generous struggle for the rights of men, yet I am not in arms as an American, nor am I in pursuit of riches. My fortune is liberal enough, having no wife nor family, and having lived long enough to know that riches cannot insure happiness. I profess myself a citizen of the world, totally unfettered by the little, mean distinctions of climate or of country, which diminish the benevolence of the heart and set bounds to philanthropy. Before this war was begun, I had, at an early time of life, withdrawn from sea service, in favor of 'calm contemplation and poetic ease.' I have sacrificed not only my favorite scheme of life, but the softer affections of the heart, and my prospects of domestic happiness, and I am ready to sacrifice my life also with cheerfulness, if that forfeiture could restore peace and goodwill among mankind.

"As the feelings of your gentle bosom cannot but be congenial with mine, let me entreat you, Madam, to use your persuasive art with your husband's, to endeavor to stop this cruel and destructive war, in which Britain never can succeed. Heaven can never countenance the barbarous and unmanly practice of the Britons in America, which savages would blush at, and which, if not discontinued, will soon be retaliated on Britain by a justly enraged people. Should you fail in this, (for I am persuaded that you will attempt it,—and who can resist the power of such an advocate?) your endeavors to effect a general exchange of prisoners, will be an act of humanity which will afford you golden feelings on a death-bed.

"I hope this cruel contest will soon be closed; but, should it continue, I wage no war with the fair. I acknowledge their force, and bend before it with submission. Let not, therefore, the amiable Countess of Selkirk regard me as an enemy. I am ambitious of her esteem and friendship, and would do anything, consistent with my duty, to merit it.

"The honor of a line from your hand, in answer to this, will lay me under a singular obligation; and if I can render you any acceptable service in France or elsewhere, I hope you see into my character so far as to command me without the least grain of reserve.

"I wish to know exactly the behavior of my people; as I determine to punish them, if they have exceeded their liberty.

"I am, Madam, with sentiments of the highest respect,

"Your Ladyship's most obedient, humble servant,

"PAUL JONES."

On the subject of Captain Jones's offer to restore the plate taken from the residence of Lord Selkirk, there is a letter from Dr. Franklin, evincing rather a proud disposition in the Scotch peer, and indicative of his disinclination to accept a favor of the kind from Jones. It follows:—

"*Passy, Feb.* 24*th*, 1779.

"DEAR CAPTAIN,

"Mr. Alexander called here this morning to deliver a little message to be communicated to you, from Lord Selkirk. The purport was, that his lordship had written an answer to your letter: which answer, after having been detained many months in the post-office, had been sent back to him. That, as to the proposition of returning the plate, if it was made by order of Congress, or any public body, he would accept of it, and endeavor to make suitable returns for the favor; but if by a private person's generosity, the captain's, for instance, he could by no means receive it. You will now judge whether it is worth while to give yourself any farther trouble about that matter.

"I am, with great regard, dear Sir,

"Your most obedient humble servant,

"B. FRANKLIN."

On the 1st of March, 1780, Jones wrote again to Lady Selkirk, as follows:—

"*L'Orient, March* 1*st*, 1780.

"The Right Hon. the Countess of SELKIRK,
&c. &c. St. Mary's Isle, Scotland.

"MADAM,

"It is now ten or eleven months since his Excellency Benjamin Franklin, Esq., Minister Plenipotentiary for the United States of America at the Court of France, communicated to me a message from the earl, your husband, in a letter to his friend, Mr. Alexander, at Paris, in substance as follows:—That he, the Earl of Selkirk, had written an answer to the letter that I had the honor to write to your ladyship in May, 1778, from Brest, respecting your plate; which answer, after being detained for several months at London, in the general post-office, had been returned to Scotland. He, therefore, wished Mr. Alexander to inform the concerned, that if the plate was to be restored by Congress, or by any public body, it would be accepted, &c.; but if, through the generosity of an individual, his delicacy would scruple to receive it, &c.

"The true reason why I have not written to you since I received the above information, has been, because the plate is but now come into my possession from the public agents; and I have, besides, been, for the greatest part of the time, absent from this kingdom.

"I have now the satisfaction to inform you, that Congress has relinquished their real or supposed interest in the plate, and, for my own part, I scorn to add to my fortune by such an acquisition. As for the part claimed by the few men who landed with me on St. Mary's Isle, it is of little consequence, and they are already satisfied. Thus you see, madam, that the earl's objection is removed.

"The plate is lodged here in the hands of Messrs. Gourlade & Moylan, who hold it at your disposal, and will forward it agreeable to your orders, by land or by water to Holland, Ostend, or any other port you think proper.

"I shall be happy, by my conduct through life, to merit the good opinion of the Earl and Countess of Selkirk; for I am, with great esteem and profound respect, Madam, your ladyship's most obedient and most humble servant,

"Paul Jones."

"*Paris, Sept.* 24*th*, 1784.

"To Capt. Paul Jones, Paris.

"Sir,

"M. the Count de Vergennes has delivered to me the letter which you had written to him, to ask his permission to transport by land from L'Orient to Calais the plate of Lady Selkirk, which you had permitted to be taken by your people during the last war, and which you afterward purchased to return to her ladyship.

"That action, sir, is worthy of the reputation which you acquired by your conduct, and proves that true valor perfectly agrees with humanity and generosity.

"It gives me pleasure to concur in the execution of this honorable proceeding.

"I have, therefore, given orders to the Farmer's General to permit the transportation of the plate from L'Orient to Calais, free of duty, and you may write to your correspondent at L'Orient to deliver it to the director of the posts, who will take upon himself the care of having it transported to Calais, and to fulfil all the necessary formalities.

"I have the honor to be, &c.

"De Calonne."

"*Paris, Nov.* 8*th*, 1784.

"The Right Hon. the Countess of Selkirk.

"Madam,

"Since the moment when I found myself under the necessity to permit my men to demand and carry off your family plate, it has been my constant intention to restore it to you, and I wrote to you to that effect from Brest, the moment I had arrived there from my expedition in the Irish Sea.

"By the letter which I had the honor to write to Lork Selkirk, the 12th of February last, which will accompany this, I have explained the difficulties that prevented the plate from being restored until that time. I had expectation, all the last summer, that opportunities would have offered to send it by sea from L'Orient to London; but being disappointed, I applied to government for leave to transport it through the kingdom by land, and the Duke of Dorset has been so obliging as to write to the custom-house at Dover, requesting them to let it pass to London, without being opened. It is now arrived here, and will be forwarded immediately to your sister in London, under the lead that has been affixed to the case that contains it, by the Farmer's General at L'Orient, and the seal of the Duke of Dorset, that has been affixed to it here. The charges to London are paid, and I have directed it to be delivered at the house of your sister.

"I could have wished to have ended this delicate business by delivering the plate to you at St. Mary's Isle, in Scotland; but I conform to the arrangement made between Lord Selkirk and Mr. Alexander, because I have no person in London whom I can charge with the transportation of the plate from thence. Enclosed is the inventory that I have just received from Mr. Nesbitt, from L'Orient, which I presume you will find to correspond with the one he sent last year to Lord Dare, and with the articles which you put into the hands of my men.

"I am, Madam, with sentiments of the highest respect,

"Your Ladyship's most obedient

"And most humble servant,

"Paul Jones."

"*From the Count* D'ESTAING, *Commander of the Fleet of His Most Christian Majesty.*

"*Paris, Dec.* 18*th*, 1785.

"To Mr. PAUL JONES, Commodore in the Navy of the United States.

"SIR,

"It is impossible not to take advantage of your kindness. Never lend me your journal again, for I must warn you that I shall read it over and over, and always with renewed pleasure. It is one of the things which one absolutely wants to know by heart. It is not only a lesson of naval and military heroism, but, by your conduct to Lord and Lady Selkirk, also one of generosity.

"I am very far from regretting the homage which I have been obliged to render to the engagement between the Bon Homme Richard and the Serapis; and although I did not suppose, while writing it,* that it might be of any other use than that of procuring an admission into the Society of the Cincinnati, I can but be flattered that you have thought it proper to insert it among the pieces which are annexed to your journal.

"I have the honor to be,
"With the most perfect attachment,
"Your most obedient servant,
"ESTAING."

"*London, August* 4*th*, 1789.

"Monsieur le Chevalier PAUL JONES, à Paris.

"SIR,

"I received the letter you wrote to me at the time you sent off my plate, in order for restoring it. Had I known where to direct a letter to you, at the time it arrived in Scotland, I would then have wrote to you; but not knowing it, nor finding that any of my acquaintance at Edinburgh knew it, I was obliged to delay writing till I came here; when, by means of a gentleman connected with America, I was told M. le Grand was your banker at Paris, and would take proper care of a letter for you; therefore I enclose this to him.

"Notwithstanding all the precautions you took for the easy and uninterrupted conveyance of the plate, yet it met with considerable delays: first at Calais, next at Dover, then at London; however, it at last arrived

* In his recommendation of Captain Edward Stack for admission into the Society of Cincinnati.

at Dumfries, and I dare say quite safe, though as yet I have not seen it, being then at Edinburgh.

"I intended to have put an article in the newspapers about your having returned it; but before I was informed of its being arrived, some of your friends, I suppose, had put it in the Dumfries newspaper, whence it was immediately copied into the Edinburgh papers, and thence into the London ones. Since that time, I have mentioned it to many people of fashion; and, on all occasions, sir, both now and formerly, I have done you the justice to tell, that you made an offer of returning the plate very soon after your return to Brest; and, although you yourself was not at my house, but remained at the shore with your boat, that yet you had your officers and men in such extraordinary good discipline, that your having given them the strictest orders to behave well, to do no injury of any kind, to make no search, but only to bring off what plate was given them; that in reality they did exactly as ordered, and that not one man offered to stir from his post on the outside of the house, nor entered the doors, nor said an uncivil word; that the two officers staid not a quarter of an hour in the parlor and butler's pantry, while the butler got the plate together, behaved politely, and asked for nothing but the plate, and instantly marched their men off in regular order, and that both officers and men behaved in all respects so well, that it would have done credit to the best disciplined troops whatever.

"Some of the English newspapers at that time having put in confused accounts of your expedition to Whitehaven and Scotland, I ordered a proper one of what happened in Scotland to be put in the London newspapers, by a gentleman who was then at my house, by which the good conduct and civil behavior of your officers and men was done justice to, and attributed to your order, and the good discipline you maintained over your people. "I am, Sir, your must humble servant,

"SELKIRK."

So highly did Dr. Franklin and John Adams, the American commissioners to the Court of France, appreciate the descent upon Whitehaven, that they proposed to recommend the persons engaged in it to the Congress, and wrote a letter to Captain Jones to that effect, of which the subjoined is an extract:

"*Extract of a letter from their Excellencies Benjamin Franklin and John Adams, to Captain John Paul Jones, dated Passy, August* 10*th*, 1778.

"We shall recommend the men who landed with you at Whitehaven to the favor of Congress, because we think they merited it; but lest our recommendation should miscarry, we wish you to recommend them, and enclose in your letter an extract of this paragraph of ours. As they have done themselves so much honor in this expedition, perhaps Congress would approve of the deduction of the advance at the time of entry, which they all received from me, being made from their wages in America, that the men may have their prize money here."

Captain Jones, indeed, according to a letter which he addressed to the Marine Committee of Congress, was the first to suggest to the American commissioners the propriety of rewarding the brave men who had been concerned in that enterprise. Less anxious about his own fortune than that of those who served with him, and merited an extraordinary recompense; he was the invariable friend of the praiseworthy seamen, whose rights he was ever ready to support, and whose interests he never failed to advance, when a favorable opportunity offered itself for his interposition:

"*Brest, August* 18*th*, 1778.

"To the Honorable the MARINE COMMITTEE.

"GENTLEMEN,

"It is evident from the above extract, that the letter from which it is taken was written in compliance with my particular request to the Commissioners. It was my intention, from the beginning, to beseech you also to recommend the men who landed with me at Whitehaven, to the bounty of Congress. That service being unprecedented in latter wars, accounts for the extreme difficulty which I found prevailing with the handful of men, who, at last, reluctantly undertook it.—The men, however, have in my judgment well merited a reward, and the bestowing it liberally on so few would, I hope, have a happy effect in prompting others to attempt still greater enterprises, with such spirit and unanimity as will generally ensure success, and lead to the most glorious victory.

"For me, if I have done my duty, the continued approbation of Congress, and the Marine Committee, will make me rich indeed, and far more than reward me for a life of service devoted from principles of philanthropy, to support the dignity of human nature.

"The Court of France having made application without my knowledge to the commissioners, that I should remain for a little time in Europe, and they having consented, Congress will, I flatter myself, approve of my having also consented to oblige a court, who has asked such a trifle, as a favor, and to whom America owes such superior obligations. I will, however, command only under freedom's flag, which I have endeavored to support since it was first displayed. I will be always ready to return to America, and I hope with some improvement and increase of knowledge in Marine affairs.

"I am, with unfeigned sentiments of esteem,
"and grateful respect,
"Gentlemen, yours, &c."

The Ranger returned from her cruize, and came to anchor in the road of Brest, on the 9th of May, 1778. Unhappy differences still prevailed between Captain Jones and his first lieutenant, whom he accused of disobedience of orders, and of incessant efforts to introduce insubordination among the seamen. Prior to Captain Jones's taking command of the Ranger, at Portsmouth, New Hampshire, his first lieutenant, whose name was Simpson, had instilled into the minds of the crew that Jones was not the real commander of the vessel; that he was, indeed, to have the control during the passage, but that, on his arrival in France, the command was to devolve on the lieutenant. Disquietudes arose among the men; Jones and Simpson had personal quarrels; and to such extremities were these unhappy differences carried, that the expedition against Whitehaven was near miscarrying, and the Drake escaping the capture which awaited her. The enterprises of Capt. Jones being out of the ordinary routine of naval service, the seamen did not always relish them; and, carrying their notions of civil government on board of a man-of-war, thought they had a just claim to be consulted on any occasion when extraordinary duty was to be performed. Jones, on the contrary, was a strict disciplinarian, required everything to be done in time and place, and enforced rigid obedience to the orders of superiors. It is very probable, also, that Lieut. Simpson, understanding that Jones was repairing to France to take the command of a vessel of a large class, did really believe that he was there to leave the Ranger under the direction of the Lieutenant, who might have supposed that he was to re-conduct her to America. Whatever the impressions of Simpson were, and whatever the deportment of Jones, it is certain that great jealousy and animosity prevailed between them, which resulted in the arrest of the former while navigating the Drake to a port in France. Capt. Jones accused Lieut. Simpson of disregarding his instructions and signals, and by the following written order suspended him from command :—

"*By* JOHN PAUL JONES, ESQ. *Captain in the American Navy, &c.*

"SIR,

"You are hereby appointed Commander of our prize, the English ship-of-war the Drake, of 20 guns. You are to put Lieut. Simpson under arrest for disobedience of orders. You are to keep company with me, and to pay punctual attention to the signals delivered herewith for your government. You are to superintend the navigation and defence of the ship under your command, and to support me as much as possible should we fall in with and engage any of the enemy's ships.

"The honor of our flag is much concerned in the preservation of this prize, therefore keep close by me, and she shall not be given *tamely up*.

"You will take your station on the Ranger's starboard quarter, at or about the distance of a cable's length. Should bad weather, or any accident, separate you from the Ranger, you are to make the best of your way to France, and I recommend the port of Brest to your preference. You will secure all the books, charts, instruments, and effects, belonging to the deceased captain and officers, &c.; for which this shall be your order.

"Given on board the American Continental ship-of-war the Ranger, off Ushant, the 7th day of May, 1778.

"JOHN PAUL JONES.

"*To Lieut.* ELIJAH HALL, *of the American Navy, commanding the prize ship the Drake.*"

"I certify the above to be a true copy of the original in my possession.

ELIJAH HALL.

Portsmouth, September 8, 1824.

When Capt. Jones on his arrival at Brest with his prize, found it convenient to put the prisoners of war on board the Drake, he deemed it necessary to remove Lieut. Simpson to a ship lying in the port, called the Admiral, in which he had a good state-room, and liberty to walk the deck. He was, however, quite restless, and sent a message to the officers and crew of the Ranger, that he had been put in prison. This excited a considerable sensation, and such was Simpson's behavior subsequently that Jones, upon a representation of the necessity of it, from Count D'Orvilliers, the French Admiral, actually placed the lieutenant in close confinement. Capt. Jones, nevertheless, cherished no enmity to Lieut. Simpson. On the contrary, he afterwards assented to his liberation; and, when a question arose as to who should command the Ranger on her return to America, and it was proposed to give it to another, it was Jones who interfered in his behalf, and urged the propriety of placing Lieut. Simpson in command for the purpose of navigating her back to Portsmouth. He accordingly took charge of that vessel on the 29th of July, 1778, and arrived at Portsmouth on the 16th of October following, having made several prizes on the passage home.

The apprehension which Jones infused along the coasts of Great Britain and Ireland by the extraordinary boldness of his enterprises against Whitehaven and St. Mary's Isle, and the capture of the Drake, is almost inconceivable. Look-out vessels were constantly kept in motion; the public attention was immediately turned to the construction of fortifications; troops were called out; and the population on the sea board was kept in the most fearful state of alarm. The following paragraphs, copied from the "*Cumberland Packet,*" of the 28th April, 1778, give but a faint idea of the frightful impressions that Capt. Jones had made upon the minds of the British and Irish public.

"LONDON.

(From the "Cumberland Packet," of April 28, 1778.)

"*Whitehaven, April* 28.—Last Thursday, in consequence of the alarm occasioned by the Ranger privateer, Lieut. Hollingsworth, at the request of the merchants, took the command of the Hussar, James Gurley, master, (a cruizer under the inspection of Charles Lutwidge, Esq.) with an intent to dodge the privateer. She sailed about 10 o'clock in the morning, two hours after which she got sight of the privateer which was then steering to the north-westward, under an easy sail, the wind about N.N.E. and moderate weather. They chased her till they came within two or three miles, spoke a boat and sent her express to Kirkcudbright, to alarm the coast. About 4 o'clock the ship brought to, being then about a league from Borough-Head. She several times altered her position, going off and hauling her wind occasionally, which the Hussar observing, acted in the same manner, being then two or three miles from her, until about seven, when the privateer made all the sail she could to the W.S.W. At half past nine the cruizer lost sight of her, then tacked and stood for Whitehaven, not knowing (it being night), but she might have stood for this place, in order to do more damage.

"At daylight, perceiving she had not come here, they stood towards Kirkcudbright, hoisted out the boat, and sent her on shore to inquire if any account had been received of her there. The boat returned with intelligence of the pirates having landed about eleven in the forenoon, on St. Mary's Isle, and plundered the house of Lord Selkirk, of plate, &c. to the amount of 650*l*.

"Friday night the Hussar returned, after looking into Wigton Bay, fully satisfied that the privateer had steered up the South Channel, and consequently quitted these coasts.

"At the request of the Committee, the Hussar, Capt. Gurley, sailed from hence on Sunday night for Belfast, to inquire into the report of the taking of his Majesty's sloop the Drake, after which and getting what intelligence he can of the Ranger privateer (or any other enemy in the channel), he is to return and report the same. And, at the request of the Committee, Capt. Perry and Capt. Sharpe are also on board the Hussar in this necessary expedition.

"David Freeman who may, in some respects, be considered as the savior of this town, says, 'that the captain of the Ranger declared that the destruction of Whitehaven was his first object, seizing the person of Lord Selkirk was the next thing he wished, after which he would sail for Brest, and on his passage, sink, burn, and destroy whatever fell in his way belonging to Great Britain.'

"Other alarming intelligence arrived here on Sunday morning, brought by the Mary Ann, Capt. Robinson, from Belfast. He arrived about nine, and reported on oath, that, on Saturday afternoon, he spoke a boat in the Lough of Belfast belonging to the Draper brig of that place, who informed him that the Drake sloop-of-war was taken on Friday afternoon, and carried away to the northward. Soon after he spoke four fishing boats, who all gave the same disagreeable information, having seen the engagement between her and three privateers, two rigged as ships, and the other a brig. The engagement lasted near two hours. Capt. Robinson further says, that soon after he got clear of the Lough, he saw the above ships to the northward of him, their courses hauled up, and the top-sails on the cap; but at too great a distance for him to ascertain their force.

"A vessel from the Isle of Man (arrived yesterday) brings an account of the Drake having two companies of soldiers on board; that she was taken by a privateer (supposed to be the Ranger); she made a stout resistance, and in the engagement lost her bowsprit and fore-top-mast.

"The account of the Drake being taken was also brought express from the shore to Belfast at 12 o'clock on Friday night. The Drake sailed from Belfast on Friday morning full of men.

"Four companies of the militia are now here.

"The guns at the forts are all cleaned and put into order; some are also planted on the north wall, and the present measures, it is hoped, will be persevered in till the fortifications are thoroughly completed. A committee of gentlemen is appointed, and a subscription opened, for defraying whatever expenses may be incurred in the defence of the town.

"Sunday last, a company of gentlemen volunteers were formed for the protection of the town, exclusive of the ten companies of seamen, &c.

"The Olive-Branch, which arrived here on Saturday last, brings an account of a large man-of-war being in the channel, and standing this way.

"Saturday last, about twelve at night, a boat full of men attempted to land at Workington. Same time a cutter stood in between the perches; but being hailed by the people on guard, who threatened to fire on them, they sheered off."

The following anecdote pertinent to the occasion, and illustrating the influence of the terrors inspired by the visit of Jones to the coast of Cumberland, is copied from the work of

Mr. Henderson, who having explored the whole of Scotland, England, and Wales, was perfectly acquainted with that part of the country which was the scene of Capt. Jones's exploits in 1778. On a reference to Jones's account of his cruize in the Ranger, in a preceding page, it will be seen that the wind did change at the time of the clergyman's extraordinary prayer to the Divinity, which must have confirmed his parishioners in the belief that their parson was a particular favorite of heaven:

"About the time that Jones visited Whitehaven, he went round to the Firth of Forth, and made his appearance off the harbor of Kirkaldy, a noted small town on the borders of Fifeshire (called by the Scotch '*Lang toun o' Kirkaldy*,' owing to its length). No other enemy, however formidable, could have created in the minds of the inhabitants such consternation and alarm as that which then approached. Paul Jones was the dread of all, old and young (and pamphlets of his depredations were as common in every house as almanacs). He was looked upon as a sea-monster, that swallowed up all that came in his power. The people all flocked to the shore to watch his movements, expecting the worst consequences. There was an old Presbyterian minister in the place, a very pious and good old man, but of a most singular and eccentric turn, especially in addressing the Deity, to whom he would speak with as much familiarity as he would to an old farmer, and seemingly without respect, as will appear from the following. He was soon seen making his way through the people with an old black oak arm-chair, which he lugged down to low water mark (the tide flowing), and sat down in it. Almost out of breath, and rather in a passion, he then began to address the Deity in the following singular way :—

"'Now *deed* Lord, *dinna* ye think it's a shame for *ye* to send this vile *pireet* to *rub* our *folk o' Kirkaldy ;* for ye *ken* they're *a' puir* enough already, and *hae naething* to *spare.* They are *a' gaily guid*, and it *wad* be a *peety* to serve them in *sic in a wa.* The *wa* the *wun blaws*, he'll be here in a *jiffie*, and *wha kens* what he may do. He's *nane* too *guid* for *ony* thing. *Meickle's* the mischief he has *dune* already. *Ony pecket gear* they *hae* gathered *thegither* he will *gang wi' the heal o't ;* may burn their *hooses*, *tak* their *vary claes*, and *tirl* them to the *sark ;* and *waes me! wha kens* but the *bluidy* villain might *tak* their lives. The *puir weemen ere maist freightened* out o' their *wuts*, and the *bairns skirling* after them. *I canna' tho'lt! I canna' tho'lt!* I *hae* been *lang* a *faithfu'* servant to *ye*, *Laird ;* but *gin ye dinna* turn the *wun* about, and *blaw* the

5

scoundrel out of our *gate*, I'll *na stur a fit*, but will *juist* sit here, until the tide comes and *drouns* me. *Sae tak yere wull o't.*' "

When Captain Jones left the United States for France he understood that he was destined eventually to take command of a frigate of the first class, which had been built for the United States in Holland. In this he was disappointed; and was for some time kept in a situation of inactivity and suspense, ill suited to his genius and disposition. He had been sent for to Paris, and had suggested a number of enterprises to the French ministry; but they were slow in their determinations, and Jones, for a time, considered himself neglected, and, in some degree, badly treated. His drafts on the American Commissioners, also, had been protested,* and he felt chagrined at the apparent indifference shown to his claims to employment, which was aggravated by an opinion which he entertained that he was regarded at Brest as an officer in disgrace. But Captain Jones was not a man to yield to adverse circumstances. He combated every difficulty, repeated and reiterated his applications to the minister of the French marine, wrote to Dr. Franklin, remonstrated with Mr. Arthur Lee, addressed himself to influential persons about the French court, and actually wrote a spirited letter to the King of France, Louis XVI., which doubtless had its effect. His feelings and thoughts under the various embarrassments which he endured, his views and reflections, from the period of his arrival at Brest after the capture of the Drake, whilst at Paris, and on his return to Brest from that capital until his appointment to the command of the Bonhomme Richard, and his return from the cruize which

* The commissioners explained to Commodore Jones that they had neither authority nor funds to make the advances of money which he required. They, however, did all in their power, and even exceeded their instructions in assisting him.

ended in the capture of the British frigate Serapis, are so well expressed in the subjoined letters and documents, that no apology is requisite for their insertion. No writer can so well portray the incidents of any transaction as an intelligent individual who is personally concerned in it, who originates it, and under whose control it is consummated. Captain Jones was particularly attentive in committing to paper every public event of his life, was remarkably clear in his explanations, and extremely precise in communicating his sentiments to those with whom he corresponded:

"*Ranger*, *Brest*, *March* 31*st*, 1778.

"M. De Sartine, Minister, and Secretary of State for the Marine Department.

"Honored Sir,

"As I have not the honor of being known to you, I hope you will pardon the liberty I take of enclosing the copy of a letter from the secret committee of Congress to the American commissioners in Europe. I must, however, acknowledge that the generous praise which is therein bestowed on me by Congress, far exceeds the merit of my services.

"My reason for laying this letter before you is, because I am destined by Congress to command a frigate of a very large construction lately built at Amsterdam,—and as political reasons made it necessary for that frigate to become French property, I am now induced to hope that on her arrival in France she will again become the property of America, and of course be put under my command.

"The within extract of a letter dated 10th Feb. last, to the American commissioners will, I hope, prove to you the real satisfaction with which I have anticipated the happy alliance between France and America.—I am, sir, convinced that the capture of Lord Howe's light ships and frigates in America, and the destruction of the enemy's fishery at Newfoundland, which might be easily effected this summer, would effectually destroy the sinews of their marine, for they would afterward be unable to man their fleet:—and as to their army in America, that must fall of course.

"I should be ungrateful did I forget to acknowledge the polite attentions and favors which I have received from Compte d'Orvilliers, M. De la Porse, M. la Motte Picquet, and every officer in this place.

"The Admiral Count d'Orvilliers has, I doubt not, communicated to you a project of mine. I am, sir, ambitious of being employed in active and enterprising services;—but my ship is of too small a force, and does not sail so fast as I could wish. If I am successful I will return to France, and hope for your countenance and protection.

"I have addressed you, sir, with the same freedom which has ever marked my correspondence with Congress. The interests of France and America are the same; and as I hope to see the common enemy humbled, I shall be happy if I can furnish any hint whereby that event can be effected. Meantime,

"I have the honor to be,
"with profound respect, &c.

"*Brest, June* 1*st*, 1778.

"His Excellency, BENJAMIN FRANKLIN.

"HONORED AND DEAR SIR,

"Accept my grateful thanks for your much esteemed favor of 27th ult. Such a mark of your good opinion and approbation really affords me the most heartfelt satisfaction. It shall always be my ambition to do my duty as far as my judgment and small abilities enable me;—but you will see by the within papers that my roses are not without thorns; and, perhaps, it will seem romance that I have succeeded, which I am sure I should not have done had I not been my own counsellor.

"Nothing would give me more pleasure than to render essential services to America, in any measure which you may find expedient. Should I be able to lead my present crew, it can be done only by the seldom failing bait for sordid minds, *great views of interest.*

"If, in bringing about the plan you propose, I may take the liberty to assure them of the protection of the French flag, in the channel, against enemies of superior force, with the free liberty to attack, and take under that sanction such of the enemy's ships of war or merchantmen as may be met with of equal or inferior force, perhaps I may succeed and gain them over by that means, nor will it be necessary to tell them our real object.

"If I am not at liberty to give them such assurances, and their *home-sickness* should continue, I could wish that such officers as may appear *dangerously ill*, might have liberty to lay down their commissions and warrants,—and that others may be given to men of stronger nerves, who would be too proud to think themselves servants by the year. I believe many such may be found among American subjects in France.

"If it should be consistent to order the Boston frigate here from Bordeaux, perhaps such exchanges might be made as would be for the interest and harmony of the service; and we might perhaps be able to assemble a sufficient number of officers to form a court.

"The Duc de Chartres has shown me sundry attentions, and expressed his inclination to facilitate my obtaining the ship built at Amsterdam. I believe I could easily obtain letters to the same effect from the principal people here, but shall take no step without your approbation. If the prisoners should be exchanged in Europe, I believe it would be possible to man that ship with Americans. I could have manned two such with French volunteers since I arrived.

"The Ranger is crank, sails slow, and is of a trifling force. Most of the enemy's cruizers are more than a match, yet I mean not to complain. I demand nothing; and, although I know that it was the intention of Congress to give me that ship, I am now ready to go wherever the service calls me.

"If two or three fast sailing ships could be collected, there is a great choice of private enterprises, some of which might succeed and add more to the interest and honor of America, than cruizing with twice the force. It appears to me to be the province of our infant navy to surprise and spread alarms with fast sailing ships. When we grow stronger we can meet their fleets, and dispute with them the sovereignty of the ocean. These are my private sentiments, and are therefore submitted with the utmost diffidence to your superior understanding.

"I have the honor to be, &c.

Extract of a Letter from Com. John Paul Jones to the American Commissioners at the Court of France, dated Brest, June 3, 1778.

"I hope you do not mean to impute to me a desire to receive presents of the public money, or even to touch a dollar of it for my own private use; on the contrary, I need not now assert, that I stepped forth at the beginning from *nobler motives.*

"My accounts before I left America testify that I am more than 1500*l.* in advance for the public service, exclusive of any concern with the sloop-of-war Ranger; and as for wages I have never received any.

"The Rules whereby Congress have been pleased to command me to regulate my conduct in the navy, authorize me to issue my warrant to the agent, &c., and I humbly conceive that it is his province to furnish me with an estimate of the amount of expenses. A space of sixteen months is now elapsed since Congress thought of me, and placed under my command *seven times* my present force, leaving me at full liberty how and where to apply it. And if I am not now capable of supporting the internal government of a single sloop-of-war, I wish that some person more deserving had my place, and I in America to answer for my misconduct. I have 'well considered,' and yet shall persist in justifying the steps which I have taken, and to which you allude.

"I am happy in having it in my power to furnish you with the inclosed resolution of Congress, respecting the capture of the enemy's ships-of-war, agreeably to your desire; and, if you are in possession of any resolution of Congress which will authorize me to * * * * * send to America, I should be obliged to you for a copy of it."

Passy, June 5, 1778.

Plan for Expeditions submitted by Com. Jones to the American Plenipotentiaries, and to the French Minister of Marine.

"As the first proposed will be impeded for some time, in the interval a great variety of projects present themselves, some of which might prove of great utility to France and America by distressing the common enemy at a small expense.

"Three very fast sailing frigates, with one or two tenders, might enter the Irish channel, and burn at Whitehaven from two to three hundred ships, besides the town which contains 50,000 inhabitants; this would render it difficult, if not impossible, to supply Ireland with coal the ensuing winter.

"The same force would be sufficient to take the bank of Ayr in Scotland, and to destroy the town, or perhaps the whole shipping in the Clyde with the towns and stores of Greenock and Port-Glasgow, provided no alarm was first given at other places. The fishery at Cambletown is an object worthy attention, and in some of the ports of Ireland ships may perhaps be found worth from 150,000 to 200,000*l.* sterling each.

"It might perhaps be equally expedient to alarm Britain on the east side, which might be effected with equal and perhaps inferior force, by destroying the coal shipping of Newcastle, &c. which would occasion the utmost distress for fuel in London; and there are many towns of consequence on the east and north coasts of England and Scotland which are defenceless, and might be either burnt or laid under contribution.

"The success of either these or the like enterprises will depend on surprising well, and on despatch both in the attack and in the retreat; therefore it is necessary the ships should sail fast, and that their force should be sufficient to repel any of the enemy's cruizing frigates, two of which may perhaps be met at a time.

"It is scarcely conceivable how great a panic the success in any one of these projects would occasion in England. It would convince the world that their coasts are vulnerable, and would consequently hurt their public credit.

"If alarming the coast of Britain should be thought inexpedient, to intercept the enemy's West India or Baltic fleets, or their Hudson Bay ships, or to destroy their Greenland fishery are capital objects, which promise success if well adopted, and any one of them might be finished before the first can take place."

Passy, July 17, 1778.

"M. De Sartine.

"My Lord,

"I should be ungrateful, did I not return my thanks for your kind and generous intentions in my favor. My greatest ambition would be to merit your future approbation, by my services against the common enemy of France and America. Had your first plan taken effect, the most pleasing prospect of success would have been before me. But that now seems a distant object.

"I have no doubt but that many projects, which would promise success, might be formed from the hints I had the honor of sending lately for your inspection. Had I been intrusted with the chief command, I would have been responsible for the consequences.

"I am bound in honor to communicate faithfully to Congress the generous offer which the king now makes of lending the Epervier, in the mean time to be employed under my command and under the flag of the United States of America. I would thankfully have accepted this offer the moment it was communicated to me, had no difficulties occurred on account of the situation of the American funds. I have now under my command a ship bound to America. On my arrival there, from the former confidence of Congress, I have reason to expect an immediate removal into one of their best ships. I have reason, also, to expect the chief command of the first squadron destined for an expedition. I have in my possession several similar appointments; and when Congress sees fit to appoint admirals, I have assurances that my name will not be forgot.

"These are flattering prospects to a man who has drawn his sword only from motives of philanthropy, and in support of the dignity of human nature. But, as I prefer a solid to a shining reputation—a useful to a splendid command,—I hold myself ready, with the approbation of the American Commissioners at Paris, to be governed by you in any measures that may tend to distress and humble the common enemy.

"I have the honor to be, &c.

"J. P. Jones."

"*Brest*, *August* 24, 1778.

"His Highness the Prince De Nassau.

"My Prince,

"The honor which you propose to do me, by accompanying me on the ocean, fills my heart with the warmest sentiments of gratitude.

"When your intentions were communicated to me I had under my command a ship bound in company with two fine frigates for America, where there are now two new ships of 80 guns each, and eight frigates of 40 guns each, nearly ready for sea.

"On my arrival there, from the former confidence of Congress, I had assurance of an immediate removal into one of their best ships, and to have been appointed to command the first squadron which they thought fit to destine for any private expedition. Before I came to Europe, Congress honored me with several such appointments, and I had assurance that when admirals were appointed my name would be remembered.

"These, my Prince, were flattering prospects to a man who drew his sword only from principles of philanthropy and in support of the dignity of human nature; and these are the prospects which I have voluntarily laid aside that I may pursue glory in your company.

"Suffer me not therefore, I beseech you, to continue longer in this shameful inactivity; such dishonor is worse to me than a thousand deaths. I have already lost the golden season, the summer, which in war is of more value than all the rest of the year. I appear here as a person cast off and useless, and when any one asks me what I purpose to do, I am unable to answer.

"Had this been my first or second disappointment I should have said nothing concerning it. After various other objects had misgiven before I left Passy, which M. de Sartine had thought of to keep me employed, until the scheme wherein you were concerned could take place, I was ordered down here at so short a notice, that I had not time, before my departure, to take leave of you; yet, on my arrival here, I found that what had been proposed for me was bestowed on others. I then offered to follow Count D'Orvilliers as a volunteer, agreeably to his kind invitation; but M. de la Prévaláye will not permit this, it not being mentioned in his orders.

"I have, my Prince, been unaccustomed to ask any favors, even from Congress, for I am not in pursuit of interest;—yet, let me beseech you to represent my situation to the best of kings, that I may, with you, be forthwith enabled to pursue glory, and humble the common enemy of humanity.

"If the ship that was at first proposed cannot with certainty be got ready for sea next month, you, my Prince, can obtain another, with the

Epervier and the Alert, tenders. There is a fine frigate at L'Orient, built on the same construction with the ship at first proposed, and mounted with eighteen-pounders. This ship has been at India, is known to sail fast, and may, perhaps, be obtained, till it is seen whether the other can be got out.

"If this ship is refused, there are many other fine frigates newly built at St. Maloes, and other places, to which I hear of no commanders being appointed. I have the greatest dependence on the generous intentions of that great minister, M. de Sartine, but I cannot every day intrude on him with letters, and, in the multiplicity and importance of his affairs, my concerns may escape his memory.

"I wish for the honor of a letter from your own hand;—though I cannot write in French, yet I understand letters which are written in that language; and I have with me now a lieutenant that speaks it well.

"My Prince, yours," &c.

"*Brest, August* 24*th*, 1778.

"His Excellency, BENJAMIN FRANKLIN.

"HONORED AND DEAR SIR,

"Had I indulged my inclination since my return, I should have already troubled you with sundry letters. I must not, however, abuse the indulgent liberty which you gave me at parting, and I have, therefore, been more troublesome to Dr. Bancroft.

"I wish not to be thought too impatient, but you know, my dear sir, that this is the nice moment, when I ought to be either in search of marine knowledge with Count D'Orvilliers, or in search of honor in attempting some private enterprise. Before I was at liberty to go, the good old count pressed me much to accompany him; but since Dr. Bancroft has informed me that it would be agreeable to the minister that I should, I have been precluded from following the fleet, as the present commandant has no orders for that purpose.

"Thus circumstanced, without employment, and, in appearance, cast off, I have written the within letter to the Prince de Nassau, which I leave open for your perusal. Should you find the whole, or any part of it, improper, I beg of you to withhold it.

"After all my disappointments, I am yet persuaded that the court had, from the beginning, and still have, intentions in my favor, since you know the connexion was not of my seeking.

"I am, with the highest sense of your friendship and goodness,

"Honored and dear Sir, yours," &c.

"*Brest, August* 28*th*, 1778.

"His Excellency, Count D'Orvilliers, General and Commander-in-Chief of the Brest Fleet.

"Honored and Dear Sir,

"When you kindly proposed that I should accompany you on board the Bretagne, I had been ordered from Paris for a private expedition. I was, indeed, sorry that I could not then think myself at liberty to accept your very polite and friendly offer.

"Though I have not, to this moment, received a word from the minister since I returned here, yet I have understood, from a friend at Paris, that M. de Sartine at last agreed that I should embark with you. On receiving this information, I immediately applied to M. de la Prévaláye for a passage in the first ship to join the fleet; but he says he will not permit my embarkation without orders from the minister, or from you.

"This, my dear sir, is the principal reason why I now trouble you. I was ambitious of the honor of attending you on the first campaign, where you acquired so much glory; but M. de Sartine would not then permit me to go. I must now, therefore, beg the favor of you, should you send in any vessel with letters, that you will give directions to M. de la Prévaláye, to permit my embarkation to join you. I ardently wish to attend you with my eyes, even to the pinnacle of fame, and to learn from so great and good a general, how I may hereafter ascend the slippery precipice beyond which the edifice is erected."

"*Brest, September* 13*th*, 1778.

"M. de Sartine.

"Honored Sir,

"When his Excellency, Dr. Franklin, first informed me that you had condescended to think me worthy your notice, I took such pleasure in reflecting on the happy alliance between France and America, that I was really flattered, and entertained a grateful sense of the honor which you proposed for me, as well as the favor which the king proposed for America, by putting so fine a ship of war as the Indien under my command, and under its flag, with unlimited orders.

"In obedience to your desire I came to Versailles; and was taught to believe that my intended ship was in deep water, and ready for sea. But, when the prince returned, I received from him the account that the Indien could not be got afloat under three months.

"To employ this interval usefully, I offered to accompany Compte D'Orvilliers as a volunteer, which you thought fit to reject. I had, then, the satisfaction to find that you approved, in general, of a variety of hints for private enterprises, which I had presented for your consideration, and was flattered with assurances from M. le Ray de Chaumont and Bodwain, that three of the finest frigates in France, with two tenders, and a number of troops, should be immediately put under my command, and I should be at liberty to pursue such of my projects as I thought proper. But this fell to nothing, in the moment when I thought that the king's signature only was wanting.

"Another inferior armament, from L'Orient, was proposed, to be put under my command, which was by no means equal to the services that were expected from it; for speed and force, both requisite, were wanting. Happily for me, this also failed, and I was saved from a dreadful prospect of ruin and dishonor.

"I had so entire a reliance that you would require nothing of me inconsistent with my rank and honor, that the moment you commanded, I came down with such haste that, although my curiosity led me to look at the armament at L'Orient, yet I was but three days from Passy till I reached Brest. Here, too, I drew a blank. But when I saw the Lively, it was no disappointment, as that ship, in sailing and equipment, is far inferior to the Ranger.

"My only disappointment here, is being precluded embarking with Compte D'Orvilliers in pursuit of marine knowledge.

"I am not a mere adventurer of fortune. Stimulated by reason and philanthropy, I laid aside the enjoyments of private life, and embarked under the flag of America when it was first displayed. In this line my desire of fame is infinite; and I must not so far forget my own honor, and what I owe to my friends and to America, as to remain inactive. My rank knows no superior in the American marine. I have long since been appointed to command an expedition with five of its ships, and I can receive orders from no junior or inferior officer whatever.

"I have been here in the most tormenting suspense for more than a month since my return, and agreeable to your desire, as mentioned to me by M. de Chaumont.

"Circular letters were sent the 8th of last month from the English Admiralty, because they expected me to pay another visit with four ships. Therefore, I trust, that if the Indien is not to be got out, you will not substitute a force unequal in strength and sailing to the enemy's cruizing ships.

"I do not wish to interfere with the harmony of the French marine; but if I am still thought worthy your attention, I shall hope for a separate command, with liberal orders:—if, on the contrary, you have no farther occasion for my services, I have then only to ask the Alert, and a few seamen, with permission to return in that small vessel to America before winter.

"I am happy to hear that the frigates from St. Malo have been successful near Shetland. Had Count D'Estaign arrived in the Delaware a few days sooner, he might have made a most glorious and easy conquest. Many other successful projects may be adopted from hints which I had the honor to draw up, and if I can still furnish more, or execute any of those furnished, so as to distress and humble the common enemy, it will afford me the truest satisfaction.

"I am ambitious to merit the honor of your friendship, and am fully persuaded that I address a noble-minded man who will not be offended with the honest freedom which has always marked my correspondence.

"I have the honor to be, with great respect, &c."

Extract to His Excellency BENJAMIN FRANKLIN, dated

"*Brest, September* 14, 1778.

"HONORED AND DEAR SIR,

"I yesterday took the resolution to write the inclosed explicit letter to the minister. I should not have mentioned my rank, had it not been hinted that it was proposed to send me from St. Maloes under command of French lieutenants. The frigates were sent in consequence of a hint from me, and though I am neglected, I hope they have been very successful.

"It is vain for the minister to pretend he has no ships to bestow, as I know to the contrary."

Extract of a Letter to the same, dated

"*Brest, September* 18, 1778.

"I have seen the Fox, mounting 24 guns (taken formerly by the Hancock and Adams), and would accept of that ship attended by the Alert, unless something better is immediately bestowed. I shall, with this command, expect unlimited orders."

Extract of a Letter to the same, dated

"*Brest, November* 27, 1778.

"Lieut. Amiel has exercised with me patience for four months in this place, without society or hospitality.

"Let them give me but powers, and I will find a ship and men without loss of time. I will undertake, if necessary, at the risk of my private property, that the seamen's wages shall be either paid from the public funds in America, or from the part of prizes usually claimed by the American Government.

"Your silence has hurt me; though I am sensible I owe much to your good offices and wishes.

"I have read and considered well all my past letters, and find nothing that I wish I had omitted, or that I conceive could have altered any person before my friend."

"*Brest, September* 21, 1778.

"His Royal Highness le Duc de CHARTRES.

"MY PRINCE,

"I should be ungrateful did I not entertain the deepest sense of the obligation which you conferred on me by your letters to the Palais Royal aud Versailles, in June last.

"I was at that time happy in being sent for privately to his Excellency Dr. Franklin, at the desire of M. de Sartine, who proposed to bestow on me a very honorable command.

"I was flattered with the assurances that three frigates, two tenders, and a number of troops, should be immediately put under my command, to pursue such projects as I thought proper. This plan failed. Another was proposed where the force was unequal to what was expected from the service. Happily for me this also failed.

"I was then ordered to the command of the Lively to join some frigates on an expedition from St. Maloes. I arrived in Brest in three days from Passy, and found the Lively had been given to another; but this disappointment pleased me, when I found that the Lively was quite inferior to the Ranger.

"I do not wish to interfere with the harmony of the French marine; but we fight in a common cause, and it is the interest of both to distress and humble an enemy who arrogates to himself the sovereignty of the ocean. I could have been serviceable had my hands been at liberty in the summer.

"I would accept of the ——— as a ———, rather than undergo the mortification of returning to America unemployed, after having written to Congress that I am detained in Europe by the particular desire of the Court of France. If the minister has no farther occasion for my services, I have then only to ask permission to have the Alert, and to carry with me to America his good opinion, before the winter.

"As, in my present mysterious situation here, I am considered an officer in disgrace, I am persuaded I need make no farther apology to a brave officer and a noble minded prince for the liberty I take.

"The honor your letters procured me at the Palays Royal, will be ever remembered with gratitude.

"Ambitious to merit your friendship and favor,

"I am, with great esteem and profound respect, &c."

"*Brest, October* 19, 1778.

"His Excellency BENJAMIN FRANKLIN.

"HONORED AND DEAR SIR,

"I hope you will find the within letter (to the king) entirely free from asperity or ill nature. I have been, and am in the eyes of Brest and the French marine, considered as having incurred your displeasure, and being consequently in disgrace.

"The Commissioners' refusal of my bill, my journey to Paris without any visible reason, the cabals and misrepresentations of Lieutenant Simpson, and my present inactivity, are held to be so many circumstantial proofs; and my dishonor is now so firmly believed everywhere that it is in vain for me to assert the contrary; such a situation destroys my peace of mind, and is incompatible with my sensibility, yet I am far more affected by the indignity that has been shown through me to yourself and to America, than on my own account.

"My heart cannot forgive the minister, till he makes whole my injured honor by a direct apology, and atonement for the past.

"My letter to the king cannot, I think, do harm, and unless you disapprove it, I beg that it may have course. The Duchess de Chartres will, I am persuaded, undertake to deliver it into the king's hands, and as you may not think fit at present to appear in the business, either the Duc de Rochefacault or your grandson will oblige me by waiting on her at the Palays Royal. The Duc de Rochefacault as he understands English well, and is acquainted with the circumstances, would oblige me much if he could be present when the letter is presented to the king. I do not wish to trouble the Duc de Chartres about this affair, as that brave Prince has undeservedly met with vexations of his own. Let not your delicacy prevent my having the honor of hearing from you, for so far am I from blaming you as the cause of my unhappiness, that I am entirely convinced that you had no other motive than my honor and promotion as consistent with the public good. I am consequently with the veneration and affection of a son who ardently wishes to render himself worthy your regard,

"Honored and dear Sir,

"Yours, &c.

"*Brest, October* 19, 1778.

"His Most Christian Majesty, Louis,
King of France and Navarre.

"Sire,

"After my return to Brest in the American ship-of-war the Ranger from the Irish Channel, his Excellency, Dr. Franklin, informed me by letter, dated June 1st, that M. de Sartine, having a good opinion of my conduct and bravery, had determined, with your Majesty's consent and approbation, to give me the command of the ship-of-war the Indien which was built at Amsterdam for America, but afterwards for political reasons made the property of France. I was to act with unlimited orders under the commission and flag of America. And the Prince de Nassau proposed to accompany me on the ocean.

"I was deeply penetrated with a sense of the honor done me by this proposition, as well as of the favor which your Majesty intended thereby to confer on America, and I accepted the offer with the greater pleasure as the Congress had sent me to Europe in the Ranger to command the Indien, before the ownership of that vessel was changed.

"The minister desired to see me at Versailles, to settle future plans of operations, and I attended him for that purpose. I was told that the Indien was at the Texel, completely armed and fitted for sea, but the Prince de Nassau was sent express to Holland, and returned with a very different account—the ship was at Amsterdam, and could not be got afloat or armed before the September equinox.

"The American plenipotentiaries proposed that I should return to America; and as I had been appointed repeatedly to the chief command of an American squadron to execute secret enterprises, it was not doubted but that Congress would again show me a preference. M. de Sartine, however, thought proper to prevent my departure by writing to the plenipotentiaries (without my knowledge), requesting that I might be permitted to remain in Europe, and that the Ranger might be sent back to America under another commander, he having special services which he wished me to execute. This request they readily granted, and I was flattered by the prospect of being enabled to testify by my services my gratitude to your Majesty as the first prince who has so generously acknowledged our independence.

"There was an interval of more than three months before the Indien could be got afloat. To employ that period usefully, when your majesty's fleet was ordered to sail from Brest, I proposed to the minister to embark in it as a volunteer, in pursuit of marine knowledge. He objected to this, but at the same time approved of a variety of hints for private enterprises, which I had drawn up for his consideration.

"Two gentlemen were appointed to settle with me the plans that were to be adopted—who gave me assurance that three of the best frigates in France, with two tenders, and a number of boats, should be immediately put under my command, and to pursue such of my own projects as I thought proper; but this fell to nothing, when I believed that your majesty's signature only was wanting.

"Another armament, composed of cutters and small vessels at L'Orient, was proposed to be put under my command, to alarm the coasts of England, and check the Jersey privateers; but happily for me this also failed, and I was saved from ruin and dishonor; for, as I now find, all the vessels sailed slow, and their united force was very insignificant.

"The minister then thought fit that I should return to Brest to command the Lively, and join some frigates on an expedition from St. Malo to the North Sea. I returned in haste for that purpose, and found that the Lively had been bestowed at Brest, before the minister had mentioned that ship to me at Versailles. This was, however, another fortunate disappointment, as the Lively proves, both in sailing and equipment, much inferior to the Ranger, but more especially if it be true, as I have since understood, that the minister intended to give the chief command of the expedition to a lieutenant, which would have occasioned a very disagreeable misunderstanding; for, as an officer of the first rank in the American marine, who has ever been honored with the favor and friendship of Congress, I can receive orders from no inferior officer whatever. My plan was the destruction of the English Baltic fleet, of great consequence to the enemy's marine, and then only protected by a single frigate! I would have held myself responsible for its success had I commanded the expedition.

"M. de Sartine afterward sent orders to Count D'Orvilliers to receive me on board the fleet, agreeable to my former proposal, but the order did not arrive until after the departure of the fleet the last time from Brest, nor was I made acquainted with the circumstance before the fleet returned here.

"Thus have I been chained down to shameful inactivity for nearly five months. I have lost the best season of the year, and such opportunities of serving my country and acquiring honor as I cannot again expect this war; and, to my infinite mortification, having no command, I am considered everywhere an officer cast off, and in disgrace for secret reasons.

"I have written respectful letters to the minister, none of which has he condescended to answer. I have written to the Prince of Nassau with as little effect, and I do not understand that any apology has been made to the great and venerable Dr. Franklin, whom the minister has made the instrument of bringing me into such unmerited trouble.

"Having written to Congress to reserve no command for me in America, my sensibility is the more affected by this unworthy situation in the sight of your majesty's fleet. I however make no remark on the treatment I have received.

"Although I wish not to become my own panegyrist, I must beg your majesty's permission to observe, that I am not an adventurer in search of fortune, of which, thank God, I have a sufficiency.

"When the American banners were first displayed, I drew my sword in support of the violated dignity and rights of human nature; and both honor and duty prompt me steadfastly to continue the righteous pursuit, and to sacrifice to it not only my private enjoyments, but even life, if necessary. I must acknowledge that the generous praise which I have received from Congress and others, *exceeds the merit of my past services, therefore I the more ardently wish for future opportunities of testifying my gratitude by my activity.*

"As your majesty, by espousing the cause of America, has become the 'protector of the rights of human nature,' I am persuaded that you will not disregard my situation, nor suffer me to remain any longer in this insupportable disgrace.

"I am, with perfect gratitude and profound respect,

"Sire,

"Your Majesty's very obliged, very obedient,

"And very humble servant,

"J. P. JONES."

"*Brest, October* 19*th*, 1778.

"To Madame la Duchesse de CHARTRES.

"MADAM,

"The business which brought me from Brest to Paris last summer, when I had the pleasure of paying my respects to your royal highness, afforded me a very fair prospect of being enabled immediately to pay a much more successful visit to the enemy's coast than that from which I was then returned. I appeared at Versailles by the particular desire of M. de Sartine, who, in consequence of the high opinion he professed to have of my conduct and bravery, voluntarily proposed (as I understood with the consent and approbation of his majesty), to bestow on me a very honorable command; he having written a letter to their excellencies the American plenipotentiaries requesting as a favor that I might be permitted to remain in Europe. Yet the minister has made no apology for all this, either to myself (who did not seek after the commission), nor to his excellency Dr. Franklin, through whom it was accepted.

"I had the honor to furnish the minister with a number of plans, which he approved, for secret expeditions, but the various armaments which have been proposed to be put under my command to pursue my own projects, every one of these armaments have fallen to nothing, some of them even at the moment when I was taught to believe that the king's signature alone was wanting. Thus have I been trifled with for nearly five months, the best season of the year, and such opportunities of serving my country and acquiring honors, as I again expect in the course of the war, are lost. I have written to Congress to reserve no command for me in America, and to my inexpressible mortification, having no command here, I am considered everywhere as an officer in disgrace. I am not an adventurer in search of fortune; on the contrary, I laid aside my enjoyments of private life, and drew my sword at the commencement of this war only in support of the dignity and violated rights of human nature; and honored as I am with the favor and friendship of Congress, both honor and duty prompt me steadfastly to persevere till these rights are established, or lose my life in the righteous pursuit. But as I see no prospect of being soon relieved from this unworthy situation, I have written the enclosed letter to his majesty, which I must beseech your royal highness to present,—you will thereby add a singular obligation to what I already owe to your former condescending attention. I should be extremely happy to succeed through the influence of so amiable a princess and so powerful an advocate, whom I perfectly esteem and respect, being truly and always in the artless sincerity of my heart,

"Madam,

"Your Royal Highness's very obedient,

"and very humble servant,

"J. P. Jones."

"*Brest, November* 13*th*, 1778.

"The Hon. Robert Morris, Philadelphia.

"Honored and Dear Sir,

"My fortune has been so chequered since I left Quiberon Bay, that I could have sent you no general account of my situation that would not have given you more pain than pleasure, and I know that you have vexations enough of your own.

The within papers will show that my roses have not been without a superabundance of thorns, and perhaps it will appear romance that I have succeeded under circumstances; which I am sure I should not have done had I not been my own counsellor.

"I have been here in the most disagreeable situation for five months.

It has been urged that the rules of the service will not admit of giving me command of ships detached from the royal marine:—but the great obstacle is, that the French officers (though they would gladly think me in disgrace) are stung to the soul, and cannot look at me here but with rival eyes, their cabals are so high and dangerous that the minister really cannot, and dare not do what he wishes. *He has, however, authorised M. de Chaumont to purchase a ship to my liking*, if to be found in any private dock or yard in France.

"What the result of this may be I know not, but I hope it will set me, before the spring, once more afloat.

"It has been to me a most unfortunate connexion, and has, I fear, created me some enemies through jealousy, and because I am bound in honor not to publish the particulars.

"I submit the whole to your discretion, with entire confidence as the guardian of my honor, to whom I owe the most singular obligations.

"I shall have the honor to write you by future opportunities an account of what fortune attends me. Meantime, believe me,

"I am, with real esteem and affection,

"Dear Sir, yours," &c.

"*Brest, November* 21*st*, 1778.

"His Excellency, ARTHUR LEE.

"SIR,

"I have had the honor to receive your letter of the 16th current. It is my duty, and will ever afford me pleasure, to give every satisfactory information in my power respecting any circumstance that regards the public interest, and my conduct as an American officer. In my letter of the 3d of June to the commissioners, I was very particular in accounting for the prizes I had taken. On my way from America to Nantz, I took two brigs laden with fruit, from Malaga, for London. The one of which you inquire arrived at Nantz, and was sold very cheap by Messrs. Morris and Williams, the captors' moiety of which was paid them in February, agreeable to your letter. This is all that came within my knowledge; but I have understood, and believe, that the latter acted in that business by virtue of the authority which he received from the former, to whom I made application on my arrival. Should any farther account be necessary, I am always ready to give it as far as it lays in my power.

"If Mr. Lee will for a moment recur to my letter to him, dated on board the Ranger the 26th of February last, he will find no reason to charge me with want of due respect. The handbill that was enclosed, by which I became accountable to those who entered to serve under my command *for the regular payment of their wages*, having been approved of by the Marine Committee (as certified to me under their secretary's hand), the public faith was thereby pledged to put it in my power, else I should have found other means to fulfil that engagement. And this appears to have been Mr. Lee's opinion, when he wrote with his own hand a letter of credit in my favor, at Passy, the 10th of January last, now before me.

"The handful of men under my command had been led through many dangers of storms and enemies, and, though in want of clothing and money, were returned with some credit to Brest, yet when, on the 16th of May, I ventured to sign my first draft on the public funds for their relief, agreeable to my letter of advice, my signature was dishonored.

"Neither Dr. Franklin nor Mr. Adams were acquainted with my engagement to the crew; but Mr. Lee, who had been better informed, concurred to dishonor my draft, and left me with two hundred prisoners of war, a number of sick and wounded, an almost naked crew, and a ship, after a severe engagement, in want of stores and provisions, from the 9th of May till the 13th of June, destitute of any public support; yet I found means to cure my wounded, feed my people, to refit the ship, and guard my prisoners.

"The dishonor that had been done me was known through the French fleet and elsewhere; yet, though I was the first that had appeared at Brest and obtained from France the honors due the American flag, I made no public complaints, and only expressed my concern by letter to the commissioners, at the disgraceful wound which the public credit had suffered through me. And now I beg leave to ask Mr. Lee if I have deserved such treatment?

"The wretched situation of the crew occasioned murmuring, which was artfully fomented by an officer in disgrace, who succeeded too well in persuading the people that I had deceived them, and that they should cast the whole blame upon me, as the hindrance to their receiving wages, prize-money, and bounties. In this agitation of their minds he obtained from them certificates, &c. to the commissioners in his favor.

"These poor men were at last dragged away without clothing, having only received at Brest eight or nine crowns each, as prize money, the moment of their departure, and not being allowed time to lay out that trifle, and imprecating general curses on the public service, public agents, and all concerned.

"This is not the way to establish a navy. Congress has made laws for its internal government, and appointed the officers alone as magistrates to put them into execution. The standing order of the Marine Committee has been to preserve strict discipline in the fleet, and all applications of complaint, either against individuals or numbers, they have rejected without answer. It not being, as they have told me, the province of the civil power to interfere in the internal government of ships of war. *And you may now see, that listening to the people of the Ranger, instead of doing good, has destroyed even the shadow af subordination.*

"Mr. Amiel has told me that you objected to my receiving copies of some papers that concern me, because you thought I had not made a respectful application. A copy of it is enclosed, which, though not in form of an *humble petition*, I believe it will be difficult to construe into disrespect. True respect can never be extorted; and I will say of myself, that

'The tribute of respect to greatness due,
Not the bribed sycophant more freely pays.'

"I shall only add, that the dishonor of my bill of exchange has not only served to corroborate the ungrateful misrepresentations of Lieut. Simpson, but also occasioned the infamous attachment of the Ranger's prizes, for the provisions previously furnished by M. Bersolle.

"I thank you, sir, for your polite attentions while I was at Paris last winter, which I received as a proof of your good opinion, and which I have not since forfeited by any misconduct.

"The apparent mystery of my present situation cannot be imputed to me as a fault, or if it is, I am responsible to Congress. I have endeavored, in my narrow walk, to pursue a steady line of duty, wishing to offend none.

"I have the honor to be,
"With due respect, Sir, yours," &c.

" *Versailles, February 4th*, 1779.

"JOHN P. JONES, Esq., Commander of the American Navy in Europe.

"SIR,

"I announce to you, that, in consequence of the exposition which I have laid before the king, of the distinguished manner in which you have served the United States, and of the entire confidence which your conduct has merited on the part of Congress, his majesty has thought proper to place under your command the ship Duras, of forty guns, at present at L'Orient. I am about, in consequence, to issue the necessary orders for the complete armament of the said ship. The commission which was given you at your departure from America, will authorise you to hoist the flag of the United States, and you will likewise serve yourself with the powers which have been remitted to you to form your equipage with American subjects; but as you may find too much difficulty in raising a sufficient number, the king permits you to levy volunteers until you obtain a sufficient number, exclusive of those who are necessary to manœuvre the ship. It shall be my care to procure you the necessary officers, and you may assure yourself that I shall contribute everything in my power to promote the success of your enterprise.

"As soon as you are prepared for sea, you will set sail without waiting for any ulterior orders; and you will determine yourself the course you are to take, whether in the European or American seas, observing always to render me an exact account of each event that may take place during your cruize, as often as you may enter the ports under the dominion of the king.

"So flattering a mark of the confidence with which you are honored cannot but encourage you to use all your zeal in the common cause, persuaded, as I am, that you will justify my opinion on every occasion. It only rests with me to recommend to you to show to those prisoners who may fall into your hands, those sentiments of humanity which the king professes towards his enemies, and to take the greatest care not only of your own equipage, but also of all the ships which may be placed under your orders.

"I have the honor to be, most perfectly, Sir,
"Your very humble and very obedient servant,
"De Sartine.

"P.S. According to your desire, Sir, I consent that the Duras takes the name of the Bon Homme Richard."

"*Passy*, *Feb.* 6*th*, 1779.

"M. de Sartine, Minister of Marine, Versailles.

"My Lord,

"I have had the honor to receive your excellency's letter dated the 1st, by the hands of Mr. Garnier. I take the earliest opportunity to offer you my sincere and grateful thanks for so singular and honorable a mark of your confidence and approbation.

"It shall be my duty to represent in the strongest terms to Congress, the generous and voluntary resolution which their great ally, the protector of the rights of human nature, and the best of kings, has taken to promote the honor of their flag, and I beseech you to assure his Majesty that my heart is impressed with the deepest sense of the obligation which

I owe his condescending favor and good opinion, and which it shall be my highest ambition to merit, by rendering every service in my power to the common cause; I cannot ensure success, but I will endeavor to deserve it.

"I beg leave to assure your Excellency, that I will carefully observe your present as well as future instructions, and that I will communicate to you from time to time a faithful account of my proceedings.

"I will avail myself of the authority which you have given me to raise French volunteers to serve as marines, as I fear there may not be easily found a sufficient number of American seamen.

"It has always been my custom to treat my people and prisoners with hospitality and kindness, and you may be assured that I shall ever take pleasure in promoting the happiness of every person under my command.

"Your having permitted me to alter the name* of the ship has given me a pleasing opportunity of paying a well merited compliment to a great and good man to whom I am under obligations, and who honors me with his friendship.

"I am in the fulness and grateful affection of my heart, and with perfect esteem and respect,

"My Lord,

"Yours, &c."

"*Paris*, *April* 27, 1779.

"CAPTAIN JOHN PAUL JONES, Commander, &c.

"Your obliging letter, my dear Sir, is just coming into my hands, as I was myself going to write you by M. de Chaumont, who is determined

* It is a fact not generally known, that the late John Paul Jones, at the time that he was attempting to fit out a small squadron during the late war in one of the ports of France to cruize on the coast of England, was much delayed by neglects and disappointments from the Court that had nearly frustrated his plans. Chance one day threw into his hands an old almanac, containing *Poor Richard's Maxims*, by Doctor Franklin. In that curious assemblage of useful instruction a man is advised, "if he wishes to have any business faithfully and expeditiously performed, to go on it himself; otherwise, to send." Jones was immediately struck, upon reading this maxim, with the impropriety of his past conduct in only *sending* letters and messages to Court when he ought to have gone in person. He instantly set out, and by dint of personal representations, procured the immediate equipment of the squadron, which afterwards spread terror along the eastern coast of England, and with which he so gloriously captured the Serapis and Countess of Scarborough, British ships-of-war returning from the Baltic. In gratitude to Dr. Franklin's maxim he named the principal ship of his squadron after the name of the pretended almanac maker, "*Le Bon Homme Richard.*"

to undertake a journey to L'Orient:—I think you are extremely right in refusing such guns as would expose your reputation, the lives of your men, and even the honor of your flag; it is not without concern that I hear of cannon being promised to any other people but you, and I hope these difficulties shall be raised by the ministry. I am just going to add some lines to M. de Chaumont that he might take proper orders (if any forgotten) along with him. The expedition I want to have soon done, because my speedy return about the middle of the summer is somewhat useful to the common cause and to the American affairs; I therefore hope everything will be ready towards the 7th of the next month, and I intend to arrive about that time. I am very happy to hear that the *Monsieur* will be with us, we shall also get the *Alliance*, but, I think, we must not if possible put troops on board of her, because there would be disputes between the land officers and Capt. Landais. Don't you think, my dear Sir, we might have them divided in this way:

"On board the *Bon Homme Richard* 50 dragoons and 150 soldiers, ...	200
"On board the *Monsieur*, ...	300
"On board the *Pallas*, the artillery and . . .	150

"If you don't like it, you might have 150 men on board of the *Alliance*, but I fear disputes.

"M. de Chaumont will make the little arrangements for the table of the officers, &c.; but I direct him to take your ideas, and I don't wish anything but what will seem to you the best calculated for the common good and your own agreement.

"I will have with me a colonel, a major, three volunteering officers, and an engineer: two of the young officers may go with another ship to avoid the crowd.

"Though this command is not equal to my military rank, the love of the public cause made me very happy to take it; and as this motive is the only one which conducts all my private and public actions, I am sure I'll find in you the same zeal, and we shall do as much and more than any others would perform in the same situation. Be certain, my dear Sir, that I'll be happy to divide with you whatever share of glory may expect us, and that my esteem and affection for you is truly felt, and will last for ever.

"I am, my dear Sir, with a sincere regard,

"Yours,

"LAFAYETTE.

"I intend also to take Dr. Bancroft with us, but as I am obliged to leave many good officers to whom I am indebted, I'd rather wish the Irish gentleman might not come, unless you have a very particular affection for him, in which case I have no objection."

"*L'Orient, May* 1, 1779.

"His Excellency M. De Sartine, &c.

"My Lord,

"I have this day had the honor to receive from the hands of M. de Chaumont your Excellency's letter of 27th ult. This unsolicited mark of his Majesty's confidence and favor lays me under the deepest and most lasting obligation; the sense whereof I shall fully retain to the last hour of my life.

"If I have any abilities they shall be exerted to the utmost in the employment of the force entrusted to my command, and I hope my conduct will at least deserve success.

"I am persuaded that no misunderstanding will arise between the other* commander and myself, because we love and esteem each other, therefore it only remains that I return your Excellency sincere and grateful thanks for your polite and kind attention, beseeching you to assure the best of kings that I will faithfully communicate to Congress an account of the great honor done in France to the American flag.

"I am, and shall always be, with sentiments of grateful esteem and respect, and the highest ambition to merit the continuance of your favor,

"My Lord, &c.

"J. P. Jones."

"*L'Orient, May* 1, 1779.

"Major General De La Fayette,

"I have, my dear Marquis, this day had the singular pleasure of receiving your very esteemed letter by the hands of M. de Chaumont; so flattering and affectionate a proof of your esteem and friendship has made an impression on my mind that will attend me while I live. This I hope to prove by more than words. Where men of fine feelings are concerned there is seldom misunderstanding; and I am sure I should do violence to my sensibility if I were capable of giving you a moment's pain by any part of my conduct. Therefore, without any apology, I shall expect you to point out my errors when we are together alone with perfect freedom, and I think I dare promise you your reproof shall not be lost.

* The Marquis de Lafayette.

"M. de Chaumont is now endeavoring to settle matters with respect to the cannon. I hope he will succeed, and if so, the Bon homme Richard may soon be got ready. I could say more with respect to the accommodation of the men. I hope no difficulty will arise, for she can carry 350 or 400, should there be occasion.

"I have received from the good Dr. Franklin instructions at large which do honor to his liberal mind, and which it will give me the truest satisfaction to execute.

"I cannot ensure success, but will endeavor to deserve it.

"With sincere esteem and affection of my heart, and with the truest regard and respect, I am always,

"Yours, &c."

"*L'Orient, May* 1, 1779.

"His Excellency BENJAMIN FRANKLIN.

"HONORED AND DEAR SIR,

"The letter I had the honor to receive from you to-day, together with your liberal and noble minded instructions, would make a *coward brave.* You have called up every sentiment of public virtue in my breast, and it shall be my pride and ambition, in the strict pursuit of your instructions, to deserve success.

"Be assured that very few prospects could afford me so true a satisfaction as that of rendering some acceptable service to the common cause, and at the same time relieving from captivity (by furnishing the means of exchange,) our unfortunate fellow subjects from the hands of the enemy.

"It only remains for me to return your excellency my thanks for past instances of your friendship, especially in the last of your particular confidence.

"I am, and shall be to the end of my life, with the most affectionate esteem and respect,

"Honored and Dear Sir, Yours."

"*L'Orient, May* 13*th*, 1779.

"The Hon. JOHN ADAMS, on board the Alliance.

"SIR,

"You will confer on me a singular obligation by favoring me with your opinion and advice, respecting the unhappy misunderstanding which, I am told, prevails on board the Alliance. I ask your advice because, though I am determined to preserve order and discipline where I command, yet I wish to reprove with moderation, and never to punish while there remains a good alternative. It appears that there is fault at least in one of the parties, and I wish much to know where the fault lies, for without harmony and general good will among the officers I cannot proceed with a good prospect. I beseech you to favor me with an answer as soon as possible. When I have the honor of seeing you ashore I will put into your hands a letter which I have received; in the mean time, if you require it, I will promise to keep your answer a secret.

"I have the honor to be, with sentiments of great respect,

"Sir, your very obliged, very obedient,

"Humble servant."

"*Passy, May 9th*, 1779.

"Hon. JOHN PAUL JONES.

"DEAR SIR,

"I received yours of the 14th, and communicated to the marquis what related to him. I send you enclosed two more commissions, which I have found since your departure. It is difficult to revoke commissions once given, and there might be some inconvenience in French officers retaining those commissions unrevoked, after the occasion of giving them is past; I therefore am of opinion that the conclusion might be better thus, 'to continue in force during the expedition, or expeditions, intended under the command of the honorable J. P. Jones, Esq.' By this means they will continue if you should make more expeditions, and become void of themselves when the force is dissolved, and the French ships are withdrawn from under your command.

"I am sorry for, and ashamed of the divisions on board the Alliance. I hope these commissions will enable you to compose them. I do not know enough of the navy law to judge of the propriety of your giving commissions to lieutenants, and therefore can give no opinion about it. I send you all the warrants I have; will they not serve instead of commissions, till such can be obtained? My best wishes attend you, being ever,

"Dear Sir,

"Your faithful friend, and most

"Obedient humble servant,

"B. FRANKLIN."

"*Paris, May 22d*, 1779.

"The Hon. JOHN PAUL JONES.

"DEAR SIR,

"I dare say you will be very sorry to hear that the king's dispositions concerning our plan have been quite altered, and that instead of meeting you I am now going to take the command of the king's regiment at Jaints. What will be further determined about your squadron is yet uncertain, and the ministers are to consult it with Dr. Franklin. Political and military reasons have occasioned that alteration of things, and I am only to tell you, my good friend, how sorry I feel not to be a witness of your success, abilities, and glory. I hope everything will be altered for the best, and the more calculated for the common advantage. Be convinced, sir, that nothing could please me more than the pleasure of having again something of the kind to undertake with such an officer as Capt. Jones. That occasion I shall ever wish for, and I will, I hope, find before the end of this war.

"With the sincerest affection and esteem,

"I am, dear Sir, yours,

"LAFAYETTE.

"P.S. Whatever part of the world you will be in I hope you will let me often hear from you."

"I recognize this as a true copy.—LAFAYETTE.
" *City of Washington, February*, 1825."

"*Extracts of letters from the secret correspondence of his Excellency,* BENJAMIN FRANKLIN, *Minister Plenipotentiary of the United States to the court of Versailles.*

" *Passy, May 26th*, 1779.

"To the COMMITTEE FOR FOREIGN AFFAIRS.

"GENTLEMEN,

"The Marquis de la Fayette, who arrived here on the 11th of February, brought me yours of October 28th, and the new commission, credentials, and instructions the Congress have honored me with.

"I immediately acquainted the minister for foreign affairs with my appointment, and communicated to him, as usual, a copy of my credential letter, on which a day was named for my reception. The end of that part of the instructions which relates to American seamen taken by the French in English ships, had already been obtained; Capt. Jones having had for some time an order from court, directed to the keepers of the prisoners, requiring them to deliver to him such Americans as should be found in their hands, that they might be at liberty to serve under his command. Most of them have accordingly been delivered to him, if not all. The minister of marine having entertained a high opinion of him from his conduct and bravery in taking the Drake, was desirous of employing him in the command of a particular enterprise; and, to that end, requested us to spare him, which we did, and sent the Ranger home, under the command of his lieutenant. Various accidents have hitherto postponed his equipment, but he now has the command of a 50 gun ship, with some frigates, all under American commission and colors, fitted out at the king's expense, and will sail, it is said, about the 1st of June. The Marquis de la Fayette was, with some land troops, to have gone with him; but I now understand the Marquis is not to go, the plan being a little changed. The minister of marine requesting that the Alliance might be added to Com. Jones's little squadron, and offering to give a passage to Mr. Adams in the frigate with the new ambassador, I thought it best to continue her a little longer in Europe, hoping she may, in the projected cruize, by her extraordinary swiftness, be a means of taking prisoners enough to redeem the rest of our countrymen now in the English gaols. With this view, as well as to oblige the minister, I ordered her to join Capt. Jones at L'Orient, and obey his orders, where she now is accordingly."

From M. Le Ray de Chaumont, dated

"*L'Orient, June* 10*th*, 1779.

"M. de Chaumont presents his respects to Mr. Jones, and informs him that everything is on board except the powder, which will require only two hours, when he may set sail with a favorable wind.

"M. de Chaumont informs at the same time Mr. Jones, that he will have papers to sign before his departure, for the sundry articles which the king has furnished to his ship; therefore M. de C. earnestly entreats Mr. Jones not to neglect it, considering the immense expenses which the vessels in the port have occasioned to the king.

"M. de Chaumont reminds Mr. Jones, that M. de Sartine has left to him and to M. Landais the choice of two excellent American pilots, to be embarked on board the king's frigate La Sensible.

"M. de Chaumont thinks it his duty to remind Mr. Jones of a communication he has made to him against M. Amiel, his first lieutenant, from which it appears that, in case Mr. Jones should be so unfortunate as to be killed in battle, it would be improper to leave the command of the king's ship to M. Amiel, who does not seem to deserve so much confidence, by his conduct when commanding the ship the Ranger.

"M. de Chaumont, in addition to the preceding observations, suggests that Mr. Jones's crew, being for the most part composed of Englishmen, which M. Amiel had recruited in the prisons, cannot be kept in subjection but by the corps of French volunteers which is on board the Bon homme

Richard, and that it would be desirable these volunteers should be commanded by officers of their own nation, well skilled in the art of war, and provided with sufficient recommendations to justify the choice which will be made of them.

"M. de Chaumont has the honor," &c.

"*L'Orient*, *June* 14*th*, 1779.

"Mr. Jones, Commander of the Ship Bon homme Richard.

"Sir,

"The situation of the officers who have accepted commissions from Congress to join the armament of the ship Bon homme Richard, which you command, may be in contradiction with the interests of their own ships; this induces me to request you to enter into an engagement with me, that you shall not require from the said vessels any services but such as will be conformable with the orders which those officers shall have, and that in no case you shall require any changes to be made in the formation of their crews, which, as well the vessels themselves as their armaments, shall be entirely at the disposition of the commandants of the said vessels, who shall be answerable to those who have armed them. I also beg you to agree, that all the prizes which shall be made, be addressed to such consignees as I shall point out, for the preservation of the interests of all the concerned.

"I have the honor, &c.

"Le Ray de Chaumont."

"*Passy*, *June* 30, 1779.

"Mr. Jones, Commander of the Ship
Bon homme Richard.

"Sir,

"I have the honor of wishing you much success in your new cruize. Should you make any prizes, and take them to Bergen in Norway, I beg you to send them to the French Consul, if there be one; if there be none, then to the principal French Agent to account to me for the same. And such as you send to Ostend or Dunkirk, you will consign to M. Cailliez, senior, merchant at Dunkirk, who will account for them to me; and you may rest assured, that the interests of all those who may have a share in such prizes will be attended to in a proper manner.

"I have the honor, &c.

"Le Ray de Chaumont."

"*Passy*, *June* 30, 1779.

"Honorable Captain JONES.

"DEAR SIR,

"Being arrived at Groaix, you are to make the best of your way with the vessels under your command to the west of Ireland, and establish your cruize on the Orcades, the Cape of Derneus, and the Dogger Bank, in order to take the enemy's property in those seas.

"The prizes you may make, send to Dunkirk, Ostend, or Bergen in Norway, according to your proximity to either of those ports. Address them to the persons M. de Chaumont shall indicate to you.

"About the 15th of August, when you will have sufficiently cruized in these seas, you are to make route for the Texel, where you will meet my further orders.

"If by any personal accident you should be rendered unable to execute these instructions, the officer of your squadron next in rank is to endeavor to put them into execution.

"With best wishes for your prosperity, I am ever,

"Dear Sir,

"Your affectionate friend and humble servant,

B. FRANKLIN.

"*On board the Bon homme Richard, at anchor, Isle of Groaix, off L'Orient, July* 1, 1779.

"His Excellency BENJAMIN FRANKLIN.

"HONORED AND DEAR SIR,

"On the 19th ult., the American squadron under my command, consisting of the Bon homme Richard 42 guns, Alliance 36 guns, Pallas 30 guns, Cerf 18 guns, and the Vengeance 12 guns, sailed from hence with a convoy of merchant ships and transports with troops, &c. bound to the different ports and garrisons between this place and Bourdeaux.

"On the evening of the following day, I had the satisfaction to see the latter part of the convoy safe within the entrance of the river of Bourdeaux, the rest having been safely escorted into the entrance of Nantz, Rochefort, &c. But at the preceding midnight, while lying-to off Isle of Vew, the Bon homme Richard and Alliance got foul of one another, and carried away the head and cut-water, sprit-sail yard and jib-boom of the former, with the mizen-mast of the latter; fortunately, however, neither received damage in the hull. In the evening of the 21st, I sent the Cerf to reconnoitre two sail, and Capt. Varage was so ardent in the pursuit, that he had lost sight of the squadron next morning; and I am now told, that he had a warm engagement with one of them, a sloop of 14 guns which he took, but was obliged to abandon on the approach of another enemy of superior force. The action lasted an hour and a half; several men were killed and wounded on board the Cerf. That cutter is now fitting at L'Orient.

"On the 23d we had a rencontre with three ships-of-war. They were to windward, and bore down in a line abreast for some time, but seeing we were prepared to receive them they hauled their wind, and by carrying a press of sail got clear in spite of our utmost endeavors to bring them to action. On the 26th we lost company of the Alliance and Pallas. I am unable to say where the blame lays. I gave the ships a rendezvous off Penmark-rocks, but did not meet them there.

"I anchored here yesterday at noon, having had a rencontre the night before with two of the enemy's ships-of-war in the offing, in the sight of this island and of Belle Isle. Previous to this, I had given the Vengeance leave to make the best of her way to this road, so that the enemy found me alone in a place where I had no expectation of a hostile visit. They appeared at first earnest to engage, but their courage failed, and they fled with precipitation, and to *my mortification outsailed the Bon homme Richard, and got clear*. I had, however, a flattering proof of the martial spirit of my crew, and I am confident that, had I been able to get between the two, which was my intention, we should have beaten them both together.

"In the course of this short cruize I have endeavored to meet the views of the king. I have traversed the Golf de Gascogne over and over; I have fallen in with and chased various vessels.

"I am ready to enter with cheerfulness upon any plan or service that is consonant with the common interest, and meets with your approbation; and if I fail, it shall not be for want of attempting to succeed where an opportunity appears.

"I am, with sentiments of grateful esteem and affection,

"Dear Sir, yours, &c.

"P. S.—Please give the above information to M. de Sartine and M. de Chaumont."

"*Passy*, *July* 8, 1779.

"Honorable J. P. JONES.

"DEAR SIR,

"I received your favors of the 2d and 4th inst. I am sorry for the accidents that have obliged your little squadron to return and refit; but hope all may be for the best. Some days since, M. Chaumont handed to me the substance of a letter in French, which contained heads of the instructions that M. de Sartine wished me to give you. I had them translated and put into the form of a letter to you, which I signed and gave back to M. C. who, I suppose, has sent it to you. I have no other orders to give; for, as the Court is at the chief expense, I think they have the best right to direct. I observe what you write about a change of the destination; but when a thing has been once considered and determined on in council they do not care to resume the consideration of it, having much business on hand, and there is not now time to obtain a reconsideration.

"It has been hinted to me that the intention of ordering your cruize to finish at the Texel, is with a view of getting out that ship; but this should be kept a secret. I can say nothing about Capt. Landais' prize. I suppose the minister has an account of it, but I have heard nothing from him about it. If he reclaims it on account of his passport, we must then consider what is to be done. I approve of the careenage proposed for the Alliance as a thing necessary. As she is said to be a remarkable swift sailer, I should hope you might by her means take some privateers and a number of prisoners, so as to continue the cartel, and redeem all our poor countrymen.

"My best wishes attend you, being ever, with great esteem,

"Dear Sir,

"Your affectionate friend, and most obedient servant,

"B. Franklin.

"P. S.—If it should fall in your way, remember that the Hudson's Bay ships are very valuable.

"B. F."

Extract to Dr. Franklin.

"*L'Orient, July* 12, 1779.

"I have inspected the Bon homme Richard, and it is the constructor's opinion that the ship is too old to admit of the necessary alterations. Thus circumstanced I wish to have an opportunity of attempting an essential service to render myself worthy a better and faster sailing ship."

"*L'Orient*, *July* 26, 1779.

"His Excellency BENJAMIN FRANKLIN.

"DEAR SIR,

"I have received advice that the Jamaica fleet will sail homewards, escorted by a fifty gun ship and two strong frigates. Should we fall in with that force we will certainly engage and, I hope, overcome it. We shall probably be so much cut up as to be unable to prevent the escape of the convoy. If the ship Monsieur could be added to my force, it would give us a superiority, and perhaps enable us to take and destroy the Jamaica fleet. I submit this idea, however, to your superior wisdom.

"I have the honor, &c."

"*Passy*, *July* 28, 1779.

"Hon. Capt. JONES.

"DEAR SIR,

"I have just received yours of the 25th. I was yesterday with M. de Sartine at Versailles, who appeared uneasy at some accounts he had received of a mutinous disposition in your crew. He desired me to acquaint M. de Chaumont that he wished to see him that evening. This morning M. de Chaumont sent me a note of which I enclose a copy; I understand he goes down with a view to provide you a better set of hands. You must have heard that 119 American prisoners are arrived in a cartel at Nantes; perhaps out of them you may pick some very good seamen. But if this affair should be likely to take time, the Alliance will have my orders to make a cruize alone, agreeable to the minister's desire. But I hope the reports of your crew are not founded, and that your joint cruize will still take place, and be successful.

"I have the honor to be, with sincere esteem,

"Dear Sir,

"Your most obedient and most humble servant,

"BENJAMIN FRANKLIN."

"The Honorable JOHN P. JONES, commander-in-chief of the American ships-of-war, now in Europe.

"To ———,

"You are hereby directed and required forthwith, to hold yourself in readiness to proceed in company with me to sea. You are to show careful attention to every signal that shall be made on board here for your government, as well as to all future orders that you may from time to time receive from me. To prevent separation or surprise, you are to endeavor always to keep in your station: and you are never to chase so as to lose company with the squadron. I place great dependance on your zeal for the honor of the American flag, and the interests of our common cause, as well as your abilities and inclination to support me in my duty; which, I hope, you will very soon have occasion to manifest, so as to afford me the supreme pleasure of rendering justice to your merit in the account which I shall faithfully transmit both to our great ally, his Most Christian Majesty, and to the Senate of America. Should you unfortunately be separated from the Bon homme Richard, you are to open the letter of rendezvous No. 1, and to proceed to that place as soon as possible, but if the squadron has previously passed that place, you are to open the letter No. 2; and should you be taken, or in great danger of being taken, you are to burn, or otherwise effectually destroy the letters of rendezvous. For all which, this shall be your order.

"Given on board the American ship-of-war, the Bon homme Richard, at anchor in the road of Groaix, August 10, 1779."

"*On board the Bon homme Richard, at anchor in the road of Groaix, August* 11, 1779.

"His Excellency M. De Sartine.

"My Lord,

"The moment I returned from the late cruize to this road, I wrote the history of my proceedings to his Excellency Dr. Franklin, and requested him to communicate the whole to you. I have also rendered him an exact account of everything that has affected this ship, and every other vessel under my command while at L'Orient: all which, I conclude, has been submitted to your inspection. I am now, however, sorry that I did not address letters to your Excellency on the same subject, especially as Dr. Franklin has lately acquainted me that you were uneasy at some accounts of a mutinous disposition in my crew. I did not at the beginning advise it as a prudent measure to take on board so great a proportion of English seamen. But M. de Chaumont can inform you that *he* thought it expedient, and that it would be attended with no risque after the embarkation of the troops under the orders of the Marquis de la Fayette. When that expedition was laid aside, and I was forbidden to enlist French seamen, I had no means to replace the English, and they remained on board from necessity, not from choice. When they saw that I had observed their mutinous disposition, and taken measures to prevent its bad consequences, I must do them the justice to say that they manifested a true martial spirit when, being alone in this ship off Belle

Isle in the evening of the 29th of June, I met with and chased two large frigates that were in company, and durst not wait for our approach, but fled notwithstanding their great superiority both in force and sailing.

"I have the satisfaction to assure your Excellency that this second journey of M. de Chaumont was altogether unnecessary; as I had, before his arrival at L'Orient, sent officers to Nantes to enlist Americans, and had also enlisted as many of the strangers as were willing to embark at L'Orient. My crew now in this ship consists of 380 officers, men, and boys, inclusive of 137 marine soldiers.

"I expect to sail this evening or to-morrow morning, and, I hope, the Monsieur will go in company. I have also reason to expect the General Mifflin, having sent the Vengeance to Belle Isle with a letter to the captain of the privateer to invite him to join this little squadron. When I depart I hope to be able to do my duty, thereby to testify to his Majesty and to your Excellency the high sense which I shall ever entertain of the honorable attentions which have been shown towards me in France, and to prevent future misrepresentations, I will myself transmit to your Excellency, from time to time, an account of my proceedings and situation.

"I am with the highest sentiments of esteem and respect,

"My Lord,

"your Excellency's very obliged,

"very obedient,

"and most humble servant.

"N. B.—I have seen with surprise various letters in the hands of persons here, on the subject of my destination!"

"*Ship Bon homme Richard, at anchor in the Road of Groaix, August* 13, 1779.

"The Hon. Major General, the Marquis de

LAFAYETTE, at Havre de Grace.

"Although, my dear Marquis, I have not lately written to you, yet there is no man for whom I entertain a greater share of esteem and respect. By what I have felt myself since our expedition was laid aside, I can easily imagine how much concern it has given you; and I assure you that I have met with few disappointments that have equally affected my sensibility and my health. As the object of our expedition was imprudently communicated to almost every person who should have been concerned in it, as well as to others who would not have been actors, I had determined, for some time before I had the honor to receive your last letter, to propose to you another project when we met at L'Orient, which I am persuaded you would have adopted, and communicated to no person until we had been ready the next hour to put it into execution.

"I am highly honored by your expressing hopes that such an expedition between us will yet take place in the course of this war. I ardently join you in that wish, and assure you that few prospects could afford me equal pleasure, or more entirely gratify my ambition. I will write to you, my dear Marquis, and communicate my thoughts when the subject is of consequence, agreeable to the within dictionary. I expect to sail this evening, and you will perhaps hear of me soon. I was happy in the acquaintance of your two Aids-de-Camp; and I thank you, with reason, that I now have the company and assistance of Messrs. Weibert and Chamillard.

"I am happy in being ranked among the number of your friends, and shall ever endeavor to merit your regard, being always, my dear Marquis,

"Your most obliged,
"and very obedient,
"humble servant.

"*Washington City, February* 1825.

"True copy to the best of my remembrance.

"LAFAYETTE."

"*Ship Bon homme Richard, at anchor in the Road of Groaix, August* 13, 1779.

"His Excellency BENJAMIN FRANKLIN.

"HONORED AND DEAR SIR,

"It is but this moment that the Court Martial has finished the affair of the Bon homme Richard and the Alliance on account of their having run foul of each other. I enclose you the result of the proceedings of that court, which being the only one of consequence, it is unnecessary to trouble you with bundles of papers where the conclusions have only amounted to whipping, which has been executed.

"The within paper respecting the prize-money of this little squadron is submitted to your regulations, and from the enclosed paper, addressed to me by the captain and officers of the Vengeance, I am persuaded that you will think it unreasonable that *he* (the captain), should share *equally* with Captain Landais, or the captain of the Pallas,—and not rather that each ship and vessel should first share in proportion to the number and calibre of her guns, and the number of her men;—and that they should afterward divide their respective shares by the laws of their flag, or otherwise to their mutual satisfaction. The within state of the force of each ship and vessel, will be useful in forming your decisions.

"M. de Chaumont has made an useless journey here, as I had taken all the necessary measures to engage the men that were wanting before his appearance, even at Nantes. I am, however, much obliged to him and to the minister for that attention, as well as for all former favors. I shall certainly sail to-morrow at daybreak, and I hope shortly to find opportunities to testify my gratitude to our great and good ally, for the honor which he has conferred on the American flag, and on myself. The enclosed dictionary will be useful, when I write to you on particular subjects. This little squadron appears to be unanimous, and, if that good understanding continues, we are able to perform essential service. I look forward with pleasing expectation, and an ardent desire to merit your friendship, and that of America, being ever, with the highest esteem and respect,

"Dear Sir,
"The most obliged of
"Your obedient servants."

"*Ship Bon homme Richard, at sea off Ushant, August* 18*th*, 1779.

"M. Le Ray de Chaumont.

"I have, my friend, the honor to forward this letter by our prize ship die Verwagting, bound from Barcelona to Dunkirk with a cargo of wine and brandy, and several cases of silks, &c.

"This prize was taken eight days ago, by the privateer brig Eagle, belonging to Poole, in England, and is therefore a lawful prize to the flag of the United States.

"We have met several other vessels, neutral property, but have learned no news except by one, a Portuguese snow, yesterday, that the English fleet had put back to Portsmouth, and that the snow passed through the French and Spanish fleet in number 114 ships, steering N.N.E., fifteen leagues south from Lizard. You will please to communicate this, with my respects to the minister, and to Dr. Franklin.

"I have the honor to be,
"with great esteem and respect, your obliged
"friend and humble servant.

"P.S. I enclose you a paper which the commander of the Monsieur has given, contrary to my orders, and without my knowledge or consent, to the person whom he appointed master of this prize, which was taken under my orders and in my sight,—yet he takes no notice of this in that paper, and probably was his intention to keep the whole as his own property. He has now left the squadron, after plundering this prize and detaining me 24 hours by his lagging behind the squadron. This is the result of being concerned with privateers, where good faith and honor are generally strangers."

"I certify that the original of the preceding letter was duly received by my father, from Com. John Paul Jones.

"LE RAY DE CHAUMONT.
"*New York, December*, 1824."

"*Bon homme Richard, at Sea, off the S. W. of Ireland, August 24th*, 1779.

"M. LE RAY DE CHAUMONT.

"The enclosed copies of papers will show you, my friend, that on the 18th I sent in a prize ship for L'Orient, laden with brandy, &c.; and that on the 21st I sent also for L'Orient a prize brig, laden with Irish beef and butter. I send this by the prize brig Fortune, bound for England from Newfoundland, and laden chiefly with oil, blubber, and staves. I have ordered this prize for Nantz, or if circumstances will admit, for St. Malo, as the best market. I have sent on board the prize a man who is perfectly acquainted with the coast between Brest and St. Malo, and will, in consequence, I hope, elude the Jersey privateers. By the captain of the Mayflower I am told that there is now an encampment of 30,000 troops in Ireland, at a place called Clonmell, about midway between Waterford and Limerick; I do not, however, credit this report.

"I beseech you to present my respects to M. de Sartine, and his excellency, M. Franklin, and apologize for my not writing them. It is now calm: when the breeze returns I shall embrace it to proceed directly to my destination.

"I am, with sentiments of esteem and respect,
"Your very obliged friend and servant."

"I certify that the original of the preceding was duly received by my father, from Commodore J. Paul Jones.

"LE RAY DE CHAUMONT.
"*New York, December*, 1824."

"*On board the Ship of War the Serapis, at anchor without the Texel, October 3d*, 1779.

"M. LE RAY DE CHAUMONT, à Passy.

"The original of the enclosed copy of my last letter, written on board the Bon homme Richard, off the S.W. coast of Ireland, the 24th of August, as well as the papers which preceded it, and to which it alludes, I hope duly reached the hands of my friend M. de Chaumont, and explained to his satisfaction my conduct from the time I left Groaix until that date. For the full history of my expedition I must beg leave to refer you to a letter of this date, which accompanies this, to his excellency, Dr. Franklin, who will, if you demand it, furnish you with a copy.

"I wish to act a candid part towards all men, and therefore wish you to have a copy of that letter, that you may see my sentiments respecting the 'Concordat,' which you imposed upon me in the moment of my departure from Groaix. What could have inspired you with such sentiments of distrust towards me, after the ocular proofs of hospitality which I so long experienced in your house, and after the warm expressions of generous and unbounded friendship which I had constantly been honored with in your letters, exceeds my mental faculties to comprehend. I am, however, yet willing to give you an opportunity of rendering justice to my character. I cannot think you are personally my enemy. I rather imagine that your conduct towards me at L'Orient has arisen from the base misrepresentation of some secret villany; therefore, I am, with unaltered sentiments of good will and affection for yourself and family,

"My dear friend,

"Your obliged, humble servant."

"I certify that the original of the preceding letter was duly received by my father.

"Le Ray de Chaumont.

"*New York, December*, 1824.

Commodore Jones was now approaching the scene of his greatest glory, which, in other respects than the affair of the Serapis, would have been much more complete, had the captains of his squadron, and particularly Landais, of the frigate Alliance, cordially co-operated with him. In perusing the narrative of this cruize, which is from the pen of Jones himself, the reader will observe that he had designed to lay the town of Leith under contribution, which intended enterprise would in all probability have succeeded, had the winds not been adverse; and even with that hindrance, under the energetic direction of Commodore Jones, it might perhaps have been effected. He had prepared everything for the purpose, and assigned to each vessel of his squadron its appropriate duty. The landing was to have been made by Lieut. Col. Chamillard, with one hundred and thirty men, furnished with a white and a red flag, the display of the former of which was to be the signal that the inhabitants submitted to the terms proposed by the commodore; and of the latter, that they had refused. The display of both flags together was to indicate that the party under Chamillard was compelled to retreat; in which case their re-embarkation was to have been covered by the ships of war. A contribution of 100,000*l.* sterling was to have been levied upon Leith, the payment of 50,000*l.* of which was to have been insisted on instantly, and hostages from among the principal inhabitants taken for the speedy payment of the remaining moiety. The undertaking failed from the causes described by Jones; but the summons written for the occasion will serve to show the humanity with which he proceeded, and it is therefore presented for perusal, together with the terms of capitulation, both documents, in blank, having been found among the papers of Jones, now in possession of the author of this volume. It will be remarked that Commodore Jones, in this, as in every other instance, ascribed the severity of his operations to the outrages committed by the British troops in America; thus giving to his actions a national, and not a vindictively personal complexion. It will be seen in the sequel, that Dr. Franklin himself justified these retaliatory measures, and almost regretted the mildness of the instructions which he had previously addressed to the commodore for the government of his conduct towards the enemy, so deeply was that venerable man affected by the atrocities of the English soldiers. In no particular did Jones transcend these instructions, but seems, in every situation, to have endeavored to assuage the miseries of war by the kindest possible treatment to his prisoners.

The Honorable Captain JONES, Commander-in-Chief of the American squadron now in Europe, on board the American ship of war the Bon homme Richard, at anchor in the Road of Leith, September the ——, 1779.

"To the Worshipful the Provost of Leith, or, in his absence, to the Chief Magistrate who is now actually present and in authority there.

"SIR,

"The British marine force that has been stationed here for the protection of your city and commerce, being now taken by the American arms under my command, I have the honor to send you this by my officer, Lieutenant Colonel de Chamillard, who commands the vanguard of my troops. I do not wish to distress the poor inhabitants; my intention is only to demand your contribution towards the reimbursement which Britain owes to the much injured citizens of America. Savages would blush at the unmanly violation and rapacity that has marked the tracks of British tyranny in America, from which neither virgin innocence nor helpless age has been a plea of protection or pity.

"Leith and its port now lays at our mercy; and did not the plea of humanity stay the hand of just retaliation, I should, *without advertisement*, lay it in ashes. Before I proceed to that stern duty as an officer, my duty *as a man* induces me to propose to you, by the means of a reasonable ransom, to prevent such a scene of horror and distress. For this reason I have authorized Lieut. Col. de Chamillard to conclude and agree with you on the terms of ransom, allowing you exactly half an hour's reflection before you finally accept or reject the terms which he shall propose.

"If you accept the terms offered within the time limited, you may rest assured that no farther debarkation of troops will be made, but that the re-embarkation of the vanguard will immediately follow, and that the property of the citizens shall remain unmolested.

"I have the honor to be," &c.

"CAPITULATION.

"We the subscribers, the Provost, Recorder, and principal Magistrates of the city or corporation of Leith, in Scotland, promise and swear in honor and good faith, agreeable to the laws of war, according to which we submit to the Honorable Captain Jones, Commander-in-Chief of an American squadron now in Europe, to perform faithfully the articles of the present capitulation.

"*Art.* 1*st.* There shall not be any act of hostility committed against any ship or vessel, or against any person whatsoever that is belonging to the American squadron under the command of Capt. Jones, either by the inhabitants of Leith, by regular or irregular troops, or by any person or persons whatsoever, during the term which he may be compelled by contrary winds, or other insuperable causes, to remain with his squadron within the Firth of Forth.

"*Art.* 2*d.* In case of any contravention or breach of this capitulation on our part, it is agreed that the commander-in-chief of the American squadron aforesaid, shall use vigorous measures towards the subjects of his Britannic Majesty who are in his hands, either as prisoners, or hostages; and the magistrates and principal inhabitants of Leith agree to submit themselves exactly to this article.

"*Art.* 3*d.* As soon as the terms of ransom are fulfilled on the part of the Magistrates of Leith, Captain Jones shall embrace the first fair wind and depart, with his squadron, from Leith, without molesting the inhabitants.

"Done at Leith this   day of September, 1779."

Nothing can be more characteristic of the determined resolution of Commodore Jones to obtain the object on which he was once bent, than his perseverance in remaining on his cruizing ground off the enemy's coast, in defiance of the singular behavior of Captain Landais, and the lukewarmness of the other commanding officers in the squadron. The fortunate issue of every enterprise of the sort depends mainly upon the spirit and harmony that prevail among those who have been appointed to act in concert, and, at the same time, in subordination. The deportment of Captain Landais throughout the engagement with the Serapis was well calculated to give the victory to the British flag; and there is good ground for believing that it was, from envy or jealousy, in the contemplation of Landais to tear the laurels from the brow of Jones, or to subject him to disgrace by allowing the Bon homme Richard and Serapis, in their close encounter, so to disable each other, that keeping the Alliance uninjured, in the event of the Bon homme Richard's striking her colors to her antagonist, Captain Landais might have made prizes of both ships, and, returning victorious to France, have figured as the principal hero of the bloody combat. Certain it is, that he manœuvred so as to cripple the Bon homme Richard, and actually shed the blood of some of the valiant crew. The fact does not admit of dispute. It is established by the testimony of those who witnessed his manœuvres, and who, it will be found in the subsequent pages, specifically verify all the allegations made by Commodore Jones against Landais. Such a mass of evidence is irresistible, and leaves nothing to reflecting minds but regret that the bad passions of the human heart, unrestrained by reason, should, at a critical moment, have had such influence over a naval officer, honored with a commission from the American Congress, as to have rendered the triumph of the flag of the United States dubious for several hours. Had Captain Landais employed himself in capturing and destroying the ships of the Baltic fleet, whilst Jones was engaged with the Serapis, it can scarcely be considered as doubtful that very few of them would have escaped.

"*On board the Ship Serapis, at anchor without the Texel in Holland, October* 3, 1779.

"His Excellency BENJAMIN FRANKLIN.

"HONORED AND DEAR SIR,

"When I had the honor of writing to you on the 11th of August, previous to my departure from the Road of Groaix, I had before me the most flattering prospect of rendering essential service to the common cause of France and America. I had a full confidence in the voluntary inclination and ability of every captain under my command to assist and support me in my duty with cheerful emulation; and I was persuaded that every one of them would pursue glory in preference to interest.

"Whether I was or was not deceived will best appear by a relation of circumstances.

"The little squadron under my orders, consisting of the Bon homme Richard of 40 guns, the Alliance of 36 guns, the Pallas of 32 guns, the Cerf of 18 guns, and the Vengeance of 12 guns, joined by two privateers, the Monsieur and the Granville, sailed from the Road of Groaix at daybreak on the 14th of August; the same day we spoke with a large convoy bound from the southward to Brest.

"On the 18th we retook a large ship belonging to Holland, laden chiefly with brandy and wine that had been destined from Barcelona for Dunkirk, and taken eight days before by an English privateer. The captain of the Monsieur, however, took out of this prize such articles as he pleased in the night, and the next day being astern of the squadron and to windward, he actually wrote orders *in his proper name*, and sent away the prize under one of his own officers. This, however, I superseded by sending her for L'Orient under my orders in the character of commander-in-chief. The evening of the day following the Monsieur separated from the squadron.

"On the 20th we saw and chased a large ship, but could not overtake her, she being to windward.

"On the 21st we saw and chased another ship that was also to windward, and thereby eluded our pursuit. The same afternoon we took a brigantine called the Mayflower, laden with butter and salt provisions, bound from Limerick in Ireland for London; this vessel I immediately expedited for L'Orient.

"On the 23d we saw Cape Clear and the S.W. part of Ireland. That afternoon, it being calm, I sent some armed boats to take a brigantine that appeared in the N.W. quarter. Soon after in the evening it became necessary to have a boat ahead of the ship to tow, as the helm could not prevent her from laying across the tide of flood, which would have driven us into a deep and dangerous bay, situated between the rocks on the south called the Skallocks, and on the north called the Blaskets. The ship's boats being absent, I sent my own barge ahead to tow the ship. The boats took the brigantine, she was called the Fortune, and bound with a cargo of oil, blubber, and staves, from Newfoundland for Bristol; this vessel I ordered to proceed immediately for Nantes or St. Malo. Soon after sunset the villains who towed the ship, cut the tow rope and decamped with my barge. Sundry shots were fired to bring them to without effect; in the mean time the master of the Bon homme Richard, without orders, manned one of the ship's boats, and with four soldiers pursued the barge in order to stop the deserters. The evening was clear and serene, but the zeal of that officer, Mr. Cutting Lent, induced him to pursue too far, and a fog which came on soon afterwards prevented the boats from rejoining the ship, although I caused signal guns to be frequently fired. The fog and calm continued the next day till towards evening. In the afternoon Capt. Landais came on board the Bon homme Richard and behaved towards me with great disrespect, affirming in the most indelicate manner and language, that I had lost my boats and people through my imprudence in sending boats to take a prize! He persisted in his reproaches, though he was assured by Messrs. De Weibert and De Chamillard that the barge was towing the ship at the time of elopement, and that she had not been sent in pursuit of the prize. He was affronted, because I would not the day before suffer him to chase without my orders, and to approach the dangerous shore I have already mentioned, where he was an entire stranger, and when there was not sufficient wind to govern a ship. He told me he was the only American in the squadron, and was determined to follow his own opinion in chasing when and where he thought proper, and in every other matter that concerned the service, and that, if I continued in that situation three days longer, the squadron would be taken, &c. By the advice of Capt. De Cottineau, and with the free consent and approbation of M. De Varage, I sent the Cerf in to reconnoitre the coast, and endeavor to take the boats and people the next day, while the squadron stood off and on in the S.W. quarter, in the best possible situation to intercept the enemy's merchant ships, whether outward or homeward bound. The Cerf had on board a pilot well acquainted with the coast, and was ordered to join me again before night. I approached the shore in the afternoon, but the Cerf did not appear; this induced me to stand off again in the night in order to return and be rejoined by the Cerf the next day; but to my great concern and disappointment, though I ranged the coast along, and hoisted our private signals, neither the boats nor the Cerf joined me. The evening of that day, the 26th, brought with it stormy weather, with an appearance of a severe gale from the S.W., yet I must declare I did not follow my own judgment, but was led by the assertion which had fallen from Captain Landais, when I in the evening made a signal to steer to the northward and leave that station, which I wished to have occupied at least a week longer. The gale increased in the night with thick weather; to prevent separation, I carried a top light and fired a gun every quarter of an hour. I carried also a very moderate sail, and the course had been clearly pointed out by a signal before night; yet, with all this precaution, I found myself accompanied only by the brigantine Vengeance in the morning, the Granville having remained astern with a prize; as I have since understood the tiller of the Pallas broke after midnight, which disabled her from keeping up, but no apology has yet been made in behalf of the Alliance.

"On the 31st, we saw the Flamie Islands situated near the Lewis on the N.W. coast of Scotland; and the next morning, off Cape Wrath, we gave chase to a ship to windward, at the same time two ships appearing in the N.W. quarter, which proved to be the Alliance and a prize ship which she had taken, bound, as I understood, from Liverpool to Jamaica. The ship which I chased brought to at noon; she proved to be the Union letter of Marque, bound from London for Quebec, with a cargo of naval stores on account of government, adapted for the service of British armed vessels on the lakes. The public dispatches were lost, as the Alliance very imprudently hoisted American colors, though English colors were then flying on board the Bon homme Richard. Capt. Landais sent a small boat to ask whether I would man the ship, or he should, as in the latter case he would suffer no boat nor person from the Bon homme Richard to go near the prize. Ridiculous as this appeared to me, I yielded to it for the sake of peace, and received the prisoners on board the Bon homme Richard, while the prize was manned from the Alliance. In the afternoon another sail appeared, and I immediately made the signal for the Alliance to chase; but, instead of obeying, he wore and laid the ship's head the other way. The next morning I made a signal to speak with the Alliance, to which no attention was shown; I then made sail with the ships in company for the second rendezvous which was not far distant, and where I fully expected to be joined by the Pallas and the Cerf.

"The second of September we saw a sail at daybreak, and gave chase; that ship proved to be the Pallas, and had met with no success while separated from the Bon homme Richard.

"On the 3d the Vengeance brought to a small Irish brigantine, bound homeward from Norway. The same evening I sent the Vengeance in the N.E. quarter to bring up the two prize ships that appeared to me to be too near the islands of Shetland. While with the Alliance and Pallas, I endeavored to weather Fair Isle, and to get into my second rendezvous, where I directed the Vengeance to join me with the three prizes. The next morning, having weathered Fair Isle, and not seeing the Vengeance nor the prizes, I spoke the Alliance and ordered her to steer to the northward and bring them up to the rendezvous.

"On the morning of the 4th the Alliance appeared again, and had brought to two very small coasting sloops in ballast, but without having attended properly to my orders of yesterday. The Venegance joined me soon after, and informed me that in consequence of Captain Landais' orders to the commanders of the two prize ships, they had refused to follow him to the rendezvous. I am to this moment ignorant of what orders these men received from Captain Landais, nor know I by virtue of what authority he ventured to give his orders to prizes in my presence, and without either my knowledge or approbation. Captain Ricot further informed me that he had burnt the prize brigantine, because that vessel proved leaky; and I was sorry to understand afterward that though the vessel was Irish property, the cargo was property of the subjects of Norway.

"In the evening I sent for all the captains to come on board the Bon homme Richard, to consult on future plans of operation. Captains Cottineau and Ricot obeyed me, but Captain Landais obstinately refused, and after sending me various uncivil messages, wrote me a very extraordinary letter in answer to a written order which I had sent him, on finding that he had trifled with my verbal orders. The next day a pilot boat came on board from Shetland, by which means I received such advices as induced me to change a plan which I otherwise meant to have pursued; and as the Cerf did not appear at my second rendezvous, I determined to steer towards the third in hopes of meeting her there.

"In the afternoon a gale of wind came on, which continued four days without intermission. In the second night of that gale the Alliance, with her two little prizes, again separated from the Bon homme Richard. I had now with me only the Pallas and the Vengeance, yet I did not abandon the hopes of performing some essential service. The winds continued contrary, so that we did not see the land till the evening of the 13th, when the hills of the Cheviot in the S.E. of Scotland appeared. The next day we chased sundry vessels, and took a ship and a brigantine, both from the Firth of Edinburgh, laden with coal. Knowing that there lay at anchor in Leith road an armed ship of 20 guns, with two or three fine cutters, I formed an expedition against Leith, which I purposed to lay under a large contribution, or otherwise to reduce it to ashes. Had I been alone, the wind being favorable, I would have proceeded directly up the Firth, and must have succeeded, as they lay there in a state of perfect indolence and security, which would have proved their ruin. Unfortunately for me, the Pallas and Vengeance were both at a considerable distance in the offing, they having chased to the southward; this obliged us to steer out of the Firth again to meet them. The captains of the Pallas and Vengeance being come on board the Bon homme Richard, I communicated to them my project, to which many difficulties and objections were made by them; at last, however, they appeared to think better of the design after I had assured them that I hoped to raise a contribution of 200,000 pounds sterling on Leith, and that there was no battery of cannon there to oppose our landing. So much time, however, was unavoidably spent in pointed remarks and sage deliberation that night, that the wind became contrary in the morning.

"We continued working to windward up the Firth without being able to reach the road of Leith, till, on the morning of the 17th, when, being almost within cannon shot of the town, having everything in readiness for a descent, a very severe gale of wind came on, and being directly contrary, obliged us to bear away, after having in vain endeavored for some time to withstand its violence. The gale was so severe, that one of the prizes that had been taken on the 14th sunk to the bottom, the crew being with difficulty saved. As the alarm by this time had reached Leith by means of a cutter that had watched our motions that morning, and as the wind continued contrary (though more moderate in the evening), I thought it impossible to pursue the enterprise with a good prospect of success; especially as Edinburgh, where there is always a number of troops, is only a mile distant from Leith, therefore I gave up the project.

"On the 19th, having taken a sloop and a brigantine in ballast, with a sloop laden with building timber, I proposed another project to M. Cottineau, which would have been highly honorable though not profitable; many difficulties were made, and our situation was represented as being the most perilous. The enemy, he said, would send against us a superior force, and that if I obstinately continued on the coast of England two days longer, we should all be taken. The Vengeance having chased along shore to the southward, Captain Cottineau said he would follow her with the prizes, as I was unable to make much sail, having that day been obliged to strike the main-top-mast to repair damages; and as I afterward understood, he told M. De Chamillard that unless I joined them the next day, both the Pallas and the Vengeance would leave that coast. I had thoughts of attempting the enterprise alone after the Pallas had made sail to join the Vengeance. I am persuaded even now, that I would have succeeded, and to the honor of my young officers, I found them as ardently disposed to the business as I could desire; nothing prevented me from pursuing my design but the reproach that would have been cast upon my character, as a man of prudence, had the enterprise miscarried. It would have been said, was he not forewarned by Captain Cottineau and others?

"I made sail along shore to the southward, and next morning took a coasting sloop in ballast, which, with another that I had taken the night before, I ordered to be sunk. In the evening, I again met with the Pallas and Vengeance off Whitby. Captain Cottineau told me he had sunk the brigantine, and ransomed the sloop, laden with building timber, that had been taken the day before. I had told Captain Cottineau the day before, that I had no authority to ransom prizes.

"On the 21st we saw and chased two sail, off Flamborough Head, the Pallas in the N. E. quarter, while the Bon homme Richard followed by the Vengeance in the S. W. The one I chased, a brigantine collier in ballast, belonging to Scarborough, was soon taken, and sunk immediately afterward, as a fleet then appeared to the southward: it was so late in the day that I could not come up with the fleet before night; at length, however, I got so near one of them as to force her to run ashore, between Flamborough Head and the Spurn. Soon after I took another, a brigantine from Holland, belonging to Sunderland; and at daylight the next morning, seeing a fleet steering towards me from the Spurn, I imagined them to be a convoy, bound from London for Leith, which had been for some time expected, one of them had a pendant hoisted, and appeared to be a ship of force. They had not, however, courage to come on, but kept back, all except the one which seemed to be armed, and that one also kept to windward very near the land, and on the edge of dangerous shoals where I could not with safety approach. This induced me to make a signal for a pilot, and soon afterward two pilot boats came off; they informed me that the ship that wore a pendant was an armed merchant ship, and that a king's frigate lay there in sight, at anchor within the Humber, waiting to take under convoy a number of merchant ships bound to the northward. The pilots imagined the Bon homme Richard to be an English ship of war, and consequently, communicated to me the private signal which they had been required to make. I endeavored by this means to decoy the ships out of the port, but the wind then changing, and with the tide becoming unfavorable for them, the deception had not the desired effect, and they wisely put back. The entrance of the Humber is exceedingly difficult and dangerous, and as the Pallas was not in sight, I thought it not prudent to remain off the entrance; I therefore steered out again to join the Pallas off Flamborough Head. In the night we saw and chased two ships, until three o'clock in the morning, when being at a very small distance from them, I made the private signal of recognizance, which I had given to each captain before I sailed from Groaix, one half of the answer only was returned. In this position both sides lay to till daylight, when the ships proved to be the Alliance and the Pallas.

" On the morning of that day, the 23d, the brig from Holland not being in sight, we chased a brigantine that appeared laying to to windward. About noon we saw and chased a large ship that appeared coming round Flamborough Head, from the northward, and at the same time I manned and armed one of the pilot boats to sail in pursuit of the brigantine, which now appeared to be the vessel that I had forced ashore. Soon after this a fleet of forty-one sail appeared off Flamborough Head, bearing N. N. E.; this induced me to abandon the single ship which had then anchored in Burlington Bay; I also called back the pilot boat and hoisted a signal for a general chase. When the fleet discovered us bearing down, all the merchant ships crowded sail towards the shore. The two ships of war that protected the fleet, at the same time steered from the land, and made the disposition for the battle: in approaching the enemy I crowded every possible sail, and made the signal for the line of battle, to which the Alliance showed no attention. Earnest as I was for the action, I could not reach the commodore's ship until seven in the evening, being then within pistol shot, when he hailed the Bon homme Richard, we answered him by firing a whole broadside.

"The battle being thus begun, was continued with unremitting fury. Every method was practised on both sides to gain an advantage, and rake each other; and I must confess that the enemy's ship being much more manageable than the Bon homme Richard, gained thereby, several times an advantageous situation, in spite of my best endeavors to prevent it. As I had to deal with an enemy of *greatly superior force*, I was under the necessity of closing with him, to prevent the advantage which he had over me in point of manœuvre. It was my intention to lay the Bon homme Richard athwart the enemy's bow, but as that operation required great dexterity in the management of both sails and helm, and some of our braces being shot away, it did not exactly succeed to my wishes; the enemy's bowsprit, however, came over the Bon homme Richard's poop by the mizen mast, and I made both ships fast together in that situation, which by the action of the wind on the enemy's sails, forced her stern close to the Bon homme Richard's bow, so that the ships lay square alongside of each other, the yards being all entangled, and the cannon of each ship touching the opponent's side. When this position took place it was eight o'clock, previous to which the Bon homme Richard had received sundry eighteen pounds shot below the water, and leaked very much. My battery of 12-pounders, on which I had placed my chief dependance, being commanded by Lieut. Dale and Col. Weibert, and manned principally with American seamen, and French volunteers, were entirely silenced and abandoned. As to the six old 18-pounders that formed the battery of the lower gun-deck, they did no service whatever; two out of three of them burst at the first fire, and killed almost all the men who were stationed to manage them. Before this time, too, Col. De Chamillard, who commanded a party of twenty soldiers on the poop, had abandoned that station, after having lost some of his men. These men deserted their quarters. I had now only two pieces of cannon, 9-pounders, on the quarter deck that were not silenced, and not one of the heavier cannon was fired during the rest of the action. The purser, Mr. Mease, who commanded the guns on the quarter deck, being dangerously wounded in the head, I was obliged to fill his place, and with great difficulty rallied a few men, and shifted over one of the lee quarter-deck guns, so that we afterwards played three pieces of 9 pounders upon the enemy. The tops alone seconded the fire of this little battery, and held out bravely during the whole of the action; especially the main top where Lieut. Stack commanded. I directed the fire of one of the three cannon against the main-mast with double-headed shot, while the other two were exceedingly well served with grape and canister-shot to silence the enemy's musketry, and clear her decks, which was at last effected. The enemy were, as I have since understood, on the instant of calling for quarters, when the cowardice or treachery of three of my under officers induced them to call to the enemy. The English commodore asked me if I demanded quarters, and I having answered him in the most determined negative, they renewed the battle with double fury; they were unable to stand the deck, but the fire of their cannon, especially the lower battery, which was entirely formed of 18 pounders, was incessant. Both ships were set on fire in various places, and the scene was dreadful beyond the reach of language. To account for the timidity of my three under officers, I mean the gunner, the carpenter, and the master-at-arms, I must observe that the two first were slightly wounded, and as the ship had received various shots under water, and one of the pumps being shot away, the carpenter expressed his fear that she would sink, and the other two concluded that she was sinking, which occasioned the gunner to run aft on the poop, without my knowledge, to strike the colors; fortunately for me, a cannon ball had done that before, by carrying away the ensign staff; he was, therefore, reduced to the necessity of sinking,—as he supposed,—or of calling for quarter, and he preferred the latter.

"All this time the Bon homme Richard had sustained the action alone, and the enemy, though much superior in force, would have been very glad to have got clear, as appears by their own acknowledgments, and their having let go an anchor the instant that I laid them on board, by which means they would have escaped, had I not made them well fast to the Bon homme Richard.

"At last, at half past nine o'clock, the Alliance appeared, and I now thought the battle at an end; but to my utter astonishment, he discharged a broadside full into the stern of the Bon homme Richard. We called to him for God's sake to forbear firing into the Bon homme Richard; yet he passed along the off side of the ship, and continued firing. There was no possibility of his mistaking the enemy's ship for the Bon homme Richard, there being the most essential difference in their appearance and construction; besides, it was then full moonlight, and the sides of the Bon homme Richard were all black, while the sides of the prizes were yellow; yet, for the greater security, I showed the signal of our reconnoissance, by putting out three lanthorns, one at the head (bow), another at the stern (quarter), and the third in the middle, in a horizontal line. Every tongue cried that he was firing into the wrong ship, but nothing availed, he passed round, firing into the Bon homme Richard's head, stern, and broadside, and by one of his vollies killed several of my best men, and mortally wounded a good officer on the forecastle. My situation was really deplorable. The Bon homme Richard received various shots under water from the Alliance; the leak gained on the pumps; and the fire increased much on board both ships. Some officers persuaded me to strike, of whose courage and good sense I entertain a high opinion. My treacherous master-at-arms let loose all my prisoners without my knowledge, and my prospect became gloomy indeed. I would not, however, give up the point. The enemy's main-mast began to shake, their firing decreased, ours rather increased, and the British colors were struck at half an hour past ten o'clock.

"This prize proved to be the British ship-of-war the Serapis, a new ship of 44 guns, built on their most approved construction, with two complete batteries, one of them of 18 pounders, and commanded by the brave Commodore Richard Pearson. I had yet two enemies to encounter far more formidable than the Britons:—I mean fire and water. The Serapis was attacked only by the first, but the Bon homme Richard was assailed by both: there were five feet water in the hold, and though it was moderate from the explosion of so much gunpowder, yet the three pumps that remained could with difficulty only keep the water from gaining. The fire broke out in various parts of the ship, in spite of all the water that could be thrown to quench it, and at length broke out as low as the powder magazine, and within a few inches of the powder. In that dilemma, I took out the powder upon deck, ready to be thrown overboard at the last extremity, and it was 10 o'clock the next day, the 24th, before the fire was entirely extinguished. With respect to the situation of the Bon homme Richard, the rudder was cut entirely off the stern frame, and the transums were almost entirely cut away; the timbers, by the lower deck especially, from the main-mast to the stern, being greatly decayed with age, were mangled beyond my power of description; and a person must have been an eyewitness to form a just idea of the tremendous scene of carnage, wreck, and ruin that everywhere appeared. Humanity cannot but recoil from the prospect of such finished horror, and lament that war should produce such fatal consequences.

"After the carpenters, as well as Capt. de Cottineau, and other men of sense had well examined and surveyed the ship (which was not finished before five in the evening), I found every person to be convinced that it was impossible to keep the Bon homme Richard afloat so as to reach a port if the wind should increase, it being then only a very moderate breeze. I had but little time to remove my wounded, which now became unavoidable, and which was effected in the course of the night and next morning. I was determined to keep the Bon homme Richard afloat, and, if possible, to bring her into port. For that purpose the first lieutenant of the Pallas continued on board with a party of men to attend the pumps, with boats in waiting, ready to take them on board, in case the water should gain on them too fast. The wind augmented in the night and the next day, on the 25th, so that it was impossible to prevent the good old ship from sinking. They did not abandon her till after 9 o'clock; the water was then up to the lower deck, and a little after ten, I saw with inexpressible grief the last glimpse of the Bon homme Richard. No lives were lost with the ship, but it was impossible to save the stores of any sort whatever. I lost even the best part of my clothes, books, and papers; and several of my officers lost all their clothes and effects.

"Having thus endeavored to give a clear and simple relation of the circumstances and events that have attended the little armament under my command, I shall freely submit my conduct therein to the censure of my superiors and the impartial public. I beg leave, however, to observe, that the force that was put under my command was far from being well composed; and as the great majority of the actors in it have appeared bent on the pursuit of interest only, I am exceedingly sorry that they and I have been at all concerned. I am in the highest degree sensible of the singular attentions which I have experienced from the court of France, which I shall remember with perfect gratitude until the end of my life, and will always endeavor to merit, while I can, consistent with my honor, continue in the public service. I must speak plainly. As I have been always honored with the full confidence of Congress, and as I also flattered myself with enjoying in some measure the confidence of the Court of France, I could not but be astonished at the conduct of M. de Chaumont, when, in the moment of my departure from Groaix, he produced a paper, a concordat, for me to sign, in common with the officers whom I had commissioned but a few days before. Had that paper, or even a less dishonorable one, been proposed to me at the beginning, I would have rejected it with just contempt, and the word *deplacement*, among others, should have been necessary. I cannot, however, even now suppose that he was authorized by the Court to make such a bargain with me; nor can I suppose that the minister of the marine meant that M. de Chaumont should consider me merely as a colleague with the commanders of the other ships, and communicate to them not only all he knew, but all he thought, respecting our destination and operations. M. de Chaumont has made me various reproaches on account of the expense of the Bon homme Richard, wherewith I cannot think I have been justly chargeable. M. de Chamillard can attest that the Bon homme Richard was at last far from being well fitted or armed for war. If any person or persons who have been charged with the expense of that armament have acted wrong, the fault must not be laid to my charge. I had no authority to superintend that armament, and the persons who had authority were so far from giving me what I thought necessary, that M. de Chaumont even refused, among other things, to allow me irons for securing the prisoners of war.

"In short, while my life remains, if I have any capacity to render good and acceptable services to the common cause, no man will step forth with greater cheerfulness and alacrity than myself, but I am not made to be dishonored, nor can I accept of the *half confidence* of any man living; of course I cannot, consistent with my honor and a prospect of success, undertake future expeditions, unless when the object and destination is communicated to me alone, and to no other person in the marine line. In cases where troops are embarked, a like confidence is due alone to their commander-in-chief. On no other condition will I ever undertake the chief command of a private expedition; and when I do not command in chief, I have no desire to be in the secret.

"Captain Cottineau engaged the Countess of Scarborough, and took her after an hour's action, while the Bon homme Richard engaged the Serapis. The Countess of Scarborough is an armed ship of 20 six-pounders, and was commanded by a king's officer. In the action, the Countess of Scarborough and the Serapis were at a considerable distance asunder; and the Alliance, as I am informed, fired into the Pallas and killed some men. If it should be asked why the convoy was suffered to escape, I must answer, that I was myself in no condition to pursue, and that none of the rest showed any inclination, not even Mr. Ricot, who had held off at a distance to windward during the whole action, and withheld by force the pilot boat with my lieutenant and 15 men.* The Alliance, too, was in a state to pursue the fleet, not having had a single man wounded, or a single shot fired at her from the Serapis, and only three that did execution from the Countess of Scarborough, at such a distance that one stuck in the side, and the other two just touched and then dropped into the water. The Alliance killed one man only on board the Serapis. As Captain de Cottineau charged himself with manning and securing the prisoners of the Countess of Scarborough, I think the escape of the Baltic fleet cannot so well be charged to his account.

"I should have mentioned that the mainmast and mizentopmast of the Serapis fell overboard soon after the captain had come on board the Bon homme Richard.

"Upon the whole, the captain of the Alliance has behaved so very ill in every respect, that I must complain loudly of his conduct. He pretends that he is authorized to act independent of my command: I have been taught the contrary; but supposing it to be so, his conduct has been base and unpardonable. M. de Chamillard will explain the particulars. Either Captain Landais or myself is highly criminal, and one or the other

* This is founded on a report that has proved to be false; for it now appears that Capt. Ricot expressly ordered the pilot boat to board the Bon homme Richard, which order was disobeyed.

must be punished. I forbear to take any steps with him until I have the advice and approbation of your excellency. I have been advised by all the officers of the squadron to put M. Landais under arrest; but as I have postponed it so long, I will bear with him a little longer, until the return of my express.

"We this day anchored here, having since the action been tossed to and fro by contrary winds. I wished to have gained the Road of Dunkirk on account of our prisoners, but was overruled by the majority of *my colleagues.* I shall hasten up to Amsterdam, and there if I meet with no orders from my government, I will take the advice of the French ambassador. It is my present intention to have the Countess of Scarborough ready to transport the prisoners from hence to Dunkirk, unless it should be found more expedient to deliver them to the English ambassador, taking his obligation to send to Dunkirk, &c. immediately an equal number of American prisoners. I am under strong apprehensions that our object here will fail, and that through the imprudence of M. de Chaumont, who has communicated everything he knew or thought on the matter to persons who cannot help talking of it at a full table. This is the way he keeps state secrets, though he never mentioned the affair to me.

"I am ever, &c.

"JOHN P. JONES."

"*Particulars of the bloody engagement between the U. S. Frigate Bon homme Richard and British Frigate Serapis, written for the author by his late friend, Commodore Richard Dale, First Lieutenant of the Bon homme Richard.*

"On the 23d of September, 1779, being below, was roused by an unusual noise upon deck. This induced me to go upon deck, when I found the men were swaying up the royal yards, preparatory to making sail for a large fleet under our lee. I asked the coasting pilot what fleet it was? He answered, 'The Baltic fleet, under convoy of the Serapis of 44 guns, and the Countess of Scarborough of 20 guns.' A general chase then commenced of the Bon homme Richard, the Vengeance, the Pallas, and the Alliance. The latter ship being then in sight after a separation from the squadron of nearly three weeks, but which ship, as usual, disregarded the private signals of the commodore. At this time our fleet headed to the northward, with a light breeze, Flamborough head being about two leagues distant. At 7 P.M. it was evident the Baltic fleet perceived we were in chase, from the signal of the Serapis to the merchantmen to stand in shore. At the same time, the Serapis and Countess of Scarborough, tacked ship, and stood off shore, with the intention of drawing off our attention from the convoy. When these ships had separated from the convoy about two miles, they again tacked and stood in shore after the merchantmen. At about eight, being within hail, the Serapis demanded, 'what ship is that?' He was answered, 'I can't hear what you say.' Immediately after the Serapis hailed again, 'what ship is that? Answer immediately, or I shall be under the necessity of firing into you.' At this moment I received orders from Commodore Jones to commence the action with a broadside, which indeed appeared to be simultaneous on board both ships. Our position being to windward of the Serapis, we passed ahead of her, and the Serapis coming up on our larboard quarter, the action commenced abreast of each other. The Serapis soon passed ahead of the Bon homme Richard, and when he thought he had gained a distance sufficient to go down athwart the fore foot to rake us, found he had not enough distance, and that the Bon homme Richard would be aboard him, put his helm a-lee, which brought the two ships on a line, and the Bon homme Richard, having headway, ran her bows into the stern of the Serapis. We had remained in this situation but a few minutes when we were again hailed by the Serapis, 'Has your ship struck?' To which Captain Jones answered, 'I have not yet begun to fight.' As we were unable to bring a single gun to bear upon the Serapis, our topsails were backed, while those of the Serapis being filled, the ships separated. The Serapis wore short round upon her heel, and her jibboom ran into the mizen rigging of the Bon homme Richard; in this situation the ships were made fast together with a hawser, the bowsprit of the Serapis to the mizenmast of the Bon homme Richard, and the action recommenced from the starboard sides of the two ships. With a view of separating the ships, the Serapis let go her anchor, which manœuvre brought her head, and the stern of the Bon homme Richard to the wind, while the ships lay closely pressed against each other. A novelty in naval combats was now presented to many witnesses, but to few admirers. The rammers were run into the respective ships to enable the men to load after the lower ports of the Serapis had been blown away, to make room for running out their guns, and in this situation the ships remained until between 10 and 11 o'clock P.M., when the engagement terminated by the surrender of the Serapis.

"From the commencement to the termination of the action, there was not a man on board the Bon homme Richard ignorant of the superiority of the Serapis, both in weight of metal, and in the qualities of the crews. The crew of that ship was picked seamen, and the ship itself had been only a few months off the stocks; whereas the crew of the Bon homme Richard consisted of part American, English, and French, and a part of Maltese, Portuguese, and Malays, these latter contributing, by their want of naval skill and knowledge of the English language, to depress rather than elevate a just hope of success in a combat under such circumstances. Neither the consideration of the relative force of the ships, the fact of the blowing up of the gun-deck above them by the bursting of two of the 18 pounders, nor the alarm that the ship was sinking, could depress the ardor or change the determination of the brave Captain Jones, his officers and men. Neither the repeated broadsides of the Alliance, given with the view of sinking or disabling the Bon homme Richard, the frequent necessity of suspending the combat to extinguish the flames, which several times were within a few inches of the magazine, nor the liberation by the master-at-arms of nearly 500 prisoners, could change or weaken the purpose of the American commander. At the moment of the liberation of the prisoners, one of them, a commander of a 20 gun ship taken a few days before, passed through the ports on board the Serapis, and informed Captain Pearson that if he would hold out only a little while longer, the ship alongside would either strike or sink, and that all the prisoners had been released to save their lives. The combat was accordingly continued with renewed ardor by the Serapis.

"The fire from the tops of the Bon homme Richard was conducted with so much skill and effect as to destroy ultimately every man who appeared upon the quarter-deck of the Serapis, and induced her commander to order the survivors to go below. Nor even under shelter of the decks were they more secure. The powder-monkeys of the Serapis finding no officer to receive the 18 pound cartridges brought from the magazines, threw them on the main-deck, and went for more. These cartridges being scattered along the deck, and numbers of them broken, it so happened that some of the hand-grenades thrown from the main-yard of the Bon homme Richard, which was directly over the main-hatch of the Serapis, fell upon this powder, and produced a most awful explosion. The effect was tremendous; more than twenty of the enemy were blown to pieces, and many stood with only the collars of their shirts upon their bodies. In less than an hour afterward, the flag of England, which had been nailed to the mast of the Serapis, was struck by Captain Pearson's *own hand*, as none of his people would venture aloft on this duty; and this, too, when more than 1500 persons were witnessing the conflict, and the humiliating termination of it, from Scarborough and Flamborough head.

"Upon finding that the flag of the Serapis had been struck, I went to Captain Jones, and asked whether I might board the Serapis? to which he consented; and, jumping upon the gunwale, seized the main-brace pennant, and swung myself upon her quarter-deck. Midshipman Mayrant followed with a party of men, and was immediately run through the thigh with a boarding-pike by some of the enemy stationed in the waist, who were not informed of the surrender of their ship. I found Captain Pearson standing on the leeward side of the quarter-deck, and, addressing myself to him, said—'Sir, I have orders to send you on board the ship alongside.' The first lieutenant of the Serapis coming up at this moment, inquired of Captain Pearson whether the ship alongside had struck to him? To which I replied, 'No, sir, the contrary; he has struck to us.' The lieutenant renewing his inquiry, have you struck, sir? was answered, 'Yes, I have.' The lieutenant replied, 'I have nothing more to say;' and was about to return below, when I informed him he must accompany Captain Pearson on board the ship alongside. He said, "If you will permit me to go below, I will silence the firing of the lower-deck guns.' This request was refused, and with Captain Pearson was passed over to the deck of the Bon homme Richard. Orders being sent below to cease firing, the engagement terminated, after a most obstinate contest of three hours and a half.

"Upon receiving Captain Pearson on board the Bon homme Richard, Captain Jones gave orders to cut loose the lashings, and directed me to follow him with the Serapis. Perceiving the Bon homme Richard leaving the Serapis, I sent one of the quarter-masters to ascertain whether the wheel-ropes were cut away, supposing something extraordinary must be the matter, as the ship would not pay off, although the head sails were aback, and no after sail; the quarter-master returning, reported that the wheel-ropes were all well, and the helm hard a-port. Excited by this extraordinary circumstance, I jumped off the binnacle, where I had been sitting, and falling upon the deck, found to my astonishment I had the use of only one of my legs: a splinter of one of the guns had struck and badly wounded my leg, without my perceiving the injury until this moment. I was replaced upon the binnacle, when the sailing-master of the Serapis coming up to me, observed that from my orders he judged I must be ignorant of the ship *being at anchor*. Noticing the second lieutenant of the Bon homme Richard, I directed him to go below and cut away the cable, and follow the Bon homme Richard with the Serapis. I was then carried on board the Bon homme Richard to have my wound dressed."

ADMIRALTY OFFICE,

October 12, 1779.

A letter from Capt. Richard Pearson, of his Majesty's ship Serapis to Mr. Stephens, of which the following is a copy, was yesterday received at this office.

"*Pallas, French Frigate, in Congress service, Texel, October* 6, 1779.

"SIR,

"You will be pleased to inform the Lords Commissioners of the Admiralty, that on the 23d ult., being close in with Scarborough, about 4 o'clock, a boat came on board with a letter from the bailiffs of that corporation, giving information of a flying squadron of the enemy's ships being on the coast, and a part of the said squadron having been seen from thence the day before, standing to the southward. As soon as I received this intelligence I made the signal for the convoy to bear down under my lee, and repeated it with two guns; notwithstanding which the van of the convoy kept their wind, with all sail stretching out to the southward from under Flamborough Head, till between twelve and one, when the headmost of them got sight of the enemy's ships, which were then in chase of them; they then tacked, and made the best of their way under the shore for Scarborough, &c. letting fly their top-gallant sheets, and firing guns; upon which I made all the sail I could to windward, to get between the enemy's ships and the convoy, which I soon effected. At 1 o'clock we got sight of the enemy's ships from the masthead, and about 4 we made them plain from the deck to be three large ships and a brig, upon which I made the Countess of Scarborough a signal to join me, she being in shore with the convoy. At the same time I made the signal for the convoy to make the best of their way, and repeated the signal with two guns: I then brought to, to let the Countess of Scarborough come up, and cleared ship for action. At half past 5 the Countess of Scarborough joined me, the enemy's ships bearing down upon us with a light breeze at S.S.W., at 6 tacked, in order to keep our ground the better between the enemy's ships and the convoy: soon after which we perceived the ships bearing down upon us to be a two-decked ship and two frigates, but from their keeping end on, and bearing upon us, we could not discern what colors they were under; at about 20 minutes past 7 the largest ship of the three brought to on our larboard bow, within musket-shot. I hailed him and asked what ship it was; they answered in English, 'The Princess Royal.' I then asked where they belonged to, they answered evasively; on which I told them, if they did not answer directly I would fire into them; they then answered with a shot which was instantly returned with a broadside; and, after exchanging two or three broadsides, he backed his topsails, and dropt upon our quarter within pistol shot, then filled again, put his helm-a-weather, and run us on board upon our weather quarter, and attempted to board us, but being repulsed, he sheered off; upon which I backed our topsails, in order to get square with him again, which, as soon as he observed, he then filled, put his helm a-weather, and laid us athwart hause; his mizen-shrouds took our jib-boom, which hung him for some time until at last it gave way, and we dropt alongside of each other, head and stern, when the fluke of our spare anchor hooking his quarter, we became so close fore and aft that the muzzles of our guns touched each other's sides. In this position we engaged from half past 8 till half past 10, during which time, from the great quantity and variety of combustible matters which they threw in upon our decks, chains, and, in short, into every part of the ship, we were on fire no less than ten or twelve times in different parts of the ship, and it was with the greatest difficulty and exertion imaginable at times that we were able to get it extinguished. At the same time the largest of the two frigates kept sailing round us the whole action and raking us fore and aft, by which means she killed or wounded almost every man on the quarter and main decks. About half past 9, either from a hand-grenade being thrown in at one of our lower-deck ports, or from some other accident, a cartridge of powder was set on fire, the flames of which running from cartridge to cartridge all the way aft, blew up the whole of the people and officers that were quartered abaft the main-mast; from which unfortunate circumstance all those guns were rendered useless for the remainder of the action and, I fear, the greatest part of the people will lose their lives. At 10 o'clock they called for quarters from the ship alongside, and said they had struck; hearing this I called upon the captain to know if he had struck, or if he asked for quarters; but no answer being made, after repeating my words two or three times, I called for the boarders and ordered them to board, which they did; but the moment they were on board her, they discovered a superior number laying under cover with pikes in their hands, ready to receive them, on which our people retreated instantly to their guns again till past 10, when the frigate coming across our stern, and pouring her broadside into us again, without our being able to bring a gun to bear on her, I found it in vain, and indeed impracticable from the situation we were in, to stand out any longer with the least prospect of success. I therefore struck (our main-mast at the same time went by the board). The first lieutenant and myself were immediately escorted into the ship alongside, when we found her to be an American ship-of-war, called the Bon homme Richard of 40 guns and 375 men, commanded by Capt. Paul Jones, the other frigate which engaged us to be the Alliance of 40 guns and 300 men, and the third frigate which engaged and took the Countess of Scarborough, after two hours' action, to be the Pallas, a French frigate of 32 guns and 275 men, the Vengeance an armed brig of 12 guns and 70 men, all in Congress service and under the command of Paul Jones. They fitted out and sailed from Port L'Orient the latter end of July, and came north about; they have on board 300 English prisoners which they have taken in different vessels in their way round since they left France, and have ransomed some others. On my going on board the Bon homme Richard I found her to be in the greatest distress; her counters and quarter on the lower deck entirely drove in, and the whole of her lower deck guns dismounted; she was also on fire in two places, and six or seven feet water in her hold, which kept increasing upon them all night and the next day, till they were obliged to quit her, and she sunk with a great number of her wounded people on board her. She had 306 men killed and wounded in the action; our loss in the Serapis was also very great. My officers and people in general behaved well, and I should be very remiss in my attention to their merit, were I to omit recommending the remains of them to their Lordships' favor.

"Herewith I enclose you the most exact list of the killed and wounded I have as yet been able to procure, from my people being dispersed among the different ships, and having been refused permission to muster them; there are, I find, many more both killed and wounded than appears in the enclosed list, but their names I find as yet impossible to ascertain; as soon as I possibly can, I shall give their Lordships a full account of the whole.

"I am, Sir, &c.

"R. PEARSON." *

A more perfect idea of the dreadful havoc on board the Serapis may be obtained from the official list of the wounded prisoners taken in that ship; and it may gratify the curiosity of those readers who are desirous of learning more particularly the multiplied afflictions to which persons engaged in naval warfare are exposed:—

"*List of wounded prisoners on board the Serapis.*

"*September* 30*th*, 1779.

James Clerk, . . . thigh fractured.
Richard Angel, . . . wounded hand.

* On Paul Jones' arrival in New York, after his capture of the *crack* British Frigate Serapis of 50 guns, off Flamborough Head, after six hours' fight yard arm and yard arm, by moonlight, he was informed by a friend that Captain Pearson of the Seraphishad been *knighted*. "Well," said Jones, "he deserved it; and should I have the good fortune to fall in with him again, I will make a *Lord* of him."

John Robertson, . .	wounded hand.
Abraham Cornish, . .	wounded leg and scorched.
John Robertson, . .	wounded legs.
William Rogers, . .	wounded arm.
Leonard Addison, . .	wounded legs.
Richard Williams, . .	wounded shoulder.
James Ashworth, . .	wounded shoulder.
John M'Lean, . .	wounded side.
Cumberland Ward, .	wounded thigh and scorched.
Charles Jebb, . .	arm shot off and much scorched.
Richard Mason, . .	wounded arm.
Benjamin Rushton, .	wounded shoulder and scorched.
William Hudson, . .	wounded shoulder.
Edward Morgan, . .	wounded shoulder.
Mr. Brownhill, . .	wounded arm and side.
Mr. Wightman, . .	both arms wounded.
Robert Ozord, . .	scorched slightly.
Mr. Bannatyne, *Surgeon*,	fingers slightly scorched.
Mr. M'Knight, Mr. Kitchen, } *his Mates*,	much scorched in the face.
Stephen Maggot, . .	wounded back.
John Clark, . . .	wounded wrist.
Thomas Rubbish, . .	wounded shoulder.
Charles Brooks, . .	shoulder much bruised.
John Campbell, . .	shot in the hand.
Charles Davis, . .	wounded haunch.
William Pubbelon, .	shot in the back.
Anthony Franks, . .	arm amputated.
Robert Man, . . .	leg wounded.
John Oliver, . . .	shot in the back.
Thomas Mersell, . .	arm and thigh wounded.
William Guerney, . .	slightly wounded.
Samuel Davis, . .	arm and thigh wounded.
Harry Hook, . .	arm and breast wounded.

"*The following miserably scorched.*

Abraham Portsmouth,	William Searcher,
Mr. Mycock,	Thomas Sandwell, *Boy*,
Mr. Popplewell,	Benjamin Pickersgill,
Thomas Rivers,	Thomas Hyslop,
William Bennet,	Jeremy Murphy,
Joseph Springale,	Charles Metcalf,

John Lawrence,	Richard Seaton,
George Lever,	Alexander Hutchinson,
James Caw,	William Crow,
John Paul,	Thomas Weeks,
Robert Ingram,	John Ashby,
James Hall,	Seven or eight Lascars.

"*Dead of their wounds.*

Mr. Brown, *Master's Mate*,	Patrick Sulivan,
Mr. Plaice, *Boatswain*,	John Ellison,
John Jones, *Marine, Private*,	John Appleby,
Edward Vernon,	Michael ——, *Capt. Servant.*

"Besides one or two others whose names could not be ascertained.

"WM. BANNATYNE, *English Surgeon.*"

"*Sir Joseph Yorke, the British Ambassador, presented the following memorial to their High Mightinesses, on the 9th inst.*

"*Hague, Oct. 13th,* 1779.

"HIGH AND MIGHTY LORDS,

"The undersigned, ambassador extraordinary and plenipotentiary of the King of Great Britain, has the honor to communicate to your High Mightinesses, that two of his majesty's ships, the Serapis and the Countess of Scarborough, arrived some days ago in the Texel, having been attacked and taken by force by a certain Paul Jones, a subject of the king, who, according to treaties and the laws of war, can only be considered as a rebel and a pirate. The undersigned is, therefore, in duty bound to recur to your High Mightinesses, and demand their immediate orders that those ships, with their officers and crews, may be stopped, and he especially recommends to your humanity, to permit the wounded to be brought on shore, that proper attention may be paid to them, at the expense of the king his master.

"YORKE."

"*Resolutions of their High Mightinesses relative to Paul Jones's squadron and prizes, delivered to the English ambassador at the Hague, on the 25th October,* 1779.

"That their High Mightinesses, being informed that three frigates had lately arrived at the Texel, namely, two French and one called an American, commanded by Paul Jones, bringing with them two prizes taken by them in the open sea, and called the Serapis and the Countess of Scarborough described in the ambassador's memorial. That their High Mightinesses, having for a century past strictly observed the following maxim, and notified the same by placards, viz., that they will in no respect whatever pretend to judge of the legality or illegality of the actions of those who have on the open sea taken any vessels which do not belong to this country, and bring them into any of the ports of this republic; that they only open their ports to them to give them shelter from storms or other disasters; and that they oblige them to put to sea again with their prizes without unloading or disposing of their cargoes, but letting them remain exactly as when they arrived. That their High Mightinesses will not examine whether the prizes taken by the three frigates in question belong to the French or the Americans, or whether they are legal or illegal prizes, but leave all that to be determined by the proper judges, and will oblige them to put to sea, that they may be liable to be retaken, and by that means brought before the proper judge, particularly as his excellency the ambassador must own he would have no less a right to reclaim the above mentioned ships if they had been private property, than as they have been king's ships; therefore their High Mightinesses are not authorised to pass judgment either upon these prizes, or the person of Paul Jones; that, as to what regards acts of humanity, their High Mightinesses have already made appear how ready they are to show them towards the wounded on board of the vessels, and that they have given orders accordingly. That an extract of the present resolution be given to Sir Joseph Yorke, by the agent, Vander Burch de Spierinxhock."

"*Extract of a memorial presented by Sir Joseph Yorke, His Majesty's Ambassador at the Hague, to their High Mightinesses, requesting the delivering up the Serapis and Countess of Scarborough, taken by Paul Jones.*

"High and Mighty Lords,

"In thanking your High Mightinesses for the orders which your humanity dictated relative to the wounded men on board the two king's ships, the Serapis and the Countess of Scarborough, I cannot but comply with the strict orders of his majesty, by renewing in the strongest and most pressing manner his request that these ships and their crews may be stopped and delivered up, which the pirate Paul Jones, of Scotland, who is a rebel subject and a criminal of the state, has taken.

"The king would think he derogated from his own dignity, as well as that of your High Mightinesses, were he to enter into the particulars of a case so notorious as that in question, or to set before the eyes of the ancient friends and allies of his crown, analogous examples of other princes and states, but will only remark that all the placards even of your High Mightinesses require that all the captains of foreign armed vessels shall, upon their arrival, present their letters of marque, or commission: and authorizes, according to the custom of admiralties, to treat all those as pirates whose letters are found to be illegal, for want of being granted by a sovereign power.

"The quality of Paul Jones, and all the circumstances of the affair, are too notorious for your High Mightinesses to be ignorant of them. The eyes of all Europe are fixed upon your resolution; your High Mightinesses know too well the value of good faith not to give an example of it in this essential rencontre. The smallest deviation from so sacred a rule by weakening the principle of neighbors may produce serious consequences.

"JOSEPH YORKE,

"*Done at the Hague, Oct. 29th,* 1779.

The answer which their High Mightinesses caused to be given to the above memorial was in brief:—"that they will in no respect take upon them to judge of the legality or illegality of those who have on the open sea taken any vessels which do not belong to their country; that they only open their ports to give them shelter from storms, or other disasters; and that they oblige them to go to sea again with their prizes, without suffering them to unload or dispose of any part of their cargoes, that they may be liable to be retaken in the same state they were taken; but do not think themselves authorised to pass judgment upon those prizes, or the person of Paul Jones."

A statement of Mr. Van Berckel, Grand Pensionary of Amsterdam, and of Mr. Dumas, Agent of the United States in Holland.

"The Commodore John Paul Jones, commanding a light squadron, equipped at the expense of his most Christian Majesty, under the flag and commission of the United States of America, made sail from France, August the 14th, 1779: about the same time that the grand combined fleets of France and Spain, of 66 vessels of the line, under the command of his excellency the Count d'Orvilliers, appeared in the channel between France and England. As they expected that a French army, under the protection of this fleet, would make a descent upon the southern coast of

England, the Commodore having a carte-blanche, believed it to be his duty to make a strong diversion, in order to facilitate the enterprise. To this effect he alarmed and insulted the coast and ports of the enemy from Cape Clear along the western coast of Ireland, by the north of Scotland, to Hull, the east of England. In the course of this service, as difficult as important, he made many armed captures, and destroyed a number of merchant vessels belonging to the enemy. The great object of the Commodore was to intercept the British fleet returning from the Baltic, and consequently to deprive the enemy of the means of equipping their vessels of war. There is every reason to believe that he would have completely effected this object, if he had not been abandoned on the coast of Ireland by a considerable part of his forces, and if his frigate, the Bon homme Richard, had been in the least assisted in this memorable combat with the Serapis, a two-decker, and against the frigate the Countess of Scarborough. But after the commodore had fought these two vessels during one hour, the distance of pistol-shot, whilst the rest of his forces sheltered themselves from any damage, notwithstanding the advantage of the wind, the American frigate the Alliance traitorously fired three broadsides of grape-shot into the Bon homme Richard. During the whole affair the Alliance took care not to expose herself to receive a single shot, nor to have a single man killed or wounded on board. The Bon homme Richard was, during three hours, lashed to the Serapis, and after the battle, which lasted four hours, sunk, riddled as a vessel had never been before. The battle taking place at one league from Scarborough, it was not possible, under the circumstances above mentioned, to hinder the entrance into that port of the enemy's convoy, which arrived in safety.

"The Commodore entered the Texel with the remainder of his squadron, and his two last prizes, the 3d of October, 1779. The one half of the crews, as well of the Bon homme Richard as of the Serapis having been killed or wounded, the Commodore addressed himself to their High Mightinesses for permission to establish a hospital at the Helder, in order to cure his wounded. But the Magistracy of the place being opposed, their High Mightinesses assigned for this purpose the fort of the Texel, and as the Commodore had the permission to garrison the fort by a detachment of his soldiers, he granted a commission of commandant of the place, for as long a time as was necessary, to one of his officers. The combined fleet having entered Brest, the English, filled with the terror of an invasion, with which they perceived themselves menaced, let loose all their animosity against the Commodore. The English ambassador at the Hague, by his repeated memorials to the States General, did not cease to reclaim peremptorily the restitution of the vessel of war and the frigate taken by the Commodore, and to demand likewise that the *Scotch Pirate*,

Paul Jones, should be delivered up to the King his master. This step of the ambassador not succeeding, he did all in his power with the magistrates and private citizens of Amsterdam to cause them to lay hands upon the person of the Commodore, and to deliver him up to him, but in vain; no person had the baseness or the courage to undertake his desire in this respect.

"The English despatched many light squadrons to intercept the Commodore. Two of these squadrons cruised continually in sight of the Texel, and of the Ulie, whilst the others were stationed in such a manner as to cause the belief that it would be impossible for him to escape. The object of the court of France in causing the Commodore to enter the Texel was, that he might escort from thence to Brest a numerous fleet, loaded with materials for the arsenal of that port, but his situation rendered this service impracticable; above all, as the minister had not taken care to keep the matter secret. The situation of the Commodore engaged the attention of all Europe, and profoundly affected the politics of the belligerent powers. But this situation became infinitely more critical, when the Prince of Orange deprived Mr. Riemersma of the command of the Dutch fleet, consisting of thirteen men-of-war, and sent the Vice-Admiral Rhyust to succeed him, and to expel the Commodore from the Texel, in sight of the British squadrons. This engaged the Court of Versailles to send to the ambassador of France at the Hague a commission from his most Christian Majesty for the Commodore, which authorized him to hoist the French flag, but to this the Commodore would not consent. On his arrival, he had declared himself an officer of the United States of America; he was not authorized by Congress to accept the offered commission: in fine, he conceived it would be dishonorable and disadvantageous, as well for himself as for America, to change his flag, especially under existing circumstances. With the exception of the frigate Alliance, the remainder of the squadron under the command of the Commodore belonged to his most Christian Majesty, and the French ambassador had, in consequence, the right to dispose of them. The American minister, at Paris, addressed an order to the Commodore to deliver all his prisoners to the French ambassador; and, to obey this order, the Commodore was obliged to deliver also the Serapis and Countess of Scarborough, because the other vessels could not contain the great number of his prisoners. The Commodore continued to carry the American flag on board the Alliance, and as soon as the wind permitted, the Vice-Admiral, having rendered his stay in the Texel as disagreeable as possible, obliged him to set sail in this frigate. The Commodore had the address and the good fortune to escape the vigilance of the enemy; and the English, enraged at this, and also because the States General had granted an escort for the fleet which carried out the naval stores from the Texel to Brest, declared, a short time afterward, war against the united low countries. They made use of the stay and the conduct of the Commodore at the Texel for the first article of their declaration.

"The facts above stated are of public notoriety throughout all Europe, and my motive in giving this testimony to America in favor of the Commodore, proceeds from the desire to render justice to his zeal and good conduct for the honor and interest of the United States in the affairs which have come immediately under my own cognizance. At the Hague, March 10th, 1784.

"E. P. Van Berckel."

"I, the undersigned, knowing not only the exact truth of all which is above stated, but having been officially present, during nearly three months, on board the American squadron in the Road of the Texel, attest to it with pleasure, this 11th of March, 1784, at the Hague.

"M. F. Dumas,
"Agent of the United States of America."

The brilliant result of the terrible contest with the Serapis filled Europe and America with the renown of Commodore Jones. The British Government was incensed and the national pride wounded at finding one of the finest frigates in the English navy captured so near the coast of Great Britain, and in the view, by moonlight, of numerous spectators. The subjoined comparative statement of the relative force of the two ships and their crews will show that the advantage was decidedly in favor of the Serapis:

"*Statement of the Force of the Bon homme Richard on the* 23*d September*, 1779.

" Six	18	pounders on the		lower gun deck,
Fourteen	12	"	"	middle gun deck,
"	9	"	"	" " "
Two	6	"	"	quarter " "
"	6	"	"	spar, or upper deck,
One				in each gangway,

Two 6 pounders upon the forecastle.
380 men and boys.

"*Force of the Serapis on the same day.*

"Twenty	18 pounders	on her	lower	gun deck,		
"	9	"	"	upper	"	"
Six	6	"	"	quarter		"
Four	6	"	"	forecastle,		

305 men, and about 15 lascars."

The officers and men who so gallantly distinguished themselves in this memorable affair deserve to be immortalized. The annexed roll contains the names of the whole of them from an official source, and it is with pleasure that the opportunity is embraced of inserting them in a work which is a record of the achievements and prowess of their intrepid commander. The roll includes also a specification of those who were killed and wounded, together with the respective countries of which they were natives:—

"Roll *of the Officers, Seamen, Marines, and Volunteers, who served on board the Bon homme Richard, commanded by Commodore John Paul Jones, in her cruize made in* 1779.

NAMES.	COUNTRY.	RANK.	REMARKS.
John Paul Jones,	Scotch,	Commodore,	
Richard Dale,	Maryland,	1st Lieut.	badly wounded.
Henry Lunt,	Mass.	2d do.	
Cutting Lunt,	Mass.	3d do.	
Samuel Stacey,	N. H.	Master,	
Laurence Brooks,	do.	Surgeon,	
Mathurin Mease,	Mass.	Purser,	badly wounded.
——— Stack,	French,	Lt. Col. Marines,	
——— Macarty,	do.	Lieut. do.	
——— O'Kelly,	Irish,	do. do.	
John White,	American,	Mate,	

NAMES.	COUNTRY.	RANK.	REMARKS.
Thomas Potter,	American,	Midshipman,	wounded.
Nathaniel Fanning,	do.	do.	
Benjamin Stubbs,	Mass.	do.	
Reuben Chase,	do.		
Beaumont Groube,	do.	Midshipman,	
Jonah Carvell,	American,		killed.
William Daniel,	do.		
John Mayrant,	S. C.	Midshipman,	wounded.
Robert Coram,	N. H.	do.	
John L. White,	American,		
Richard Wat,	do.		
Gilbert Wat,	do.		
John Robinson,	English,		
John Gunnion,	American,	Carpenter,	
William Clarke,	do.	Sailmaker,	wounded.
Jacob True,	do.	2d Gunner,	
Ichabod Lord,	Mass.	Carpenter,	
Daniel Russel,	do.	Steward,	
Thomas Turner,	English,	Boatswain,	killed.
Edward Garret,	do.	do.	
Thomas Miller,	do.	Carpenter,	
William Physic,	do.	do.	killed.
James Connor,	Irish,	do.	
Robert Steel,	English,	Qr. Master,	killed.
Robert Towers,	do.	do.	
William Thompson,	Scotch,	do.	
John Woulton,	English,	do.	
Robert Stevens,	do.	Cook,	
Arthur Randall,	do.	Gunner,	
Thomas Macarthy,	Irish,	do.	killed.
Jonathan Wells,	American,	do.	
William Lee,	English,	do.	
John Murphy,	Irish,	do.	killed.
John Pearce,	English,	do.	
Thomas Jones,	do.	do.	
Francis Campbell,	do.	do.	
Michael Longstaff,	American,	Qr. Master,	killed.
Henry Gardiner,	do.	Gunner,	wounded.
Elijah Perkins,	English,	Surg. Mate,	
Hugh Wonton,	do.	Sail Maker,	killed.
John Williams,	do.	Qr. Master,	killed.

NAMES.	COUNTRY.	RANK.	REMARKS.
John Peacock,	Irish,	Surg. Mate,	
Stephen Lee,	American,	Clerk,	
John Burbank,	do.	Master-at-arms,	
Josiah Brewster,	Mass.	Armorer,	killed.
William Sturgess,	Irish,	do.	
John Thomas,	American,	Cook,	wounded.
John Maden,	Irish,	Armorer,	
John Haguet,	English,	do.	
Thomas Davis,	do.	do.	killed.
William Roberts,	do.	do.	
Thomas Knight,	American,	Carpenter.	

SEAMEN.

NAMES.	COUNTRY.	REMARKS.
Peter Nolde,	Swede,	
Gilbert Crumb,	American,	
James Smith,	English,	
Thomas Wythe, or White,	do.	wounded.
Henry Martin,	American,	killed.
Edward Lewis,	do.	
John Brown,	English,	wounded.
William Fox,	do.	
Duncan Taylor,	Scotch,	
John M'Kinley,	do.	
George Walker,	English,	
Robert Hill,	do.	killed.
Lewis Brown,	Norway,	
James Evans,	English,	
John Earl,	Irish,	
Robert Dougherty,	English,	killed.
Richard Huguet,	do.	
John Brown,	do.	wounded.
William Clisdall,	American,	
James Nicholson,	do.	killed.
John Connor,	Irish,	wounded.
Richard Taylor,	English,	
John Walker,	American,	
George Johnston,	Norway,	wounded.
Alexander Cooper,	English,	

NAMES.	COUNTRY.	REMARKS.
David Pritchard,	English,	
Andrew Ryan,	do.	
Samuel Mathews,	Irish,	
Laurence Furlong,	do.	wounded.
Thomas Forrest,	English,	
Jas. M'Kinley, or M'Kinsay,	Providence,	wounded.
John M. Coffery,	American,	
Thomas Mehany,	Irish,	
John Colbraith,	English,	
James Riley,	Irish,	
James Lenn,	English,	wounded.
Joseph Collinson,	do.	do.
Jones Haraham,	do.	
Joseph Wiera,	Portugal,	wounded.
Antoine Alcantara,	do.	
Joseph Mare,	do.	killed.
Joachim Joseph,	do.	do.
Vincent Ignace,	do.	do.
James Quint, or Quin,	New Hampshire,	
John Weaver,	American,	
David Cross,	Massachusetts,	
John Turpin,	American,	
John Carrico,	do.	
John Burnet,	do.	wounded.
John Thompson,	do.	
John Frankford,	do.	
Charles Peterson,	Swede,	wounded.
Daniel Emblon,	do.	
Peter Biorkman,	do.	
Benjamin Gartineau,	do.	
Peter Molin,	do.	
Oliver Gustaff,	do.	
Elijah Johnstone,	American,	
Jacob Henrio,	Swiss.	

BOYS.

Baptist Travaillier,	Paris,	
Anthony Jeremiah,	India,	
John Ridway,	English,	killed.

NAMES.	COUNTRY.	REMARKS.
James Powert,	English,	
John Jordan,	do.	wounded.
Jeremiah Crooks,	do.	killed.
James Parry,	Irish,	
William Garret,	English,	
William Listera,	do.	
Thomas Davis,	do.	
Peter Richardson,	do.	
Joseph Steward,	do.	
Isaac Hobshaw,	American,	
Samuel Flatcher,	do.	
Thos. Honnet, or Hammett,	New Hampshire,	wounded.
Stephen Loley,	American,	killed.
John Downs,	New Hampshire,	
Nicholas Rogers,	American,	
Aaron Goodwin,	Massachusetts,	
Andrew Mason,	American,	do.
Nathaniel Kennard,	do.	
William Cullingwood,	English,	wounded.
Benjamin Bickets,	New Hampshire,	
James Cunningham,	American,	
John Holliday,	Massachusetts,	do.
James M'Michan,	American,	do.
Robert Upham,	do.	do.
Joseph Bartlett,	New Hampshire,	
William M'Cullough,	American,	do.
John Kilby,	do.	
William Simpson,	do.	do.
Nicholas Caldwell,	do.	
Jeremiah Evans,	do.	
Richard Lawson,	do.	
Patrick Quin,	Massachusetts,	
William Earth,	American,	
Daniel Prior,	do.	
Joseph Cooper,	do.	
William Murphy,	do.	killed.
Mark Paul,	do.	
Manuel Quito,	Portugal,	
Robert Lyon,	American,	wounded.

ORDINARY SEAMEN.

NAMES.	COUNTRY.	REMARKS.
Laurent Verness,	Norway,	
Daniel Swain,	English,	wounded.
John Brussen,	Naples,	
John Jones,	English,	
Joseph Burns,	do.	
John Duffy,	Irish,	
John Pinkman,	do.	
William Knox,	do.	
Abraham Martel,	English,	
Henry Humphreys,	do.	
Nathaniel Bailey,	Massachusetts,	killed.
James Mehanny,	Irish,	
William Wilkinson,	English,	
Elijah Middleton,	do.	
George Harroway,	Scotch,	do.
John Jordan,	Bengal,	wounded.
Francis Perkins,	American,	killed.
John Hacket,	English,	
Antoine Francisque,	Portugal,	wounded.
Francois Darros,	do.	
Ignace Silveyra,	do.	
Mathieu Antoine,	do.	
Joseph Rodrique,	do.	killed.
Antoine Carriero, or Corrisque,	do.	do.
Mathieu Joseph,	do.	
Jean Ignace,	do.	
Jean Pracia,	do.	
Joseph Maurda,	do.	do.
Manuel Vieza,	do.	
Thomas Clarke,	English,	do.
James Fogg,	do.	
Jean Silveyra,	Fayal,	
Manuel Priera,	Portugal,	
Jonan Joseph,	do.	do.
Antoine Foustade,	do.	
Manuel Antoine,	do.	do.
Mathieu Francisque,	do.	
Joseph Ignace,	do.	do.
Antoine Silvestre,	do.	do.

Names.	Country.	Remarks.
Joseph Joachim,	Portugal,	
Manuel Castaino,	do.	
Louis Antoine,	do.	killed.
John Minant,	Irish.	

SERVANTS.

George Campbell,	Cook,	Charles Priestly,	Cook."
Joseph Holland,	do.		

The following persons, according to the roll kept by the first lieutenant of the Bon homme Richard, belonged to the ship, but for some cause not known were not included in the distribution of the prize money.

KILLED.	WOUNDED.
Alexander Antoine,	Thomas Wat,
Jacques Loria,	John Lyons,
John B. Frerry,	George Trefathen,
Lewis Role Tomis,	Richard Williams,
Jacques Baterga,	John M'Intyre,
Joham Gorrica,	Hugh Euroney,
Perry Carreau.	Aaron Smith,
	Richard Hughes,
	George Johnson,
	William Hamilton.

Roll of the Officers and Crew of the Frigate Alliance, Captain Peter Landais, October 3d, 1779.

NAMES.	RANK.
Peter Landais, ...	Captain.
James Degges, ...	1st Lieutenant.
John Buckley, ...	2d Lieutenant.
James Linds, ...	3d Lieutenant.
John Lachar, ...	Master.
Arnold Winship, . . .	Surgeon.
John Swain,	
Arthur Robinson,	

Names.	Rank.
John Patten,	
Thomas White,	
Nathaniel Watson,	
Alexander Moore,	
James Logham,	
Freight Arnold,	
Park, ...	Captain of Marines.
Thomas Ehlenwood, . .	1st Lieutenant.
James Warren, . . .	2d Lieutenant.
Thomas Hinsdale, . . .	2d Mate.
Thomas Fitzgerald, . . .	3d Mate.
Lewis Larchard, . . .	4th Mate.
Isaac Carr, ...	Master Sail-Maker.
James Bragg, ...	Master Carpenter.
John Green, ...	Carpenter's Mate.
James Peter, ...	Gunner.
John Orr, ...	2d Mate.
Chauncey Wheeler, . . .	3d Mate.
Alexander Darling, . . .	Boatswain.
Thomas Taylor, . . .	2d Mate.
John Epet, ...	3d Mate.
Joseph Frederick, . . .	4th Mate.
Robert Embleton, . . .	Quarter Master.
Jacob Nuttar, ...	do.
George Fenwick, . . .	do.

SEAMEN.	SEAMEN.
James Buright,	George Cock,
James Haslam,	John Doyle,
George Allen,	John Wethabe,
Joseph Plumer,	John Wire,
John Carebis,	John Sadler,
James Richardson,	Evan Evans,
Thomas Luce,	John Dickson,
James Rody,	Thomas Chase,
John Pall,	John Morrow,
William Shackford,	James Forrester,
Gardner Hammond,	Samuel Platt,
Charles Hisbert,	Edward Flinn,
James Chester,	Thomas Duane,

SEAMEN.	SEAMEN.
Samuel Dale,	Jacob Arnold,
John M'Lean,	John Neale,
John Graves,	John Fitzgerald,
Richard Hughes,	Peter Lunt,
John Downing,	Joseph Choat,
John Thomas,	Jeremiah Perry,
John Shalf,	Stephen Turner,
Joseph Poor,	Daniel Hancock,
Samuel Nach,	Robert Smith,
John Collington,	Richard Woodron,
John Davis,	John Simpson,
Kirtland Griffing,	Charles Brown,
Henry Nalander,	John Jones,
John Diraud,	Peter Greenwood,
James Whitney,	Juba Blodgett,
Samuel Gray,	Zadock Bell,
John Fraker,	David Iron,
Patrick Martin,	John M'Gaham,
Alexander Augist,	William Barrett,
Jacob Wendel,	Thomas Bolton,
Prince Pattison,	John Sorry,
Jacob Wendel, Jr.	Owen Hewitt,
Abraham Bradley,	Thomas Jones,
Robert Calder,	Owen Rues,
Lewis Russel,	Samuel Gethel,
Benjamin Carr,	Walter Dumphy,
John Kelly,	Juba Bourne,
Michael Lyons,	Henry Callaghan,
Gibman Wails,	Elisha Ozal,
Zachariah Rodgers,	Joseph Scudman,
Ebenezer Brown,	Moses Stocking,
Nathan Dorter,	Richard Mowbray,
William Laper,	John Watkins,
Joseph Still,	John Cochran,
Hugh Fleming,	John Leggins,
Thomas Malony,	Archibald Martin,
Daniel Moncor,	James Fearam,
Thomas Bayley,	John Blean,
John Smith,	Robert Hamilton,
William Scott,	John Kelly,
William Neale,	John Lake,

SEAMEN.	SEAMEN.
Arthur Bennett,	William Taylor,
Joseph Shillaber,	Alexander Galoway,
Richard Pricand,	James Heath,
Pheones Baker,	Andrew Witham,
David Jackson,	Thomas Andrews,
Daniel Knight,	John Ambrose,
James Brown,	Barry Clarke,
Ebenezer Edwards,	Samuel Wall,
Ozere Hone,	Samuel Rodgers,
Joseph Batter,	Richard Parish,
Thomas Walsh,	Benjamin Taylor,
James Bounds,	William M'Cassett,
John Kennedy,	Thomas Cox,
John Mayne,	John Hannibal,
George Skipper,	Asher Cranded,
Peter Lyons,	Charles Ross,
John Kirks,	Samuel Lambert,
Henry Wrightington,	Richard Lunt,
Benjamin Youlin,	William Patton,
Nathaniel Warner,	William Brown,
Henry Wilson,	Stephen Rodgers,
Moses Hilton,	Luther Breck,
John Adams,	Ephraim Clark,
Abraham Simmonds,	Edward Jarvis,
Daniel Nicholson,	Samuel Carroll,
David Hoye,	Joseph Stricker,
John Dalson,	John Diamond,
Zachariah Bassett,	Paul Noyes,
Robert Ellis,	Alexander Libby.

SUPERNUMERARIES.

Nathan Blodgett, ...	Secretary.
Samuel Guild, ...	Surgeon's Mate.
James Daly, ...	do.
John Holeky, ...	do.
Shipman Bangs, ...	Clerk.
Fitz Pool, ...	do.
Ebenezer Pild, ...	Armourer.
Chase Rodgers,	
Benjamin Bowers,	

Peter Adams, ...	Cook,
Michael Baptist, . . .	do.
John Farman, ...	1st Sergeant.
Alexander Ogden, . . .	2d Sergeant.
Matthew Ingram, . . .	Volunteer.
John Spencer, ...	do.

The following letters present so interesting a view of the motives and feelings of Com. Jones both in adverse and prosperous circumstances, and of the opinions entertained by others of his conduct and bravery in the matter referred to, that, in justice to his memory, they are now made public:

"*Passy, October* 17, 1779.

"James Lovell, Esq.

"Sir,

"Enclosed I send you a copy of the instructions I gave to Com. Jones, when it was intended to send with him some transports and troops to make descents in England. Had not the scheme been altered by the more general one of a grand invasion, I know he would have endeavored to put some inconsiderable towns to a high ransom or burnt them. He sailed without the troops, but he nevertheless would have attempted Leith, and went into the Firth of Edinburg with that intention, but a sudden hard gale of wind forced him out again. The late provocations, by the burning of Fairfield and other towns, added to the preceding, have at length demolished all my moderation; and were such another expedition to be concerted, I think so much of that disposition would not appear in the instructions.

"Instructions to the Hon. John Paul Jones, Esq. commander of the American Squadron, in the service of the United States, now in the port of L'Orient.

"1. His Majesty having been pleased to grant some troops for a particular expedition, proposed to annoy our common enemy, in which the sea force under your command might have an opportunity of distinguishing itself, you are to receive on board your ships-of-war, and the other vessels destined for that purpose, the troops that shall present themselves to you, afford them such accommodations as shall be most proper for preserving their health, and convey them to such port or place as their commander shall desire to land them at.

"2. When the troops are landed, you are to aid by all means in your power their operations, as they will be instructed in like manner to aid and support those you may make with your ships, that so by this concurrence and union of your different forces, all that such a compounded strength is capable of, may be effected.

"3. You are, during the expedition, never to depart from the troops, so as not to be able to protect them, or to secure their retreat in case of a repulse; and, in all events, you are to endeavor their complete re-embarkation on board the ships and transports under your command when the expedition shall be ended.

"4. You are to bring to France all the English seamen you may happen to take prisoners, in order to complete the good work you already have made such progress in, of delivering by an exchange the rest of our countrymen now languishing in the gaols of Great Britain.

"5. As many of your officers and people have lately escaped from English prisons, either in Europe or America, you are to be particularly attentive to their conduct towards the prisoners which the fortune of war may throw into your hands, lest the resentment of the more than barbarous usage by the English in many places towards the Americans, should occasion a retaliation and imitation of what ought rather to be detested and avoided for the sake of humanity and for the honor of our country.

"6. In the same view, although the English have wantonly burnt many defenceless towns in America, you are not to follow this example, unless when a reasonable ransom is refused, in which case your own generous feelings as well as this instruction, will induce you to give timely notice of your intention, that sick and ancient persons, women, and children may be first removed.

"Given at Passy, this 28th day of April, 1779.

"B. Franklin,

"Minister Plenipotentiary from the United States at the Court of France."

"*Amsterdam, October* 25, 1779.

"The Hon. Commodore Jones.

"Dear Sir,

"I am with your favor of the 20th. The following lines are an abstract of a letter from the great man at the Hague.

"'I am extremely glad to find that the affair which caused me so much uneasiness, has not been followed by any disagreeable circumstances. I rely confidently on the circumspection of Mr. Jones, and I am well persuaded that he will not give me occasion for the slightest complaint, and what is equally as important, is that he experiences here the most favorable treatment. The States of Holland have unanimously adopted the advice of the Admiralty, which is in perfect conformity with that of the particular College of Amsterdam, of which you have been informed. In all probability the resolution of the province will be confirmed on Monday by that of the States General, and the answer highly satisfactory for the Congress transmitted to Mr. Yorke. I learn with great pleasure that Mr. Jones has received orders which are agreeable to him, relative to Capt. Landais.'"

"They want here your answer respecting the five deserters, who are seized, and your promise to pardon them when you will have them in your power.

"After having read with attention the copy of your letter, dear sir, to his excellency Dr. Franklin, of the 3d of October, intended for M. de Capelle, I think it highly improper to be sent to the gentleman so as it is presently, and that he must not be acquainted with your complaints against M. de Chaumont. I think I must tell you also, dear sir, that I am not in any connection with this gentleman respecting America, and that nobody has the secret of my negotiations here, besides two great men, with whom this gentleman is not intimate. He is a very good republican, but by his circumstances he cannot do any good towards an alliance between the two republics. He is a well thinking private, but that is all; being excluded from any share of government in his country. This between us. I am, &c.,

"DUMAS.

"P. S. The great man desires to know when you think to be ready to sail."

"*On board the Serapis at the Texel, October 26th*, 1779.

"M. LE RAY DE CHAUMONT, Jun.:

"You will pardon, my dear friend, my not having written to you earlier since my arrival here; my silence has not, I assure you, been the effect of the little misunderstanding which unhappily took place between your father and myself when he imposed upon me a '*Concordat*' at Groaix, which I thought, and think still, I dishonored my hand by signing. The ticklish and uncertain situation of the politics of this country as affecting the flag of America, has hitherto so much occupied my attention, that I have found little leisure to write. My fears in that respect being now entirely removed by an unanimous resolution of the States General, that is far more favorable to our cause than I had reason to expect,—I employ this breathing space with great pleasure to assure you that my regard and affection for all the family of de Chaumont is far from diminished: I earnestly wish your father to give to oblivion the past misintelligence. I am persuaded that he will now see the impropriety of communicating *too early* the intended enterprises and operations of a partisan, and no longer blame me for avoiding free conversations on such subjects. It is not, indeed, my characteristic to be free of words. My heart, however, is no stranger to the sentiments and duties of friendship, though my situation as a servant of the public leaves me without the power of obliging my private friends, except in the pleasure which I am persuaded they take in hearing of my success, when they have furnished me with the means.

"It affords me pleasure to assure you that I cannot too much praise the gallant behavior of the young volunteer Baptiste Travallier whom you sent to L'Orient. In the engagement a sailor called for a wad in loading one of the great guns; he furnished him immediately by substituting his coat, which he then wore, and soon afterward, when the Bon homme Richard was on fire, he instantly took off his shirt, and dipped it in water and applied it with great dexterity to smother the flames.

"Present my best respects to Madame de Chaumont and to your sisters. I beseech them and you to love me, and that your father will forgive my past fault, which was the effect only of my believing that he had less confidence in me than he had taught me to expect, and had always said I had merited.

"I am, affectionately and truly, &c."

"I certify that the original, of which the preceding is a copy, was duly received by me.

"LE RAY DE CHAUMONT.

"*New York*, *Dec.* 1824."

"*On board the Serapis at the Texel*, *Oct.* 26*th*, 1779.

"EDWARD BANCROFT, ESQ.

"MY DEAR FRIEND,

"Your warm and affectionate letter of the 14th is doubly welcome; and although it overrates and praises my services beyond their real merits, yet the commendation of superior understanding, and from the man whom I entirely love and esteem, cannot but afford me the truest pleasure.

"M. de Chaumont has written me a very affectionate letter; but then he had written me many equally affectionate letters, even from the first of our acquaintance, offering me always the most disinterested services, until that of the 14th of June, whereof I enclose a copy. He has not yet offered me an apology respecting the dishonorable '*Concordat*' which he afterwards imposed upon me at Groaix. I love him, however, notwithstanding; and his excellency tells me that M. de Chaumont has still 'a great regard for me.' That assurance revives all my former friendship, and will confirm it, if you think the answer which I have here inclosed is proper, and that the delivery of it will put a final end on his part to our misunderstanding. At any rate, I pray you to present my warmest respects to the whole family, for whom I shall ever retain a grateful affection.

"I am happy, my dear sir, in being able to assure you that, in spite of Sir Joseph,* the flag of freedom is highly respected indeed at the Texel. I had yesterday the honor to receive authority, by an unanimous resolution of the States, and by an order of *the Prince of Orange*, to land as many prisoners as I please, to place sentinels to guard them in the fort on the Texel, to haul up the drawbridge of that fort, and to take them away again from thence whenever I think proper, and dispose of them afterwards as though they had never been landed. Huzza, America!

"Captain Landais has been ashore for some days past, but I believe is not yet set out from the Helder. I understand that he has been and is trying to excite the compassion of the people, and in that mode to obtain certificates in his favor. It is natural also to conclude that the late captain of the Serapis will continue to stretch a point, and save his own credit if he can, by speaking of damage done to him by the Alliance. Let them do their utmost. I shall forward the necessary proof.

"Yours, &c."

"*On board the Bon homme Richard's prize, the ship of war Serapis of* 44 *guns, at the Texel, Oct.* 28*th*, 1779.

"To Madam LE RAY DE CHAUMONT.

"I can no longer, my dear madam, refrain from writing to you, although I have not been honored with a line from you since my letter from L'Orient, dated 13th June.

"I congratulate you on my late success, because I know it affords you pleasure; and knowing this is, I assure you, a very singular addition to my satisfaction. What has given me more pain, however, than words can express, has been a *want of confidence* on the part of M. de Chaumont after he had honored me with strong proof of his friendship and good opinion. The 'concordat' which, to my great surprise, he imposed upon me in the moment of my departure from L'Orient, was the most humiliating paper that ever a friend forced upon the commander of a squadron,

* Sir Joseph Yorke, English minister at the Hague.

and even my success has not wiped off the dishonor of my having signed it!

"I am willing to believe that my friend did not see the concordat in the same light, and that the idea was not originally his own, but only by him adopted from the misrepresentations of persons who were constantly buzzing in his ear, and showing an infinity of theory which they have not since been quite so happy in reducing to practice. I say, as I verily believe, that the idea was not originally his own; and as I love him still with undiminished and grateful affection, I earnestly wish him to forgive the complaints which I have made, and to continue towards me his first warmth of friendship and confidence.

"My departure from hence is extremely uncertain; my destination, too, is better known to Dr. F. than myself at present. Our ships are now in a severe storm. I mention this only to show that I can, in no situation, forget how much I owe to the polite attentions and friendship of the amiable family at Passy, which I beseech you to believe I shall ever remember with sentiments of the most lively esteem and affection, being very truly,

"Your obliged friend, &c."

"I certify that the original of the foregoing letter was duly received by my mother.

"Le Ray de Chaumont.

"*New York, December*, 1824."

"*On board the Bon homme Richard's prize, the ship of war Serapis, at the Texel, October 28th*, 1779.

"The Marquis De Lafayette, Paris.

"A thousand thanks to my loved and noble friend for the very kind and affectionate letter that he did me the honor to write me from the Havre, which greatly rewards me for the dangers which I have lately overcome. Words are wanting to express how much I esteem, how highly I value, and how much I wish to merit the friendship and affection of the American General Marquis De Lafayette.

"I am very much concerned and ashamed to understand that my 'numbers,' that you received from L'Orient, were so ill composed. It is proof that their ladyships the Muses, however condescending they may be on the banks of the Helicon, will not dispense their favours to the sons of Neptune, especially while they are

By bounding billows and rude winds that blow,
Alternate tossed in air, or sunk to sands below.

"In truth, my dear General, I am *almost* as sorry that you have not been able to understand my meaning as if I had been addressing myself to—a fair lady! The enclosed key will, however, I hope unlock the past difficulty, and enable you fully to see what I so much wish you to understand.

"I will send you very soon a little work that shall be better finished than that from L'Orient; and in the mean time a machine, to which the present key is adapted, is forwarded through the hands of Dr. Bancroft, in case you should have spoiled or thrown away the one formerly sent.

"The late brutalities of the Britons in America fills me with horror and indignation. They forget that they are men; and I believe that nothing will bring them to their senses but the most exemplary retaliation. Landais is ordered to Paris to answer for his past conduct.

"I wish to answer very particularly the three points which you have propounded. 1st. I never meant to ask a reward for my services, either from France or America: consequently the approbation of the Court and of the Congress is all the gratification I can wish for. 2dly. I yet intend to undertake whatever the utmost exertion of my abilities will reach in support of the common cause, as far as any force that may in future be entrusted to my direction may enable me to succeed; I hope, however, my future force will be better composed than when I sailed from L'Orient. I must sail from the Texel in course of next month, because ships cannot afterward remain here in this road. My destination or route from hence I yet know not; but I need not tell you that I wish to see your face! 3dly. It is now in vain to say what might have been done two years ago, with the force you mention; but I believe, if properly supported by sea, such a force might yet perform very essential service. There is no guarding, you know, against storms; and one would wish either to avoid or to outsail a superior sea force. As I believe you know my way of thinking on such subjects, I shall offer you no argument. I know you want no prompter.

"I beg Captain Ricot's pardon for having said in the extract of my journal that, in the engagement with the Serapis, he prevented my officers and men in the pilot boat from coming to my assistance. I now find that this did not happen till the pilot boat had returned to the Vengeance, about the middle of the action, without having boarded the Bon homme Richard according to Captain Ricot's orders. I was a little vexed, too, that Captain Ricot did not come on board the Bon homme Richard the next day, to offer me his assistance, when I was in the greatest imaginable distress, and the signal was flying. But these are trifles—and I am much more obliged to him for not firing, than to Landais for killing my men and sinking my ship. Upon the whole Captain Ricot has acted as became a sensible and prudent officer, and is a man with whom I wish to be further connected. At Leith he was destined to cover the descent, and I am fully convinced that he would have executed it with great honor to himself, had not the gale of wind in the critical moment rendered the design impracticable. I shall correct the error in my letter to the minister, and do his character justice. I have a very good opinion of the abilities of Captain Cottineau, and I wish to be concerned with them both in future with better ships. But I must speak plainly my opinion, since you desire it. I do not think that the desire of glory was the uppermost sentiment in the breast of any captain under my command, at the time we left L'Orient.

"I shall ever be proud to merit the just title of, my dear marquis,

"Your very affectionate and faithful friend and servant, &c.

"I remember to have received such a letter.

"LAFAYETTE.

"*February* 10*th*, 1825."

"*Texel, on board the Serapis, November* 5, 1779.

"M. DUMAS, &c. &c. &c.

"I have, my dear Sir, your two esteemed favors of the 3d. I am much obliged to M. de Neufville for his good intentions; but duty must take the precedence of pleasure, and therefore I have no desire at present to revisit either Amsterdam or even the Hague. I must wait a more favorable opportunity to kiss the hands of the fair.

"As I had the honor to write you fully last night, I have now very little to add respecting my situation, only that I have resolved to send up the purser of the Alliance immediately to Amsterdam, in order to hasten the sending down a few articles that are really wanted, and that can be got without any loss of time, and before we get the mast secured. If the weather permits, what remains to be done, may be effected within four or five days, and then I shall not remain idle here. In the mean time I wish the *Great Man* would order the two French cutters here to attend our motion. I believe it will not be difficult to persuade them.

"With respect to the powers of Capt. Pearson, I am convinced that he has received no authority from Sir Joseph Yorke. His powers, however, must be as ample as mine; and I should not, I assure you, have made such a convention with him, if Captain Remirsma, on the part of the States General, had not given me verbally, free liberty to land the wounded prisoners, and to guard them in the fort on the Texel by my soldiers with drawn swords, and with the bridges hauled up at our pleasure, and with free liberty to embark them again, and dispose of them as though they had not been landed in Holland. You see therefore that my convention with Capt. Pearson does not bind me to continue the prisoners ashore; I can embark them again whenever I please, and it was only intended on my part as a security against elopement. They have hitherto been guarded with the drawbridges hauled up or let down at the sovereign will and pleasure of the 'Governor General.' If my wishes succeed, it will afford America matter of exultation; and, at the worst, we can only lose eighteen or nineteen dangerously wounded prisoners which, I think, will be made up by our having had possession of a fort on the Texel. I shall only add that my meaning has been good, and that I thought I might rely on the guaranty that I had on the part of the States General while we could keep the prisoners from making their escape from the fort.

"I am with respect and attachment, yours, &c."

"*Alliance, at sea, December* 27, 1779.

"M. DUMAS,

"I am here, my philosopher with a good wind at east, and under my best American colors; so far you have your wish. What may be the event of this critical moment I know not. I am not, however, without good hopes. Through the ignorance or drunkenness of the old pilot, the Alliance was last night got foul of a Dutch merchant ship, and, I believe, the Dutchman cut our cable. We lost the best bower anchor, and the ship was brought up with the sheet anchor so near the shore, that this morning I have been obliged to cut the cable in order to get clear of the shore, and that I might not lose this opportunity of escaping from purgatory.

"I wish Mr. Hoogland would have the sheet and best bower anchors taken up, that they may be sent to France or sold, as M. De Neufville may find most expedient. The pilot knows where the anchors lay, and unless he assists willingly in taking them up, he ought not in my opinion to be paid for his services on board her.

"Adieu, my dear friend; present my best respects to your fireside, and to the good patriot, &c.; and believe me to be always affectionately, &c."

The consternation and uproar produced in Great Britain, and particularly on the coasts of that island and of Ireland, by the rumors of this unparalleled exploit, were amazing. It naturally associated itself in the public mind with the descent upon

Whitehaven and the capture of the Drake. Orders were expedited in every direction for ships-of-war to put to sea in quest of Jones, with instructions to take him at all hazards. The annexed extracts from newspapers of that day, will demonstrate what aggravating annoyance a single intelligent, brave, and skilful officer may give to a very large portion of the subjects of a great empire :—

"*London, September* 27, 1779.

"A letter from Sunderland, dated 20th September, says, that an express arrived there on the 18th from Aymouth with information that Paul Jones was off there, with five sail of ships-of-war, and 2000 troops on board; that, on the 19th, they appeared off Sunderland, and came up within two miles, which put the inhabitants into great confusion, as they expected them to land every hour, or destroy the ships in the harbor."

Extract of a letter from Stockton, September 21st.

"The undermentioned ships have appeared off this place under the command of Paul Jones; we have sent the bearers to inform all light colliers they may meet with to take harbor as soon as possible, and there to remain till they receive advice of their being off the coast.

"On Saturday noon two gentlemen of the corporation of Hull arrived express at the Admiralty with the alarming account that the celebrated American Corsair Paul Jones had entered the River Humber on Thursday last, and chased a vessel to within a mile of the pier, where he sunk, burned, and destroyed 16 sail of valuable vessels, which threw the whole town and neighborhood into the utmost consternation. He had taken 9 or 10 colliers and other vessels a day or two before he appeared at Hull. The following is the force of Jones's squadron.

"A Boston built frigate with 40 guns upon one deck (Jones's ship).
A French ship (an old Indiaman), of 44 guns.
Two American frigates of 32 guns each, new.
One 20 gun "
Two brigantines of 18 guns each,
And two small tenders.

"On Saturday night another express arrived at the Admiralty from Hull with the further disagreeable intelligence, that Paul Jones's squadron, after having done more mischief in the shipping on Friday, had fell in with the Baltic fleet, and had taken their convoy the Serapis man-of-war of 44 guns, Captain Pearson, and the armed ship the Countess of Scarborough, Captain Piercy, of 24 guns. This action was seen by thousands of spectators. The other ships of Jones's squadron were making havoc among the fleet, most of which, however, had taken shelter near Flamborough and the Head.

"From four captured Americans it was discovered that it was Jones's plan to alarm the coasts of Wales, Ireland, the western parts of Scotland, and the North Channel. Jones took several prizes on the coast of Ireland, (particularly two armed transports with stores for New York,) in the North sea, and near the Firth of Forth, and had it in his power to have burnt Leith, but his orders are only to burn shipping. His squadron is now but weakly manned, owing to the great number of prizes he has taken, and it therefore may fall an easy conquest to the 16 sail of men-of-war who have orders to go after him.

"The Serapis man-of-war lost her main-mast, bowsprit, and mizen top-mast before she struck, and the Countess of Scarborough made an exceeding good defence against one of the 32 gun frigates. The enemy's 44 gun ship was not in the action, and the Serapis struck to Jones's ship and the other 32 gun frigate.

"Expresses also arrived on Saturday from Sunderland, stating that Paul Jones had taken 16 sail more of colliers. In consequence of the capture of so many colliers and the interruption of the trade, the price of coals will be enormous. Instead of having the dominion of the sea, it is now evident that we are not able to defend our own coast from depredations.

"The master of a sloop from Harwich, who arrived yesterday, saw on Saturday last, no less than eleven sail of men-of-war going in search of Paul Jones, and among them was the Edgar of 74 guns.

"By the examination of the four men belonging to one of Paul Jones's squadron, it appears that Jones's orders were not to burn any houses or towns. What an example of honor and greatness does America thus show to us! While our troops are running about from town to town on their coast, and burning everything with a wanton, wicked barbarity, Dr. Franklin gives no orders to retaliate,—he is above it; and there was a time when an English minister was above it; when an English minister would have disdained to make war in so villainous a mode. It is a disgrace to the nation. Paul Jones could have burned Leith the other day with the greatest ease, and another little town near it.

"Yesterday Lord Sandwich informed some Russian merchants who waited on him, that twenty of his Majesty's ships were sent in quest of Paul Jones.

September 28.—Capt. Pearson who commanded the Serapis of 44 guns which was taken by Paul Jones, was appointed to the Endymion of 44 guns, lately launched at Limehouse and fitting out there for sea, and was coming from off his station in the North sea to go on board of her.

"*Philadelphia, January* 19*th*, 1780.

Extract of a letter from L'Orient, October 20*th*, 1779.

"The brave Captain Jones, on the 23d of last month, attacked the Baltic fleet of 60 sail, under convoy of the Serapis of 44 guns, and the Scarborough of 20."

From L'Orient, dated October 22*d.*

"The gallant behavior of Captain Paul Jones, at present engages the whole attention here. In my last I informed you that he had the command of a small squadron then on a cruize. He sailed round Ireland and Scotland, spreading terror and devastation in every part. He took, burnt, and sunk a great number of vessels, among them a ship bound to Quebec extremely rich.

"On the 23d of September in the evening, he fell in with the Baltic fleet under convoy of the Serapis 44 guns, and the Countess of Scarborough 20 guns. The Pallas, after an engagement of about an hour, took the latter, and Jones in the poor Richard attacked the former,—they fought for three hours and a half, with inconceivable rage; two hours of which time they were fast to each other, and almost all the time one or the other was on fire. The Serapis is a fine new ship, sheathed with copper, on an entire new construction, and thought to be the fastest sailing vessel in Europe; she has two entire batteries, the lower of which is 18 pounders, so that she may be said to be almost double the force of the Poor Richard."

Extract of another letter from the same place.

"The Poor Richard, with all the assistance afforded from the other ships after the action, could not be kept above water, and Jones had the mortification to see her go down. He has made a good exchange, but he wished to have got the Poor Richard into port, shattered as she was, as a picture of curiosity and distress."

On the return of the squadron to the Texel, Captain Landais

propagated a report that he, and not Commodore Jones, had caused the Serapis to surrender. To give plausibility to the story, he referred to his having raked the British frigate, which, in part, was true; but it was equally true that he fired more repeatedly, and with more fatal effect into the Bon homme Richard; nor did he, at any period of the action, lay the Serapis along side, as he was directed, or take such a position as would have caused the enemy to strike his flag at an earlier moment. Had Landais closed with the Serapis, as Commodore Jones did, she must have almost immediately yielded, and the lives of many valuable men would have been spared. His omission to embrace the chance offered by the Commodore to secure or destroy the merchantmen of the convoy was altogether unpardonable. The vain boasting of Captain Landais, and his misconduct during the battle as well as previously thereto, induced Jones to recur to the testimony of the officers of his squadron, who had been eyewitnesses of Landais's behavior, and their evidence was collected, in coincidence with the advice of Dr. Franklin, and incorporated in the annexed documents, the tenor of which will remove every scruple of doubt as to the disobedient and reprehensible procedure of the captain of the Alliance.

" *Charges and Proofs respecting the Conduct of Peter Landais.*

"We, the officers, &c. of the American squadron now at the Texel, this 30th day of October, 1779, do attest and declare, upon our words of honor as gentlemen, that all the following articles, which we subscribe, respecting the conduct of Peter Landais, Captain of the frigate Alliance, are really and truly matters of fact. In witness whereof we hereunto sign our names and qualities; and will, at any time hereafter, be ready to prove the same upon oath if required.

"1. The Captain of the Alliance did not take the steps in his power to prevent his ship from getting foul of the Bon homme Richard, in the Bay of Biscay; for instead of putting his helm a-weather, and bearing up to make way for his commanding officer, which was his duty, he left the deck to load his pistols.

"2. When in chase of a ship, supposed an English East Indiaman, on the —— day of August, 1799, Captain Landais did not do his utmost to overtake that ship, which he might easily have done before night, but put his helm a-weather, and bore away several times in the day, after the Alliance had gained the wake of the chase, and was overtaking her very fast.

"3. Captain Landais behaved with disrespect and impertinence towards the commander-in-chief of the squadron, on frequent occasions.

"4. He disobeyed his signals.

"5. He very seldom answered any of them.

"6. He expressed his fears and apprehensions of being taken on the coast of Ireland, and insisted on leaving sight of it immediately, when we had cruized there only two days.

"7. His separation from the squadron the first time, must have happened either through ignorance or design; because though he distinctly saw the signal for the course before night, yet he altered it, first two, and then four points of the compass, before morning.

"8. His separation from the squadron the second time, must also have happened through ignorance or design; because the wind being at N.W., and the other ships, *to his knowledge*, lying to, and being astern of the Alliance, what less than separation could be the consequence of his obstinacy in ordering the weather main-brace to be hauled in, and the ship to be steered S.W., and S.W. by S., in the trough of the sea, which was done from ten at night till morning; and he would not then permit the ship to be tacked, in order to regain the squadron, as was proposed to him by the officers.

"9. On the morning of the 23d September, when the Bon homme Richard, after being off the Spurn, came in sight of the Alliance and Pallas, off Flamborough Head, Captain Landais distinctly told Captain Cottineau, that if it was, as it appeared, a fifty gun ship, they must run away; although he must have been sure that the Pallas, *from her heavy sailing*, must have fallen a sacrifice.

"10. In the afternoon of the same day, Captain Landais paid no attention to signals, particularly the signal of preparation, and for the line; which was made with great care, and very distinctly, on board the Bon homme Richard.

"11. Although the Alliance was a long way ahead of the Bon homme Richard, when bearing down on the Baltic fleet, yet Captain Landais lay out of gunshot to windward, until the Bon homme Richard had passed by and closely engaged the Serapis, and then, instead of coming to close action with the Countess of Scarborough, the Alliance fired at very long shot.

"12. He continued to windward, and, a considerable time after the action began, fell astern and spoke the Pallas, leaving the Countess of Scarborough in the wake of the ships engaged, and at free liberty to rake the Bon homme Richard.

"13. After the Bon homme Richard and Serapis were made fast along side of each other (which was not done till an hour after the engagement began), Captain Landais, *out of musket shot*, raked the Bon homme Richard with crossbar and grape shot, &c., which killed a number of men, dismounted sundry guns, put out the side lights, and silenced all the 12 pounders.

"14. The Alliance then ran down towards the Pallas and Scarborough, that were at the time engaged at a considerable distance to leeward of the Bon homme Richard and Serapis, and Captain Landais hovered about there out of gunshot, and without firing, till some time after the Countess of Scarborough had struck; and then bore down under her topsails, and spoke, first the prize, and then the Pallas, asking a number of questions.

"15. At last Captain Landais made sail under his topsails, to work up to windward, but made tacks before he (being within the range of grape-shot, and, *at the longest*, three quarters of an hour before the Serapis struck) fired a second broadside into the Bon homme Richard's larboard quarter, the latter part whereof was fired when the Alliance was not more than three points abaft the Bon homme Richard's beam, although many tongues had cried from the Bon homme Richard that Captain Landais was firing into the wrong ship, and prayed him to lay the enemy alongside. Three large signal lanthorns, with proper signal wax candles in them, and well lighted, had also, previously to his firing, been hung over the bow, quarter, and waist of the Bon homme Richard in a horizontal line, which was the signal of reconnoissance; and the ships, the one having a high poop, and being all black, the other having a low stern, with yellow sides, were easily distinguishable, it being full moon.

"16. The Alliance then passed at a very considerable distance along the larboard or off side of the Bon homme Richard, and having tacked and gained the wind, ran down again to leeward, and, in crossing the Bon homme Richard's bow, Capt. Landais raked her with a third broadside, after being constantly called to from the Bon homme Richard not to fire, but to lay the enemy alongside.

"17. Sundry men were killed and wounded by the broadsides mentioned in the two last articles.

"18. Captain Landais never passed on the off side of the Serapis, nor could that ship ever bring a gun to bear on the Alliance at any time during the engagement.

"19. The leaks of the Bon homme Richard increased much after being fired upon by the Alliance; and as the most dangerous shot which the Bon homme Richard received under the water were under the larboard bow and quarter, they must have come from the Alliance, for the Serapis was on the other side.

"20. Several people on board the Alliance told Captain Landais, at different times, that he fired upon the wrong ship; others refused to fire.

"21. The Alliance only fired three broadsides, while within gun shot, on the Bon homme Richard and Serapis.

"22. The morning after the engagement, Captain Landais acknowledged on board the Serapis, that he raked each time with grape-shot, which he knew would scatter.

"23. Captain Landais has acknowledged, since the action, that he would have thought it no harm if the Bon homme Richard had struck, for it would have given him an opportunity to retake her, and to take the Serapis.

"24. He has frequently declared that he was the only American in the squadron, and that he was not under the orders of Captain Jones.

"25. In coming into the Texel he declared that if Captain Jones should hoist a broad pennant, he would, *to vex him*, hoist another.

"I attest the articles number 2, 4, 5, 10, 11, 15, 16, and 22, to be matters of fact, and I believe all the rest.

"ROBERT CORAM, Midshipman."

"I attest the articles number 2, 3, 4, 5, 9, 10, 11, 13, 15, 16, 17, 19, 21, and 22, to be matters of fact, and I believe all the rest.

"J. W. LINTHWAITE, Midshipman."

"I attest the articles number 2, 3, 4, 5, 6, 10, 11, 13, 15, 16, 17, 19, 21, and 22, to be matters of fact, and I believe all the rest.

"JOHN MAYRANT, Midshipman."

"I attest the articles number 1, 2, 3, 4, 5, 6, 7, 8, 10, 13, 15, 16, 17, 18, 19, 20, 22, 23, and 24, to be matters of fact, and I believe all the rest.

"Lieut. Col. WEIBERT."

"I attest the articles number 2, 3, and 11, to be matters of fact, and I believe all the rest.

"BENJAMIN STUBBS, Midshipman."

"I attest the articles number 2, 3, 4, 5, 6, 10, 11, 13, 15, 16, and 17, to be matters of fact, and I believe all the rest.

"THOMAS POTTER, Midshipman."

"I attest the articles number 2, 3, 4, 5, 10, 11, 13, 15, and 19, to be matters of fact, and I believe all the rest.

"NATHANIEL FANNING, Midshipman."

"I attest the articles number 3, 4, 5, 10, 11, 13, 15, 16, 17, 19, and 21, to be matters of fact, and I believe all the rest.

"THOMAS LUNDY, Midshipman."

"I attest the articles number 2, 3, 4, 5, 6, 10, 11, 13, 15, 16, and 17, to be matters of fact, and I believe all the rest.

"BEAUMONT GROUBE, Midshipman."

"I attest the articles number 2, 3, 4, 5, 10, 11, 15, 16, 17, 18, and 23, to be matters of fact.

"STACK, Lieut. of Walsh's Reg."

"I attest the articles number 2, 3, 4, 5, 6, 10, 11, 13, 15, 19, 23, and 24, to be matters of fact.

"MACARTHY, Officer of Walsh's Reg."

"I attest the articles number 2, 3, 4, 5, 15, 16, 17, 18, 19, and 21, to be matters of fact.

"RICHARD DALE, First Lieutenant."

"I attest the articles number 2, 3, 4, 5, 11, 14, and 22, to be matters of fact.

"HENRY LUNT, Second Lieutenant."

"I attest the articles number 2, 3, 4, 5, 10, 11, 13, 15, 16, 17, 18, 19, and 21, to be matters of fact.

"SAMUEL STACEY, Master."

"We attest the articles number 2, 3, 4, 5, 7, 8, 11, 12, 18,* 20, and 21, to be matters of fact.

"JAMES DEGGE, Lieutenant,
"JOHN BUCKLEY, Master, } Alliance."
"JOHN LARCHER, Master's Mate,

"I attest to the articles number 11, 12, 14, and 24; as to the 4th article, I know that he refused to obey the signals for going on board the Bon homme Richard; and with respect to the 9th article, I recollect that he said, 'If it is a ship of more than fifty guns, we have nothing to do but to run away.'

"DE COTTINEAU DE KLOGUENE, Captain of the Pallas."

"I attest the articles number 2, 5, 11, 12, 20, and 22, to be matters of fact.

"M. PARK, Captain of Marines of the Alliance."

"I, the subscriber, being sent for by the Commodore on the 23d day of September, to repair immediately on board his ship, the Bon homme Richard, there to examine and find out the leaks of his ship, which was within an hour after her engagement with the Serapis, an English ship of war, I accordingly obeyed the Commodore's orders, and repaired on board his ship, when, after searching diligently without and within the said ship, I found it was impracticable to stop the leaks, the ship's bottom being so much shattered.

"Dated on board the ship Serapis, at sea, September 24th, 1779.

"JAMES BRAGG, Master Carpenter of the Alliance."

"I, the subscriber, late midshipman on board the late American ship of war the Bon homme Richard, but now acting in that capacity on board the ship of war the Serapis, which ship was taken by the Bon homme Richard, on the night of the 23d of September last, the same night I was stationed in the Bon homme Richard's main-top the whole of the action. About two hours after the engagement commenced, I saw, to my great surprise, the Alliance come under the Bon homme Richard's stern, and fire her whole broadside into the Bon homme Richard; she then came along the off side of the Bon homme Richard, and came under her bow, wheu she discharged another volley of both grape and round shot, which I heard

* The Alliance never passed on the off side of the Serapis.

strike the rigging, masts, &c., on board the Bon homme Richard. Though previous to the Alliance firing the second time into the Bon homme Richard, I heard some of our officers and men call to the Alliance, which was then within hail, for God's sake not to fire into the Bon homme Richard, for, said they, you have killed several of our men already. Notwithstanding all this, she fired a number of shot afterward into the Bon homme Richard. But as to the number of men the Alliance killed on board the Bon homme Richard, I cannot ascertain; however, as to what I have written here, I can attest to as a fact.

"Given under my hand this 23d day of October, 1779.

"NATHANIEL FANNING."*

*"An intelligent, sensible officer. He had the good fortune and the merit of aiding to overcome the enemy stationed in the main-top of the Serapis. He commanded afterward, and until the close of the war, the privateer Eclipse, belonging to Dunkirk.

"J. P. JONES."

"I, late a midshipman on board of the Bon homme Richard, and aid-de-camp to the Honorable John Paul Jones in the action of the 23d of September, off Flamborough Head, do certify, that an hour after the commencement of it, I was on the main-deck, where there was a brisk firing kept up until a ship raked us, when I saw two men drop dead, and several running from their quarters, crying out, 'The Alliance is manned with Englishmen, and firing upon us.' I went up immediately, and saw her pass by us. She then, in about two hours' time, came under our stern, and while we were hailing her, she fired into our larboard quarter, and went ahead of us; then came before the wind, athwart our bows, when she was hailed by Captain Jones's orders, to lay the enemy on board, but they returning no answer, were hailed once or twice again, to which they answered, 'aye, aye,' and immediately fired several guns, but they being at too great a distance to damage the enemy without hurting us, when she might have come half as near again without any danger of running foul of us or damaging us. But, previous to the above-mentioned engagement, a signal was hove out from the Bon homme Richard to form a line of battle, to which the Alliance paid no attention, but during the whole cruise the Alliance very seldom attended to any of Captain Jones's signals. It is my sincere opinion on the conduct of the commander of the said ship, together with her manœuvres during the time of action, on the 23d of last September, that his motive must have been to kill Captain Jones, and distress the Bon homme Richard, so as to cause her to strike to the Serapis, that he might himself be able to take the Serapis, and honor himself with the laurels of that day.

"In witness whereof, I have hereunto subscribed my name, on board the Serapis, lying in the Texel, the 24th of October, 1779.

"JOHN MAYRANT."*

* "A young gentleman of fortune, of South Carolina, whose conduct in the engagement did him great honor.

"J. P. JONES."

"I, late midshipman on board of the American ship of war le Bon homme Richard, commanded by the Honorable John Paul Jones, at present on board of the Serapis, prize to the above ship, do certify, that while at my station in the mizen-top, after we had engaged about two hours and a half, I saw, to my great surprise and astonishment, the Alliance frigate fire several guns into our larboard quarter. Some time after, being ordered from my station in the mizen-top on deck, I saw from the forecastle the Alliance standing athwart our bows, before the wind. Mr. Linthwaite was then hailing her, by Captain Jones's orders, to lay the enemy on board, but hearing no answer to his repeated hail, I hailed her in the same words, 'lay the enemy on board;' no answer being yet made, I asked them if they heard us, to which they replied, 'aye, aye,' and fired several guns at that distance that part of her grape and cannister shot damaged us as well as the enemy; whereas, it is my opinion, had the Alliance come half the distance nearer the Serapis than she did, she might have cleared the enemy's deck, and not have raked the Bon homme Richard.

"Previous to the afore mentioned engagement, a signal was hove out by Capt. Jones's orders to form a line of battle to which no attention was paid on the part of the Alliance. If I may be allowed to give my opinion on the general conduct of the commander, together with the manœuvres of the said ship during the action, it appears to me his motive must have been to distress the Bon homme Richard, so as to cause her to strike to the Serapis, and by boarding the Serapis to retake the Bon homme Richard, and thereby claim the laurels of that day.

"In testimony whereof, I hereunto subscribe my name, on board the Serapis, lying in the Texel, the 24th of October, 1779.

"ROBERT CORAM."*

* "A brave, steady officer of South Carolina, whose conduct in the engagement did him much honor.

"J. P. JONES."

"I, the undersigned, Philip Ricot, captain of a vessel in the service of the United States of America, and commander of the tender Vengeance,* in conformity to the request of Com. Paul Jones, my commander, do communicate to him, and affirm to the different circumstances, hereafter declared, in which M. Landais, captain of the frigate Alliance, has, in this cruize, appeared to have deviated from that subordination which the service requires.

"I observed that, on the 31st of August, at half past four in the afternoon, a signal was made him by the commodore to chase a sail in sight, which M. Landais did not obey.

"The next day, September 1st, the commodore made him a signal to come under his stern that he might speak with him; this M. Landais did not do.

"The 5th of September the captains of the division being on board of the commodore, according to his orders, M. Landais was the only one who refused to go, and although Messrs. de Chamillard and Cottineau went on board of the Alliance, to persuade him to it, he persisted in his refusal.

"That, in the night of the 23d and 24th of said month, during the engagement between the Bon homme Richard and the Serapis, the Alliance remained within cannon-shot of the enemy's ship, from about half past eight till ten o'clock, without my having seen her fire. I shall add, that October the 1st, at eight at night, I received orders from the commodore to go and tell M. Landais, who was to windward, to take post astern of him; to which I received this answer, and which was repeated by M. Landais himself: 'Go tell the commodore that he may go where he pleases.' The inconsistence of this answer, and his rudeness to me, have since obliged me to testify my dissatisfaction to M. Landais, who appeared to have forgot it. I affirm to the facts above declared.

"Texel, October 25th, 1779.

"P. Ricot."

* "The Vengeance was to windward, just out of gun-shot during the whole action. The Captain was a sensible man and a good officer.

"J. P. Jones."

"These are to certify, that I, Henry Lunt, second lieutenant of the American ship-of-war, the late Bon homme Richard, but now of the Serapis, commanded by the Honorable John Paul Jones, having, on the 23d of September, 1779, been ordered in a pilot boat with a party of men after a brig, but some time after I set out from alongside, a signal was made for me to return back to the Bon homme Richard, she being then in chase of two British ships-of-war, the Serapis and Countess of

Scarborough, and before I could get on board the Bon homme Richard she commenced the engagement with the Serapis. It being night, I thought it not prudent to go alongside in time of action. Being in the boat near, I had an opportunity of seeing some part of the Alliance's behavior above three quarters of an hour after the action began between the Richard and Serapis. The Alliance was to windward of them, and appeared to be lying to, about one mile distant. At the same time the Pallas was engaging the Countess of Scarborough to leeward of the Alliance, and out of my sight. Presently after the Pallas and Countess of Scarborough had ceased firing, the Alliance bore down for them, and disappeared out of my sight. What she did there I cannot tell; but she was gone, as near as I can judge, one hour and three quarters, and then appeared to me to be going up to assist the Bon homme Richard, but was half an hour from that time before she fired; and after she got up to the Richard and Serapis, she fired, and stood off from them to the eastward some distance, and, as near as I can judge, was gone better than half an hour, then returned back to the Richard and Serapis, and fired again.

"On board the Serapis, at the Texel, 25th of October, 1779.

"HENRY LUNT.*

* "This certificate of Lieut. Lunt, who was a mere spectator, is of great weight and importance, it being only in the power of this gentleman or of Capt. Ricot, who in the Vengeance was also a mere spectator, to give a true account of the respective positions and manœuvres of the ships engaged.

"J. P. JONES."

"I, the undersigned, certify, that I was extremely surprised in the evening of the 23d of September, when I did not hear the Alliance begin the engagement with the Serapis or Countess of Scarborough, having remarked just before I went to the main-top (where I commanded a detachment during the action), that she appeared to me to be very near them. M. Landais had pressed sail during the whole afternoon without orders. M. Cottineau hailed us, and asked what station he should take during the action, and complained to M. Jones that M. Landais, instead of forming the rear as it had been agreed, took the van which was his (M. Cottineau's) from him. M. Jones, however, made the signal for forming the line; and I well recollect that he caused a manœuvre to be made in order the Alliance might clearly see his signal, but M. Landais, *as usual*, paid no attention to it, and we all thought the Alliance engaged a long time before us. After taking my station in the main-top, I thought no more of the Alliance, because the main-top-sail hid her from me. A little while after the Serapis hailed us, and I then perceived the Serapis and the Countess of Scarborough pretty nigh each other. We immediately began the engagement with the Serapis, and I did not perceive the Alliance till about two hours afterwards, when I saw her rake us with her whole broadside, a little to larboard of us; and, at the same time, I heard a hundred voices hailing the Alliance, and telling them that it was on board the Bon homme Richard she was firing. A moment after she passed us on our larboard side, and it was with difficulty that I hindered the people whom I commanded from firing upon her. I hailed M. Landais as loud as I could, saying to him, 'I beg you will not sink us.' I, at the same time, thought that M. Landais was taking advantage of our circumstances to destroy M. Jones, and thereby save himself the trouble he must have expected for having disobeyed M. Jones in chasing without orders, and in edging off to shape a contrary course, when the signal was made to chase, and on several other occasions, such as refusing to come on board the Bon homme Richard to consult on the necessary operations, &c. The Alliance then came athwart our bow, and began afresh to cannonade us very smartly; I then had not the least doubt of his intention to sink us, and should have fired on the Alliance in preference to the Serapis, but that the main-top-sail and other sails concealed her from us. At the instant when they cried that the Serapis had struck, I came down, and was informed that the Alliance had killed us a number of people and, amongst others, an officer who was upon the forecastle. In my opinion there was not a soul on board the Bon homme Richard, who did not believe that M. Landais knew us before he fired, as we were higher out of the water than the Serapis; that it was moonlight, and that we had made the signal by which we must have been known during the action.

"The first lieutenant of the Countess of Scarborough told me some days since, that he had remarked, during the action with the Pallas, that the Alliance was for some time athwart and to windward of them; that, as soon as the Scarborough had struck, the Alliance came and hailed them and asked them 'what vessel that was which was engaged?' He was answered 'the Serapis.' He asked her force, but they would not tell him; he then tacked and shaped his course under his *top-sails only* to join us.

"Done on board the Serapis in the Texel, this 27th of October, 1779.

"Edward Stack,*

"Lieutenant of Walsh's Regiment.

* "Mr. Stack had the distinguished advantage of commanding in the main-top, and the post was essentially useful in the engagement. His merit obtained such a certificate from his Commodore, as, being presented to the Minister of War at Versailles, procured him promotion from sub-lieutenant to the rank of

captain with a pecuniary gratification for the loss of his effects when the Bon homme Richard sunk ; and, since the war, his Most Christian Majesty has, *for his behavior* in the Bon homme Richard, granted to him an annuity of four hundred livres for life.

"J. P. JONES."

"I, late midshipman on board the Bon homme Richard, and aid-du-camp to the Honorable John Paul Jones, in the action of the 23d of September last, off Flamborough Head, do certify, that about an hour after the commencement of it, I heard some of the men that were stationed on the forecastle cry out, 'the Alliance rakes us, and has wounded Mr. Caswell, the master's mate, with several men;' this report was afterward confirmed by Mr. Caswell, and he declared in his dying words, he received his wound from the Alliance. The ship then disappeared, and did not return till an hour and a half. As soon as she was discovered, Capt. Jones ordered the signal lanthorns of reconnoisance to be placed at proper distances from each other, on the larboard side, which order was obeyed by the master, notwithstanding which, she came up to our larboard quarter and fired into us, then shot ahead and stood athwart our bow, when I hailed by order from Captain Jones to lay the enemy on board, to which no answer was made. Mr. Coram also repeated the same order, then asked them if they heard us, their reply was, 'ay, ay;' the instant after she raked without apparently drawing any nearer the distance, then being only within the range of grape-shot, and the two ships lying parallel with their sides touching each other, several of his shot were drove into the Bon homme Richard. The conclusion I shall make relative to Captain Landais's conduct, on the 23d of September, and previous to that time, is, that his principal object was to kill Capt. Jones, and to cause the Richard to strike, that he might step in and claim the honor of the day.

"Given under my hand, on board the Bon homme Richard's prize the Serapis of 44 guns, at the Texel, the 27th of October, 1779.

"J. W. LINTHWAITE."

* "Of South Carolina, and a brave officer, whose conduct in the engagement did him great honor.

"J. P. JONES."

"Capt. Landais has oftentimes, in my presence, spoken disrespectfully and even impudently of Capt. Jones. On one occasion, about the beginning of September last, on the coast of Scotland, I went on board the Alliance frigate by desire of Captain Jones, and told Captain Landais that he requested of him to be furnished with the names of the officers and men he had a day or two before that put on board the prize ship the

Union, Capt. Johnston, that he (Capt. Jones) might be enabled to despatch her; or, to be informed what directions he had given, if any, as well with respect to that vessel, as also with respect to the prize ship the Betsey, Capt. Fisher, which also had been manned from the Alliance. Capt. Landais, in reply, told me very pertly, that Capt. Jones had no business at all with any of those vessels, for that both of them had already received proper instructions from him, and that the orders he had given were agreeable to the direction he had received from Capt. Jones. I told him I was of opinion no commander in the squadron, except Capt. Jones, was authorized to send away a prize, or otherwise dispose of her, when in his presence, but by virtue of particular orders obtained from him for that purpose. Capt. Landais, in a *sneering* manner, again replied, that he would let Capt. Jones know that he had as good a right to despatch prizes as he had; that they were captains of equal rank; and that the only difference between them was seniority on the part of Capt. Jones, which he held of little consideration; and at last Capt. Weibert, who had accompanied me on board, and myself, returned on board the Bon homme Richard totally unable to inform Capt. Jones what Capt. Landais had ordered with respect to those two ships. A short time after this, a signal was made on board the commodore's ship for the captains of the squadron to come on board. Capt. Cottineau and Capt. Ricot accordingly came on board. Capt. Landais not obeying, Capt. Jones desired me to go again on board the Alliance, and deliver Capt. Landais a letter which he then handed to me, and which I understood contained an order for him to come immediately on board; accordingly, I went on board the Alliance, and delivered Captain Landais the letter, which he took with him to the cabin, and in a few minutes returned and delivered me another for Capt. Jones; this I brought instantly on board and delivered to him. It contained a second refusal on the part of Capt. Landais, and very much offended the gentlemen who had politely obeyed the signal, and were then waiting for him. Capt. Jones, chagrined by the obstinacy of that officer, would have proceeded to the business he had in view, without paying any further attention to him; but being still anxious to have his opinion on, and approbation of the measure, conjointly with the other officers of the squadron, a further attempt to obtain his company was resolved on. For this purpose, at the desire of Capt. Jones, Capt. Cottineau, M. Chamillard, and myself, went on board the Alliance, to try the effect of persuasion upon Capt. Landais; but in vain did those gentlemen represent to him the absolute necessity there was for his joining in consultation with his brother officers; that the good of the service demanded his compliance, as an enterprise of some moment was to be deliberated on; but alas! in vain did they waste an hour or more in arguments to this end—in vain did they attempt to persuade him—in vain did they entreat him—in vain did they tell him what he had to dread from the consequences of his obstinately persisting to disobey the orders of his commanding officer. Instead of paying polite attention to the advice given him, he, on the contrary, not only disregarded it, but gave himself the liberty to speak of Capt. Jones in terms highly disrespectful and insolent, and said he would see him on shore, when they must kill one or the other, &c.

"On the 23d of September last, when the signal for a general chase was given to pursue the Baltic fleet, the Alliance frigate was the headmost ship of our squadron, and continued to keep ahead until she began to near the enemy, when Capt Landais very unexpectedly and agreeably surprised Capt. Jones by hauling his ship's wind, thereby politely leaving room for his commander to approach the largest ship, which he instantly engaged, Captain Landais still keeping at a respectful distance from his commander, which respect he, however, continued to observe, mal-apropos, until very late in the engagement. The action had lasted more than an hour, and the Bon homme Richard and the Serapis had been made fast alongside each other by Captain Jones, head and stern together, for some time, before I received the wound which obliged me to quit the deck, at which time the Bon homme Richard still continued alone with a force much superior to herself, and although she had been most severely treated by her enemy, she nevertheless continued to hug her in close embrace. The behavior of our consorts upon this day was very mysterious; but that of Capt. Landais was of such a cast, as, in my opinion, must unavoidably announce him to the public a man devoid of conduct—a man of infamous principles—or, a rank coward.

"The Alliance having received no shot from the enemy, her captain had the *advantage* to have none of his men either killed or wounded during the whole engagement. And it is highly worthy of remark, that before the Alliance raked the Bon homme Richard by firing alternately into her head and stern, the enemy had been dislodged and driven from the tops and quarterdeck of the Serapis to her first and second batteries, where they were under cover. The discharge of the second battery of the Serapis having beat in one side of the Bon homme Richard and blown out the other, made a breach from before the mainmast to the stern, cutting off the sternpost and rudder, and dislodging every one from that situation. These retreated to the forecastle of the Bon homme Richard, where they could not be fired upon from the Serapis, and with those stationed there, were exposed to the fire of the Alliance.

"Serapis, at the Texel, November 13th, 1779.

"MATTHEW MEASE."*

* "Mr. Mease, of Philadelphia, was a gentleman of worthy character. He

was not bred a seaman, but had many times crossed the ocean, being a merchant and owner of ships. His love for America (his country) induced him to embark in the Bon homme Richard, and, the other offices being previously filled, he accepted the place of purser. In the engagement with the Serapis, he commanded the quarterdeck guns of the Bon homme Richard, and behaved with distinguished coolness and intrepidity, till he was dangerously wounded in the head by a grape-shot. The next day his skull was trepanned in six or seven places; but, immediately after the surgeon had tied up his head in the action, which lasted three hours after his misfortune, he returned again upon deck.

"J. P. JONES."

"Whereas, since the campaign of 1779, there have been various and partial reports secretly spread against the private and social character of Commodore Paul Jones, formerly commanding the squadron of the Bon homme Richard; and as, among other hearsays and groundless stories, I have sometimes heard that the above mentioned officer had formally given the lie to M. Landais, formerly captain of the Alliance, relating to the loss of a boat in sight of the coast of Ireland:—therefore I declare and affirm, that the aforesaid commodore did not say to M. Landais, 'You lie,' but no more than these very words: 'It is an untruth;' which M. Landais was pleased to interpret as a *formal giving the lie*, who was never able to overcome his peevish, obstinate, turbulent, and ungovernable temper, which he constantly showed during the whole of the campaign. Moreover, I certify, that Commodore Paul Jones, far from commanding with haughtiness or brutality, as certain persons have endeavored to circulate, was always (though very strict and sharp in the service) affable, genteel, and very indulgent, not only towards his officers, but likewise towards the sailors and soldiers, whom he ever treated with humanity. As I was a witness to the before-mentioned quarrel, I must in conscience confess that M. Landais gave, at the time, great cause for it, by the arrogant manner which he assumed towards his commander in answer to the peaceable, good, and fair reasons to which he would never yield; so far to the contrary, that he (M. Landais) answered the commodore (Lieut. Chamillard and myself both being present) in the most gross and insulting terms —at first in English, which he immediately rendered in French, that M. Chamillard might not be ignorant of anything that passed. The whole of the aforesaid quarrel happened in the round house of the Bon homme Richard, the 23d and 25th of August, in the above mentioned year. I conclude by saying, that M. Landais accompanied or affirmed his offensive and very scandalous discourse by the most provoking gestures.

"*Philadelphia, November 28th*, 1781.

"Lieut. Col. WEIBERT,

"Of the corps of American Engineers."

"Being on board the Alliance on the 23d of September, 1779, and stationed on the quarterdeck in the time of the action with the Serapis and Countess of Scarborough, do certify, that I saw the Countess of Scarborough rake the Bon homme Richard, but cannot say whether she raked her more than once.

"JOHN SPENCER.*

"October 30, 1779."

* He said he was a lieutenant-colonel in the service of the State of South Carolina.

The Bon homme Richard and Serapis had been from the beginning, and still were closely engaged, broadside to broadside. The Alliance being just within long cannon shot to windward of the Countess of Scarborough, could easily have prevented that ship's raking fire into the stern of the Bon homme Richard. The Pallas was at this time to windward of the Alliance, of course out of gun-shot of the enemy. But Capt. Cottineau, of the Pallas, bore down, and having spoken the Alliance as he passed that frigate, he engaged, and after a considerable action took the Countess of Scarborough.

On the 9th of May, 1777, Captain John Paul Jones was directed to proceed to France (by the Marine Committee), and to obey the orders of the Secret Committee. Being arrived in Europe, it was the intention of Congress "that he should be invested with the command of a *fine fast sailing frigate, or larger ship*." In pursuance of this plan, the Secret Committee of Congress wrote to the Honorable Benjamin Franklin, Silas Deane, and Arthur Lee, Esq'rs. Commissioners, &c. at Paris, as follows:—

"*Philadelphia, May 9th*, 1777.

"HONORABLE GENTLEMEN,

"This letter is intended to be delivered to you by John Paul Jones, Esq., an active and brave commander in our navy, who has already performed signal services in vessels of little force; and, in reward for his zeal, we have directed him, &c. You will assign him some good house or agent to supply him with everything necessary to get the ship speedily and well equipped and manned: somebody that will bestir themselves vigorously in the business, and never quit it until it is accomplished. You see by this step how much dependence Congress place in your advices, and you must make it a point not to disappoint Capt. Paul Jones's wishes and our expectations on this occasion.

"We are, Honorable Gentlemen,

"Your obedient, humble servants,

"Robert Morris,
"Richard H. Lee,
"William Whipple,
"Philip Livingston."

The ship in question was the *Indien*, then on the stocks at Amsterdam, belonging to the United States; but this having been discovered to the British minister by some of Mr. Arthur Lee's papers, of which they had got possession just before Com. Paul Jones arrived at Paris, and the treaty of alliance being on the point to be concluded, he consented to their assigning over the property of that ship to the King of France. Among the political reasons which operated this arrangement was the great opposition made to the equipment of the Indien, by the British ambassador in Holland. The command of the Indien was, however, reserved for Captain Jones, till (subsequent to his campaign of 1779) he had made an arrangement of a plan with the Count de Maurapas, which promised much greater importance to the common cause. After this his majesty lent the use of the Indien to the Prince de Luxembourg for three years, and the prince *chartered* her, for the term prescribed, to Mr. Gillon, of South Carolina, under the commission of that state.—This was the ship that Mr. Gillon came in to Philadelphia, under the name of the *South Carolina*.

Extract of a letter from Captain J. P. Jones to the Honorable John Adams,* dated L'Orient, May 13th, 1779.

"You will confer a singular obligation on me, by favoring me with

* The Honorable Mr. Adams was then, and had been for some time, on board the Alliance.

your opinion and advice respecting the unhappy misunderstanding which I am told prevails on board the Alliance. I ask your advice, because, though I am determined to preserve order and discipline where I command, yet I wish to reprove with moderation, and never punish while there remains a good alternative. It appears that there is a fault at least in one of the parties, and I wish much to know where the fault lies; for without harmony and general good will among the officers, I cannot proceed with a good prospect."

In relation to Captain Landais, Dr. Franklin's opinion was decidedly against him. He communicated to that officer himself his objections to him, and in the most unequivocal terms refused to him the command of a ship of war, giving his reasons.

His Excellency BENJAMIN FRANKLIN to Captain LANDAIS, dated Passy, March 12th, 1780.

"No one has ever learned the opinion I formed of you from the inquiry made into your conduct. I kept it entirely to myself—I have not even hinted it in my letters to America, because I would not hazard giving to any one a bias to your prejudice. By communicating *a part of that opinion* privately to you, I can do no harm, for you may burn it. I should not give you the pain of reading it, if your demand did not make it necessary: I think you then so imprudent, so litigious, and quarrelsome a man, even with your best friends, that peace and good order, and consequently the quiet and regular subordination so necessary to success, are, where you preside, impossible; these are within my observation and apprehension: your military operations I leave to more capable judges. If, therefore, I had twenty ships of war in my disposition, I should not give one of them to Captain Landais. The same temper which *excluded* him from the French marine would weigh equally with me; of course I shall not replace him in the Alliance. I am, &c.,

"B. FRANKLIN."

The subjoined correspondence will illustrate the friendly disposition of Holland towards the United States, the difficulties which the states of that republic experienced in the manifestation of it, so as to avoid an open rupture with Great Britain;

the influence of Commodore Jones at the Hague; the exclusively American feelings by which he was governed; the high estimation in which he was held by Dr. Franklin, by some of the principal men in Europe, and by all the Americans of note within the sphere of his acquaintance. His patriotism and philanthropy cannot be questioned, when it is observed with what anxiety he sought for the liberation of the American prisoners in England, regarding his successes chiefly as the means of procuring their exchange. Although not insensible to pleasure, he was never negligent of business, was eminently discreet, and always at the post which duty required.

"*On board the ship of war Serapis, at anchor in the road of the Texel, October 5th,* 1779.

"His Excellency the Duke DE LA VAUGUYON,
Ambassador of France, at the Hague.

"MY LORD,

"I am but this moment arrived here, otherwise I should have sent you a more early account of my late expedition. I now enclose herewith a copy of the account which I have forwarded by express to his excellency the Minister of the Marine at court. As we have on board the different vessels here, I believe (for I have not yet been able to procure an exact return) three hundred and fifty prisoners, and of that number I suppose an hundred and thirty wounded, I would esteem it a particular favor to have your opinion on the measures that are most expedient to be adopted in that respect. Whether it would be proper to set them at liberty here, upon such security as may be obtained, that the English government will immediately expedite an equal number of Americans to France? Unless such security as may be fully depended upon can be obtained, I think these prisoners must be sent immediately for Dunkirk. We are now preparing the Countess of Scarborough and the Vengeance to transport them to France, in case it should be necessary. The Countess of Scarborough not being fit for war, can remain in France, while the Vengeance brings back all our people, and as many more as can be obtained to replace the great number that I have lost out of the crew of the Bon homme Richard, in killed and wounded, not less I suppose than one hundred and fifty men.

"I have had the honor to receive by the hand of our agent, Mr. Dumas, such orders from his Excellency Dr. Franklin, as it will be impossible for me to fulfil, unless I meet with great and immediate assistance to enable me to depart before the end of this month. The Serapis must be entirely new masted and rigged; nothing being left above deck that is capable of sustaining a passage of any length in the approaching season. She wants also sails, rigging, boats, and provision. The hull, though considerably damaged, may easily be repaired.

"As soon as I have made some necessary arrangements here, I mean to do myself the honor of paying your Excellency my personal respects, and to receive your orders at the Hague. In the mean time, I beseech you to favor me with a line respecting my wounded, whether of France or America, as well as respecting the prisoners of war, and the treatment that they ought to receive in point of provision and otherwise.

"I have the honor to be, with profound respect, &c."

"*Amsterdam, October* 11*th*, 1779.

"His Excellency BENJAMIN FRANKLIN.

"I had the honor to write your Excellency a line from the Hague, on the 8th. His Excellency the French ambassador and the agent have, no doubt, marked the situation of affairs with respect to the squadron as concerned with this government and with the enemy. I am doing everything in my power towards fulfilling the advice which I have received from his Excellency; and as I am informed that Captain Cunningham is threatened with unfair play by the British government, I am determined to keep in my hands the captain of the Serapis, as an hostage for Cunningham's release as a prisoner of war. With respect to the other prisoners now in my hands, if the English ambassador, Sir Joseph Yorke, will give us security, in his public character, that an equal number and denomination of Americans shall be sent immediately to France, I believe it will be good policy to set them at liberty here; and I shall endeavor indirectly to inform myself immediately how that matter can be managed. Landais is come up here, and purposes, after gadding about in this city, to figure away at the Hague. He continues to affect an entire independence of my control, and has given in here an extraordinary demand for supplies of every kind. This famous demand, however, I have ventured to disapprove, and reduced to, I believe, a fourth part of its first extent. I hope to account to your satisfaction for my reasons—among which is his having been so plentifully and so lately furnished. I wish heartily that poor Cunningham, (whom I am taught to regard as a continental officer,) was exchanged, as with his assistance I could form a court-martial, which I believe you will see unavoidable. I go down to the Texel to-night, and will from thence forward the return of killed and wounded with the prisoners. I think the prisoners will not fall much short of four hundred; and I hope my loss in killed and wounded will be less than I at first imagined. I believe, also, that the enemy's loss will considerably exceed ours.

"I am ever, with sentiments of the highest esteem and respect, &c."

"*Zwol, October* 13*th*, 1779.

"The Hon. PAUL JONES.

"Having the honor to be an old and tried friend of America, I hope you will pardon, on that account, the liberty I take to address you these lines.

"It was with unspeakable satisfaction I received the tidings of the many successes during your expedition on the coasts of Britain; but particularly was I struck with admiration by your late engagement with the Serapis, of which M. De Neufville has given me some incomplete account. Do not therefore wonder, Sir, that I long to hear directly from yourself an authentic and circumstanced one, containing all the particulars relating to a sea fight rather to be found in the books of a former century than in our present age on the ocean. What emboldens me, moreover, to ask you the favor of such an account is, that I have the mortification to see a despicable party spirit endeavoring to deprive you of a praise which even your antagonist, the commander of the Serapis, if he be as just as he seems valorous, will not deny you. As I am very desirous to do you justice wherever occasion shall offer itself, you will, by supplying me the necessary means, and sending your answer to M. De Neufville, very much oblige,

"Sir, your most humble and obedient servant,

"J. D. VANDER CAPELLEN.

"Address to the Baron Vander Capellen, Member of the House of Nobles of the province of Overyssel.

"*Passy, October* 15*th*, 1779.

"DEAR SIR,

"I received the account of your cruize and engagement with the Serapis, which you did me the honor to send me from the Texel. I have since received your favor of the 8th from Amsterdam. For some days after the arrival of your express, scarce anything was talked of at Paris and Versailles but your cool conduct and persevering bravery during that terrible conflict. You may believe that the impression on my mind was not less strong than that of others, but I do not choose to say in a letter to yourself, all I think on such an occasion.

"The ministry are much dissatisfied with Capt. Landais, and M. de Sartine has signified to me in writing that it is expected I should send for him to Paris, and call him to account for his conduct, particularly for deferring so long the coming to your assistance, by which means, it is supposed, the States lost more of their valuable citizens, and the King lost many of his subjects, volunteers in your ship, together with the ship itself.

"I have accordingly written to him this day, acquainting him that he is charged with disobedience of orders in the cruize, and neglect of his duty in the engagement; that a court martial being at this time inconvenient, if not impracticable, I would give him an earlier opportunity of offering what he has to say in his justification, and for that purpose direct him to render himself immediately here, bringing with him such papers or testimonies as he may think useful in his defence. I know not whether he will obey my orders, nor what the ministry will do with him if he comes, but, I suspect, that they may by some of their concise operations save the trouble of a court martial. It will be well however for you to furnish me with what you may judge proper to support the charges against him, that I may be able to give a just and clear account of the affair to Congress.

"In the meantime it will be necessary, if he should refuse to come, that you should put him under an arrest, and in that case as well as if he comes, that you should either appoint some person to command his ship, or take it upon yourself; for I know of no person to recommend to you as fit for that station.

"I am uneasy about your prisoners, I wish they were safe in France. *You will then have completed the glorious work of giving liberty to all the Americans that have so long languished for it in the British prisons: for there are not so many there as you have now taken.*

"I have the pleasure to inform you that the two prizes sent to Norway are safely arrived at Berghen.

"With the highest esteem, I am, &c.

"B. FRANKLIN.

"P. S.—I am sorry for your misunderstanding with M. de C. who has a great regard for you."

"*Pallas, Tuesday evening, October* 19*th*, 1779.

"CAPTAIN JONES, Serapis.

"Captain Pearson presents his compliments to Captain Jones, and is sorry to find himself so little attended to in his present situation, as not to have been favored with either a *Call* or a line from Captain Jones since his return from Amsterdam. Captain P. is sorry to say that he cannot look upon such behavior in any other light than as a breach of that *Civility* which his rank, as well as behavior on all occasions, entitles to; he, at the same time, wishes to be informed by Captain Jones whether any *Steps has* been taken towards the enlargement or exchange of him, his officers, and people, or what is intended to be done with them. As he cannot help thinking it a very unprecedented circumstance their being *keeped* here as prisoners on board of ship, being so long in a neutral port."

"*Serapis, Wednesday, October* 20*th*, 1779.

"CAPTAIN PEARSON,

"SIR,

"As you have not been prevented from corresponding with your friends, and particularly with the English ambassador at the Hague, I could not suppose you to be unacquainted with his memorial of the 8th to the States General, and therefore I thought it fruitless to pursue the negotiation for the exchange of the prisoners of war, now in our hands.

"I wished to avoid any painful altercation with you on that subject; I was persuaded that you had been in the highest degree sensible that my behavior 'towards you had been far from a breach of civility.' This charge is not, Sir, a civil return for the polite hospitality, and disinterested attentions which you have hitherto experienced.

"I know not what difference of respect is due to 'Rank' between your service and ours; I suppose, however, the difference must be thought *very great* in England, since I am informed that Captain Cunningham, of equal denomination, and who bears a senior rank in the service of America than yours in the service of England, is now confined at Plymouth *in a dungeon and in fetters.*

"Humanity, which has hitherto superseded the plea of retaliation in American breasts, has induced me (notwithstanding the procedure of Sir Joseph Yorke), to seek after permission to land the dangerously wounded, as well prisoners as Americans, to be supported and cured at the expense of our Continent. The permission of the government has been obtained, but the magistrates continue to make objections. I shall not discontinue my application. I am ready to adopt any means that you may propose for their preservation and recovery, and, in the meantime, we shall continue to treat them with the utmost care and attention, equally, as you know, to the treatment of our people of the same rank.

"As it is possible that you have not yet seen the memorial of your ambassador to the States General, I enclose a paper which contains a copy, and I believe he has since written what, in the opinion of good men, will do still less honor to his pen.

"I cannot conclude without informing you that, unless Captain Cunningham is immediately better treated in England, I expect orders in consequence from His Excellency, Dr. Franklin; therefore, I beseech you, Sir, to interfere.

"I am, Sir, &c."

"*On board the Serapis at the Texel,*
October 24*th*, 1779.

"M. Le Ray de Chaumont.

"I owed you, my dear friend, an earlier reply to your much esteemed favor of the 11th, from Passy. Although I am sensible that I have not yet merited the many compliments and generous praises that you have there bestowed on my past conduct, yet I should be very unworthy indeed if I did not return you my most grateful and sincere thanks. There is a warmth of expression in your compliments which affords me the truest pleasure, as a proof that I still enjoy a share of your affection; and, although Capt. Landais has lately told me at Amsterdam that you proposed to him to displace me from the Bon homme Richard, yet I believe the assertion false, and calculated to serve a base and selfish purpose. I pity and despise his narrow and jealous mind, that could form an idea of my character so far beneath it as to suppose that I sought to supplant him in the command of the Alliance. It must be his punishment to be informed, as he will by his Excellency Dr. Franklin, that I have always written in his favor, and you well know that I took every possible pains to establish him in that command, and to gain back to him the confidence of his people which, when he first came to serve under my orders, he had entirely lost. I can now tell besides that, although my officers in the Bon homme Richard were the only persons blamed for the damage sustained when the two ships ran foul of each other, yet Capt. Landais could and should have prevented that accident. He was on deck, and it was his duty to make way for his senior officer and commander, instead of running below, as I am assured he did, with trepidation to load his pistols! On our late expedition he left off to chase a ship thought to be an English East-Indiaman, without my order, having first bore away several times while he could easily have overtaken her. And to his fears and remonstrances on the coast of Ireland, is owing the escape of the eight East-India ships that arrived at Limerick three days after I had gratified him by leaving sight of the entrance of that harbor.

"His separation from the squadron afterward, is owing, as the officers of the Alliance inform me, to his altering the course both times in the night. Captain Landais has told me at Amsterdam that he saw the Countess of Scarborough rake the Bon homme Richard, early in the engagement. He ought to be ashamed to confess that he lay to windward and permitted this! It is certain that the Bon homme Richard then was raked by a full broadside, besides sustaining the whole fire of the Serapis.

"Many people are of opinion that Captain Landais also about that time raked the Bon homme Richard:—however that was, I verily believe that in firing the two last broadsides upon the Bon homme Richard, he did not wish all the shot to miss Captain Jones, and also that the worst shot which the Bon homme Richard received under water came from the Alliance. He has since our arrival here, told Col. de Weibert and others of my officers, that 'he was in no haste to come to our assistance, because there would have been no harm if we had been taken, to give him an opportunity of retaking the Bon homme Richard.' None but a fool, a madman, or a villain would have raked at that distance, while a friend and an enemy were made fast alongside of each other. If he had wished to act the part of an officer or a man, he would have come to my assistance long before the two ships were in a situation that to rake the one at the range of grape shot, he must necessarily rake the other.

"But why should I dwell on a subject which can afford neither you nor me pleasure! I am now convinced that I now enjoy your friendship and affectionate wishes; therefore I beseech you to pardon the freedom of my letters, that I forwarded by M. de Chamillard; which, though a proof of the honest pride which will ever attend an independent and disinterested spirit, is also, I hope, a proof that my mind is far above the little arts of falsehood and double dealing.

"It shall be my pride to acknowledge everywhere how much I owe to the attentions of France, and to the personal friendship of M. de Chaumont, for furnishing me with the means of giving liberty to all the American prisoners now in Europe:—for that is the greatest triumph which a good man can boast, and is therefore a thousand times more flattering to me than victory.

"I ardently wish for future opportunities to render real services to our common cause; which is the only way I can hope to prove my gratitude to France, to America, and to my much loved friend M. de Chaumont, and his amiable family, with whom I sincerely desire to live henceforth in the fullest confidence and affection. In the fullness of my heart, I am, with the highest respect, my dear Chaumont, your truly obliged friend, &c."

"*New York, December*, 1824.

"I certify that the original of the preceding letter was duly received by my father.

"LE RAY DE CHAUMONT."

The determinations of the French court, which appear to have been too tardy for Jones's ardent wish for active employment at this period of his history, seem to have occasioned him some uneasiness. He had, moreover, as every celebrated man will have, rivals and enemies, who felt rebuked beneath his superior genius, instilled suspicions into the minds of the French ministry, and contested his claim to an independent command, where the cost of a cruize or expedition was to be defrayed by the treasury of France. Jones did not conceal his sensations. He refused to accept of any other commission than one from the Congress, or to fight under any other flag than that of the United States. He expressed his sentiments freely, and began to think of returning to America. The Duke de la Vauguyon was apprised of the commodore's dissatisfaction, and wrote to him a soothing letter, of which the following is a correct translation:

"*Hague, December* 21*st*, 1779.

"Commodore JONES, in the road of the Texel.

"I have received, my dear commodore, the letter which you have addressed to me. I perceive with pain that you do not view your situation in the right light; and I can assure you that the ministers of the king have no intention to cause you the least disagreeable feelings, as the honorable testimonials of the esteem of his majesty which I send you, ought to convince you. I hope you will not doubt the sincere desire with which you have inspired me, to procure you every satisfaction you may merit. It cannot fail to be precious to you, and to incite you to give new proofs of your zeal for the common cause of France and America. I flatter myself to renew before long the occasion, and to procure you the means to increase still more the glory you have already acquired; I am already occupied with all the interest I promised you, and if my views are realized, as I have every reason to believe, you will be at all events perfectly content; but I must pray you not to hinder my project, in delivering yourself to the expression of that bitter grief to which you appear to have given way, and which has no real foundation. You appear to possess full confidence in the justice and kindness of the king, rely also on the same sentiments on the part of the ministry; my friendship for you, my dear commodore, requires that neither your conduct nor conversation announce the least doubt in this respect.

"LE DUC DE LA VAUGUYON."

To this letter Commodore Jones thus answered:

"*Alliance, Texel, December 25th,* 1779.

"The Duke de VAUGUYON.

"MY LORD,

"I have not an heart of stone, but am duly sensible of the obligations conferred on me by the very kind and affectionate letter that you have done me the honor to write me the 21st current.

"Were I to form my opinion of the ministry from the treatment that I experienced while at Brest, or from their want of confidence in me afterward, exclusive of what has taken place since I had the misfortune to enter this port, I will appeal to your Excellency as a man of candor and ingenuousness, whether I ought to desire to prolong a connexion that has made me so unhappy, and wherein I have given so very little satisfaction? M. le Chev. de Lironcourt has lately made me reproaches on account of the expense, that he says France has been at, *to give me reputation*, in preference to twenty captains of the royal navy, better qualified than myself, and who, each of them, solicited for the command that was lately given to me! This, I confess, is quite new and indeed surprising to me, and had I known it before I left France, I certainly should have resigned in favor of the twenty men of superior merit. I do not, however, think that his first assertion is true; for the ministry must be unworthy of their places, were they capable of squandering the public money, merely to give an individual reputation! and, as to the second, I fancy the Court will not thank him for having given me that information, whether true or false. I may add here that with a force so ill composed, and with powers so limited, I ran ten chances of ruin and dishonor for one of gaining reputation; and had not the plea of humanity in favor of the unfortunate Americans in English dungeons superseded all considerations of self, I faithfully assure you, my lord, that I would not have proceeded under such circumstances from Groaix. I do not imbibe hasty prejudices against any individual, but when many and repeated circumstances, conspiring in one point, has inspired me with disesteem towards any person, I must see very convincing proofs of reformation in such person, before my heart can beat again with affection in his favor. For the mind is free, and can be bound only by kind treatment.

"You do me great honor as well as justice, my lord, by observing that no satisfaction can be more precious to me than that of giving new proofs of my zeal for the common cause of France and America; and the interest that you take to facilitate the means of my giving such proofs by essential services, claims my best thanks. I hope I shall not through any imprudence of mine, render ineffectual any noble design that may be in contemplation for the general good. Whenever that object is mentioned, my private concerns are out of the question; and where I cannot speak exactly what I could wish with respect to my private satisfaction, I promise you in the mean time to observe a prudent silence.

"With a deep sense of your generous sentiments of personal regard towards me, and with the most sincere wishes to merit that regard by my conduct through life,

"I am, my lord, &c."

Commodore Jones had previously written to his friend, Mr. Morris, on the 5th of December. To him he said: "By the within despatches for Congress, I am persuaded you will observe with pleasure that my connexion with a Court is at an end, and that my prospect of returning to America approaches. The great seem to wish only to be concerned with tools who dare not speak or write truth. I am not sorry that my connexion with them is at an end. In the course of that connexion I ran ten chances of ruin and dishonor for one of reputation; and all the honors or profit that France could bestow should not tempt me again to undertake the same service with an armament equally ill composed and with powers equally limited. It affords me the most exalted pleasure to reflect that, when I return to America, I can say that I have served in Europe at my own expense, and without the fee or reward of a Court. When the prisoners we have taken are safely lodged in France, I shall have no further business in

Europe, as the liberty of all our fellow citizens who now suffer in English prisons will then be secured; and I shall hope hereafter to be usefully employed under the immediate direction of the Congress."

Jones was a man of ardent temperament, felt the value of his own talents, and was restless under the least appearance of indifference towards him. He did not justly estimate the obstacles which the French ministry had to remove in assigning to him the honorable command which he had already held. He was a foreigner, and the officers of the French navy must have had their prejudices against him. Many of them longed for employment as well as Jones, and putting in their claims to a preference, on account of rank and nativity, was no doubt the principal cause of that neglect of which he complained. He, nevertheless, retained the esteem of the king and of the most enlightened of his subjects, who felt the benefit, both to America and France, of the splendid services of the Commodore.

Commodore Jones at length departed from the Texel, and arrived at Corogne about the middle of January, 1778, when he immediately wrote to General Lafayette the following letter. His skill and hardihood in eluding the vigilance of the squadron by which he was blockaded, and in braving the dangers of the British Channel were conspicuous, and he speaks of his good fortune in his usual strain of manliness and naval gallantry:—

"*Alliance, Corogne, January* 16*th*, 1780.

"The Hon. Marquis DE LA FAYETTE.

"Notwithstanding my hopes of leaving the Texel immediately after I had the honor of writing to my noble friend on the 30th of November a letter of which the within is a copy, yet I was detained in that detestable road until the 27th of December. I made my passage safe through the Channel, in spite of all their cruizing ships and squadrons, and had the pleasure of looking at them in the Downs, and in passing in sight of the Isle of Wight, &c. I steered this way in hopes of meeting some of their cruizers off Cape Finisterre, but am hitherto disappointed. It being very stormy weather I this evening anchored here, where I mean only to scrub the bottom and take a little fresh water, after which I purpose to cruize towards France, and on my arrival at L'Orient I shall be happy to hear from you again.

"Since my last to you, while I remained at the Texel, I was greatly astonished, and indeed mortified, at a proposition from Court, communicated to me by the Duc de Vauguyon; his Excellency afterwards, on the 21st of December, wrote me a most affectionate letter, a copy with my answer is enclosed. I shall make no remark, but leave you, my dear Marquis, to judge of my feelings, and how much I must have been shocked at the treatment I received from the Court, particularly in the Texel. I am always, with the most lively affection and esteem,

"Yours, &c.

"I remember this letter to me.

"LAFAYETTE.

"*Washington City*, *February*, 1825."

On the 28th of January the Commodore sailed from Corogne, and after a short cruise, which is explained in the annexed letter to Dr. Franklin, he arrived at Groaix on the 10th of February, when he left the Alliance and, on account of impaired health, went up to L'Orient:—

"*L'Orient*, *Feb.* 13*th*, 1780.

"His Excellency BENJAMIN FRANKLIN.

"Honorable and Dear Sir,

"I had the pleasure of writing to your Excellency on my arrival at Corogne. Having refreshed my people, and shunned a gale of wind in that port, I sailed again the 28th ult. I took a turn to the westward of Cape Finisterre, in hopes of intercepting some of the enemy's ships, but without success; and meeting with Mr. Haywood, in the Livingston, on his return from Virginia, I thought it my duty to take him under convoy. On the passage from Boston for Brest the Alliance was broached-to, and very near being lost. In that situation the sea struck with such violence against the head that the cutwater was wrenched considerably out of its place. When the ship was hove down here, it would have been an easy matter to have secured the head. I did not, however, then know the circumstance, nor did my health permit me to attend, and as I understood Captain Landais only ordered the part of the cutwater that projected on one side of the stem to be dubbed off. When he parted from me off the west of Ireland, and again in the North Sea, the Alliance was steered in the trough of the swell, so that the ship was greatly fatigued in every part, but particularly in the cutwater, which was much loosened. At the Texel we did all that was possible in such a road to secure the head, but notwithstanding, it became necessary to lash it with an hawser, after we got clear of the channel. This was, of course, an inducement for me to steer sooner for this port than I had otherwise proposed, though I had yet other reasons. Among these I may mention that I have found it impossible to regain the trim of the ship without altering the arrangement of the ballast, which I understand Captain Landais has extended along the ceiling from the stern-post to the stem; an idea that I believe he may without vanity call his own. Besides, to my great surprise, there is not a good sail, nor, I may almost say, a good rope in the Alliance. Even the cables were in so wretched a condition, that had it not been for a timely supply of three new ones that I ordered from Amsterdam, I should infallibly have lost the ship in the severe weather I found at the Texel. In short, the situation in which I found the Alliance appears to me to have been the effect of slothfulness and ignorance. I procured a second anchor at Corogne, and we arrived at Groaix on the 10th, where the ship still remains, the wind not permitting her to enter the harbor. From my late fatigues my health is rather impaired; and being also, when we anchored, almost blind with sore eyes, I the next evening came up here at the desire of my friends. I have found some benefit from the change of air, otherwise I could not now have seen to write.

"As soon as the ship can be brought into Port Louis, we shall begin to refit without loss of time. The head, in my opinion, cannot be secured without heaving down; therefore I wish it could be afforded to sheathe the bottom with copper, as the ship would be doubly serviceable afterward.

"I ordered some canvas and cordage from Amsterdam, which did not appear before I left the Texel, nor is yet arrived here. As I suppose M. de Neufville means to send these articles after me, perhaps you will now see fit to contradict the order, as I am assured they can be had on as easy terms here. I wish to know if I am to apply here, as I do in the mean time to Messrs. Gourlade and Moylan; and the Serapis being arrived here, I wish she could be made the property of America.

"I have the honor to be always, with the highest respect and most affectionate esteem, "Your Excellency's most obliged, &c."

At L'Orient the commodore learned that rumors were circulated to his disadvantage, that he did not like the French nation; in consequence of which he addressed letters to the Marquis de la Fayette and to the Duke de la Vauguyon, wherein he explains his principles, and vindicates his character. These letters place Jones in a very amiable light, demonstrating that he was not only a valiant captain and a person of enlarged views, but one who felt the miseries incident to war, and was desirous of a durable peace on just grounds, as the main object of the contest:

"*L'Orient, February* 18*th*, 1780.

"The Hon. General M. LE MARQUIS DE LA FAYETTE, &c.

"I had, dear Marquis, the honor to write you sundry letters before I left the Texel: I also wrote you on my arrival at Corogne. I arrived at Groaix the 10th, and landed here the day after, almost blind with sore eyes, and not otherwise in a very good state of health. I am now a little recovered, but it is with difficulty that I can yet look on paper;—therefore I should not at this instant have taken up my pen, had I not this day understood by a friend that my attachment and esteem for this nation had been called in question.

"Withdrawn as I am at present from the public attention, and having endeavored only by my past conduct to prove my zeal for the common cause, it is strange that I cannot escape the malicious attacks of little minds. If any person who has himself deserved well of his country, can accuse me of ingratitude, let him step forth like a man, and I will answer in homme d'honneur. M. Weibert has, I understand, taken great pains to promulgate that I do not love France. He is not surely among the most worthy part of the nation, yet he partook both of my purse and my table, till the moment of separation, after I had provided for him a free passage in a ship destined for America, from a situation where he had but little danger to apprehend from the enemy.

"To come to the point, here follows my political profession. I am a citizen of the world, totally unfettered by the little mean distinctions of country or of climate; which diminish or set bounds to the benevolence of the heart. Impelled by principles of gratitude and philanthropy, I drew my sword at the beginning of the American Revolution, and when France so nobly espoused that great cause, no individual felt the obligation with truer gratitude than myself. When the Court of France soon after invited me to remain for a time in Europe, I considered myself as highly honored by the application that was made to the American commissioners. Since that time I have been at every instant, and I still am ready to do my utmost for the good of the common cause of France and America. As an American officer, and as a man, I affectionately love and respect the character and nation of France, and hope the alliance with America may last forever. I owe the greatest obligation to the generous praises of the French nation on my past conduct, and shall be happy to merit future favor. I greatly love and esteem his most Christian Majesty as the great ally of America, the best of kings, and the amiable friend and 'protector of the rights of human nature,' therefore he has very few of his own subjects who would bleed in his present cause with greater freedom than myself, and none who are more disinterested. At the same time I lament the calamities of war, and wish above all things for an honorable, happy, and lasting peace. My fortune is not augmented by the part I have hitherto acted in the revolution (although I have had frequent opportunities of acquiring riches), and I pledge myself to the worthy part of mankind, that my future conduct in the war shall not forfeit their good opinion. I am ever with great and sincere affection, happy in your friendship," &c.

"I remember such a letter being received.

"LA FAYETTE.

"*Washington City, February,* 1825."

"*L'Orient, February* 18*th,* 1780.

"His Excellency M. LE DUC DE VAUGUYON.

"MY LORD,

"I had the honor of writing to your excellency a day or two before I left the Texel, in answer to your very kind letter on the subject of my discontent. I sent my letter to the Helder by my pilot, to the care of M. le Chevalier de Lirencourt, and I hope it came safe to your hands. I have been here since the 10th of this month, but being almost blind with sore eyes, I could not sooner look on paper, otherwise I should not have failed to repeat how much I feel the obligation conferred on me by your attentions while I remained in Holland.

"There are, my lord, some of my secret enemies base enough to insinuate that I do not love the nation of France; but be assured that though I felt myself hurt by some measures that were adopted towards me, and for which I cannot yet see any good reason, yet I have never written, spoken, or even thought disrespectfully of the nation. On the contrary, I owe the greatest obligation to France for the generous friendship of the nation towards America, and for the generous praises bestowed on my late conduct, which I should be very happy to merit, by future services in the common cause. Above all, as an individual I am deeply sensible of the great honor conferred on me by the personal esteem and approbation of the best of kings. I shall through life be happy in every circumstance where I can manifest how much I wish to merit his majesty's good opinion; and when I thank you in particular, my lord, for the affectionate manner in which you communicated to me his majesty's sentiments in my favor, I speak not words without meaning, but my heart overflows with gratitude, and will ever be ambitious to merit your friendship.

"I am with an artless sincerity, my lord," &c.

By a preceding letter from Commodore Jones, it will have been observed that the Alliance required many repairs. Dr. Franklin had expected that these would have been made without loss of time, and wrote to Jones accordingly. In the following letters the cause of the delay will be shown, and that no blame could be properly ascribed to the commodore:

"*Passy, February 19th*, 1780.

"Honorable Capt. JONES.

DEAR SIR,

"I received yours from Corogne of the 16th past, and from L'Orient of the 13th inst. I rejoice that you are safely arrived in France, malgré all the pains taken to intercept you.

"As to refitting your ship at the expense of this court, I must acquaint you that there is not the least probability of obtaining it, and therefore I cannot ask it. I hear too much already of the extraordinary expense you made in Holland to think of proposing an addition to it, especially as you seem to impute the damage she has sustained more to Capt. Landais's negligence than to accidents of the cruize. The whole expense will therefore fall upon me, and I am ill provided to bear it, having so many unexpected calls upon me from all quarters. I therefore beg you would have mercy on me, put me to as little charge as possible, and take nothing that you can possibly do without. As to sheathing with copper, it is totally out of the question. I am not authorised to do it, if I had money;

and I have not money for it, if I had orders. The purchase of the Serapis is in the same predicament. I believe the sending canvas and cordage from Amsterdam has already been forbidden; if not, I shall forbid it. I approve of your applying to Messrs. Gourlade and Moylan for what repairs you want, having an exceeding good opinion of those gentlemen; but let me repeat it, for God's sake be sparing, unless you mean to make me a bankrupt, or have your drafts dishonored, for want of money in my hands to pay them.

"We are likely to obtain 15,000 stand of good arms from the government. They are much wanted in America. M. de la Fayette has just now proposed that you should take them as ballast. You know best if this is practicable.

"Mr. Ross acquaints me that he has 120 bales of public cloth for our army, and wishes it may likewise go in the Alliance. Can this be done? It is undoubtedly an article of great necessity; but I have mentioned to him the room required in a ship of war for the men, their provisions, water, &c., and the difficulty thence of finding place for goods. You will judge of this likewise.

"Mr. Ross also requests to be permitted to take his passage with you. As he has been a servant of the States in making their purchases in Europe, it seems to me that it would be wrong to refuse him. There is also a particular friend of mine, Mr. Samuel Wharton, of Philadelphia, who desires to go with you. These gentlemen will doubtless lay in their own stores, and pay as customary for their accommodations; and I am persuaded you will find them agreeable company.

"Mr. Lee and Mr. Izard propose also to take their passages in your ship, whom I hope you can likewise accommodate. Pray write me immediately your sentiments on these particulars, and let me know at the same time when you think you can be ready, that I may forward my despatches.

"I am glad to hear that your indisposition is wearing off. I hope your health will soon be re-established, being, with sincere esteem, dear sir,

"Your most obedient and most humble servant,

"B. Franklin."

"*L'Orient, February 25th,* 1780.

"His Excellency Benjamin Franklin.

"I am honored with your Excellency's letter of the 19th. I feel your reasons for urging frugality, and as I have not hitherto been among the most extravagant servants of America, so you may depend on it my regard for you will make me particularly nice in my present situation. It will give me very great pleasure to be able to carry to America the supplies of arms and clothing you mention, and I hope to be able to cram a great part, if not the whole, into the Alliance. Should any remain, I hope Captain Bell will be able to take them on board the Luzerne, and it is likely that he will sail with the Alliance. I will pay the most cheerful regard to the accommodation of the four gentlemen that you mention as passengers. I hope they will agree together, and I shall be happy in showing them attentions. I am in the greatest want of a lieutenant.

"With the most affectionate respect and esteem,

"I am your Excellency's very obliged, humble servant."

"*Passy, June 1st*, 1780.

"The Honorable Commodore JONES, Commander of the Alliance frigate, in the service of the United States.

"SIR,

"I have received a letter from the Board of Admiralty, containing their orders for the return of the Alliance, a copy of which is annexed for your government; and I hereby direct that you carry the same into execution with all possible expedition.

"With great regard, I am, sir,

"Your most obedient and most humble servant,

"B. FRANKLIN."

"*Board of Admiralty,*
"*Philadelphia, March 28th*, 1780.

"His Excellency BENJAMIN FRANKLIN.

"Sir,

"By the annexed list you will perceive the present disposition of the continental navy in North America. The detachment of four ships to guard the harbor of Charlestown has subjected our coasts to the depredations of the enemy's armed vessels from New York, who of late have frequently appeared in our bays and made many captures.

"For these reasons the Board think it will be necessary that the frigate Alliance should be forthwith ordered to proceed for this port, and should any supplies for our navy be ready in France, a part may be sent in the Alliance, and the residue in other armed vessels under her convoy.

"I have the honor to be,

"Your Excellency's most obedient servant,

"By order. "FRA. LEWIS.

P. S.—The Board would be highly obliged to your Excellency to send them a set of drafts of the new ships in the royal navy of France for the use of our master builders."

In writing to the President of Congress, on the 4th of March, 1780, Dr. Franklin informs Mr. Huntington that the Commodore was to return to America in the Alliance, and elucidates the course that had been taken with respect to the exchange of prisoners captured by Jones :—

"*Passy, March 4th*, 1780.

"SAMUEL HUNTINGTON, Esq. President of Congress.

"SIR,

"In my last I gave some account of the success of our little squadron under Commodore Jones. Three of their prizes sent into Bergen, in Norway, were, at the instance of the British minister, seized by order of the Court of Denmark, and delivered up to him. I have, with the approbation of the ministry here, drawn up and sent to that Court a memorial reclaiming the prizes. In the absence of Captain Landais from the Alliance, Commodore Jones took command of her, and on quitting the Texel, made a cruize through the Channel to Spain, and is since returned to L'Orient, where the ship is now refitting in order to return to America. Capt. Landais had not applied to me to be replaced in her, and I imagine has no thought of that kind, having before, on several occasions, expressed to me and others his dissatisfaction with his officers, and his inclination on that account to quit her. Capt. Jones will, therefore, carry her home, unless he should be prevailed with to enter another service, which, however, I think is not likely; though he has gained immense reputation all over Europe for his bravery. When the squadron of Commodore Jones arrived in the Texel with 500 English prisoners, I proposed exchanging there, but this was declined, in expectation, as I heard from England, of retaking them on their way to France. The stay of our ships in Holland, through the favor of the States, being prolonged, and the squadrons being stationed to intercept us, being tired of cruising for us, the British ministry consented at length to a cartel with France, and brought Frenchmen to Holland to exchange for these prisoners, instead of Americans. These proceedings have occasioned our poor people to be kept longer in confinement; but the minister of marine having given orders that I shall have as many English, another cartel with Americans is now daily expected, and I hope in a few months to see them all at liberty.

"I have the honor to be, &c.

"B. FRANKLIN."

On his visit to Paris the Commodore seems to have enjoyed the esteem of the French sovereign in a higher degree than ever. He was received with the utmost distinction at Court, and the following letter from M. de Sartine to the President of Congress, testifies that the king voluntarily presented him with a superb sword, and proposed to Congress to decorate him with the Order of Military Merit, a proposition which that body assented to:—

From M. DE SARTINE to Mr. HUNTINGTON, President of the Congress of the United States.

"*Versailles, May 30th*, 1780.

"Commodore Paul Jones, after having shown to all Europe, and particularly to the enemies of France and the United States, the most unquestionable proofs of his valor and talents, is about returning to America to give an account to Congress of the success of his military operations. I am convinced, Sir, that the reputation he has so justly acquired will precede him, and that the recital of his actions alone will suffice to prove to his fellow citizens that his abilities are equal to his courage. But the king has thought proper to add his suffrage and attention to the public opinion. He has expressly charged me to inform you how perfectly he is satisfied with the services of the Commodore, persuaded that Congress will render him the same justice. He has offered, as a proof of his esteem, to present him with a sword which cannot be placed in better hands, and likewise proposes to Congress to decorate this brave officer with the Cross of Military Merit. His Majesty conceives that this particular distinction, by holding forth the same honors to the two nations, united by the same interests, will be looked upon as one tie more that connects them, and will support that emulation which is so precious to the common cause. If, after having approved the conduct of the Commodore, it should be thought proper to give him the command of any new expedition to Europe, his Majesty will receive him again with pleasure, and presumes that Congress will oppose nothing that may be judged expedient to secure the success of his enterprises. My personal esteem for him induces me to recommend him very particularly to you, Sir, and I dare flatter myself that the reception he will receive from Congress and you, will warrant the sentiments with which he has inspired me.

"I have the honor of being, &c.

"De Sartine."

The following resolution of Congress shows the sense of that exalted body of the services rendered by Commodore Jones, and permits his acceptance of the Cross of Military Merit offered to him by His Most Christian Majesty :—

"In Congress, *February 27th*, 1781.

"The Committee to whom was referred the letter of May 30th, 1780, from M. de Sartine, delivered in a report, whereupon

"*Resolved*, That the Congress entertain a high sense of the distinguished bravery and military conduct of John Paul Jones, Esq. captain in the navy of the United States, and particularly in his victory over the British frigate Serapis on the coast of England, which was attended with circumstances so brilliant as to excite general applause and admiration:

"That the minister plenipotentiary of these United States at the Court of Versailles, communicate to His Most Christian Majesty the high satisfaction Congress have received from the conduct and gallant behavior of Captain John Paul Jones, which have merited the attention and approbation of His Most Christian Majesty, and that His Majesty's offer of adorning Captain Jones with a Cross of Military Merit is highly acceptable to Congress.

[Extract from the minutes.]

"C. Thompson, *Secretary*."

In consequence M. de la Luzerne gave a fête to all the members of Congress, and to the principal inhabitants of Philadelphia, and in their presence he, in the name of His Majesty, invested the Commodore with the Order of Military Merit.

The naval means of America in 1780 were exceedingly limited, and the necessity of detaching four ships to guard the harbor of Charleston, rendered it expedient to recall the Alliance to the United States to aid in the protection of the coasts from the depredations of the enemy's armed vessels, especially from New York, whence they cruised in the bays of the continent, making a number of captures. An order was despatched by the Board of Admiralty, on the 28th of March, 1780, to our minister in France to send the Alliance home, which order Dr, Franklin communicated to Commodore Jones on the 1st of June, 1780. On the same day that minister prepared and gave to the Commodore the annexed unequivocal letter of approbation:

"*Passy, June* 1, 1780.

"SAMUEL HUNTINGTON, Esq. President of Congress.

"SIR,

"Commodore Jones, who by his bravery and conduct has done great honor to the American flag, desires to have that also of presenting a line to the hands of your Excellency. I cheerfully comply with his request, in recommending him to the notice of Congress and to your Excellency's protection, though his actions are more effectual recommendations, and render any from me unnecessary. It gives me, however, an opportunity of showing my readiness to do justice to merit, and of professing the esteem and respect with which I am, &c.

"B. FRANKLIN."

On the 30th of May, Dr. Franklin had written to M. de Sartine for the purpose of ascertaining whether his Majesty would consent that one of his vessels should accompany the Alliance for the conveyance of supplies for the United States. In reply, on the 30th of June, M. de Sartine intimated the king's willingness, and assured the American minister that directions had been given at L'Orient to afford to Commodore Jones every facility that he might require for his armament and departure. The Commodore had stated to M. de Sartine, that seamen for the additional vessel might be obtained from the Alliance.

On the 28th of June, 1780, M. de Sartine addressed a very flattering letter to Commodore Jones, apprising him that the Cross of the Institution of Military Merit, agreeably to the king's previous determination, was enclosed in a despatch to M. de la Luzerne, the minister of France near the United States, of which Jones was to be the bearer, and with which cross he was to be invested by a chevalier of the order as soon as Congress had assented to his acceptance of it. M. de Sartine likewise informed him that His Majesty had directed a golden headed sword to be made for him, which would be immediately delivered to him. The letter is in the following words:—

"*Versailles, June 28th*, 1780.

"Mr. PAUL JONES, Commodore in the Navy of the United States of America.

"SIR,

"The king has already testified his approbation of the zeal and valor which you have displayed in Europe, in support of the common cause between the United States and his majesty, and he has also informed you of the distinguished proofs he is disposed to give you thereof. Persuaded that the United States will give their consent that you should receive the cross of the institution of Military Merit, I send you in the packet addressed to M. de la Luzerne, the one designed for you. You will be pleased to deliver him this packet, and he will confer on you this distinction by a chevalier of the institution, agreeably to his majesty's orders. But at any rate that you should have a proof of the king's approbation and munificence, his majesty has ordered a gold headed sword to be made for you, which will be immediately delivered to you, and he has the greatest confidence in the use you will make of it for his glory and that of the United States. I have the honor, &c.

"DE SARTINE."

Commodore Jones was extremely grateful for the marks of distinction thus conferred upon him, and expressed his feelings in the most fervent manner in his correspondence with his friends. To one of them, Mr. Genet, he wrote under date of the 19th of July, 1780, "I am bound by gratitude and honor to give every proof in my power of my affection to France. Tell M. de Sartine, and the rest of the king's ministers, that I would rather be shot to death than suffered to pine away in idleness, while our glorious cause is undetermined. I shall not die happy, unless they give me an opportunity to prove by my actions how much I wish always to merit the favor of the king, his ministers, and the nation. My best wishes will ever attend my friends in this kingdom, for their liberal minds do honor to human nature."

Arrived at L'Orient, from Paris, Jones found that Landais, who seemed to be his evil genius, had, in his absence, excited a refractory disposition in the crew of the Alliance, which had the effect of preventing the commodore from taking the command of that frigate, and obliged him to sail for America on board the Ariel. The board of admiralty afterward took cognizance of the dispute between Commodore Jones and Captain Landais: and having propounded questions to Dr. Franklin, in order to elicit information, that minister answered them, explained the circumstances which had occasioned so much chagrin to Jones, and produced the unprofitable dissensions between him, Landais, and the crew of the Alliance. With his answers was forwarded a copy of the "*concordat*," the signing of which Jones so deeply regretted, and from which sprung almost all his disagreements with Captain Landais, and M. Le Ray de Chaumont. The former, he conceived, had availed himself of the community of interests established by the "*concordat*," to treat his orders with contempt, and the latter he thought had not acted correctly towards him in relation to the prizes taken from the enemy. In illustrating more particularly the sources of all the commodore's disquietudes, a date is here anticipated, to lay at once before the reader Dr.

Franklin's letter and answers to the board of Admiralty, and a copy of the "*concordat*," which will render more intelligible the allusions in some of Jones's letters written previously to that of Dr. Franklin to Francis Lewis, Esq.

"*Passy, March* 17*th*, 1781.

"FRANCIS LEWIS, Esq., and the Board of Admiralty.

"GENTLEMEN,

"I received the honor of yours, dated January the 2d, containing sundry questions relative to the ship Alliance, and the expedition under the command of John Paul Jones, Esq.

"I would remark as to the expedition in general that this court having, I suppose, some enterprise in view, which Captain Jones, who had signalized his bravery in taking the Drake, was thought a proper person to conduct, had soon after the action requested we would spare him to them, which was the more readily agreed to, as a difference subsisted between him and his lieutenant, which laid us under a difficulty that was by this means got over. Some time passed, however, before any steps were taken to employ him in a manner agreeable to him, and possibly the first project was laid aside, many difficulties attending any attempt of introducing a foreign officer into the French marine, as it disturbs the order of their promotion, &c., and he himself choosing to act rather under the commission of Congress. However, a project was at length found, by furnishing him with some of the king's ships, the officers of which were to have temporary American commissions, which being posterior in date to his commission, would put them naturally under his command for the time, and the final intention, after various changes, was to intercept the Baltic fleet: the Alliance was, at that time, under orders to carry Mr. Adams back to America, but the minister of the marine, by a written letter, requesting I would lend her to strengthen the little squadron, and offering a passage to Mr. Adams in one of the King's ships, I consented to their request, hoping that, besides obliging the minister, I might obtain the disposition of some prisoners, to exchange for our countrymen in England."

Questions of the Admiralty Board, respecting the squadron under the Chevalier John Paul Jones, answered.

"*Question.* Whether any agreement was made by you, or any person in your behalf, with the owners of the ships *concerted* with the Alliance in that expedition, respecting the shares they were severally to draw of the prizes which might be taken during that expedition?

"*Answer.* I never made such an agreement, nor any person in my behalf. I lent the Alliance to the King, simply at the minister's request, supposing it would be agreeable to Congress to oblige their ally; and that the division, if there should be anything to divide, would be according to the laws of France, or of America, as should be found most equitable. But the Captains, before they sailed, entered into an agreement, called the concordat, to divide according to the rules of America, as they acted under American commissions and colors.

"*Ques.* What orders were given to Captain Landais?

"*Ans.* That he should obey the orders of Captain Jones.

"*Ques.* What was the ground of the disputes between Captain Jones and him?

"*Ans.* That when at sea together, he refused to obey Captain Jones's orders.

"*Ques.* Why did the Alliance lay so long at Port L'Orient after her arrival there from the Texel, and in general every information in your power respecting the Alliance and the expedition referred to?

"*Ans.* Her laying so long at L'Orient was first occasioned by the mutinous disposition of the officers and men, who refused to raise the anchors until they should receive wages and prize-money. I did not conceive they had a right to demand payment of wages in a foreign country, or anywhere but at the port they came from, no one here knowing on what terms they were engaged, what they had received, or what was due to them. The prize-money I wished them to have, but as that could not soon be obtained, I thought it wrong in them to detain the vessel on that account, and as I was informed many of them were in want of necessaries, I advanced 24,000 livres on account, and put it into Captain Jones's hands to relieve and pacify them, that they might go more willingly. But they were encouraged by some meddling passengers to persist. The King would have taken the prizes, and paid for them, at the rate per gun, &c., as he pays for warlike vessels taken by his ships; but they raised a clamor at this, it being put into their heads that it was a project for cheating them, and they demanded a sale by auction. The minister, who usually gives more when ships are taken for the King than they will produce by auction, readily consented to this, when I asked it of him; but then this method required time to have them inventoried, advertised in different ports, to create a fuller concurrence of buyers, &c.; Captain Jones came up to Paris to hasten the proceedings; in his absence Capt. Landais, by the advice of Mr. Lee and Commodore Gillon, took possession of the ship, and kept her long in writing up to Paris, waiting answers, &c.

"As the ministry had reasons, if some of the first plans had been pursued, to wish the expedition might be understood as American, the instructions were to be given by me, and the outfit was committed to Monsieur de Chaumont, known to be one of our friends, and well acquainted with such affairs. Monsieur le Marquis de la Fayette, who was to have been concerned in the execution, can probably acquaint you with those reasons; if not, I shall do it hereafter. It afterward continued in the hands of M. de Chaumont to the end. I never paid or received a farthing, directly or indirectly, on account of the expedition; and the captains having made him their trustee and agent, it is to him they are to apply for their proportions of the captures."

Concordat made between Captain John Paul Jones and the officers of the Squadron.

"*Agreement* between Messieurs John Paul Jones, captain of the Bon homme Richard; Pierre Landais, captain of the Alliance; Dennis Nicolas Cottineau, captain of the Pallas; Joseph Verage, captain of the Stagg; and Philip Nicolas Ricot, captain of the Vengeance; composing a squadron that shall be commanded by the oldest officer of the highest grade, and so on in succession in case of death or retreat. None of the said commanders, whilst they are not separated from the said squadron, by order of the minister, shall act but by virtue of the brevet, which they shall have obtained from the United States of America, and it is agreed that the flag of the United States shall be displayed.

"The division of the prizes to the superior officers and crews of the said squadron, shall be made agreeable to the American laws; but it is agreed, that the proportion of the whole, coming to each vessel in the squadron, shall be regulated by the minister of the marine department of France, and the Minister Plenipotentiary of the United States of America.

"A copy of the American laws shall be annexed to the present agreement, after having been certified by the commander of the Bon homme Richard; but as the said laws cannot foresee nor determine as to what may concern the vessels and subjects of other nations, it is expressly agreed, that whatever may be contrary to them should be regulated by the minister of the French marine, and the Minister Plenipotentiary of the United States of America.

"It is likewise agreed that the orders given by the Minister of the French Marine, and the Minister Plenipotentiary of the United States, shall be executed.

"Considering the necessity there is of preserving the interests of each individual, the prizes that shall be taken shall be remitted to the orders of Monsieur Le Ray de Chaumont, honorary intendant of the Royal Hotel of Invalids, who has furnished the expenses of the armament of the said squadron.

"It has been agreed, that M. le Ray de Chaumont be requested not to give up the part of the prizes coming to all the crews, and to each individual of the said squadron, but to their order, and to be responsible for the same in his own and proper name.

"Whereas the said squadron has been formed for the purpose of injuring the common enemies of France and America, it has been agreed that such armed vessels, whether French or American, may be associated therewith by common consent, as shall be found suitable for the purpose, and that they shall have such proportion of the prizes which shall be taken, as the laws of their respective countries allow them.

"In case of the death of any of the before mentioned commanders of vessels, he shall be replaced agreeably to the order of the tariff, with liberty, however, for the successor to choose whether he will remain on board his own vessel, and give up to the next in order the command of the vacant ship.

"It has moreover been agreed, that the commander of the Stag shall be excepted from the last article of this present agreement, because in case of a disaster to M. de Varage it shall be replaced by his second in command, and so on by the other officers of his cutter the Stag.

"J. P. JONES,
"P. LANDAIS,
"DE COTTINEAU,
"DE VARAGE,
"LE RAY DE CHAUMONT,
"P. RICOT."

The controversy between Commodore Jones and Captain Landais, respecting the command of the Alliance, was, as Jones believed, secretly fomented by Mr. Arthur Lee, who, acting as an umpire in the case, assigned the command of the frigate to Landais. The annexed letter from that gentleman to Commodore Jones will explain his avowed reasons for this preference:

"*L'Orient, June 13th*, 1780.

"Captain J. P. JONES.

"SIR,

"When you showed me yesterday the authorities under which you conceive you had a right to command the Alliance frigate, I told you it was not in my power to give you an opinion upon them without seeing those of Captain Landais; and that I would not give an opinion in this matter but in writing. Since that I have seen the authorities of Captain Landais, and I now shall state them both, with my opinion upon them; which I hope may be of use in preventing any farther contest, which cannot but be disgraceful and injurious to the service, as well as to those who are in the wrong.

"The authorities you showed me, consisted of a commission from Congress appointing you a captain in the marine of the United States, and a late order from Dr. Franklin to you, to take command of the Alliance, and carry her where she is ordered by the Admiralty. This order from Dr. Franklin does not recite or allege any power from Congress to take the command from Captain Landais, and put another in his place.

"The authorities Captain Landais laid before me, were a commission from Congress, like yours, appointing him captain in the service;—a resolve of Congress giving him the command of the Alliance frigate; and a letter of instructions for that purpose from the Marine Committee.

"From these documents it is clear, beyond a possibility of doubt, that Captain Landais commands that ship under the full, direct, and express order of Congress; and that no such authority appears to dismiss him from the command. In this situation Captain Landais must answer at his peril for the frigate entrusted to him till he receives an order of Congress to deliver her to another. If any such order exists, those who have it do infinite wrong to the service in not producing it, to prevent any disturbance. If there is no such order, the subjects of the United States who attempt to divest Captain Landais of the command he holds from the sovereign power, or to disturb him by violence in the exercise of it, commit a high crime against the laws and sovereignty of the United States, and subject themselves to a proportionable punishment.

"This, Sir, is my opinion founded upon a cool and candid consideration of the authorities on both sides; which alone ought to determine our judgment and our actions. You are at liberty to show this letter to whom you please, or to send it to Dr. Franklin. Should it prevail upon you to urge this matter no farther till you know whether there is authority of Congress for what you are doing, I shall think I have rendered no less service to you personally, in preventing you from committing a rash and illegal action, than to the public, the honor of which must be committed by such a contest in a foreign port. When I see such things threatened, my duty to my country, and the love of law and order, call upon me to do whatever is in my power to prevent them.

"I have the honor to be, &c.

"Arthur Lee."

Mr. Lee, however, was unquestionably in the wrong. Landais had resigned the command of the Alliance, had requested and obtained money from Dr. Franklin to repair to America, under the pretext of having his conduct investigated, and Jones had received instructions both from Dr. Franklin and the court of France, to carry the frigate back to the United States. An order, in fact, was issued by the French minister of marine to stop the sailing of the Alliance, if she attempted to proceed under the directions of Landais. But Commodore Jones, justly apprehending the consequences of violent measures, declined employing the means within his power to prevent her departure. Jones himself attributed the partiality of Mr. Lee for Landais to improper motives. "I am convinced," said he in a letter to Mr. Morris, of the 27th of June, 1780, "that Mr. Lee has acted in this matter merely because I would not become the enemy of the venerable, the wise, and good Franklin, whose heart and head does, and always will do honor to human nature. I know the great and good in this kingdom better, perhaps, than any other American who has appeared in Europe since the treaty of alliance: and if my testimony would add anything to Franklin's reputation, I could witness the universal veneration and esteem with which his name inspires all ranks, not only at Versailles and all over this kingdom, but also in Spain and in Holland: and I can add, from the testimony of the first characters of other nations, that, with him, envy itself is dumb, when the name of Franklin is but mentioned."

Dr. Franklin was aware of Mr. Lee's proceedings. He had given directions that he should have a passage home to America in the Alliance; but on learning that he had been instrumental in promoting disaffection among the crew, he wrote to Jones, revoking the order:

"*Passy, June 17th*, 1780.

"Honorable Commodore Jones,

"Sir,

"Having been informed by several gentlemen of and from L'Orient, that it is there generally understood the meeting on board your ship has been advised or promoted by the Hon. Arthur Lee, Esq. whom I had ordered you to receive as a passenger; I hereby withdraw that order so far as to leave the execution of it to your discretion; that if from the circumstances which have come to your knowledge, it should appear to you, that the peace and good government of the ship during the voyage may be endangered by his presence, you may decline taking that gentleman; which, I apprehend, need not obstruct his return to America, as there are several ships going under your convoy, and no doubt many of their passengers may be prevailed with to change places. But if you judge these suspicions groundless, you will comply with the order aforesaid.

"I have the honor to be, &c.

"B. Franklin."

Jones was the more mortified at the delay which these bickerings occasioned in the sailing of the Alliance, as she had on board stores for the use of the United States, which were much wanted for the supply of the American army. In a letter to Madame T———, of the 24th of July, 1780, he adverted to the affair between himself and Landais in the following manner:—

"*L'Orient, July 24th*, 1780.

"Madam,

"When you did me the honor to ask my promise to write to you a particular account of my services in this revolution and of my late expedition, I thought myself very happy indeed in enjoying that pleasing proof of your attention; and it was my firm intention to have fulfilled my promise with you on that head, immediately after my return here. Had I undertaken to write my own history to a lady of a less elevated mind than Madame T———, I should have run too great a risk, especially in what relates to my last battle; many circumstances of which are not yet known to the world, and are of such a nature as not to be believed by an ordinary mind upon the evidence of an individual. With you, Madam, I have not the remotest doubt, and the extraordinary event that took place here with respect to the Alliance is the only reason that has withheld my pen. I confess to you I feel rather ashamed that such an event should have happened, although God knows it was not owing to any fault of mine. The true reason was, M. le Ray de Chaumont unjustly detained from the brave Americans who had so well served in the squadron under my command, not only their wages but also their prize-money; and he has not, even to this hour, given the means of paying them their just claims. One or two envious persons here, taking advantage of these circumstances, persuaded these poor people that I had joined with M. de Chaumont to detain from them their just dues; and that it was besides my intention to carry them on new expeditions in Europe, and not to suffer them to return to their families in America during the war. These insinuations were false and groundless. I had disapproved the conduct of M. le Ray de Chaumont so much as neither to speak nor write to him after my return to France. My sole business at Court was to obtain the free sale of the prizes, which I effected. And far from being then bound on new expeditions in Europe, I was ordered by the Board of Admiralty in America to return forthwith to Congress, and had in consequence received the public despatches both from Mr. Franklin and the Court. The Alliance, however, was hurried out of this port before the crew had time for reflection; yet before they sailed from the Road of Groaix many of them, seeing their error, refused to weigh anchor, and were carried to sea confined hands and feet in irons. The government of France had taken measures to stop the ship, but I interposed to prevent bloodshed between the subjects of the two allied nations. I am now again almost ready to sail in the Ariel, and I know, soon after my arrival in America, that Congress will render me impartial justice. I will then have the happiness to furnish you with the account I promised, and the circumstances will be supported by the fullest evidence. I dare promise that it will then appear that I have only been to blame for having returned here from Paris, without having insisted absolutely on the previous payment of my men. Money is essential in war: in love, you will tell me perhaps, the case may be otherwise. I have still in contemplation to return to France soon after I arrive in America, for I have the most ardent desire to give the court, the nation, and my friends, farther proofs of my gratitude by my services in the glorious cause of freedom that France has so nobly espoused in concert with America. The singular honors I have lately received from the king have made the deepest and most lasting impression on my heart, and it shall be my constant care to deserve the continuance of His

Majesty's esteem. Although my departure is near, yet I hope to have the honor of a letter from you, before I sail. I hope my conduct will always merit your good opinion, and that you will honor me in consequence with your attention, and permit me to consider you as one of my best friends.

"I am, Madam,

"With the most profound respect, yours, &c."

As the name of the Alliance and that of Capt. Landais have been frequently introduced into this volume, in connexion with the occurrences incident to the life of Commodore Jones, it may not be unacceptable to the reader to be made more particularly acquainted with the history of the captain and of the ship. The only account of the former, within the reach of the author, is from the pen of Commodore Jones—and, as it is from that source, should be received with some degree of caution. In a memorandum, dated at Versailles, on the 17th of June, 1780, Jones stated, that, "When the treaty of alliance with France arrived in America, Congress, feeling the most lively sentiments of gratitude towards France, thought how they might manifest the satisfaction of the continent by some public act. The finest frigate in the service was on the stocks, ready to be launched, and it was resolved to call her the Alliance. M. Landais, a French subject, who had then arrived in America from France as master of a merchant ship laden with public stores, had reported that he had been a captain in the royal navy of France, had commanded a ship of the line, been a chief officer of the port of Brest, and was of such worth and estimation for his great abilities that he could have had any honors or advancement in his own country that he pleased to accept; but that his desire to serve America had induced him to leave his own country, and even to refuse to receive the Cross of St. Louis, that he might be at liberty to abjure the religion of his forefathers, which he did accordingly. Congress, believing M.

Landais to be in high esteem at the Court of Versailles, and thinking with reason that it would give pleasure to His Majesty to find that one of his worthy subjects had been treated with distinction in America, appointed him captain of the Alliance."

Capt. Landais was well known to the citizens of the United States, especially during the latter years of his life. He died on Long Island in the State of New York. For a considerable time prior to his death he was an annual petitioner to Congress, on whose sessions he often attended, to urge his claim for indemnity on account of his portion of the prize-money which ought to have accrued from three prizes sent into Norway, whilst he was in command of the Alliance in Europe. His temper, even in old age, appeared to be severe; for whilst at Washington he could not avoid betraying his irritability. A remarkable instance of this unhappy constitutional excitability is related of him with respect to a member of Congress who had spoken rather slightingly of him. Landais dressed himself in his uniform with a small sword by his side, and repaired to the gallery of the House of Representatives, when in session; indicating thereby, as well as in conversation with his acquaintances, that he was prepared to give any gentleman satisfaction who might be offended with him. He afterwards observed, quoting a remark ascribed to Henry IV. of France, that "if there was bad blood in Congress he would draw it." He affirmed to the last, that he, and not Jones, captured the Serapis, attributing her surrender entirely to his having raked her from the Alliance,—about which the reader has seen that his assertion was entirely void of foundation.

On the 2d of August, 1780, Jones addressed the following letter to the Count de Vergennes, and a similar one to the Count de Maurepas. The contents denote the activity of his mind, his continual anxiety for the furtherance of the American cause, and his accurate views of the best method of annoying the enemy. Of the ideas or plan to which he alludes in this letter there is no written statement in possession of the author, farther than what is contained in the answer of the Count de Maurepas which is subjoined :—

"*L'Orient*, *August 2d*, 1780.

"His Excellency M. le Compte de VERGENNES, &c.

"MY LORD,

"I should be unworthy of the illustrious marks that I have lately received of the royal favor, if I were not constantly impressed with the most ardent zeal to merit the continuance of his majesty's approbation, by an invariable attention to the mutual interests of France and America. Although my departure for America has been protracted by unforeseen events, it is not yet too late for government to pray the Congress that I may, during the remainder of this war, be constantly employed on active and useful services, tending to distract and distress the common enemy. After having been so highly honored by the kind attentions of the king's ministers, and their approbation of my poor services, I am convinced that I shall still find such support and protection from this government, as may enable me to prove my gratitude by my future actions.

"Since I had the honor of laying before your excellency, in the month of May last, my project for future expeditions, the events of the war have not so altered circumstances as to render my ideas inexpedient: on the contrary, the farther the war advances, I am the more confirmed in the utility that would result to the common cause from such services as I have therein hinted at. I was then happy in finding that your excellency approved of my ideas: It is therefore that I now enclose a copy, which I beseech your excellency to reconsider and lay before his majesty's privy council. If such expeditions as I wish to command were to be fitted out *in America*, I might be able with the greater certainty to strike the first blow by a complete surprise. Before the fleet of his majesty sailed from Brest the first time, under Count D'Orvilliers, M. de Chaumont told me it was the desire of government to have my ideas on private expeditions in writing. I gave him with great pleasure many ideas, from my long knowledge of the enemy's trade and situation, that might have proved of great advantage to our cause, and I wish M. de Chaumont had given all my then ideas to the court, although I am told he has taken credit for some of them as *his own*. I am now nearly ready for the sea with his majesty's sloop of war the Ariel, and I should be happy to carry with me to Congress the interest of this government for my promotion; but especially that I may be henceforth constantly employed in the most active and enterprising services, with such a force under my command as may enable me effectually to promote the interest of our glorious cause. This, my lord, would be my supreme ambition, actuated by no mean views of self-interest, but inspired by the purest principles of gratitude and philanthropy. It is upon this ground alone that I depend on the constant protection of the king, your excellency, and this government.

"It is absolutely necessary, my lord, to destroy the foreign commerce of the English, especially their trade to the Baltic, from whence they draw all the supplies for their marine. It is equally necessary to alarm their coasts, not only in the colonies abroad, but even in their islands at home. These things would distress and distract the enemy much more than many battles between fleets of equal force. England has carried on the war against America in a far more barbarous form than she durst have adopted against any power of Europe. America has a right to retaliate; and by our having the same language and customs with the enemy, we are in a situation to surprise their coasts and take such advantage of their unguarded situation, under the flag of America, as can never be done under the flag of France. This is not theory, for I have proved it by my experience; and if I have opportunity I will yet prove it more fully.

"I shall be happy, my lord, to be honored with your excellency's determination as soon as possible, as I purpose to proceed with the utmost expedition to Philadelphia, and as there is no time to lose in preparing for the operations of the next campaign.

"I am, my lord, your excellency's most obliged,

"Most obedient, and most humble servant."

" *Versailles, August* 15*th*, 1780.

"Com. Paul Jones.

"Sir,

"I have received with great pleasure, and read with attention, the letter wrote me the 2d instant from L'Orient. I have remarked therein the continuation of your zeal for the common cause. I have examined and communicated to M. de Sartine the project annexed to your letter, and we have no manner of doubt of the good effect that would result, were it entrusted to you. But at present it could not be said what number of frigates might be employed, they being all actually armed on account of the king, and the plan of the approaching campaign is not yet sufficiently determined, positively to say how many frigates may be given to you. But this need not prevent, if you have the consent of Congress, the execution of the first part of your scheme, to come here as you propose with the Alliance, and the other vessels which you may have, and with a sufficient American crew to arm the frigates which may join you. I will endeavor here to secure some for you, or to substitute privateers in their place. This is all I can inform you of for the present. The conduct you have observed, and the zeal you have shown for the service, must assure you of the readiness with which I shall always aid any enterprise in which you may be concerned. Be assured, sir, of the desire I have of rendering you any service, and convincing you of the sentiments with which,

"I am, &c.

"Maurepas."

On the 21st of September the commodore replied to the Count de Maurepas evincing the same resolute spirit of perseverance in the cause of American Independence, for which, from his first entrance into the service, he had been remarkable:

"*Ariel, Groaix, September 21st*, 1780.

"His Excellency M. le Compte de Maurepas, &c.

"My Lord,

"I received in its due course the letter that your excellency condescended to write me from Versailles the 15th ult., I having been detained in this road by contrary and stormy winds ever since the 4th current. I have postponed writing to you until I could tell you at the same time, the wind being fair, that I was immediately about to depart. The prospect is become promising this evening, and I hope to set sail to-morrow. My lord, I want words to express my thanks for your very kind letter; but it shall be the ambition of my life to merit your excellency's protection, and to exert all my abilities, such as they are, with double ardor, to prove my grateful attachment and zeal for the glory and interest of the king, his ministers, and this generous minded nation. By the four late ships that are arrived at L'Orient from Philadelphia, I learn that the Congress and all America were warmly my friends. This cannot but afford me real satisfaction as a citizen of America; and more especially because I shall be the better able to accomplish the first part of my project, agreeable to your excellency's proposal,—by providing the frigates and men in question in America, which will I fondly hope enable me effectually to promote the glory and success of the common cause. With the most lively sentiments of esteem and respect, I am,

"My lord," &c.

Commodore Jones proceeded from L'Orient to Groaix, on the 4th of September, and was detained in that road, by storms and contrary winds, until the 7th of October, 1780, when he put to sea in the Ariel the first time. She had the misfortune to be dismasted, which occasioned his return. To the dangers he escaped, he alludes in a letter to Dr. E. Bancroft, of the 17th of October:

"*L'Orient, October 17th*, 1780.

"E. Bancroft, Esq.

"Dear Sir,

"I am, my dear Sir, returned to France without laurels, and which is worse, *without having been able to render service to our cause.* I must refer you to Count de Vauban, the bearer of this letter, for a description of the late storm. I shall only say, it far exceeded all my former ideas of tempest. We must console ourselves that no lives were lost,—an event remarkably fortunate under such circumstances. You have no doubt received news from America. I have seen some of the papers, but find nothing very agreeable, except the address of the assembly of Rhode Island to the Count de Rochambeau and the answer. Mr. Wharton and myself would be glad to hear from you anything you find interesting. Lee had reached Philadelphia the night before one of Captain Hall's passengers left it; but we know nothing farther, except that no guns were fired, no bells were rung, nor bonfires made in consequence of so great an event! Your affairs are dry and safe, though many of our things are damaged, I mean our clothing and books, &c. Part of the powder, arms, and bread, &c. are wet. Count de Vauban behaved remarkably well, and appears to me to be a very worthy character. He is determined to use his interest with the Duke de Orleans, that the *Terpsicore* may be substituted for the Ariel.

"I am not less a friend now than I was formerly to Madam Chaumont and her family. Pray have you seen my fair friend the Countess of N.— she is, I understand, returned from Aix, and I am very anxious to hear from her.

"I am," &c.

A more particular account of this calamity is contained in the following document:

"We, the officers of the ship of war Ariel, in the service of the United States of America, do hereby declare, that having been detained in the road of Groaix by stormy and contrary winds from the 4th ult., so that it was impossible to proceed on our voyage to America before the 7th current; we on that day weighed anchor at 2 in the afternoon, the wind being at N.N.W. and the weather having a very good appearance. We had under convoy two brigantines belonging to America, named the Duke of Leinster and Luke, partly laden with public stores, and one lugger named the ——, belonging to France. In the night the wind fell very moderate, and the weather was very serene. At — o'clock in the morning of the 8th the wind sprung up a moderate breeze at S. by W. At 8 o'clock the island of Groaix bore by compass N.E. by E. distance 5 leagues. It was then squally weather with showers of rain, the wind at S. by W., and immediately afterward we lost sight of the land. The weather became very thick and the wind increased. By this time the storm had become so violent that the lee fore yard-arm was frequently under water. The lee gangway was laid entirely under the water, and the lee side of the waist was full. The water in the hold flowed into the cockpit, notwithstanding the utmost efforts of the chain pumps. In this distress at 11 we let drop the best bower anchor in 30 fathoms, but it would not bring the ship's head to the wind. The captain ordered the weather shrouds of the foremast to be cut, and the ship then brought up and rode head to the wind. The heel of the foremast carried away from the bow the stream and kedge anchors. The agitation of the elements was so violent that the mainmast could not stand, but reeled about like a man drunk. Orders were therefore given to cut away the starboard shrouds so as to let it fall over the larboard side to save, if possible, the mizenmast. Before this could be done the larboard shrouds and chain-plates gave way, and the mainmast fell over the starboard side, carrying with it the mizenmast and quarter gallery. The mainmast had worked the heel out of the step. The ship leaked, though less than might have been expected, and the people were employed at the pumps and to clear away the wreck; on the 9th, at noon, saw the sun, and observed the latitude 47 deg. and 47 min. The storm continued with very little intermission until the morning of the 10th, and the agitation rendered it impossible to erect jury-masts; we made the best preparation we could for that purpose, and succeeded so as to be able to cut our cable at 1 o'clock in the morning of the 11th. The wind had then come round to W.N.W., and we steered out S.S.W. till 4 o'clock, and finding then 10 fathom water, we bore away E.S.E. At 8 o'clock, steered easterly; at 10 o'clock saw the island of Groaix bearing E.N.E., and at 6 in the evening anchored in the road of Groaix. In the morning of the 12th we got a pilot from L'Orient, who, at 3 o'clock, brought the Ariel to an anchor in the harbor of L'Orient, where we now attest and subscribe all the circumstances of the within declaration as matters of fact. And we apprehend that part of the public stores on board are damaged. Done on board the Ariel in the harbor of L'Orient, this 13th of October, 1780."

Signed by the officers.

He sailed again on the 18th of December, and arrived safely in the United States.

The following extract from the journal, given by him to his majesty the King of France, will illustrate the dexterity with which on the following occasion he extricated himself from peril, and the more so at this particular time, as the Ariel was deeply laden with military stores for the use of the army :—

"After having met several vessels, I at last met the frigate Triumph of 20 guns, belonging to the British Navy.

"As that frigate sailed much faster than the Ariel I could not avoid an engagement, but I so well manœuvred and so well concealed my preparations for an engagement that the enemy thought of nothing else than making an easy conquest and a good prize.

"As the night approached the Triumph hailed the Ariel, and the enemy was much surprised to find he had to contend with a force so nearly equal to his own. As the two frigates carried the English flag, there ensued a conversation between the commander of the Triumph and me, by which I learned the situation of the English affairs in America. At last I pretended not to believe that the Triumph belonged to the British navy, and I insisted that the captain should come on board the Ariel to show me his commission. The captain excused himself by saying that his boats leaked, and that I had told him neither my name nor that of my frigate. I answered I had no account to give to him, and that I allowed him only five minutes to determine. That time having expired, and the Ariel being situated abreast and to leeward, about 30 feet distant, I hoisted the American flag and began the engagement. Never was I in any preceding action so much pleased as in this of the Ariel, with the regular and vigorous fire of the tops and the deck guns. This proceeded from the arrangement and preparation which had preceded the action, by placing the officers and passengers of the Ariel in different parts of the ship to prevent the men from deserting their posts, and to encourage them to do their duty; which proves the advantage of having good officers, for there never was a more indifferent crew than that of the Ariel.

"After a short resistance the enemy struck his colors; the captain of the Triumph begged for quarters, saying that he surrendered, and that half of his people were killed. I immediately ordered the firing to cease, and there were several huzzas on board the Ariel, as is usual after a victory; but a minute afterward the captain of the Triumph had the baseness to fill his sails and run away. It was not in my power to prevent this, the Triumph sailing much faster than the Ariel. But if the British government had that feeling of honor and justice which becomes a great nation, they would have delivered up to the United States that frigate as belonging to them; and would have punished in the most exemplary manner her captain, for having thus violated the laws of war, and the custom of civilized nations."

Complaints by Mr. Lee and Captain Landais had, no doubt, preceded him; for he was immediately afterward called upon by the Board of Admiralty to answer forty-seven interrogatories, the answers to which would embrace the whole of his public transactions, from the period of his departure from Portsmouth in the Ranger, until his return to the United States in the Ariel. On the 20th of February, 1781, Mr. John Brown enclosed the interrogatories to him in the subjoined terms:

"*Admiralty Office, February 20th*, 1781.

"Captain Paul Jones is hereby required to answer the following questions in writing, as soon as possible; and to produce the original orders.

"By order of the Board.

"JOHN BROWN, *Secretary*."

With this requisition Jones complied on the 21st of March, and as the copy of the answers is in his own handwriting, being indeed the original thereof, they are here introduced, as containing a precise narrative of the incidents of his life during a very interesting period of it:—

"*Philadelphia, March* , 1781.

"JOHN Brown, Esq., Secretary of Admiralty.

"SIR,

"I have the honor to give the following answers to the questions proposed to me by the Board of Admiralty, February 20th, and March 1st, 1781:—

"*Answer* 1*st.* I sailed from Portsmouth in New Hampshire, the first day of November, 1777, by order of the Marine Committee, dated September 6th, 1777; having on board the despatches respecting the victory of Saratoga, and being bound for France, to take command of a large ship then building for America at Amsterdam, agreeable to orders from the Secret Committee, dated May 9th, to the commissioners at Paris.

"2. I took two brigantines on the passage, laden with fruit, wine, &c., bound from Malaga for London. I ordered the prize masters to deliver them to the Continental agents, Mr. Thomas Morris and Mr. Alderman Lee, in France, in conformity to the orders I had formerly received from the Committee of Congress. One of these prizes arrived at Bordeaux, the other at Nantes. Being at Nantes myself, I proposed to send the one arrived there to America, finding she would fetch very little in France, but this Mr. Morris would not agree to. I believe Mr. Dunlap had his authority either from the agents or the commissioners. He had no appointment from me. He accounted at last for the captors' part of the sale to Mr. Williams, who paid them before the Ranger left France for America; and I suppose he accounted for the Continental part to the commissioners. The commissioners sent for me to Paris, to consult on future operations respecting the ship of war Indien, built for America at Amsterdam, and proposed to be put under my command; but after I had remained at Paris three weeks, the commissioners informed me they had assigned over the property of that ship to the King of France, whose property she still seems to be. As nothing had been hitherto done for the relief of the unfortunate Americans confined in English dungeons, I determined if possible to effect their exchange, and to put an end to the cruel burnings of our enemies on this continent. The commissioners were not in my secret, as appears by the unrestraining papers I then received from them, dated, Paris, January 15th, 16th, 17th, and 18th, 1778.

"I returned to Nantes, and sent the commissioners the scheme that was afterward adopted for Count d'Estaing's expedition. I also demanded and obtained a salute from the flag of France, both at Quiberon and at Brest, before the treaty of alliance was announced. I sailed from Brest in the Ranger into the Irish channel, made a descent at Whitehaven with 30 men only, surprised and took two strong forts, with 30 pieces of cannon, and set fire to the shipping, where there lay 300 or upwards, in the dry pier. That both the shipping and town, containing from forty to fifty thousand inhabitants, was not burnt to ashes, was owing to the backwardness of some persons under my command. I landed the day afterward in Scotland, in order to take some nobleman prisoner, as a hostage for the good treatment and exchange of our countrymen in England. The Earl of Selkirk lived near the shore, and it was my intention to take him; but he being from home, I was obliged to give way to the murmurs of my party, and suffer them to bring away the family plate. I have since purchased it, and restored it to the fair owner. We took the sloop of war Drake of 20 guns, and an hundred and seventy-five men, sent in pursuit of the Ranger. I had but an hundred and twenty-three men and 18 guns in the Ranger. We took also five other prizes, sunk three of them, and arrived with the Drake, the other two, and 200 prisoners, at Brest, May 7th, 1778, having been absent only 28 days.

"3. I am unable to say with certainty by whom the then agents were appointed. Mr. Morris was dead, and Mr. Sweighauser informed me by letter that Mr. Williams had nothing to do with public affairs, and that Mr. Alderman Lee, before he went to Germany, had appointed him (Mr. Sweighauser) as his deputy agent, &c. His conduct was not satisfactory to me, because his inquiry was only respecting the prizes; because he left me for a month, to cure my wounded, to feed my people, to guard my prisoners, and to refit the Ranger on my own credit; because my prizes were actually attached afterward for provision that had been furnished to the Ranger, by Monsieur Bersole, before that ship sailed on the expedition from Brest; because he sold my prizes at last, without my proper authority, and without giving the public proper notice of that sale; and because I believe he has not yet accounted to the crew of the Ranger for their share in their prizes, that were, I understand, while in his hands, shamefully plundered, and at last given away rather than sold. The second year after these transactions were ended, I authorized Mr. Williams to receive from Mr. Sweighauser what he pleased to allow as my share in these prizes, and Mr. Williams gave me credit in his account, in part of the moneys I had been obliged to borrow from my private friends. I do not remember the amount of what Mr. Williams received; nor do I find the account among my papers, that have been several times broken open.

"Perhaps Mr. Sweighauser had Alderman Lee's appointment confirmed by the commissioners, for his deputy assumed the agency at L'Orient immediately on the revolt of the Alliance, and went to a considerable expense, which he has since repented, as I understand, his bills having been refused by Mr. Franklin.

"4. The prisoners were guarded on board one of my prizes by French soldiers, and none escaped from the month of May until the middle of September. This guard cost America nothing; I obtained it on my own credit, and the soldiers were even fed at the King's expense. Many of them escaped afterward while they remained under the care of Mr. Sweighauser, and the remainder were at last exchanged for American seamen.

"5. I left the Ranger in the beginning of June, 1778, on an invitation from the Court of France, communicated to me by His Excellency B. Franklin, Esq., (which was afterward approved of by the commissioners,) in order, as it then appeared, to command the ship built for America at Amsterdam, that had been assigned over to the King by the commissioners. That ship to be, as I understood, presented to America, and supported under our flag by the King.

"6. I took command of the Bon homme Richard the 4th of February, 1779, agreeable to a letter of that date, addressed to me by His Excellency M. de Sartine.

"7. The Bon homme Richard was the property of the King, and all the squadron I commanded was at the expense of the crown of France. This is clear from a letter I received from His Excellency B. Franklin, Esq., dated 12th of August, 1780, &c.

"8. I have never borne nor acted under any other commission than that of the Congress of America.

"9. The squadron I commanded was at the first left entirely at my discretion, as well as the French troops that government proposed to embark. I had a variety of objects in view, and should have endeavored to execute some of the projects I had laid before the minister of the marine. But when the Marquis de la Fayette arrived in France, the court again sent for me express to L'Orient. It was determined the Marquis should command the troops;—the Alliance was made part of the squadron, and I received orders for an expedition, from His Excellency Benjamin Franklin, Esquire.

"10. The Alliance was put under my orders by His Excellency B. Franklin, Esq.

"11. The squadron being at first committed to my discretion, I had, as I have already said, a variety of objects, but no person was in my secret. I hope it is not doubted it was my intention to distress the enemy, and promote to the utmost of my ability the mutual interests of France and

America, and it is not improbable I might have appeared seasonably on this coast.

"12. I have already said I had a variety of objects in view. This will best appear by a general review of my correspondence. My first object was the cause of humanity to effect the liberty and exchange of our unfortunate fellow-citizens confined as 'pirates, felons, and traitors,' in the dungeons of England, and to put a stop to the savage burnings and wanton cruelties of the enemy on this continent. My second and last object has been the honor of the American flag. The orders I received in Europe will best explain the objects of the Court of France, and of the American minister at that court.

"13. The expense of the armament was paid by the Court of France, (the men's wages who belonged to the Bon homme Richard, and were carried away from L'Orient in irons on board the Alliance excepted,) these poor men were not paid owing to the revolt on board that ship, and the trifling idle excuses formerly made from time to time by M. le Ray de Chaumont, to whom government had entrusted the funds as a commissary for the expense of that armament. The Alliance appears to have been provided with stores and provision at the expense of the court from the time of joining the squadron until her return to L'Orient from Spain, the 10th day of February, 1780. But I did not find that the Court meant to pay the men's wages of that ship, though I endeavored to obtain that payment. I am uncertain whether the expense of the Alliance, after her return to L'Orient, was on account of the Court or of the United States: sometimes I believed the one, and sometimes the other.

"14. The Alliance was undoubtedly to share in prizes taken by the squadron, in proportion to the number of her men, and the number and calibre of her guns.

"15. I know of no ordinance made by the King respecting the squadron His Majesty put under my command. But as the squadron was under the flag of America, the officers appeared entitled to every advantage that any other officers may or can claim under the establishment of the marine laws of America, and the rules of the continental navy.

"16. I have given a particular account of my expedition from L'Orient round the west of Ireland, north of Scotland, and east of England, to the Texel, in a letter to the Minister of these States at the Court of Versailles, and to the Minister of the Marine, dated on board the Serapis, off the Texel, the 3d of October, 1779, copies whereof were sent to the President of Congress. I find on the return of 405 prisoners at the Texel, November 4th, 1779, 13 masters of merchantmen, so that the squadron took 15 sail, including the Serapis and Countess of Scarborough. I need not observe how much might have been done, if due subordination had prevailed in the squadron.

"17. A ship and two brigantines, taken by the squadron off the entrance of the Channel and west of Ireland, were ordered for France. The brigantines arrived at L'Orient, and were sold there. The ship was not heard of afterward. Two rich letter-of-marque ships were taken off the coast of Scotland, and Capt. Landais took upon himself, *even under my nose*, and without my knowledge, to order them to Bergen, in Norway, where they were given up to the English. A brigantine collier was sent, as I understand, to Dunkirk by Capt. Landais, during his second separation from the squadron in the East Sea. The Countess of Scarborough arrived, and was publicly sold at Dunkirk. The Serapis arrived, and was publicly sold at L'Orient. The rest of the prizes taken were either sunk, burnt or destroyed, except one brigantine from Holland for England that was retaken, and a small collier that I gave up to the master, on account of his attachment to America, and the faithful information and important services he rendered me by his general knowledge of the east coast of Britain, particularly in the Firth of Forth, in my projected enterprise against Leith and Edinburg. I had given orders to sink the old vessel, when the tears of that honest man prevailed over my intention. He became security for the good behavior and *payment* of the pilots of the Pallas and Vengeance.

"18. The officers and men of the Bon homme Richard and Alliance appointed Messrs. Gourlade and Moylan their agents for prizes. I had nothing to do with that appointment. I can give no certain account respecting the appointment of agents for the United States. But I hope my correspondence, which I wish to be examined respecting these prizes, will show I have done my utmost for the general good.

"19. I never received any account of the nett proceeds of the prizes taken by the squadron.

"20. The American officers and men did, I believe, receive from their agents, some part of their shares arising from the sale of the prizes taken by the squadron under my command; but what part they received I cannot say, it being their own private transaction.

"21. His Excellency Benjamin Franklin, Esq. wrote me the 4th of December, 1780, 'he understood the prize-money was not then received from the King.' My correspondence will, I hope, show I have done my best to obtain payment.

"22. I have always considered, and now consider the prisoners taken by the squadron I commanded as the property of the United States; and, I believe, Mr. Franklin had assurance from government to receive an equal number of prisoners in France to exchange for the Americans in England, before he sent me orders to deliver up the prisoners I had taken to the Duke de la Vauguyon, Ambassador of France in Holland. After

I returned to France, a cartel arrived at Morlex with an hundred Americans from England. I had occasion to lay before government a paper mentioning the American prisoners remaining in England, and nothing was either said or written to me by the king's ministers that could bear an unfavorable construction. On the contrary, Count Maurepas wrote me a very kind letter, expressing his general approbation of that paper.

"23. I had command of the Serapis from the time the Bon homme Richard sunk until she was remasted, repaired, and fit for sea at the Texel.

"24. When ready for sea, I received a letter from his Excellency, Benjamin Franklin, Esq. referring me to the ambassador of France who sent for me to Amsterdam, and, after a dispute of thirteen hours, I yielded to go from on board the Serapis to the command of the Alliance. This, as I afterward understood, was brought about through M. le Ray de Chaumont. This will best appear by my correspondence on that subject.

"25. When Capt. Landais received orders to appear at Paris, His Excellency Benjamin Franklin, Esq. wrote me either to appoint a commander for the Alliance, or take it upon myself. I had applied to him to name a commander, and he said he had no fit person. I was in the same predicament. Lieut. Degge was the senior officer on board, and my giving him an order to act as commander, was matter of necessity, not of choice; for, as I then expected to bring the Serapis to America, after having landed the prisoners in France, and as the Alliance was abominably dirty and out of order, I did not choose to go on board that ship as captain.

"26. I took command of the Alliance at last, by the authority and repeated order of His Excellency Benjamin Franklin, Esq. I may add I had also all the authority that could be given me by the Ambassador of France; and I conceive my own authority, as commander-in-chief of the squadron, might justify me, had I acted in consequence of it.

"27. The Alliance left the Texel the 27th of December, 1779.

"28. The Alliance arrived in Spain the 16th of January, 1780, and at Groaix without L'Orient, the 10th of February, 1780.

"29. At L'Orient the Alliance required very considerable repairs. She had not one good sail,—had left the Texel with only one anchor, and had I not procured two new cables from Amsterdam after I left the Serapis, I should have lost the Alliance at the Texel. I never found a frigate in so bad a condition. Epidemical disorders raged among the crew. The cutwater was loosened by laying in the trough of the swell in a gale of wind, while separated from the squadron in the North Sea. I was obliged to secure it with a hawser. The bowsprit was too long, ran out too much in a horizontal line, and was loose. The ballast was, a considerable part of it, laid before the magazine in the fore-peak, and on the breast hooks; the rest was ranged along the wings, cleeted up at a very considerable distance from the keel, and above the dead-rising. The remainder of it was laid in the afterpeak, and on the transums. The two foreguns had been carried and run out over the bow; the after guns run out at the stern ports. The top-masts, yards, and rigging were large enough for a sixty gun ship, and the tops were so ill made, and so narrow, as to give the masts no proper support. It is impossible to imagine a worse arrangement than that of the store-rooms. They were divided and subdivided into little closets, nooks, and winding passages, and, instead of being adapted to contain the ship's stores, appeared only fit to lodge dirt, and increase the quantity of rats, already immense. The magazine was not only inconvenient, but very insecure from fire, &c. There was no fit orlop for the cables, and the sail-room could contain at most only *one* of the spare courses. The deck was burnt through under the hearth, and the bottom of the copper burnt out. Many obstructions of useless hatchways, &c. were in the way of the recoil of the guns; and the gangways were so ill contrived as neither to afford a convenient passage from the quarter-deck to the forecastle, nor cover the men at the guns in the waist. The mizen-mast stood too close to the mainmast. The ship was very crank—plunged very deep in a head sea, and could neither sail nor work as a frigate. I began to put that ship in order immediately on my taking command; and after my arrival at L'Orient the essential repairs were finished early in April, by the crew of the ship and four or five American carpenters, hired from the Luzern to assist ours. The materials of the old arrangement did not fall much short of finishing the new. Judges have allowed that, when the business was finished, every thing about that frigate was perfect. I know not what was the amount of the disbursements. The accounts were never shewn to me; but I understand from Mr. Ross, an expense of 30 or 40,000 livres was contracted afterward, by Capt. Landais and his advisers, which Mr. Franklin refused to pay. I took on board the Alliance 28 18-pounders and 12 9-pounders that I had myself contracted for at Angouleme for the Bon homme Richard; also 76 chests of arms, and 216 barrels of powder from the king's magazine, and I had allotted a place for the bales of clothing, afterwards shipped in the brig Luke, which the Alliance could have carried without any inconvenience, and I should also have endeavored to take in part of the clothing that was made up.

"30. M. le Ray de Chaumont had promised from day to day, to remit the government monies to L'Orient, for the payment of wages, and also 100,000 livres, in part of prize-money, to be divided among the Americans of the squadron, then on board the Alliance; but at last, instead of complying with either, he prevailed on the Minister of the Marine to order the Serapis to be valued in the French way, for account of the King, and without giving the captors any satisfaction whatever, or obtaining their leave or consent, the workmen in the port began to rip up the orlop deck, and all the interior work of that ship. Messrs. Gourlade and Moylan did not interfere to prevent this. Mr. Lee took much pains to persuade the people they had been sailing with me *in a privateer*, would be detained in Europe during the war, and get nothing at last. I found it impossible to reason them into good humor, so as to go to sea; they positively declared they would not weigh anchor till they were fully paid, and wrote to this effect to Mr. Franklin. I was then greatly disgusted with the treatment that, *in appearance*, I had met with from M. de Sartine, but which in reality did not prove to be his fault but that of M. le Ray de Chaumont. But as I saw no way of overcoming my difficulties by remaining at L'Orient, I, with the advice of Mr. Samuel Wharton, and the majority of the Americans then assembled at L'Orient, waiting to proceed with me to America, went up to court to demand the free sale of our prizes, agreeable to the laws of the American navy. Mr. Franklin went with me to the minister who, contrary to my expectation, gave me the most friendly welcome, and sent immediate orders to publish the inventories and advertise the sale of all the prizes. This, however, took up more time than had been imagined. I improved this moment and the favorable disposition of government to ask for and obtain the Ariel, to assist the Alliance in transporting the clothing, &c. for our armies. I purposed to mount the Ariel with only 16 guns, with 60 or 80 men; and as I had left near 400 men in the Alliance, I had a crew sufficient for both ships. Thus the Ariel would have carried a large quantity of public stores, and no additional expense would have been incurred on account of that ship. The men must have been fed, whether in the Alliance or the Ariel, and being in part removed to the latter ship, the former would have had so much the less water and provision to carry. Upon learning that the sale of the prizes was protracted beyond expectation, I returned to L'Orient in the beginning of June, and as the sale was published, I hoped to be able to remove the idea of their having sailed in a '*privateer*,' and to be able to prevail with the people to leave the prize money to be settled by their agents in France, and to sail immediately with the two frigates and merchant ships that waited my convoy; but, to my great mortification, my scheme was entirely defeated by Mr. Lee, Capt. Landais, and his party.

"31. I know not exactly the date of Admiral de Terney's sailing from Brest for America, but think it was about the latter end of May.

"32. I understood it was proposed to charter two ships from Messrs. Bondfield and Haywood, for the purpose of transporting from France the clothing and stores for our armies, which was not concluded, because the terms were thought too extravagant.

"33. I know the Marquis de la Fayette took much pains to obtain clothing and stores from government. I never understood that the funds for such purchase were put into the hands of the minister plenipotentiary of these States. The arms and powder came directly from the King's manufactories. I understood M. le Ray de Chaumont was principally concerned in the purchase of the clothing, and that he employed Mr. Williams of Nantes, who drew his bills on M. le Ray de Chaumont, at sundry usances; but I am unable to say who employed M. le Ray de Chaumont, or who is now charged to ship the clothing and stores for America. Mr. Joseph Wharton, who was at Passy, and intimate both with Mr. Franklin and M. le Ray de Chaumont, when the purchase of clothing was made, and is now here, can, I believe, give a satisfactory answer respecting that transaction.

"34. The reasons already assigned will show why Admiral de Terney's convoy was not embraced for the Alliance.

"35. Captain Landais repossessed himself of the Alliance the 13th of June. Mr. Lee and the rest of his council can best answer why he sailed contrary to my orders, as well as the orders of Mr. Franklin. The passengers he had on board were, Mr. Lee and his two nephews, Mr. M. Livingston, Major Frazer, Mr. Brown, and three French officers now with the Marquis de la Fayette; I heard of no others. I cannot answer as to what private property might have been on board the Alliance, at the time she left France.

"36. The brig Luke appeared to be in very good condition when she left France—was, I understood, owned by Mr. James Moylan. I believe she had some private freight on board.

"37. I took command of the Ariel the beginning of June, when lent by the King, whose property she is, for a voyage from France to America, for the purpose I have already mentioned.

"38. I have already explained what was the object of my taking command of the Ariel. If I had any personal view, it was to appear here to answer for my past conduct. I have obeyed orders, and refer to my correspondence.

"39. I have already said I never commanded under any other commission than that of the Congress of these United States.

"40. I sent from France to the Board of Admiralty a declaration of my officers and men, showing that the Ariel sailed from L'Orient to Groaix the 4th of September, and was detained in that road by storms and contrary winds till the 7th of October, when I put to sea the first time.

"41. The Ariel had on board for the United States four hundred and thirty-seven barrels of powder, one hundred and forty-six chests of arms, a quantity of medicine, a quantity of 12 and 9 pound shot, and a small quantity of sheet lead.

"42. It was well known at Nantes and L'Orient what time I was ready to sail. The Luke, Duke of Leinster, and a French lugger, all bound here, sailed under my convoy. I had no official information, nor indeed any private certainty, respecting captains or agents having charge of the public stores of any kind—therefore I could not write to such persons *officially*.

"43. I put to sea with the Ariel the second time the 18th of December last.

"44. I had on board, when I last sailed, the articles I have mentioned in my last answer but two, except the arms, which being wet when the Ariel was dismasted, were left under the care of Messrs. Gourlade and Moylan.

"45. I never knew officially in Europe who were the American agents. The brig Luke sailed the second time about the last of October, before the Ariel was again masted. The clothing lay in the warehouse of Messrs. Gourlade and Moylan, the military stores being in the hands of the King's officers at Port Louis. Both were well acquainted with my time of sailing: I waited ten or twelve days with a fair wind for the despatches. I do not believe either the King's officers, or Messrs. Gourlade and Moylan, were authorized to ship any part of the public stores in their hands in any merchant ships that have, in the course of last year, been bound from France to America.

"46. No private merchandise came over in the Ariel to my knowledge. There was on board some 8 or 10 small trunks and boxes, which I conceive to have been presents to the gentlemen of Congress. Mr. Ross, an old servant to the public, had his books and accounts on board. The passengers had but little baggage. These trifling articles were put into my own store room: and I am above deriving any benefit or profit whatever either from the passengers or the articles here mentioned.

"47. The officers and crew of the Ariel are at the expense of the United States, they are enlisted for three years, except some few who entered at L'Orient for one year after the ship put back there, as will best appear by the entry book.

"Having thus endeavored to answer all the questions that have been put to me by the Board of Admiralty, I lay all my correspondence on the subject of this inquiry before that Board. I submit with the utmost deference my own conduct to the impartial inspection of the Board, and am, with great respect, sir,

"Yours, &c."

On the 14th of April ensuing, Congress, then in session, passed the following vote of thanks:

"By the UNITED STATES in CONGRESS assembled.

"*Saturday, April 14th*, 1781.

"On the report of a committee, consisting of Mr. Varnum, Mr. Houston, and Mr. Matthews, to whom was referred a motion of Mr. Varnum:

"The United States in Congress assembled, having taken into consideration the report of the Board of Admiralty of the 28th of March last, respecting the conduct of John Paul Jones, Esq., captain in the navy, do

Resolve, That the thanks of the United States in Congress assembled, be given to Captain John Paul Jones, for the zeal, prudence, and intrepidity with which he has supported the honor of the American flag; for his bold and successful enterprises to redeem from captivity the citizens of these States who had fallen under the power of the enemy; and in general for the good conduct and eminent services by which he has added lustre to his character, and to the American arms:

"That the thanks of the United States in Congress assembled, be also given to the officers and men who have faithfully served under him from time to time, for their steady affection to the cause of their country, and the bravery and perseverance they have manifested therein."

The subjoined letters from the Commander-in-Chief, General Lafayette, and the Hon. John Adams, express in very handsome terms, their opinion and conduct of the services of Commodore Jones:

"*Head-Quarters, New Windsor, May 19th*, 1781.

"The Chevalier PAUL JONES, Captain in the Navy of the United States.

"SIR,

"My partial acquaintance with either our naval or commercial affairs, makes it altogether impossible for me to account for the unfortunate delay of those articles of military stores and clothing which have been so long provided in France.

"Had I any particular reasons to have suspected you of being accessory to that delay, which I assure you has not been the case, my suspicion would have been removed by the very full and satisfactory answers which you have, to the best of my judgment, made to the questions proposed to you by the Board of Admiralty, and upon which that board have, in their report to Congress, testified the high sense which they entertain of your merit and services.

"Whether our naval affairs have in general been well or ill conducted, would be presumptuous in me to determine. Instances of bravery and good conduct in several of our officers, have not, however, been wanting: delicacy forbids me to mention that particular one which has attracted the admiration of all the world, and which has influenced the most illustrious monarch to confer a mark of his favor, which can only be obtained by a long and honorable service, or by the performance of some brilliant action.

"That you may long enjoy the reputation you have so justly acquired, is the sincere wish of,

"Sir, your most obedient and very humble servant,

"George Washington."

"*Alliance, off Boston, Dec.* 22*d*, 1781.

"John Paul Jones, Esq., Chevalier of the Royal Order of Military Merit, Commander of the ship of the line America, at Portsmouth in New Hampshire.

"Sir,

"I have been honored with your polite favor, my dear Paul Jones, but before it reached me I was already on board the Alliance, and every minute expecting to put to sea. It would have afforded me great satisfaction to pay my respects to the inhabitants of Portsmouth, and the State in which you are for the present. As to the pleasure to take you by the hand, my dear Paul Jones, you know my affectionate sentiments, and my very great regard for you, so that I need not add anything on that subject.

"Accept of my best thanks for the kind expressions in your letter. His lordship's (Lord Cornwallis) downfall is a great event; and the greater, as it was equally and amicably shared by the two allied nations. Your coming to the army I had the honor to command, would have been considered as a very flattering compliment to one who loves you and knows your worth. I am impatient to hear that you are ready to sail; and I am of opinion that we ought to unite under you every continental ship we can muster, with such a body of well appointed marines (trouper de mer) as might cut a good figure ashore, and then give you plenty of provisions and *carte blanche.*

"I am sorry I cannot see you: I also had many things to tell you.

Write me by good opportunities, but not often in ciphers, unless the matter is very important. On my arrival in France I will be able to let you know about the one you gave me, but am almost certain I have got it.

"Your friends will be happy to hear from you: and I, my dear sir, need not tell you that your letters will be gratefully acknowledged by, &c.

"LAFAYETTE."

"*Hague*, *August* 12*th*, 1782.

"JOHN PAUL JONES, Esq., Commander of the America, at Portsmouth, New Hampshire.

"DEAR SIR,

"I had yesterday the pleasure of receiving your favor of the 10th of December last, and am much obliged to you for your care of the articles which Mr. Moylan, at my desire, sent to my family.

"The command of the *America* could not have been more judiciously bestowed, and it is with impatience that I wish her at sea, where she will do honor to her name. Nothing gives me so much surprise, or so much regret, as the inattention of my countrymen to their navy: it is a bulwark as essential as it is to Great Britain. It is less costly than armies, and more easily removed from one end of the United States to the other. Our minister of finance used to be a great advocate for this kind of defence. I hope he has not altered his sentiments concerning it.

"Every day shows that the Batavians have not wholly lost their ancient character. They were always timid and slow in adopting their political systems, but always firm and able in support of them, and always brave and active in war. They have hitherto been restrained by their chiefs; but, if the war continues, they will show that they are possessed of the spirit of liberty, and that they have lost none of their great qualities.

"Rodney's victory has intoxicated Britain again to such a degree that I think there will be no peace for some time. Indeed, if I could see a prospect of half a dozen line-of-battle ships under the American flag, commanded by Commodore Paul Jones, engaged with an equal British force, I apprehend the event would be so glorious for the United States, and lay so sure a foundation for their prosperity, that it would be a rich compensation for a continuance of the war.

"However, it does not depend upon us to finish it. There is but one way to finish it, and that is—Burgoynizing Carlton in New York.

"I should be happy to hear from you, and remain, &c.

"JOHN ADAMS."

After remaining a short time in the United States, Jones was appointed on the 26th of June, 1781, unanimously by ballot, to the command of the America, one of the seventy-four gun ships ordered to be built by a resolution of Congress of the 20th of November, 1776.

The following is the resolution adopted on the occasion:

"IN CONGRESS, *June 26th*, 1781.

"Congress proceeded to the appointment of a captain to command the ship America 74, and the ballots being taken, John Paul Jones, Esq. was *unanimously* elected."

In superintending the construction of this vessel, he was engaged sixteen months. But the king of France having, about this time, lost a ship of that class from his navy, the United States made a present of the America to him to supply the place of the one that was lost.

The annexed is the resolution passed by Congress on the occasion:—

"IN CONGRESS, *September 3d*, 1782.

"Whereas the Magnifique, a 74 gun ship belonging to the fleet of His Most Christian Majesty, commanded by the Marquis de Vaudreuil, has been lately lost by accident in the harbor of Boston, and Congress are desirous of testifying on this occasion to his Majesty the sense they entertain of his generous exertions in behalf of the United States:

"*Resolved*, That the agent of marine be, and he is hereby instructed to present the America, a 74 gun ship, in the name of the United States, to the Chevalier de la Luzerne for the service of His Most Christian Majesty."

The following letter from the Hon. Robert Morris was written to Jones with the intention no doubt of soothing his feelings under this severe disappointment:—

"*Marine Office, Sept. 4th*, 1782.

"Chevalier Paul Jones,

"Dear Sir,

The enclosed resolution* will show you the destination of the ship America. Nothing could be more pleasing to me than this disposition, excepting so far as you are affected by it. I know you so well as to be convinced that it must give you great pain, and I sincerely sympathize with you; but, although you will undergo much concern at being deprived of this opportunity to reap laurels on your favorite field, yet your regard for France will in some measure alleviate it, and to this your good sense will naturally add the delays which must have happened in fitting this ship for sea. I must entreat of you to continue your inspection until she is launched, and to urge forward the business. When that is done if you will come hither, I will explain to you the reasons which led to this measure and my views for employing you in the service of your country. You will, on your route, have an opportunity of conferring with the General, on the place you mentioned to me in one of your letters.

"I pray you to believe me your affectionate friend, &c.

"Robert Morris."

Jones was then left without employment; and, ever impatient, when not occupied, he addressed in 1782 a long memorial to the United States' Minister of Marine, in which he set forth his claims to promotion, and submitted some projects and suggestions, which, had they been adopted, would have had the effect to bring him once more into service. As several passages in that memorial may prove interesting to our naval officers, a few of them are inserted from the rough draft in the hands of the author. Some of the extracts here published, appear to have been crossed and cancelled by Jones himself, so that they were probably not communicated to the Board of Admiralty.

* Resolution of Congress of September 3d, 1782, directing the presentation to His Majesty the King of France, of the America, to replace the Magnifique which had been lately lost by accident in the harbor of Boston.

"*Philadelphia, September 22d*, 1782.

"The United States Minister of Marine.

"Sir,

"The beginning of our navy, as navies now rank, was so singularly small, that I am of opinion it has no precedent in history. Was it a proof of madness in the first corps of sea officers, at so critical a period, to have launched out on the ocean with only two armed merchant ships, two armed brigantines, and one armed sloop, to make war against such a power as Great Britain?

"To be diffident is not always a proof of ignorance, but sometimes the contrary. I was offered a captain's commission at the first to command the Providence, but declined it. Let it, however, be remembered, that there were three grades of sea lieutenants established by the act of Congress of the 22d of December, 1775, and as I had the honor to be placed at the head of the first of those grades, it is not quite fair to confound me with the last. I had sailed before this Revolution in armed ships and frigates, yet when I came to try my skill, I am not ashamed to own I did not find myself perfect in the duties of a first lieutenant. If midnight study, and the instruction of the greatest and most learned sea officers, can have given me advantages, I am not without them. I confess, however, I have yet to learn. It is the work of many years' study and experience, to acquire the high degree of science necessary for a great sea officer. Cruising after merchant ships, the service in which our frigates have generally been employed, affords, I may say, no part of the knowledge necessary for conducting fleets and their operations. There is now, perhaps, as much difference between a battle between two ships and an engagement between two fleets, as there is between a duel and a ranged battle between two armies.

"The English, who boast so much of their navy, never fought a ranged battle on the ocean, before the war that is now ended. The battle off Ushant was, on their part, like their former ones, irregular; and Admiral Keppel could only justify himself by the example of Hawke in our remembrance, and of Russel in the last century. From that moment the English were forced to study and to imitate the French in their evolutions. They never gained any advantage when they had to do with equal force, and the unfortunate defeat of Count de Grasse was owing more to the unfavorable circumstance of the wind coming ahead four points at the beginning of the battle, which put his fleet into the order of echiquier when it was too late to tack, and of calms and currents afterward, which brought on an entire disorder, than to the admiralship or even the vast superiority of Rodney, who had forty sail of the line against thirty, and five three deckers against one. By the account of some of the French officers, Rodney might as well have been asleep, not having made a second signal during the battle, so that every captain did as he pleased.

"The English are very deficient in signals as well as in naval tactic. This I know, having in my possession their present fighting and sailing instructions, which comprehend all their signals and evolutions. Lord Howe has, indeed, made some improvements by borrowing from the French. But Kempenfelt, who seems to have been a more promising officer, had made still greater improvement, by the same means. It was said of Kempenfelt, when he was drowned in the Royal George, England had lost her du Pavillion. That great man, the Chevalier du Pavillion, commanded the Triumphant, and was killed in the last battle of Count de Grasse. France lost in him one of her greatest naval tacticians, and a man who had besides the honor, in 1773, to invent the new system of naval signals, by which 1600 orders, questions, answers, and informations, can, without confusion or misconstruction, and with the greatest celerity, be communicated through a great fleet. It was his fixed opinion that a smaller number of signals would be insufficient.

"A captain of the line must at this day be a tactician. A captain of a cruising frigate may make shift without having ever heard of naval tactics. Until I arrived in France, and became acquainted with that great tactician Count D'Orvilliers, and his judicious assistant the Chevalier du Pavillion, who each of them honored me with instructions respecting the science of governing the operations, &c., of a fleet, I confess I was not sensible how ignorant I had been before that time of naval tactics. I have already said there were three grades of sea lieutenants established by the act of Congress, of the 22d of December, 1775. If I may be allowed at this day to judge, it would be sound wisdom to re-adopt the same number of subaltern grades, exclusive of midshipmen, under the same, or some other denomination. From the observations I have made, and what I have read, it is my opinion, that in a navy there ought to be at least as many grades below a captain of the line, as there are below a colonel of a regiment. Even the navy of France is deficient in subaltern grades, and has paid dearly for that error in its constitution, joined to another of equal magnitude, which authorizes ensigns of the navy to take charge of a watch on board ships of the line. One instance may be sufficient to show this. The Zélé, in the night between the 11th and 12th of April, 1782, ran on board the Ville de Paris, which accident was the principal cause of the unfortunate battle that ensued next day between Count de Grasse and Admiral Rodney. That accident in all probability would not have happened, had the deck of the Zélé been at the time commanded by a steady experienced lieutenant of the line, instead of a young ensign. The charge of the deck of a ship of the line should, in my judgment, never be entrusted to an officer under twenty-five years of age. At that time of life he may be supposed to have served nine or ten years, a term not more than sufficient to have furnished him with the necessary knowledge for so great a charge. It is easy to conceive that the mind of officers must become uneasy, when they are continued too long in any one grade, which must happen (if regard be paid to the good of the service) where there are no more subaltern grades than midshipman and lieutenant. Would it not be wiser to raise young men by smaller steps and to increase the number? I have many things to offer respecting the formation of our navy, but shall here limit myself to one, which I think a preliminary to the formation and establishment of a naval constitution suitable to the local situation, resources, and prejudices of the Continent.

"The constitution adopted for the navy in the year 1775, and by which it has been governed ever since, and crumbled away I may say to nothing, is so very defective, that I am of opinion it would be difficult to spoil it. Much wisdom, and more knowledge than we possess, is, in my humble opinion, necessary to the formation of such a naval constitution as is absolutely wanting. If, when our finances enable us to go on, we should set out wrong, as we did in the year 1775, but much more so after the arrangement, or rather derangement of rank in 1776, much money may be thrown away to little or no purpose. We are a young people, and need not be ashamed to ask advice from nations older and more experienced in marine affairs than ourselves. This I conceive might be done in a manner that would be received as a compliment by several or perhaps all the marine powers of Europe, and at the same time would enable us to collect such helps as would be of vast use when we come to form a constitution for the creation and government of our marine, the establishment and police of our dock-yards, academies, hospitals, &c., and the general police of our seamen throughout the Continent. These considerations induced me, on my return from the fleet of His Excellency the Marquis de Vaudreuil, to propose to you to lay my ideas on the subject before Congress, and to propose sending a proper person to Europe in a hand some frigate, to display our flag in the ports of the different marine powers, to offer them the free use of our ports, and propose to them commercial advantages, &c. And then to ask permission to visit their marine arsenals, to be informed how they are furnished both with men, provision, materials, and war-like stores, by what police and officers they are governed, how and from what resources the officers and men are paid, &c.—The line of conduct drawn between the officers of the fleet and the officers of the ports, &c.—Also the armament and equipment of the different ships of war, with their dimensions, the number and qualities of their officers and men, by what police they are governed in port and at sea, how and from what resources they are fed, clothed, and paid, &c.; and the general police of their seamen, academies, hospitals, &c. If you still object to my projects on account of the expense of sending a frigate to Europe, and keeping her there till the business can be effected, I think it may be done, though perhaps not with the same dignity, without a frigate. My plan for forming a proper corps of sea officers, is by teaching them the naval tactics in a fleet of evolution. To lessen the expense as much as possible, I would compose that fleet of frigates instead of ships of the line; on board of each I would have a little academy, where the officers should be taught the principles of mathematics and mechanics, when off duty. When in port, the young officers should be obliged to attend at the academies established at each dock-yard, where they should be taught the principles of every art and science that is necessary to form the character of a great sea officer. And every commission officer of the navy should have free access, and be entitled to receive instruction gratis at those academies. All this would be attended with no very great expense, and the public advantage resulting from it would be immense. I am sensible it cannot be immediately adopted, and that we must first look about for ways and means; but the sooner it is adopted the better. We cannot, like the ancients, build a fleet in a month, and we ought to take example from what has lately befallen Holland.

"In time of peace it is necessary to prepare, and be always prepared for war by sea. I have had the honor to be presented with copies of the signals, tactics, and police that have been adopted under the different Admirals of France and Spain during the war, and have in my last campaign seen them put in practice. While I was at Brest, as well as while I was inspecting the building of the America, as I had furnished myself with good authors, I applied much of my leisure time to the study of naval architecture and other matters that relate to the establishment and police of dockyards, &c. I however feel myself bound to say again, I have yet much need to be instructed."

Disappointed in the command of the America, and unwilling to remain an idle spectator of the passing scene, Commodore Jones exerted himself to obtain permission from Congress to join the French fleet then in the United States, under the command of the Marquis de Vaudreuil on an expedition against the Island of Jamaica. In this application he was successful, being aided by his friend the Hon. R. Morris, who procured for him the gratification of his wishes:—

"*Marine Office, October 9th*, 1782.

"Chevalier PAUL JONES, Portsmouth.

"SIR,

"I have received your letter of the 22d of last month. The sentiments contained in it will always reflect the highest honor upon your character. They have made so strong an impression upon my mind that I immediately transmitted an extract of your letter to Congress. I doubt not but they will view it in the same manner which I have done.

"I am, &c.

"ROBERT MORRIS."

"*Marine Office, Philadelphia, Nov. 29th*, 1782.

"The PRESIDENT of Congress.

"SIR,

"I do myself the honor to enclose your Excellency the copy of a letter I received this morning from the Chevalier Paul Jones. The present state of our affairs does not permit me to employ that valuable officer, and I confess that it is with no small degree of concern that I consider the little probability of rendering his talents useful to that country, which he has already so faithfully served, and with so great disinterestedness.

"His present desire to be sent with the Marquis de Vaudreuil to join Count d'Estaing on his projected expedition from Cadiz against Jamaica, &c. consists with all his former conduct; and it will, I dare say, be a very pleasing reflection to Congress that he is about to pursue a knowledge of his profession, so as to become still more useful if ever he should be again called to the command of a squadron or fleet. I should do injustice to my own feelings, as well as to my country, if I did not most warmly recommend this gentleman to the notice of Congress whose favor he has certainly merited by the most signal services and sacrifices.

"I have the honor to be, &c.

"R. MORRIS."

"By the UNITED STATES in CONGRESS assembled, December 4th, 1782.

"On the report of a committee to whom was referred a letter of the 29th November, from the agent of marine, enclosing a copy of a letter of the same date to him from Capt. J. P. Jones,

"*Resolved*, That the agent of marine be informed that Congress having a high sense of the merit and services of Capt. J. P. Jones, and being disposed to favor the zeal manifested by him to acquire improvement in the line of his profession, do grant the permission which he requests; and that the said agent be instructed to recommend him accordingly to the countenance of His Excellency the Marquis de Vaudreuil.

"Extract from the minutes.

"GEORGE BOND, *Dep. Secretary.*"

Extract from the Journal of Commodore John Paul Jones, prepared by him for His Majesty, Louis XVI.

"When I foresaw that the plan concerted between M. La Luzerne and Mr. Morris, according to all appearances, would not succeed, I addressed Congress without loss of time. On the 4th of December, 1782, I obtained an act of that body, permitting me to embark on board the fleet of your Majesty at Boston, under the command of the Marquis de Vaudreuil, for the purpose of joining the Count D'Estaing in his expedition against Jamaica.

"The appearances were very favorable, since of all those who were appointed to serve in this expedition, no one knew the island of Jamaica so well as myself; and as the Marquis D'Estaing had commanded a fleet of more than seventy sail of the line and a large body of troops, I had the flattering hope of finding myself in the first military school in the world, in which I should be able to render myself useful, and to acquire knowledge very important for conducting great military operations.

"M. de Vaudreuil received me with distinction on board his own vessel, the Triumphant, and lodged me in his chamber of council with M. le Baron de Viomenil, who commanded the troops. By order of the Marquis de Vaudreuil a squadron, consisting of ten sails of the line, two frigates, and a cutter, left Boston the 24th of December. The intention of the Marquis was to join off Portsmouth, two other ships of the line, the Augustus and the Pluto which were then in that port, and under the command of his brother (for the America was not then ready to put to sea); but a storm and contrary winds prevented this junction, and placed the squadron in a dangerous situation, from the proximity of ice and the Bay of Fundy. The Admiral then made an attempt to join the Fantasque, with the troops which he brought from Rhode Island, with the same results. The squadron having lost sight of many vessels laden with troops, and twenty merchant vessels from Boston, directed its course towards the island of Porto Rico.

"When they came within sight of this island, the Marquis de Vaudreuil learnt that Admiral Hood was cruising off Cape Francois, with 16 sail of the line, and that Admiral Pigot, with a larger force, was at St. Lucie, so that the enemy would necessarily consider the squadron of the Marquis de Vaudreuil an easy prey which could not escape from Hood or from Pigot.

"M le Marquis de Vaudreuil remained off St. John's, Porto Rico, for ten days, and made all kinds of naval evolutions, and then he took sixteen sail of merchantmen, arrived from France, and convoyed them to the west end of that island.

"Some light vessels of observation, which Admiral Hood had sent on a cruise, perceived the squadron in the Mona Passage, and went immediately to inform him that the Marquis de Vaudreuil had sailed by the south side of St. Domingo, in order to go to some port on the west of that island, or on the east of Cuba for his expedition against Jamaica. They were mistaken; the squadron directed its course to the south, more to windward, and passed in sight of the island of Curaçoa, near the coast of South America.

"The rendezvous which had been fixed between Don Solano and the Marquis de Vaudreuil at Cape Francois, after the defeat of Count de Grasse, was kept in the greatest secrecy, and no person had the least suspicion that it was Porto Cabello about 20 leagues to the windward of Curaçoa. The squadron beat against the wind for three weeks along the coast, against a current which drove the merchant vessels out of sight to the leeward; and as he had neither pilots nor good charts of this coast on board the squadron, the Burgoyne, of 74 guns, ran upon a rock in the night, about two leagues from the coast, and was entirely lost with 200 men including officers, among the number was the first lieutenant. The Triumphant arrived at Porto Cabello the 18th of February, 1783; the Augustus and Pluto had arrived some days before, and the other vessels of the fleet betook themselves, one after another, to places of safety.

"Don Solano was to have joined the Marquis de Vaudreuil at Porto Cabello in December. He did not keep his word, and no news was received of his squadron at Porto Cabello. The anxiety which this disappointment occasioned, while at the same time no news was received from Europe, so affected the spirits of many of the officers that they fell sick, and I myself was dangerously ill.

"Finally, the news of a general peace was brought from France by a frigate. The most brilliant success and the most instructive experience in the art of war could not have given me a pleasure comparable to that which I received when I learned that Great Britain, after so long a contest, had been forced to acknowledge the independence and sovereignty of the United States of America.

"On the 8th of April, 1783, the day after the cessation of hostilities, the squadron left Porto Cabello, and after a passage of eight days, arrived in safety at Capt. Francois.

"The Spanish fleet had left Havana for Porto Cabello, and, on learning the news of the peace at Porto Cabello, directed its course for Cape Francois, and arrived there some days before the Marquis de Vaudreuil.

"I delayed but little time at Cape Francois, where I received the particular attentions of M. Belle Combe, the governor. I embarked then for Philadelphia, penetrated with gratitude for all the attentions which had been shown me by the Marquis de Vaudreuil, Baron Viomenil, and the other officers, during the five months I spent on board the fleet of your majesty.

"My health was not confirmed during the rest of the summer. I recovered it in the autumn from the use of the cold bath.

"I addressed myself then to Congress for authority to return to Europe, and there to arrange with the court of France the payment of the prize-money due to the officers and men who had served on board the squadron which I had commanded in Europe. And the Congress gave me the authority, by a resolution passed at Princeton, the 1st of September, 1783.

Copy of a letter from His Excellency the Marquis de Vaudreuil, Lieut. General of the Navy of France, Commander of the Royal and Military order of St. Louis, commanding the squadron of His Most Christian Majesty in the West Indies, to His Excellency the Chevalier de la Luzerne, Minister Plenipotentiary of France in America.

"*Cape Francois, April 20th*, 1783.

"Sir,

"The peace which has been so much desired, and which is going to make the happiness of America, since it puts the seal to her liberty, terminates our projects. We shall sail for France in a week with the troops under the command of the Baron de Viomenil. The other regiments will sail as soon as there will be vessels ready to transport them.

"Mr. Paul Jones, who had embarked with me, is about returning to his dear country. I was very glad to have him. His well deserved reputation had made him very acceptable to me, not doubting but that we would have had some opportunities in which his talents might have shone forth; but peace, of which I cannot but be glad, puts an obstacle in the way;—so we must part. Permit me, sir, to request of you the favor of recommending him to his superiors. The intimate acquaintance which I made with him since he has been on board the Triumphant, makes me take a lively interest in what concerns him, and I shall be very much obliged to you if you will find the means of being serviceable to him.

"Peace will not restore you to your country. On account of the great services which you render to France, it will be necessary for you to remain in America a long time; but you have the consolation to be amongst a people who love and respect you: thus it is for you a second home, which you have acquired by your virtues and talents.

"I am, &c.

"Le Marquis de Vaudreuil."

Desirous of procuring a final adjustment of the claim for prize-money due in Europe to himself and others, the Chevalier Jones applied to Congress to be appointed agent for the settlement of that business. The Congress consented, and, on the first of November, 1783, passed the following resolution:—

"In Congress, *November 1st*, 1783.

"On the report of Mr. S. Huntington, Mr. A. Lee, and Mr. Duane, to whom were referred a letter from Capt. John Paul Jones to the agent of marines, of the 13th of October, and a letter from him to Congress, of the 18th of the same month,

"*Resolved*, That Capt. John Paul Jones be, and he hereby is, recommended to the Minister Plenipotentiary of the United States at the court of Versailles, as agent, to solicit, under the direction of the said minister, for payment and satisfaction to the officers and crews for all prizes taken in Europe under his command, and to which they are anywise entitled. And the said Capt. John Paul Jones shall receive the commissions usually allowed in such cases out of the money which he shall recover, as agent for the said prizes, in full compensation for his services and expenses: *Provided always*, that the said Capt. John Paul Jones, previous to his entering upon the execution of the said trust, shall give to the Superintendent of Finance, for the benefit of all concerned, sufficient bonds, with good security, for the faithful discharge thereof, and for the just payment of the same to the said Superintendent of Finance, to be by him distributed to those persons who may be entitled thereto:

"*Resolved*, That the agent of marine provide Capt. Jones with a passage to France in the ship Washington."

Repairing to Paris, he there found a competitor in M. le Ray de Chaumont, who claimed to have been the one who planned the expedition for intercepting the Baltic fleet, to have had the direction of it under the orders of the king's ministers, and insisted that, as the cost of the enterprise had been defrayed by the treasury of France, the distribution of the prize-money ought to be made in pursuance of the provisions of the ordinances of the kingdom, which would have caused a deduction of four deniers per livre, for the benefit of the Hospital of Invalids, at Paris. To these pretensions, Jones replied with considerable acrimony. He contended that the force he commanded was under the commission, laws, and flag of the United States; that the officers and men were engaged, as under his command, in the American navy; that he received his orders, as an American officer, from the Minister of Congress; and that, consequently, the captors were entitled to be treated according to the laws of the navy of the United States. He remarked, moreover, to the Marshal de Castries, the Minister of Marine, that whatever understanding there might have been between the two governments, respecting the expense of the armament, it made not the least difference to the captors. The following correspondence will evince the indefatigable industry of the commodore, the zeal with which he prosecuted the interests of the brave men who served under his command, in 1779, in endeavoring to influence the French court in favor of their rights, and the success which attended his efforts. It will show that in a just cause he was as intrepid in his contests in the cabinet as on the ocean, and that his knowledge of the human character was in each situation alike useful to him.

"To the Honorable Captain JOHN PAUL JONES, Commander in the service of the United States of America.

"In pursuance of a resolution of Congress of the first of November,

1783, a copy whereof is hereunto annexed, I do hereby authorize and direct you to solicit, as agent, for payment and satisfaction to the officers and crews, citizens or subjects of the said United States, for all prizes taken in Europe under your command, and to which they are in anywise entitled, and in whose hands soever the prize-money may be detained.

"Given at Passy, this 17th day of December, 1783.

"B. Franklin, Minister Plenipotentiary from the United States of America at the Court of France."

"*Paris, February* 1*st*, 1784.

"His Excellency the Maréchal Castries, Minister of Marine.

"My Lord Marechal,

"As I wish to give your excellency as little trouble as may be respecting the money arising from the prizes taken by the squadron I had the honor to command in Europe, I have waited since the day you did me the honor to present me to his majesty until this moment, in order to give you sufficient time for any arrangement that you might find essential, before the division should take place between the ships and vessels that composed the force under my command when the prizes were taken. I now do myself the honor to transmit you the enclosed official letter on that subject, from Mr. Franklin, Minister Plenipotentiary of the United States, containing a copy of my credentials, as agent, from Congress, of which I had occasion to render an account on my arrival. I also enclose a statement of the force, in guns and men, of each ship and vessel that composed the squadron I commanded, which is the only paper essential to the first division of the prize-money. It is the custom, in cases like the present, to multiply the number of the crew by the sum of the calibre of the cannon mounted on board each ship. The product gives the intrinsic force, in proportion to which the share of the prize-money arising to each ship is determined. On that ground it is my duty to claim the proportion arising to the Bon homme Richard and the Alliance; their proportions will afterward be divided by the American Superintendent of Finance, agreeably to the rules of the American navy, between the officers and crews of these two ships.

"The subdivision of the shares of the other ships and vessels, in proportion to their force in men and metal, of the prizes in which they are concerned, will remain with your Excellency to determine as may be most agreeable to the respective officers and men. As those ships and vessels were entirely His Majesty's property, and their officers and men composed of French subjects, I do not presume to interfere in their respect, any farther than to pray your Excellency, in the most earnest manner, to render them and all concerned that immediate justice to which all Europe knows their distinguished services so highly entitle them. As nearly four years and a half have already elapsed since those captures were made, I rely on the kind promise you gave me that the prize-money shall now be immediately settled.

"I am, with profound respect, my Lord Maréchal,

"Your most obedient and most humble servant."

"*Paris, February* 18*th*, 1784.

"His Excellency the Maréchal DE CASTRIES, &c.

"MY LORD MARECHAL,

"I have examined, as you desired, the account that was laid before your Excellency by M. Chandon, on the papers that have by your orders been put into his hands by M. le Ray de Chaumont, relative to the prizes that were made by the squadron I had the honor to command in Europe, under the flag and commission of the United States, and under the orders of Mr. Franklin, the American Minister Plenipotentiary at the Court of France.

"Permit me, my Lord, before I make any observations on the account, as it there stands, to lead back your attention to some circumstances which I presume induced the government of France to ask, first of Mr. Franklin, and afterward of the other American Commissioners, that I might be permitted to remain in Europe to command such expeditions, with a force at the expense of France, but under the flag and commission of America.

"My conduct from the beginning of the war till the capture of General Burgoyne had so much commended me to the favor of Congress, that I was sent to Europe with the news of that glorious event, and with orders to the American Minister in France to put under my command, in addition to the ship I then had, a very large frigate, mounting a battery of 36 pounders, then at Amsterdam, called the *Indien*. Soon after I came to France, the treaty of alliance was concluded, and the property of the Indien was with my consent assigned over to the King, on account of difficulties that arose in Holland about getting that ship to sail. On the 10th of February, 1778, being at Nantes, and having there received some very particular and late advice from America, respecting the pretended force of the British ships and vessels of war under Lord Howe, I wrote to Mr. Deane, and communicated the exact plan that was afterward adopted, from Toulon, under the command of the Count d'Estaing, which, had it been immediately adopted from Brest, would have put an end to the British power in America. Soon afterward, when the alliance between France and America was announced, I transmitted my ideas through Count d'Orvilliers, at Brest, to M. de Sartine. I proceeded into the Irish Channel, made several descents, took and destroyed a number of ships, and among other prizes brought in with me a British frigate of superior force, that had been sent out expressly to take me. I also made prisoners, and brought with me twice the number of my crew. It was, as Mr. Franklin informed me by a letter dated at Passy, June 1st, 1778, the account that had been given of my conduct, &c., by Count d'Orvilliers, that then determined the government of France to invite me to remain in Europe. I received from the then minister of marine the most flattering hopes and promises, but his performance fell far short. He received from me, through the hands of M. le Ray de Chaumont, many ideas on the secret expeditions I wished to have commanded; among which were the interception of the Baltic fleet, and the destruction of the Hudson's Bay establishment. I was, however, trifled with for more than a year, before I could say I had a force under my command. This was, I think, owing chiefly to the ill-judged confidence which the minister placed in M. de Chaumont, who showed neither judgment nor secrecy. On that account many enterprises were laid aside that I had brought almost to the point of execution. On the last instance of this kind a number of troops had arrived at L'Orient, and in the moment when I expected them to have embarked, with their general the Marquis de la Fayette, the expedition was laid aside. I was then charged with a convoy with troops and military stores for the different ports and garrisons in the Bay of Biscay, and on my return to L'Orient to drive the enemy's privateers out of the bay, had M. de Chaumont then remained at Paris instead of meeting me again, as he did at L'Orient, that want of subordination which was so fatal to my projects would have been avoided. If your Excellency will please to call for my official letter, written at the Texel, the 3d of October, 1779, you will be convinced that if M. de Chaumont had confined himself to his own duty, which was that of commissary of the armament, and not interfered with or caballed against mine, as the military commander, I might have rendered many more important services. I might have taken eight sail of homeward bound East India ships, which entered Limerick in Ireland without convoy, three days after I was obliged to leave the entrance of that port, and of which I had received particular advice from England, before I left France. I might have taken or destroyed the whole Baltic fleet, which would have prevented Admiral Rodney from relieving Gibraltar. I might have destroyed or laid under contribution various towns and their shipping round the Irish and British coasts. And I might have entered the Texel with my ships in such good condition as might have enabled me to take under my convoy the Indien, and a large fleet of transports, loaded with stores and materials for the marine, that then waited there for my escort for Brest. That these projects failed must stand to M. de Chaumont's account. I shall say but little of the services that were actually performed; of which, however, the prizes taken and sent into port, or destroyed, make but the least part. I expected at that moment that a great army would have made a descent in the south of England, under the cover of the combined fleets; and it was therefore of the utmost consequence to make a great diversion in the north to favor that design. I think I may say I did my duty in that respect, and though almost left alone, nothing but a tempest that arose in the moment when I should have made a descent, could have hindered me from laying Leith, and perhaps Edinburg too, under contribution. I need not mention that Admiral Rodney was detained two months in port by my affair with the Baltic fleet; or that my situation in Holland, and before I arrived there, caused no less than 42 British ships of war and frigates to be sent in pursuit of me, and posted to intercept me in every quarter. And the world knows that my conduct in the Texel was a great cause of the British resentment against Holland, and stands as the first article in the declaration of war against that republic. On the whole, my Lord, it cannot be admitted that the government of France, having generously taken by the hand the young Republic of America, and having been so beneficent as to arm and support a naval force at His Majesty's expense, under the commission and flag of America, should wish to put the Americans who served as the officers and men, under any other laws than those of Congress, which I here subjoin, and agreeably to which I pledged myself to every individual among them at the time when I engaged them, viz:

"'In Congress, Wednesday, October 30th, 1776.

"'*Resolved*, That the commanders, officers, seamen, and marines in the Continental navy, be entitled to one half of merchantmen, transports, and storeships by them taken, from and after the first day of November, 1776, to be divided among them in the shares and proportions fixed by former Resolutions of Congress: that the commanders, officers, seamen, and marines of the Continental navy be entitled to the whole value of all ships and vessels of war belonging to the crown of Great Britain by them made prize of, and all privateers authorised by his Britannic Majesty to war against these States, to be divided as aforesaid.'

"The Americans were every one of them treated at their enlistment, and during the whole service, by the laws of the American flag, and the few of them who were paid their wages, were paid by the rules of Congress, from which, neither my duty as their agent, nor my honor as their commander, can now permit me to recede. As I went into the Texel in obedience to orders, and as my prizes and prisoners were there taken out of my hands, a circumstance of inexpressible mortification to me, and remained in the direction of the Duc de la Vauguyon, they were not at the risk of the captors; and, therefore, the expenses made in Holland cannot stand against the sale of the prizes. I admit that the Serapis had need of repairs in the upper works and masts, but being a new ship that had cost the British government 50,000 guineas, I deny that she wanted either anchors or cables while in my hands. The Countess of Scarborough sustained little or no damage in the battle, and therefore had as little need of repairs. It cannot be made appear from the sale of that ship or the Serapis, that they fetched a greater price on account of any repairs at the Texel: the Serapis arrived at L'Orient dismasted and in a worse condition than when she entered the Texel, and as the officers of the port of L'Orient cut to pieces and destroyed her orlop-deck with all the magazines and storerooms, &c. before I knew anything of the matter (which obliged me to make a journey to Paris, to obtain an order from government for the sale of my prizes agreeably to the laws of the American flag), I think if the account was fairly stated there would be an indemnification due to the captors for the injury thereby done to their hardly earned property, without their leave or consent. As the captors were not consulted respecting the expense of the Serapis at Dunkirk, nor the disarmament of that ship at L'Orient, which were no advantage to her sale, those articles ought not to stand against them in the account. And I never heard that even the owners of privateers, far less an established government, had charged the captors with the expense of provision for themselves or their prisoners! The expense made by Captain Cottineau regards not the captors: it is for him to show his authority for having made that expense, and the vouchers to support the different articles. I remember that I sent M. Chamillard express from the Texel to Versailles on my arrival; but that was surely a necessary expense of the armament, and cannot regard the captors. Whether M. Le Ray de Chaumont is indebted to the government, or the government is, as he says, indebted to him, is a matter that ought not to regard the captors, but they have a right to claim the protection of government to force M. Le Ray de Chaumont to render the money with interest, which he has unjustly detained from them for four years and a half, while many of them are perishing with cold and hunger.

"In short, it can make no difference to the captors whether the ships that I commanded under the flag and commission of Congress were owned by the king or by the United States. Therefore I am ready to admit all regulations and charges on the sale of my prizes, which have been usually admitted on other prizes sold in France, and taken by frigates owned by Congress. But I am persuaded that you will not think it just that anything should be deducted from the shares of the Americans on account of the Hospital of Invalids at Paris; as they receive no benefit from that hospital, but have on the contrary been pensioned by Congress for the wounds they have received.

"I am, with full confidence in your justice and generosity, my Lord Marechal,

"Yours," &c.

"*Paris, March 6th*, 1784.

"The Marechal de Castries.

"My Lord Marechal,

"Mr. Chardon has just now put into my hands a letter written to your excellency by M. le Ray de Chaumont, dated at Passy the 9th instant;—M. le Ray de Chaumont appears by that letter to insinuate that I was under his orders. That insinuation merits nothing but my contempt. He might as well pretend that the Marquis de la Fayette, with whom I had the honor to be joined in command for an important expedition (which failed only through the unwise confidence that had been placed in the secrecy of M. le Ray de Chaumont by the minister of marine), was also under his orders. For my own part, as I had served with reputation in America from the beginning of the war, and was through Mr. Franklin, in consequence of the high opinion the minister had of my bravery and good conduct, &c., invited by the government to remain in Europe to command secret expeditions, with a force at the expense of the king, but under the commission, laws, and flag of the United States, I made it a condition that I should receive orders only from the minister, or ministers of Congress; and while I remained in Europe I never received any other. I had before that time declined to accept a captain's commission in the Royal navy, which Count d'Orvilliers had offered to procure for me; and at any time, and in every situation, I would have disdained to prostitute my honor under the orders of so light-headed a man as M. le Ray de Chaumont. He seems to claim also the idea for intercepting the British Baltic fleet, an idea which did not originate either with the minister or M. le Ray de Chaumont, but which had been, with many others, suggested to government by myself at and before the time when I was first invited to come from Brest to Versailles. But I beg leave to refer your excellency to the Marquis de la Fayette, who knows that M. le Ray de Chaumont was regarded only as a simple commissary, and was therefore under my orders, instead of my being under his. I aver, that if M. le Ray de Chaumont had not been entrusted with the secret of the service intended, the views of the minister would have been not only fulfilled, but far exceeded. I had, however, a much greater latitude given me by my orders from Mr. Franklin than M. Chaumont seems to imagine: and it is clear from the strong and pointed letter of recommendation which I carried with me to Congress, approving and applauding my whole conduct, that the king and his ministers were perfectly satisfied, and even asked of Congress to send me back again to Europe, to command a larger force, which would have been done if the circumstances of America had not rendered it impracticable.

"M. le Ray de Chaumont seems to be ignorant that the American agent in Holland had, and can have no power whatever over the property of the captors. It is a power which even Congress has not reserved, and which is contrary to the established laws of the American navy. As to deducting from the prize money four deniers per livre for the Hospital of Invalids at Paris, because the expense of the armament I commanded was taken from the funds of the royal navy, &c., I presume M. le Ray de Chaumont might, with more modesty, have spared that observation to your Excellency. It is certain that the government of France foresaw that an expense would attend the armament I was so generously invited to command under the laws and flag of America, and it is not my place, much less that of such a man as M. le Ray de Chaumont, to intrude such pitiful observations as may militate against, or diminish the value of such delicate acts of friendship between two allied nations.

"I can only recur to facts mentioned to your Excellency in my former letters, viz.—The force I commanded was under the commission, laws, and flag of the United States, and the officers and men were engaged under my command, as in the American navy. I received my orders as an American officer from the Minister of Congress, and it follows that the captors are entitled in every light to be treated exactly by the laws of the American navy. And whatever understanding there may have been between the two governments *respecting the expense of the armament*, it makes not the least difference to the captors. I but ask for justice for the brave men I commanded, and I expect no less from a generous mind like yours. I am, with profound respect, &c."

"*Paris*, *March* 26*th*, 1784.

"My Lord Marechal,

"The within copy of a letter which I had the honor to receive yesterday from Mr. Franklin, will convince you that he never consented, and could not consent to the manner proposed by your predecessor and by M.

le Ray de Chaumont for settlement of the prize money due to the American officers and men who served under my orders in Europe.

"I will not now complain that the prisoners which I took and carried to Holland were not exchanged for the Americans who had been taken in war upon the ocean, and were long confined in English dungeons by civil magistrates, as *traitors*, *pirates*, and *felons*. I will only say, *I had such a promise* from the Minister of marine. It was all the reward I asked for the anxious days and sleepless nights I passed, and the many dangers I encountered in glad hope of giving them *all* their liberty, and if I had not been assured that Mr. Franklin had made an infallible arrangement with the courts of France and England for their immediate redemption, nothing but a superior force should have wrested them out of my hands, till they had been actually exchanged for the unhappy Americans in England."

"*Passy, March 25th*, 1784.

"The Hon. PAUL JONES, ESQ., Paris.

"SIR,

"I return herewith the papers you communicated to me yesterday. I perceive by the extract from M. de Sartine's letter, that it was his intention all the charges which had accrued upon the Serapis and Countess of Scarborough should be deducted from the prize-money payable to the captors, particularly the expense of victualling the prisoners and seamen, and that the liquidation of those charges should be referred to me. This liquidation, however, never was referred to me; and if it had, I should have been cautious of acting in it, having received no power from the captors, either French or Americans, authorizing me to decide upon any thing respecting their interests. And I certainly should not have agreed to charge the American captors with any part of the expense of maintaining the 500 prisoners in Holland till they could be exchanged, when none of them were exchanged for the Americans in England, as was your intention, and as we both had been made to expect.

"With great esteem, I have the honor to be, &c.

"B. FRANKLIN."

"*Paris*, ——— *13th*, 1784.

"His Excellency the MARECHAL DE CASTRIES.

"MY LORD MARECHAL,

"I am exceedingly sensible of the favor you did me yesterday by having the goodness to relinquish the claim that was made for deducting four deniers per livre for the Hospital of Invalids at Paris, from the prize money due to the Americans who served in the squadron I had the honor to command in Europe. And as you have been so obliging as to postpone your orders for the final liquidation of the prize money till I have time to show you more particular causes than I have yet done, why the expenses incurred in the Texel should not be taken from the property of the captors, I have no doubt but that the following circumstances will induce your Excellency to relinquish that charge, which is now the only difficulty remaining.

"I was ordered by Mr. Franklin to enter the Texel the last of September, but I could not reach it, notwithstanding my best endeavours, till the 3d of October. Therefore, I had not time to have *previously* landed the prisoners in France. And as the Bon homme Richard sank after the battle, it was absolutely necessary that the prizes, the *Serapis* and *Countess of Scarborough*, should accompany the Alliance and Pallas into the Texel; for those two last mentioned ships had not sufficient water and provision, and (being crowded with the remains of the crew of the Bon homme Richard) would not contain the prisoners, which were between five and six hundred in number. During the whole time, which was three months in the Texel, the *Serapis* and *Countess of Scarborough* were employed as prison-ships, and the small repairs of those two prizes in that road make but an inconsiderable part, a sixth perhaps, of the whole expense; so that the service they performed was at least worth the repairs they received. Had it not been for the prisoners, the *Serapis* and *Countess of Scarborough*, after they were taken, might have been immediately ordered for French or American ports; for they had plenty of water and provisions, and the Serapis was made perfectly manageable, and sailed fast under her jury-masts; so that they could have been out of danger before the enemy had placed their cruising squadrons to intercept them: whereas by their being detained till the middle of winter in the Texel, where they were blockaded by the enemy, they ran an infinitely greater risk; and therefore the captors had a just right to look upon government as the assurers of those prizes. Mr. Chaumont persuaded the minister of marine to take the Serapis for the king, without exposing that prize to sale. The minister sent his orders in consequence to L'Orient; and the people of that port destroyed the orlop-deck, magazines, store-rooms, galleries, breast-works, and barricades, &c. in order to make such alterations in that prize as they thought fit. When I saw this, I came from L'Orient to court, and the minister was so much convinced that Mr. Chaumont's advice was wrong that he, without difficulty, gave immediate orders for the public sale of all my prizes, agreeably to the laws of the American navy. But the Serapis was much more damaged by the operations just mentioned that had been made previously to her sale, than the value of her repairs in the Texel; to say nothing of her having been dismasted and losing anchors and cables by violent weather, on her passage from the Texel to L'Orient: therefore, taking all circumstances together, the repairs in the Texel were far from being of any advantage to her sale. She cost the King at public sale only 240,000 livres; whereas she had when new, six months before, cost the British government 50,000 guineas. The expense in the Texel arose chiefly from the provision that was supplied from Amsterdam for the prisoners and the crews of the ships that guarded them; and from the provision, repairs, and outfits for the frigates the Alliance and Pallas, and the small brigantine Vengeance. Now if any part of those expenses were chargeable to the captors, the same principle carried a little farther, would make them liable for the first cost and second outfit of the armament before the squadron sailed from France, and oblige them to sustain the loss of the Bon homme Richard. If America had asked of France to support that armament under the Continental flag, or if I had asked for that command, the matter might have had a different complexion. But it was an act of the King's free bounty, and his Majesty is too generous to lessen it by any afterclaims that are beneath his dignity. If it were asked why Americans should be placed on a more favorable footing than the subjects of France? I would answer that question by asking why Americans should be expected to accept an *invitation* from France which should put them on a more unfavorable footing than that on which France found them? Does not France pay foreign troops in her service more than she pays her own subjects?

"Permit me, my lord, to conclude by saying that no equal expense in the war was made with so great effect, or had such good consequence, as that made by the ships I commanded in the Texel; since Holland was thereby drawn into the war, without which the world would not have been this day at peace.—Had I known any thing of the order of the minister to Mr. Chaumont respecting the expense in the Texel, I am certain that, on my representation, he would have revoked it, as he did his order to the commandant at L'Orient respecting the alteration of the Serapis; both of which Mr. Chaumont obtained by misrepresenting facts, and by falsely saying it was the desire of Mr. Franklin.

"I am, with profound respect, &c."

"*Paris, Nov.* 6*th*, 1784.

"His Excellency the MARECHAL DE CASTRIES.

"MY LORD MARECHAL,

"By the state of the liquidation and repartition of the prizes taken by the squadron I commanded in Europe, which you signed the 23d of last month, I find there is an error made in the proportion due to the Vengeance. That tender was armed with only twelve four-pounders and sixty men, as you will see by the enclosed certificate of the second lieutenant. I am exceedingly sorry for this mistake, which ought to have been avoided. I beseech your Excellency to give orders that it may be rectified.

"I am, with respect, &c."

"*Paris, June 23d*, 1785.

"His Excellency the MARECHAL DE CASTRIES.

"MY LORD MARECHAL,

"By the letter your Excellency did me the honor to write me on the 13th of May last, you were pleased to promise that as soon as M. Chardon should have sent you the liquidation of my prizes, '*which you expected without delay*,' you would take measures for the payment, and that you would let me know.

"From the great number of affairs more important that engage your attention, I presume this little matter which concerns me in a small degree personally, but chiefly as the agent of the brave men who served under my orders in Europe, may have escaped your memory. Since the first of November, 1783, when I received authority to settle this business with your Excellency, I have been waiting here for no other purpose, and constantly expecting it to be concluded from month to month. To say nothing of my expenses during so long an interval, the uncertainty of my situation has been of infinite prejudice to my other concerns. My long silence is a proof that nothing but necessity could have prevailed on me to take the liberty of reminding your Excellency of your promise. I hope for the honor of your final determination, and I am, with great respect,

"Yours, &c."

"*Paris*, ——, 1785.

"His Excellency the MARECHAL DE CASTRIES.

"MY LORD MARECHAL,

"By the letter your Excellency did me the honor to write me the 27th ult., you are pleased to desire me to address myself to the Ordonnateur at L'Orient for the payment of the prizes made by the squadron I had the honor to command, and you are pleased to inform the Marquis de la Fayette, that you had assigned the funds necessary for that object. I have the honor to remind your Excellency that I came from America to France in the character of agent for the American captors, who served in the Bon homme Richard and in the Alliance. Therefore, that no misunderstanding may ensue between myself and the Ordonnateur at L'Orient, I must pray you, my lord, to give orders that the shares due to those two ships, (after deducting what is due to the subjects of France who served in the Bon homme Richard,) may be immediately paid into my hands in mass, agreeably to your Excellency's decision, in the state of the liquidation of my prizes, which you signed the 23d of October last, and conformable to the powers with which I am vested, which were announced to you by the Minister Plenipotentiary of the United States, in a letter dated in December, 1783.

"I am, my lord, with profoundest respect, &c."

"*Paris, July* 8*th*, 1785.

"His Excellency the MARECHAL DE CASTRIES.

"MY LORD MARECHAL,

"I had the honor to reply the 23d of last month to the letter your excellency did me the honor to write me on the 17th. I enclosed a copy of my public credentials, and referred you on the subject of my mission from Congress to an official letter written to you by the minister plenipotentiary of the United States, dated the 18th of December, 1783. From these documents, and as I have already given ample security to the United States, for the faithful performance of the trust reposed in me by the act of Congress, of the 1st of November, 1783, I naturally concluded that you would immediately see the impropriety of my giving you the security of a subject of France for funds arising from my prizes, which belong to the subjects of the United States. If it were possible that any doubt could remain in your mind respecting my public mission, I should refer you to a letter which I had the honor to put into your hands on my return to France, from the Chevalier de la Luzerne. As particular reasons render it extremely inconvenient, if not impossible for me to attend this business any longer, I shall take the liberty to wait on your excellency to-morrow, to be favored with your final determination.

"I am, with great respect, yours," &c.

"*Paris, July* 10*th*, 1785.

"His Excellency the MARECHAL DE CASTRIES.

"MY LORD MARECHAL,

"I have the honor to enclose an official answer from Mr. Jefferson, minister plenipotentiary from the United States at the court of France, to a letter written to him yesterday by your excellency, on the subject of my mission from Congress, to settle with you the claims of the subjects of America on the prizes that were taken in Europe by the squadron I commanded.

"Mr. d'Umons informed me yesterday that the concerned in the privateer La Granville, had, a few days ago, claimed a share in two of my prizes, the May-Flower, and the Fortune, by virtue of a sentence given to that effect by a court of justice. To that sentence I can offer no objection; because the La Granville was present when those two prizes were taken. But since the sentence of the court has very pointedly excluded the La Granville from any share in the other prizes that were taken by the squadron after that vessel had returned to a port of France, I beg leave to submit to your excellency to decide the question, whether the captors who purchased the other prizes, and particularly the Serapis, at the expense of their blood, will not have reason to be discontented if the Cerf, that returned to a port of France at the same time with the La Granville, should be allowed to share in all the prizes?

"Whatever may be your excellency's determination on that point, it can make no difference to me, as far as I am personally concerned, and I mention it again now because, should you think fit to order a new arrangement in that respect, it can, under the present circumstances, give no additional trouble to the 'Bureau.'

"I am, with great respect, yours," &c.

"*L'Orient, July 29th*, 1785.

"His Excellency THOMAS JEFFERSON, Esq., Minister Plenipotentiary of the United States to the Court of France.

"SIR,

"I have been with M. Clonot, the Ordonnateur here, to whom the Maréchal de Castries sent orders, the 15th of this month, to pay into my hands the money arising to the subjects of the United States from the prizes taken by the squadron I commanded in Europe. I find that a French merchant, M. Puchilberg, of this place, who opposed Dr. Franklin, and did all in his power to promote the revolt that took place in the Alliance, has produced a letter of attorney, which he obtained from the officers and men of that frigate when their minds were unsettled, authorising him to receive their share in the prizes. And notwithstanding the orders of the Maréchal of the 15th, I find there is a disposition here to pay the money to M. Puchilberg in preference to me.

"When I undertook the difficult and disagreeable business of settling for the prize-money with the Maréchal de Castries, I thought it necessary, to prevent any reflection on my conduct, to give security for two hundred thousand dollars, to remit the money I recovered to the treasury of the United States, to be from thence divided among the persons concerned. Not to mention the great expense I have been at, and the loss of two years of my time since the peace, to obtain a settlement, I may be permitted to say that M. Puchilberg was at no expense, and never took any effectual steps to obtain a settlement of the prize-money; and it would have been very difficult, if not impossible, for him to have obtained any satisfaction for the concerned, because no other man but myself (except Dr. Franklin, who would not act) could have explained, at Versailles, the nature and circumstances of my connexion with that court. And I may add, that M. Puchilberg will not, and cannot, if he had the best intentions, do justice to the subjects of America. He has given no security to do them justice. He has no authentic roll of the crew of the Alliance, which can only be had in America, and he is unacquainted with the manner of classing the officers and men in the division of prize-money by the laws of the American flag.

"What I request of you, therefore, is, to write to the court to obtain an explicit order from the Maréchal de Castries to M. Clonet, to pay into my hands the whole mass of the prize-money that appears due to the Alliance, and also the share of the Bon homme Richard (after deducting the proportion due to the French volunteers, who were embarked on board the ship as marines).

"As my situation here is exceedingly disagreeable, because till this new difficulty is removed I cannot receive any part of the money that appears due, I shall hope to be relieved from my embarrassment as soon as possible, by a letter from you.

"They have objected here, that the captain of the Alliance was born in France. But he had abjured the church of Rome, and been naturalized in America (as his officers reported to me) before he took command of the Alliance, and his crew were all the subjects of the United States.

"I am sorry to give you this trouble, but I am convinced that the business would have continued in suspense for a long time, if I had not come here myself.

"I am, with great esteem and respect, sir, yours, &c.

"N.B. M. Clonet has written to court by this post, therefore it will be necessary to make your application immediately. M. Barclay can give you the character of M. Puchilberg.

"*L'Orient, July* 31*st*, 1785.

"His Excellency THOMAS JEFFERSON, Esq.

"SIR,

"I had the honor to write you the 29th of this month, praying you to address the court to prevent M. Puchilberg, a French merchant here, from receiving the prize-money due to the subjects of the United States who served on board the squadron I commanded in Europe. I have done my duty, and with great trouble and expense both of time and money, obtained a settlement in their favor from government. But if M. Puchilberg (who has taken no trouble, and been at no expense to obtain a settlement) should receive the money, the greatest part of it will never reach America, nor find its way into the pockets of the captors. Were M. Puchilberg the most honest man in the world, he cannot, at this distance from America, and being ignorant of the laws of the American flag, do justice to the concerned. Besides, a preference is due to the application of one government to another for what regards the interests of its subjects, especially where it is clear that every caution has been observed for obtaining justice to each individual.

"The enclosed copy of a letter, which has just now been communicated to me, from Monsieur de Soulanges, à M.M. les Juges Consuls, dated at Toulon, the 14th day of this month, announcing that the Algerines have declared war against the United States, is of too serious a nature not to be sent immediately to you.

"This event may, I believe, surprise some of our fellow-citizens; but, for my part, I am rather surprised that it did not take place sooner. It will produce a good effect, if it unites the people of America in measures consistent with their national honor and interest, and rouses them from that ill-judged security which the intoxication of success has produced since the revolution.

"My best wishes will always attend that land of freedom, and my pride will be always gratified when such measures are adopted as will make us respected as a great people *who deserve to be free.*

"I am, Sir, with great esteem," &c.

Copie de la lettre de M. SOULANGES, à M. M. les Juges et Consuls de Nantes.

"*Toulon, le* 14 *Juillet*, 1785.

"M. le Commandeur de Segondès, qui arrive d'Alger sur la frégate la Minérve qu'il commande, M. M. m'a rendu compte en Mouillant dans cette rade, que cette Régence faisait armer 8 batiments, tant chébecs que barques, depuis 18 jusqu' à 34 canons destinés à croiser du Cap St. Vincent aux Açores, pour y prendre les Américains, à qui ils déclarent la guerre. Je vous en donne avis sur le champ, M. M., tant pour les interets que votre place peut prendre dans ces bâtiments, que pour que vous veuillez bien en donner avis aux capitaines Américains.

"Les Algeriens ont une autre division de 4 batiments, mais trop petits pour donner de l'inquiétude dans nos mers.

"SOULANGES."

"*L'Orient*, *August* 17*th*, 1785.

"His Excellency THOMAS JEFFERSON, Esq.

"SIR,

"I am still waiting for a decision respecting the claim of M. Puchilberg. But I think it my duty to inform you that one or two of the common sailors that served on board the Alliance, when that frigate was under my orders, are now here in a merchant vessel, and, as I am this moment informed, they have been persuaded to write to M. Puchilberg, desiring that their share in the prizes may not be sent to America, but paid to them here. This, I am told, has been urged as a reason to the Maréchal to induce him to decide in favor of M. Puchilberg's claim. Those two men will, however, sail in a day or two for Boston, and perhaps may never return to France; besides, their objection is too trifling to be admitted, as it would greatly injure the other persons, both officers and men of that crew, who would, in all probability, never receive any part of their prize-money unless they should come from America to L'Orient on purpose; which would not pay their expenses.

"As the post is just going, I must defer answering the letter you did me the honor to write me on the 3d, till another opportunity.

"I am, with great esteem, &c.

"N.B. I beg you therefore to write again to the Marechal de Castries."

"*L'Orient*, *August* 19*th*, 1785.

"His Excellency THOMAS JEFFERSON, Esq.

"SIR,

"I am by this day's post honored with yours of the 13th current, which appears to have been intended to be forwarded by M. Carnes. I esteem myself particularly obliged by that mark of your attention; but as there is no mention made of my letter to you of the 31st ult., I presume it has miscarried, and it is therefore that I have now written the foregoing copy. The 6th of this month, finding a ship here bound directly for Philadelphia, I sent a copy of Monsieur de Soulanges' letter to Mr. Jay for the information of Congress. I had the honor to write to you on the 17th to inform you, that I was just then told that two of the seamen, formerly of the Alliance frigate, who are now here in a brig belonging to Boston, have been wrought upon by an expectation of immediately receiving their prize money, to desire that M. Puchilberg might, in their name, object to sending the prize-money of the Alliance to America. That brig is now at Port Louis, and will sail for Boston it is supposed to-morrow morning.

"I am, with great esteem," &c.

"*L'Orient, August 24th*, 1785.

"His Excellency THOMAS JEFFERSON, Esq.

"SIR,

"I yesterday received the letter you did me the honor to write me on the 17th, mentioning the difficulty made by the Marechal de Castries in his letter to you of the 12th, and that you had removed that difficulty by your answer. I am exceedingly sensible of the favor you do me by your attention to my situation here; and it gives me great concern that it is not in my power to send you the roll you ask for of the crew of the Alliance. The rolls were in the proper time sent to court, and put into the hands of Mr. de Sartine by M. Genet, first Commissioner of foreign affairs, the certificate of which I have among my papers at Paris; and the Marechal de Castries might remember that I showed him and that he read that certificate. Those rolls, however, have been mislaid or lost in the bureau. Copies of them were sent at the same time to Dr. Franklin, who, I suppose, put them into the hands of M. le Ray de Chaumont; but since my return, I never could obtain any account of them. A third set of the rolls I carried with me to America, and before I embarked in the French fleet at Boston I put them into the hands of Mr. Secretary Livingston; and they were sealed up among the papers of his office when I left America. It is, however, impossible that any legal demands should be made on you for French subjects in consequence of your engagement to the Marechal. The Alliance was manned in America, and I never heard of any person's serving on board that frigate who had been born in France except the captain, who, as I was informed, had in America abjured the church of Rome and been naturalized.

"I have made all the inquiry I have been able here respecting the expedition you mentioned in a former letter; but I have not obtained much satisfaction. I propose to go to Brest. "I am," &c.

"*L'Orient, September 5th,* 1785.

"His Excellency THOMAS JEFFERSON, Esq.

"SIR,

"I am just returned here from Brest, where I have passed several days. I have received your letter of the 29th ult. with the copy of that written to you by the Marechal de Castries, the 26th, and I have reason to expect in consequence, that my affairs here will be finished as soon as the formalities of the bureau will permit. I shall obtain a roll of the Alliance, conformable to the pretensions of Puchilberg; which, though perhaps not quite exact, may however answer all your purposes. I really do not believe that ever any claims will be made on you; for I never heard that any French subject had served on board that frigate except the captain, and I commanded the Alliance in person seven months.

"I am, Sir, &c.

"N.B. I take the liberty to enclose a letter for M. Ledyard. It contains a small bill. If he is not at Paris, I request you to keep the letter till I come.

"*Paris, October 8th,* 1785.

"His Excellency THOMAS JEFFERSON, Esq.

"SIR,

"As the Baron de Waltersdorff does not return here, as was expected, and I wish to apply, without farther loss of time, to the Court of Denmark, for a compensation for the prizes taken by the squadron I commanded in Europe, and given up to the British, by the people in authority at Bergen in Norway; if you approve it, I will assign the powers I received, for that business from Congress, to my friend Dr. Bancroft in London. You will oblige me therefore, if you will write to Mr. Adams, requesting him to support Dr. Bancroft's application through the Danish minister in London.

"I am, with great respect and esteem," &c.

"*Paris, February 28th,* 1786.

"His Excellency THOMAS JEFFERSON, Esq.

"DEAR SIR,

"I received the kind note you wrote me this morning, on the occasion of receiving my bust; I offered it to you as a mark of my esteem and respect for your virtues and talents. It has been remarked by professed judges that it does no discredit to the talents of M. Houdon; but it receives its value from your acceptance of it, with the assurance you give me of your particular esteem, which will ever be felt by me as an honor truly flattering.

"I am, dear Sir, with great esteem," &c.

"*Paris, August 9th*, 1786.

"His Excellency THOMAS JEFFERSON, Esq.

"SIR,

"As it now appears by the reply I have just received from Mr. Adams, dated London the 17th of last month, which I had the honor to communicate to you, that his letter to the Baron de Waltersdorff, respecting my prizes delivered up to the English at Bergen in Norway, in the year 1779, by the court of Denmark has not been answered; and as the Baron de Waltersdorff is now gone to the West Indies, and Mr. Adams advises me in his letter, to apply to the Danish minister at his court; it now becomes my duty to ask your advice and assistance in the steps that remain to be pursued, to obtain a compensation from the government of Denmark for those prizes.

"And in order to give you the necessary information on this subject, I here subjoin some extracts from the papers left in my hands by Mr. Franklin, to wit:

No. 1. Extract of a letter from Monsieur Duchezaulx, Consul of France, to M. Caillard, Chargé des affaires du Roi à Copenhagen, dated à Berghen en Norvege le 14 July 1779.

"Les deux dites prises sont considérables; elles etoient armées en guerre et en merchandises, et les commandants pourvus de commissions aux Lettres de Marque; savoir *L'Union* de Londres, du port de 400 tonneaux armé de 22 canons de 6, et 4 livres de balle, plusieurs pierriers et autres armes; chargé de cables, cordage, et toile à voile, enfin tout ce qu'il faut en ce genre pour le grément de sept Batiments de guerre, avec plusieurs autres effets, destinés pour Quebec; et le *Betsey* de Liverpool, du port de 350 tonneaux armé de 20 canons de 6, et de 2 de 9 livres de balle, 12 pierriers et autres armes, chargé de fleur de farine, bœuf, et lard salés, et autres provisions et merchandises destinés pour la Nouvelle York et la Jamaique. Les deux cargaisons peuvent être évalués au moins un million de livres."

No. 2. Extract from a letter written by the Consul of France, before mentioned, to Dr. Franklin, minister of America at the court of France, dated à Berghen le 26 Oct. 1779.

"Il m'est douloureux au-dela de toute expression, d'avoir à vous informer aujourdhui, que les deux prises, the *Betsey* and the *Union*, ont été ces jours ci restituées aux Anglais, en vertû d'une résolution emanée du Roi de Danemark : Résolution injuste et contraire au droit des gens."

No. 3. Extract from the same letter.

"La valeur de ces deux prises que l'on vous enleve injustement, est au moins de 40,000*l.* sterling, indépendamment des Frais et l'argent deboursé par les banquieurs MM. Danekert and Krohn, dont je vous remettrai le compte."

No. 4. Extract of a letter from all the American officers in Norway to Dr. Franklin, minister of America in France, dated Berghen, January 4th, 1780.

"The Brigantine *Charming Polly*, which arrived 14 days after us, was likewise delivered up in the same manner."

No. 5. Extract of a letter from the same officers to Dr. Franklin, dated at Bergen, April 11th, 1780.

"Our expenses, while on board the ships, were paid by the English Consul; and those since by the King of Denmark; which enables us to proceed without drawing bills upon France. We have also the protection of the Danish flag till our arrival in France."

"After my return here from L'Orient, you remember I was prevented by circumstances from pursuing the application to the Court of Denmark in person. The bills I had received were not yet payable, and I thought it would be necessary for me to go to America in the spring, to deposit the prize-money received from this government in the Continental treasury; so that I was prevented from going to the Court of Denmark. And there being no Danish minister here, nor expected here, during the winter, you remember your having approved of my deputizing Dr. Bancroft to solicit the Court of Denmark through the Danish minister in London; and that you was so obliging as to join me in requesting Mr. Adams to support that application.

"But as experience has now shewn that this method is slow and uncertain; and as the late order of the Board of Treasury respecting the prize-money I have recovered, makes my return to America, on that account, at present unnecessary; I presume the best thing I can do will be to proceed to Copenhagen, and there make application to that court. If you approve of this, it would be useful for me to have a letter from the Count de Vergennes to the Baron de la Houze, minister of France at the Danish Court, directing him to support my reclamation. The interference of this government may be asked for with propriety, because the King had the gallantry to support under the flag of America the squadron I commanded in Europe. It is also to be wished that I could carry letters with me from the Danish minister at this court, and it is therefore very unlucky that he is now absent at the waters. If you think fit to write to him, I can, at the same time, obtain and forward a letter from his particular friend the minister of the Duc de Wertemburg; which may have a good effect. I am persuaded that the Count de Vergennes, on my own application to him, would immediately give me a proper letter to the Baron de la Houze; but it will be more official to obtain it through your application, which I therefore request.

"As I flatter myself that the Danish Court is still disposed to make a compensation, it is necessary for us now to determine on the lowest sum to be accepted. Dr. Franklin, in his letter to me from Havre, says the result of his letter to a broker in London was, that those Quebec ships were worth 16 or 18,000 pounds each. I have reason to believe the two ships delivered up, with their cargoes and armament, worth a greater sum. And besides, you will observe that the brigantine *Charming Polly* was also delivered up. I cannot judge of the value of this last prize; and perhaps it may be necessary for me to write to Bergen to obtain information.

"I am, with respect, &c.

"*Paris, Aug.* 21*st*, 1786.

"His Excellency THOMAS JEFFERSON, Esq.

"SIR,

"I am much obliged by the letter you sent me from the Count de Vergennes to Baron de la Houze, with your own to the Baron de Blome. An indisposition that has confined me close for three days, has prevented me from observing to you sooner, that Dr. Franklin, in the letter he wrote me from Havre, says, the offer made by the Baron de Waltersdorff was ten thousand pounds sterling. As you have misapprehended the amount of that offer, I take the liberty to return your letter to the Baron de

Blome, praying you to alter the word five with your own hand. I should be glad to be favored with your opinion whether I ought to accept of any sum less than what was offered to Dr. Franklin? It is very improbable that a less sum will be offered by the Danish ministers; but supposing them less favorably disposed now than formerly, it is necessary for us to be determined beforehand.

"I have the honor to be, &c."

"*Paris, Sept. 3d,* 1786.

"His Excellency THOMAS JEFFERSON, Esq.

"SIR,

"Since I had the honor of hearing from you last, my health has not permitted me to set out for Denmark. From the information I took at the Hotel of the Baron de Blome, I understood he was to arrive from the waters the 30th ult., so that I thought it better to wait till I could see him than to forward your letter. His servants arrived at the time that he was himself expected, and informed that the Baron had made a little jaunt to Geneva, and would be at Paris the 15th of this month. I now have the honor to send you the second copy of the rolls, &c., that you lately forwarded to the Board of Treasury. There is sure opportunity for London to-morrow at two o'clock. If you have any letters to send, or if you think fit to forward the papers respecting the prize money, I will give them in charge to the person who will safely deliver them in London.

"I am, Sir, with great esteem and respect, yours, &c."

Eventually, on the 15th of July, 1785, the Marshal de Castries issued an order to pay over to Jones at L'Orient the money arising to citizens of the United States from the proceeds of the sale of the prizes taken by the squadron under his command in Europe. The sum total was 181,039 livres, 1 sous, and 10 deniers.

Although Congress had approved of the distribution of it under the French ordinance, it will be seen in one of the following letters, that the king behaved with great liberality, not even retaining what he might have kept in conformity with the regulations of Congress:—

"*Paris, May 9th*, 1786.

"The Honorable JOHN JAY, ESQ. Minister
for Foreign Affairs, New-York.

"DEAR SIR,

"The application I have made to the court of Denmark for a compensation for my prizes that were delivered up by that government to the British, not having yet produced a decision, prevents me from embarking, as was my intention, about this time for America. The prize-money arising from my negotiation with the court of France, due to the citizens and subjects of the United States, who served on board the Bon homme Richard and Alliance (amounting in the gross to 157,483 livres, 6 sous, 10 deniers), is now ready in my hands. I expect that the application which is now depending with the court of Denmark will terminate so as to enable me to embark for America before the month of September. But lest a longer delay should be found necessary in Europe, and prevent my appearance in time for a passage after that date, I shall be ready to accept the drafts of Congress at Usance, for the amount in my hands.

"I say nothing of the amount of the allowance that ought in justice to be made for the great expense, trouble, and time I have devoted to this business from the 1st of November, 1783. A commission on the sum recovered will certainly be no indemnification for my expenses, far less a recompense for my time and trouble.

"I am, with great respect and esteem, &c."

On the receipt of this information, Congress passed the subjoined resolution :—

"IN CONGRESS, *June 7th*, 1786.

"*Resolved*, That the Board of Treasury be directed to take such measures as may appear to them to be most effectual for procuring accurate returns of the officers and men serving on board the Bon homme Richard, commanded by John Paul Jones, and the frigate Alliance, commanded by Peter Landais, at the time the captures were made by the late squadron under the command of John Paul Jones :

"That the amount of the prize-money paid by Capt. John P. Jones to the order of the Board of Treasury, on account of the officers and crew of the vessels above-mentioned, be by the said Board distributed to the officers and men entitled to receive the same, or to their proper heirs or assigns, in proportion to the shares respectively due to them, agreeably to the returns above-mentioned, and the ordinances of Congress in that behalf made.

Among the papers communicated by Mr. Jefferson for this work, is a statement of the settlement, which does not exactly correspond in the total amount as communicated to Mr. Jay. This may be accounted for, by supposing a proposed deduction in his favor, for additional expenses incurred in his prosecution of the claim at the Court of France, to which he refers in his correspondence with Mr. Jefferson :—

"*Paris, July 7th*, 1786.

"Amount of prize-money belonging to the American part of the crew of the Bon homme Richard (and to some few foreigners, whose names and qualities, &c. are inserted in the roll), with the amount also of the prize-money belonging to the crew of the Alliance; received at L'Orient, by order of the Maréchal de Castries, in bills on Paris,

		"Livres. S. D.
		"181,039 01 10
"From which deduct, viz.		
"'Nett amount of my ordinary expenses since I arrived in Europe to settle the prize-money belonging to the citizens and subjects of America who served on board the squadron I commanded under the flag of the United States, at the expense of His Most Christian Majesty, stated to His Excellency Thomas Jefferson, Esq. the 4th of this month,	47,972 11 0	
"Paid the draft of M. le Jeune, for the amount of prize-money due to Jacque Tual, pilot of the Alliance.	670 13 6	
"Amount of prize-money paid M. de Blondel, Lieutenant of Marines of the Pallas, as stated on the roll of the Bon homme Richard,	283 00 0	
"Advances made to sundry persons, which stand at my credit on the roll of the Bon homme Richard,	264 09 6	
"Advances made by me to sundry persons belonging to the Bon homme		

Richard; these advances do not stand at my credit on the roll settled at L'Orient by M. le Jeune, because the commissary had neglected to send him the original roll from the Bureau at Versailles; but that commissary has rectified that omission by his certificates, dated Sept. 5th, 1785, and Feb. 22d, 1786,	6,385 00 0	
"My share by the roll, as captain of the Bon homme Richard,	13,291 05 6	68,866 19 06
"Balance nett,		112,712 02 04

"PAUL JONES."

"*Paris, July 4th*, 1786.

"His Excellency THOMAS JEFFERSON, Esq.

"SIR,

"I have the honor to enclose for your examination the documents of my proceedings with those of this government in the settlement I have obtained of the prize-money, belonging to the officers and crews of the squadron I commanded in the late war in Europe at the expense of His Most Christian Majesty, but under the flag of the United States. By those documents, I presume, you will be convinced that, from a want of sufficient knowledge of circumstances, it would have been very difficult, if not impossible, for any other man (except Dr. Franklin, who never would act in it), to have gone through this business. Mr. Barclay made no progress in it, though he was charged with it by Congress two years and a half before I undertook it. I could not obtain an allowance in favor of the captors for the service of their prizes as prison-ships in the Texel, not for the damage done to the Serapis at L'Orient, previous to her sale; but I have taken care of the honor of the American flag. The American captors pay nothing towards the support of the Royal Hospital of Invalids, and His Majesty has generously renounced, in favor of the captors, the proportion of the sale of the merchant prizes, which, by the laws of the flag of America, he might have retained. I ask the favor of you to return me those papers with your observations.

"I enclose also a note of my expenses since I arrived in Europe on this business. When I am honored with your sentiments on this subject, I will prepare copies of the within papers, and, I flatter myself, comply to your satisfaction with the order you have received from the Board of Treasury. "I have the honor, &c."

"*Paris, July 7th*, 1786.

"His Excellency THOMAS JEFFERSON, Esq.

"SIR,

"I have the honor to enclose and submit to your consideration the account I have stated of the prize-money in my hands, with sundry papers that regard the charges. I cannot bring myself to lessen the dividend of the American captors by making any charge either for my time or trouble. I lament that it has not yet been in my power to procure for them advantages as solid and extensive as the merit of their services. I would not have undertaken this business from any views of private emolument that could possibly have resulted from it to myself, even supposing I had recovered or should recover a sum more considerable than the penalty of my bond. But I was anxious to force some ill-natured persons to acknowledge that, if they did not tell a wilful falsehood, they were mistaken when they asserted 'that I had commanded a squadron of privateers!' And, the war being over, I made it my first care to show the brave instruments of my success that their rights are as dear to me as my own.

"It will, I believe, be proper for me to make oath before you to the amount charged for my ordinary expenses. I flatter myself that you will find no objection to the account as I have stated it, and that you are of opinion that after this settlement has been made between us, my bond ought to stand cancelled, as far as regards my transactions with the court of France. Should any part of the prize-money remain in the treasury, without being claimed, after sufficient time shall be elapsed, I beg leave to submit to you—to the treasury—and to Congress, whether I have not merited by my conduct since I returned to Europe that such remainder should be disposed of in my favor?

"I have the honor to be, with great esteem," &c.

"*Paris, July 10th*, 1786.

"His Excellency THOMAS JEFFERSON, Esq.

"SIR,

"After what you mentioned to me before your favor of this date, respecting the imperfect powers you have received from the Board of Treasury, I did not expect you to make a settlement with me that should be final for the prize-money I have recovered. But as I have produced, and still offer you proofs to support the charges I have made, I naturally flattered myself and I still hope you will do me the favor to receive and transmit them to Congress with your sentiments. This becomes the more necessary to me at present, because from what Dr. Bancroft tells me of the application to the court of Denmark, it will be necessary for me to continue in Europe for some time longer, and to take your advice on some farther steps to obtain an answer from that government.

"With respect to the balance of the prize-money I have recovered, you may if you please give an immediate order on me for the amount, or I will pay it into your own hands.

"I have the honor," &c.

"*Paris, August* 14*th*, 1786.

"His Excellency THOMAS JEFFERSON, Esq.

"DEAR SIR,

"I send you herewith the rolls of the Bon homme Richard and Alliance, with copies of the other papers in French, respecting the prize-money of the squadron I commanded. They are numbered from 1 to 23, and I have left them open for your inspection. I rely on the good effect of your observations that will accompany them, with the papers in your hands, to Congress, and have no doubt but that my conduct will in consequence be approved. The second set of papers are not yet finished, but will be ready in a few days so as to be forwarded by the next good opportunity, with the second set of the papers in English now in your hands.

"I have the honor," &c.

Congress afterward confirmed the division of prize money made by the French government, and directed the distribution thereof to be made amongst the officers and crews of the Bon homme Richard and Alliance, on which subject that body passed the following resolution:—

"IN CONGRESS, *October* 11*th*, 1787.

"Congress took into consideration the report of a committee consisting of Mr. Smith, Mr. Dane, Mr. Johnson, Mr. Carrington, and Mr. Clarke, to whom had been committed a report of the Board of Treasury, and a letter of the 18th of July, from Captain John Paul Jones, together with a report of the committee of accounts for the marine department relative to the division of the prize-money due to the officers and crews of the Bon homme Richard and Alliance, and the charges of Captain Jones for recovering the same.

"*Resolved*, That the quotas assigned to the several ships which were under the command of Captain John Paul Jones in Europe, by direction of the court of France, be confirmed and considered as valid, and that a distribution of the prize-money be made amongst the crews of the said ships, separately, agreeably to such quotas.

"*Resolved*, That the monies paid by Captain John Paul Jones into the hands of the Hon. Thomas Jefferson, be distributed by the Board of Treasury, as soon as may be among the captors, agreeably to the division made thereof under the direction of the court of France."

In virtue of the general authority given to the Chevalier Jones to collect all the prize-money due to American citizens in Europe, he turned his attention to the reclamation from Denmark of the value of the three ships sent into Bergen, in Norway. The Baron de Waltersdorff, the Danish minister at Paris, not returning in that capacity, and the chevalier being anxious to accomplish his object, he proposed, with the approbation of Mr. Jefferson, on the 8th of October, 1785, to transfer the powers confided to him by Congress for that purpose, to his confidential friend Dr. Bancroft, then in London, and solicited Mr. Jefferson to write to his Excellency John Adams, the American minister near the court of St. James, to lend his aid in enforcing the demand. Mr. Adams wrote to Mr. Waltersdorff on the subject, urging the justice of the claim; but no answer was returned, that minister of Denmark having departed for the West Indies. Mr. Adams advised the chevalier to apply to the new Danish minister at Paris. This minister was absent at the time at some of the watering places, and Jones was inclined to proceed directly to Copenhagen. To further his views, he procured, through the friendship of Mr. Jefferson, from the Count de Vergennes, a letter of introduction and favor to the Baron de la Houze, French minister plenipotentiary at the Danish court. This letter is in these terms:

"*Versailles, August* 15*th*, 1786.

"The Baron DE LA HOUZE, Minister Plenipotentiary to the King of Denmark.

"SIR,

"Mr. Paul Jones, an officer in the sea service of the United States of America, having some business and certain claims in Denmark, on account of prizes which he took during the last war, proposes going on these accounts to Copenhagen. You will be pleased, sir, to receive this office favorably, to hear what he may wish to communicate on the subject of his claim, and to assist him with your counsels and good offices in case he should want them, during his stay at your residence.

"I have the honor of being, with perfect regard, &c.

"DE VERGENNES."

Mr. Jefferson likewise gave the chevalier a letter of introduction and friendship to the Danish envoy, Baron Blome, who was expected to be in Paris again in a few days.

The value of the prizes sent into Bergen was estimated at the highest at about fifty thousand pounds sterling. A well informed English insurer, to whom application had been made, to ascertain for what amount they had been insured, considered them to be worth from 16 to 18 thousand pounds sterling each; and the Baron de Waltersdorff, on the part of his government, had offered to pay ten thousand pounds as an indemnification:

"*Havre, July* 21*st*, 1785.

"The Honorable PAUL JONES.

"DEAR SIR,

"The offer of which you desire I would give you the particulars, was made to me by M. le Baron de Waltersdorff, in behalf of his Majesty the King of Denmark, by whose ministers he said he was authorised to make it. It was to give us the sum of ten thousand pounds sterling, as a compensation for having delivered up the prizes to the English. I did not accept it, conceiving it much too small a sum, they having been valued to me at fifty thousand pounds. I wrote to Mr. Hodgson, an insurer in London, requesting he would procure information of the sums insured on these Canada ships. His answer was, that he could find no traces of such insurance, and he believed none was made, for that the government on whose account they were said to be loaded with military stores, never insured; but by the best judgment he could make he thought they might be worth about sixteen or eighteen thousand pounds each.

"With great esteem, &c.

"B. FRANKLIN."

In all his transactions at this period the chevalier regularly consulted Mr. Jefferson, and kept up a correspondence with Dr. Franklin. Jones, however, suddenly suspended his journey to Copenhagen, and, as will be seen in the following letter to Mr. Jay, returned to America:

"*New York, July* 18*th*, 1787.

"His Excellency JOHN JAY, Esq.,
Minister of Foreign Affairs.

"SIR,

"The application I made for a compensation for our prizes through the Danish minister in London not having succeeded, it was determined between Mr. Jefferson and myself, that the proper method to obtain satisfaction, was for me to go in person to the court of Copenhagen. It was necessary for me to see the Baron de Blome before I could leave France on that business, and he being then absent on a tour in Switzerland did not return to Paris till the beginning of last winter. I left Paris in the spring, and went as far as Brussels on my way to Copenhagen, when an unforeseen circumstance in my private affairs, rendered it indispensable for me to turn about and cross the ocean. My private business here being already finished, I shall in a few days re-embark for Europe, in order to proceed to the court of Denmark. It is my intention to go by the way of Paris, in order to obtain a letter to the French minister at Copenhagen, from the Count de Montmorin, as the one I obtained is from the Count de Vergennes. It would be highly flattering to me if I could carry with me a letter from Congress to His Most Christian Majesty, thanking him for the squadron he did us the honor to support under our flag. And on this occasion, sir, permit me, with becoming diffidence, to recal the attention of my sovereign to the letter of recommendation I brought with me from the court of France, dated 30th May, 1780. It would be pleasing to me, if that letter should be found to merit a place on the journals of Congress. Permit me also to intreat that Congress will be pleased to read the letter I received from the minister of marine, when his majesty deigned to bestow on me a golden hilted sword, emblematical of the happy alliance —an honor which his majesty never conferred on any other foreign officer. I owed the high favor which I enjoyed at the court of France, in a great degree, to the favorable testimony of my conduct, which had been communicated by his majesty's ambassador, under whose eye I acted in the most critical situation, in the Texel, as well as to the public opinion of Europe. And the letter with which I was honored by the prime minister of France, when I was about to return to America, is a clear proof that we might have drawn still greater advantages from the generous disposition of our ally, if our marine had not been lost whilst I was, by perplexing circumstances, detained in Europe, after I had given the Count de Maurepas my plan for forming a combined squadron of 10 or 12 sail of frigates, supported by the America, with a detachment of French troops on board, the whole at the expense of his majesty.

"It is certain that I am much flattered by receiving a gold sword from the most illustrious monarch now living; but I had refused to accept his commission on two occasions, before that time, when some firmness was necessary to resist the temptation. He was not my sovereign. I served the cause of freedom, and honors from my sovereign would be more pleasing. Since the year 1775, when I displayed the American flag for the first time, with my own hands, I have been constantly devoted to the interests of America. Foreigners have perhaps given me too much credit, and this may have raised my ideas of my services above their real value,— but my zeal can never be overrated.

"I should act inconsistently if I omitted to mention the dreadful situation of our unhappy fellow-citizens in slavery at Algiers. Their almost hopeless fate is a deep reflection on our national character in Europe. I beg leave to influence the humanity of Congress in their behalf, and to propose that some expedient may be adopted for their redemption. A fund might be raised for that purpose, by a duty of a shilling per month from seamen's wages throughout the continent, and I am persuaded that no difficulty would be made to that requisition.

"I have the honor to be," &c.

Jones when in France had transmitted information of the hostile designs of the Algerines against the American trade, in a copy of a letter from M. Soulanges, dated at Toulon the 14th of July, 1785, written to the consular authorities in the ports of that kingdom. Annexed is a translation of it:

"*Toulon, July 14th,* 1785.

"M. de Legordes, who has arrived from Algiers in the frigate Minerva, which he commands, has, on entering this road, given me information that that regency had armed eight vessels, xebecs, and barks, with from 18 to 34 guns each, destined to cruize from Cape St. Vincent to the Azores, to capture Americans, against whom they have declared war. I give you immediate advice of this circumstance, gentlemen, as well on account of the interest your place may have in the cruise of these vessels, as to enable you to give notice of it to American captains. The Algerines have another division of four vessels, but too small to occasion any disturbance in our seas.

"SOULANGES."

"This event," said Jones, writing to Mr. Jefferson, on the 31st July, 1785, "may, I believe, surprise some of our fellow-citizens; but for my part I am rather surprised that it did not take place sooner. It will produce a good effect if it unites the people of America in measures consistent with their national honor and interest, and rouses them from that ill-judged security which the intoxication of success has produced since the Revolution."

On the 3d of October, 1787, the Chevalier Jones wrote farther to Mr. Jay:

"*New York, October 3d,* 1787.

"His Excellency JOHN JAY, Esq., Minister of Foreign Affairs, New York.

"SIR,

"As Congress have now referred back to you for your report, the chief part of the letter I had the honor to address you the 18th of July last, I beg leave to observe on the latter part of that letter, respecting the fund I wish to see established for the redemption of our fellow-citizens at Algiers, that I had also in view at the time, a national establishment, on the plan of the Greenwich Hospital in England, or Hotel des Invalides at Paris, which would be effected from the residue of the increasing fund I have proposed. I beg you, therefore, sir, to take notice of this in your report.

"I have the honor to be, sir, yours," &c.

On perusing the subjoined resolutions and letter to the King of France, a just conception will be entertained of the high consideration in which the chevalier was held by the United States in Congress assembled. They are sufficient to refute all the calumnies circulated against him by his enemies:

"IN CONGRESS, *October* 16*th*, 1787.

"*Resolved unanimously*, That a medal of gold be struck, and presented to the Chevalier John Paul Jones, in commemoration of the valor and brilliant services of that officer, in the command of a squadron of American and French ships under the flag and commission of the United States, off the coast of Great Britain, in the late war; and that the Hon. Mr. Jefferson, Minister Plenipotentiary of the United States at the court of Versailles, have the same executed, with the proper devices.

"*Resolved*, That a letter be written to His Most Christian Majesty, informing him that the United States in Congress assembled have bestowed upon the Chevalier John Paul Jones this medal, as well in consideration of the distinguished marks of approbation which His Majesty has been pleased to confer upon that officer, as from a sense of his merit: and that, as it is his earnest desire to acquire greater knowledge in his profession, it would be acceptable to Congress, that His Majesty would be pleased to permit him to embark with his fleets of evolution, convinced that he can no where else so well acquire that knowledge which may hereafter render him more extensively useful.

"*Ordered*, That the Secretary for Foreign Affairs prepare a letter for the above purpose, to be signed by the President; and that the Chevalier Jones be the bearer of the said letter.

"IN CONGRESS, *October* 16*th*, 1787

"The Secretary for Foreign Affairs reports:

"That, agreeably to the order of the 16th, he hath prepared the following letter to His Most Christian Majesty, which, having been duly signed and countersigned, was delivered to the Chevalier John Paul Jones:

"GREAT AND BELOVED FRIEND,

"We, the United States in Congress assembled, in consideration of the distinguished marks of approbation with which your Majesty has been pleased to honor the Chevalier John Paul Jones, as well as from a sense of his merit, have unanimously directed a medal of gold to be struck and presented to him, in commemoration of his valor and brilliant services, while commanding a squadron of French and American ships under our flag and commission, off the coast of Great Britain, in the late war.

"As it is his earnest desire to acquire greater knowledge in his profession, we cannot forbear requesting of your Majesty to permit him to embark in your fleets of evolution, where only it will be probably in his power to acquire that degree of knowledge which may hereafter render him more extensively useful.

"Permit us to repeat to your Majesty our sincere assurances, that the various and important benefits for which we are indebted to your friendship will never cease to interest us in whatever may concern the happiness of your Majesty, your family, and people.

"We pray God to keep you, our great and beloved friend, under his holy protection.

"Done at the city of New York, the sixteenth day of October, in the year of our Lord, 1787, and of our sovereignty and independence the 12th."

"IN CONGRESS, *October 25th*, 1687.

"*Resolved*, That the minister of the United States, at the Court of Versailles, be and he hereby is authorised and instructed, to represent to His Danish Majesty, that the United States continue to be very sensibly affected by the circumstance of His Majesty having caused a number of their prizes to be delivered to Great Britain during the late war, and the more so, as no part of their conduct had forfeited their claim to those rights of hospitality which civilized nations extend to each other. That not only a sense of the justice due to the individuals interested in those prizes, but also an earnest desire that no subject of discontent may check the cultivation and progress of that friendship which they wish may subsist and increase between the two countries, prompt the United States to remind His Majesty of the transaction in question; and they flatter themselves that His Majesty will concur with them in thinking that, as restitution of the prizes is not practicable, it is reasonable and just that he should render, and that they should accept, a compensation equivalent to the value of them:

"That the said minister be authorized and instructed to settle and conclude the demand of the United States against His Danish Majesty, on account of the prizes aforesaid, by such composition and on such terms as may be the best in his power to obtain; and that he be directed to retain in his hands all the money so recovered till the further order of Congress:

18

"That the said minister be and he is hereby authorized, in case he shall think it proper, to despatch the Chevalier John Paul Jones, or any other agent, to the Court of Denmark, with such powers and instructions relative to the above-mentioned negotiation as, in his judgment, may be most conducive to the successful issue thereof; *provided*, that the ultimate conclusion of the business be not made by the agent without the previous approbation of the said minister:

"That the person employed shall, for his agency in the business aforesaid, be allowed 5 per cent. for all expenses and demands whatever, on that account.

"*Ordered*, That the Board of Treasury transmit to the Minister of the United States at the Court of Versailles all the necessary documents relative to the prizes delivered up by Denmark.

"In Congress, *October 26th*, 1787.

"*Ordered*, That the Secretary of Congress inform the Chevalier John Paul Jones that the business relative to the prizes taken during the late war, and sent to Denmark, is put under the management of the Hon. Thomas Jefferson, Minister of the United States at the Court of Versailles, and that he furnish Mr. Jones with a copy of such part of the Resolution as respects the appointment of an agent by Mr. Jefferson, relative to the said prizes."

Chevalier Jones, in embarking again for Europe, evidently had some dread of falling into the power of the British. From what this apprehension proceeded is uncertain; whether from incidents in his life, prior to his entering the American service, or from the injury he had inflicted on British subjects during the Revolutionary war. It could hardly have been the latter; for honored and protected as he was, by both America and France, it is not likely he would have apprehended molestation or capture for having participated in the war of the Revolution. Whatever the ground of his fears may have been, it is certain that he entertained them: for writing to Mr. Jefferson from New York, on the 24th of October, 1787, he said, "I should have embarked in the packet that will sail for Havre to-morrow morning; but an account having arrived here that the English fleet is out, and was seen steering to the westward, and that a British squadron is cruising in the North Sea, has induced me with the advice of my friends, to postpone my embarkation till the next opportunity, an American ship, about the beginning of next month."

The Chevalier reached Paris, in December, 1787, when he sent to Mr. Jefferson the annexed private note. What his "strong reasons" for temporary seclusion were, do not appear:—

(*Private*) "*Hotel de Beauvais, rue des vieux Augustines.*
"*Paris, December* 12*th*, 1787.

"His Excellency Thomas Jefferson, Esq.

"Sir,

"I am just arrived here from England. I left New York the 11th of November, and have brought public despatches and a number of private letters for you. I would have waited on you immediately, instead of writing, but I have several *strong reasons* for desiring that no person should know of my being here till I have seen you, and been favored with your advice on the steps I ought to pursue. I have a letter from Congress to the King, and perhaps you will think it advisable not to present it at this moment. I shall not go out till I hear from, or see you. And, as the people in this hotel do not know my name, you will please to ask for the gentleman just arrived, who is lodged in No. 1.

"I am, with great esteem and respect, &c."

When Jones was in Europe in 1783, he was, by a letter from Dr. Franklin, of the 17th of December of that year, authorized and directed to solicit justice from the Court of Denmark, in relation to the prizes sent into Bergen, and restored to the British. As far back as the 22d of December, 1779, Dr. Franklin had addressed a memorial to the prime minister of Denmark on the same subject. That paper is so characteristic of the philosophical turn of mind of our illustrious countryman, that it is offered to the perusal of the reader:—

Memorial sent to the Prime Minister of Denmark by B. Franklin, Minister of the United States of America at Paris, respecting the prizes given up by Denmark to the English.

"*Passy, near Paris, December 22d*, 1779.

"Sir,

"I have received letters from M. de Chezaulx, Consul of France at Bergen in Norway, acquainting me that two ships, viz. the *Betsey* and the *Union*, prizes taken from the English on their coasts by Capt. Landais, commander of the Alliance frigate, appertaining to the United States of North America; which prizes having met with bad weather at sea, that had damaged their rigging, and occasioned leaks, and being weakly manned, had taken shelter in the supposed neutral port of Bergen, in order to repair their damages, procure an additional number of sailors, and the necessary refreshments; that they were in the said port, enjoying as they conceived the common rights of hospitality established and practised by civilized nations, under the care of the above said consul, when on the 28th of October last, the said ships with their cargoes and papers, were suddenly seized by the officers of His Majesty, the King of Denmark, to whom the said port belongs, the American officers and seamen turned out of their possession, and the whole delivered to the English consul.

"M. de Chezaulx has also sent me the following as a translation of His Majesty's order, by which the above proceedings are said to be authorized, viz.:

"'The English minister having insisted on the restitution of the two vessels captured by the American frigate the Alliance, Captain Landais, and which have been brought into Berghen, viz., the *Betsey* of Liverpool, and the *Union* of London, his Majesty has granted the demand on the ground that he has not yet recognised the independence of the colonies associated against England, and because the vessels could not be considered as good and lawful prizes, the two said vessels are therefore declared free, and have liberty to depart immediately with their cargoes.'

"By a subsequent letter from the same consul I am informed that a third prize belonging to the said United States, viz., the *Charming Polly*, which arrived at Bergen after the others, had also been seized and delivered up in the same manner, and that all the people of the three vessels being thus stript of their property, (for every one of them had an interest in the prizes,) were turned on shore to shift for themselves, without money, in a strange place, no provision being made for their subsistence, or for sending them back to their country. Permit me, Sir, to observe on this occasion, that the United States of America have no war but with the English. They have never done any injury to other nations, particularly none to the Danish nation; on the contrary, they are in some degree its benefactors, as they have opened a trade of which the English made a monopoly, and of which the Danes may now have their share, and by dividing the British empire have made it less dangerous to its neighbors. They conceived that every nation whom they had not offended, was by the rights of humanity their friend; they confided in the hospitality of Denmark, and thought themselves and their property safe when under the roof of his Danish Majesty. But they find themselves stript of that property, and the same given up to their enemies, on the principle only that no acknowledgement had yet been formally made by Denmark of the independence of the United States, which is to say, that there is no obligation of justice towards any nation, with whom a treaty promising the same has not been previously made. This was indeed the doctrine of ancient barbarians; a doctrine long since exploded, and which it would not be for the honor of the present age to revive; and it is hoped that Denmark will not by supporting and persisting in this decision obtained of his Majesty apparently by surprise be the first modern nation that shall attempt to revive it.*

"The United States oppressed by, and in war with one of the most powerful nations of Europe, may well be supposed incapable in their present infant state, of exacting justice from other nations not disposed to grant it; but it is in human nature that injuries as well as benefits received in times of weakness and distress, national as well as personal, make deep and lasting impressions; and those ministers are wise who look into futurity, and quench the first sparks of misunderstanding between two nations, which, neglected, may in time grow into a flame, all the consequences whereof no human prudence can foresee, which may produce much mischief to both, and cannot possibly produce any good to either.

"I beg leave through your Excellency to submit these considerations to the wisdom and justice of His Danish Majesty, whom I infinitely respect,

* "Les Anciens," (says Vattel in his excellent treatise entitled "le droit des gens,") "ne se croyoient tenus à rien envers les peuples qui ne leur etoient unis par une traité d'amitié, enfin la voix de la nature se fit entendre aux peuples civilisés; ils reconnurent que tous les hommes étoient frères." An injustice of the same kind done a century or two since by some English in the East Indies, Grotius tells us, "ne manquoit pas de partisans, qui soutenoient que par les anciennes loix d'Angleterre, on ne punissoit point en ce Royaume les outrages contre les étrangers quand il n'y avoit point d'Alliance contractée avec eux." But this principle he condemns in the strongest terms. Hist. des troubles des Pays-bas, livre XVI.

and who, I hope, will consider and repeal the order above recited, and that if the prizes which I hereby reclaim in behalf of the United States of America, are not actually gone to England, they may be stopt and redelivered to M. de Chezaulx, the said consul of France at Bergen, in whose care they before were, with liberty to depart for America when the season shall permit. But if they shall be already gone to England, I must then reclaim from His Majesty's equity the value of the said three prizes, which is estimated at 50,000*l.* sterling, but which may be regulated by the best information that can by any means be obtained.

"I am with the greatest respect, &c.

"B. FRANKLIN, Minister Plen."

The Chevalier now received a regular appointment from Mr. Jefferson; who, it is believed, drew up a memorial which Jones carried with him. Among the papers furnished to the author by Mr. Jefferson is a memorandum, in the handwriting of Mr. Jefferson, of references to particular passages of the works of Grotius and other eminent writers on the law of nations, intended for the Chevalier's use, when he should arrive at Copenhagen. This commission ran thus:—

"To JOHN PAUL JONES, Esq., Commodore in the service of the United States of America.

"The United States of America in Congress assembled, having thought proper by their resolve of the 25th of October, 1787, to authorize and instruct me finally to settle and conclude all demands of the United States, against His Majesty the King of Denmark, on account of the prizes delivered to Great Britain during the late war;—and to despatch yourself, or any other agent, to the court of Denmark, with such powers and instructions relative thereto, as I might think proper, provided the ultimate conclusion of the business be not made by the said agent, without my previous approbation, I hereby authorize you to proceed to the court of Denmark, for the purpose of making the necessary representations on the subject, and for conferring thereon with such persons as shall be appointed on that behalf by the said court, and for agreeing provisionally on the arrangement to be taken, transmitting the same to me at Paris for final approbation.

"Given under my hand and seal at Paris, this 24th day of January, in the year of our Lord 1788, and of the independence of the United States of America, the twelfth.

"TH. JEFFERSON."

The chevalier proceeded on his mission. His health, it seems, had suffered on the way to his destination, probably from the severity of the weather. From the capital of Denmark, where he was treated with the most distinguished marks of regard, he wrote to Mr. Jefferson as follows:

"*Copenhagen, March* 11*th*, 1788.

"His Excellency THOMAS JEFFERSON, Esq.

"SIR,

"I have been so much indisposed since my arrival here, the 4th, from the fatigue and excessive cold I suffered on the road, that I have been obliged to confine myself almost constantly to my chamber. I have kept my bed for several days; but I now feel myself better, and hope the danger is over. On my arrival I paid my respects to the minister of France; he received me with great kindness. We went five days ago to the minister of foreign affairs, I was much flattered with my reception, and our conversation was long and very particular respecting America and the new constitution, of which I presented a copy; he observed, that it had struck him as a very dangerous power to make the President commander-in-chief; in other respects it appeared to please him much, as leading to a near and sure treaty of commerce between America and Denmark; it was a day of public business, and I could not do more than present your letter. I shall follow the business closely. In a few days, when I am re-established in health, I am to be presented to the whole court, and to sup with the king. I shall after that be presented to all the corps diplomatic, and other persons of distinction here: I am infinitely indebted to the attentions I received from the minister of France. I made the inquiry you desired in Holland, and should then have written to you in consequence, had I not been assured by authority (M. Van Staphorst) that I could not doubt, that letters had been sent you on the subject, that could not fail of giving you satisfaction. Mr. Van Staphorst was very obliging.

"At Hamburg I ordered the smoked beef you desired to be sent to you, to the care of the American agent at Havre de Grace: you have nothing to do but receive it, paying what little charges may be on it.

"My ill health and fatigue on the road hindered me from preparing the extract of the engagement. When you see Mr. Little Page, I pray you to present my kind compliments. It is said here, that the Empress confides the command of her fleet, that will pass the sound, to Admiral Greg; and that he means to call at an English port to take provisions, &c. The Hamburg papers, I am told, have announced the death of Dr. Franklin; I shall be extremely concerned if the account proves true—God forbid! The departure of the post obliges me to conclude. I am, with a deep sense of your kind attachment,

"Sir, yours," &c.

On the 18th of the same month he again wrote to the American minister at Paris:

"*Copenhagen, March* 18*th*, 1788.

"His Excellency THOMAS JEFFERSON, Esq.

"SIR,

"Yesterday his excellency the Baron de la Houze, minister plenipotentiary of France at this court, did me the honor to present me publicly to his majesty, the royal family, and chief personages at the royal palace here. I had a very polite and distinguished reception. The queen dowager conversed with me for some time, and said the most civil things. Her majesty has a dignity of person and deportment which becomes her well, and which she has the secret to reconcile with great affability and ease. The princess royal is a charming person, and the graces are so much her own, that it is impossible to see and converse with her without paying to her that homage which artless beauty and good nature will ever command. All the royal family spoke to me except the king, who speaks to no person when presented. His majesty saluted me with great complaisance at first, and as often afterward as we met in the course of the evening. The prince royal is greatly beloved, and extremely affable: he asked me a number of pertinent questions respecting America. I had the honor to be invited to sup with his majesty and the royal family. The company at table consisting of seventy ladies and gentlemen, including the royal family, the ministers of state, foreign ambassadors, &c. was very brilliant. The death of Dr. Franklin seems to be generally believed. Every person I have spoken with at court, laments the event as a misfortune to human nature. I have had a second conference with the minister of foreign affairs, but nothing is yet done; I will press him to conclude. I am so continually feasted, and have so many visits to pay and receive, that I have scarcely a moment to call my own; and the departure of the post does not now afford me the time necessary to compare the whole of my last. I have received no letter whatever since I came here.

"I am, with great esteem and respect, Sir, yours," &c.

"*Copenhagen, March 20th*, 1788.

"His Excellency THOMAS JEFFERSON, Esq.

"SIR,

"I embrace the occasion of a young gentleman just arrived here express from St. Petersburg, and who sets out immediately express for Paris, to transmit you the foregoing copy of my last of the 18th. I have written to Norway, and expect a satisfactory answer. The minister of France is surprised to have had no object from Versailles respecting me. I pray you, and so does he, to push that point immediately. The minister of foreign affairs will receive me on Saturday. Please to present my kind compliments to Mr. Little Page. If there is anything new from that quarter you will no doubt communicate it.

"I am, sincerely, yours," &c.

"*Copenhagen, March 25th*, 1788.

"His Excellency THOMAS JEFFERSON, Esq.

"SIR,

"I propose to send the present, under cover, to Messieurs Nicholas and Jacob Van Staphorst of Amsterdam; presuming you may be there by the time they will receive it. If you are not arrived, or fully expected to arrive there in a day or two, they will be requested to forward you my letter. My mission here is not yet at an end, but the minister has promised to determine soon, and I have wrote to claim that promise. Before you can receive this, Monsieur de Semolin will have informed you that your proposal to him, and his application on that idea, have been well received. The matter is communicated to me here, in the most flattering expressions, by a letter I have received from his excellency the Baron de Krudener. There seems, however, to remain some difficulty respecting the *letter* of Monsieur de Semolin's proposal, though it is accepted, *in substance*, with an appearance of great satisfaction. I find myself under the necessity of setting out for St. Petersburg through Sweden, in a few days, instead of returning first, as was my wish and intention, to Paris. I hope in the mean time to receive a satisfactory answer, which I shall duly communicate to you. Your future letters for me you will please to send under cover, to the minister of France at Petersburg, or rather deliver them to Monsieur de Semolin, to whom I tender my sincere and respectful thanks for his good offices, which I shall ever remember with pleasure and gratitude, and which I shall always be ambitious to merit. I esteem myself also much indebted to Mr. Little Page, and hope I may one day convince him how sensible I am of his friendly behavior. I say nothing at present of your attachment, but my feelings do you justice.

"I am, with unbounded esteem and sincere regard," &c.

Jones did not remain long at Copenhagen, but whilst there he pressed the business entrusted to him with his usual ardor. The Danish Court, either from a fear of offending Great Britain, or a desire to procrastinate, pleaded a want of full powers in the chevalier to treat, and transferred the negotiation to Paris, as will be seen in the subjoined correspondence with Count Bernstorff. Jones was impatient to go to Russia, whose sovereign, the celebrated Catharine II., had invited him thither by the most flattering promises of patronage. It was Mr. Jefferson who originally projected for the chevalier this adventure, which so admirably accorded with his chivalric disposition.

"*Copenhagen, March 24th*, 1788.

"His Excellency M. le Comte de Bernstorff, Knight of the order of the Elephant, Secretary of State for Foreign Affairs, &c., Copenhagen.

"Sir,

"From the act of Congress (the act by which I am honored with a gold medal) I had the honor to show your excellency the 21st of this month, as well as from the conversation that followed, you must be convinced that circumstances do not permit me to remain here; but that I am under a necessity either to return to France, or proceed to Russia. As the minister of the United States, at Paris, gave me the perusal of the packet he wrote by me, and which I had the honor to present to you on my arrival here, it is needless to go into any detail on the object of my mission to this court, which Mr. Jefferson has particularly explained. The promise you have given me of a prompt and explicit decision from this court, on the act of Congress of the 25th of October last, inspires me with full confidence. I have been very particular in communicating to the

United States all the polite attentions with which I have been honored at this court; and they will learn with great pleasure the kind reception I had from you. I felicitate myself on being the instrument to settle the delicate national business in question, with a minister who conciliates the views of the wise statesman, with the noble sentiments and cultivated mind of the true philosopher and man of letters.

"I have the honor to be, with great respect, yours, &c.

"*Copenhagen, March 30th*, 1788.

"His Excellency M. le Comte de BERNSTORFF.

"SIR,

"Your silence on the subject of my mission from the United States to this court leaves me in the most painful suspense; the more so as I have made your excellency acquainted with the promise I am under, to proceed as soon as possible to St. Petersburgh. This being the ninth year since the three prizes reclaimed by the United States were seized upon in the port of Bergen, in Norway, it is to be presumed, that this court has long since taken an ultimate resolution respecting the compensation demanded by Congress. Though I am extremely sensible of the favorable reception with which I have been distinguished at this court, and am particularly flattered by the polite attentions with which you have honored me at every conference, yet I have remarked, with great concern, that you have never led the conversation to the object of my mission here. A man of your liberal sentiments will not, therefore, be surprised or offended at my plain dealing, when I repeat that I impatiently expect a prompt and categorical answer, in writing, from this court, to the act of Congress of the 25th of October last. Both my duty and the circumstances of my situation, constrain me to make this demand, in the name of my sovereign the United States of America; but I beseech you to believe, that though I am extremely tenacious of the honor of the American flag, yet my personal interest in the decision I now ask, would never have induced me to present myself to this court. You are too just, sir, to delay my business here; which would put me under the necessity to break the promise I have made to Her Imperial Majesty, conformable to your advice.

"I have the honor to be, with great respect, &c."

"*Copenhagen, April 4th*, 1788.

"The Chevalier PAUL JONES, Commander in Chief of the Squadron of the United States of America.

"SIR,

"You have requested of me an answer to the letter you did me the honor to remit to me from Mr. Jefferson, minister plenipotentiary of the United States of America, near His Most Christian Majesty. I do it with so much more pleasure, as you have inspired me with as much interest as confidence, and this occasion appears to me favorable to make known the sentiments of the king my master, on the objects to which we attach so much importance. Nothing can be further from the plans and the wishes of His Majesty, than to let fall a negotiation which has only been suspended in consequence of circumstances arising from the necessity of maturing a new situation, so as to enlighten himself on their reciprocal interests, and to avoid the inconvenience of a precipitate and imperfect arrangement. I am authorized, sir, to give you, and through you to Mr. Jefferson, the word of the king, that His Majesty will renew the negotiation for a treaty of amity and commerce in the forms already agreed upon, at the instant the new constitution (this admirable plan, so worthy of the most enlightened men,) will have been adopted by the States, to which nothing more was wanted to assure to itself a perfect consideration. If it has not been possible, sir, to discuss definitively with you, neither the principal object nor its accessaries, the idea of eluding the question, or of retarding the decision, had not the least part in it. I have already had the honor to express to you, in our conversations, that your want of plenipotentiary powers from Congress, was a natural and invincible obstacle. It would be, likewise, contrary to the established custom to change the seat of negotiation, which has not been broken off, but only suspended, thereby to transfer it from Paris to Copenhagen.

"I have only one more favor to ask of you, sir, that you would be the interpreter of our sentiments in regard to the United States. It would be a source of gratification to me to think that what I have said to you on this subject, carries with it that conviction of the truth which it merits. We desire to form with them connexions solid, useful, and essential; we wish to establish them on bases natural and immovable. The momentary clouds—the incertitudes which the misfortunes of the times brought with them, exist no longer. We should no longer recollect it, but to feel in a more lively manner the happiness of a more fortunate period; and show ourselves more eager to prove the dispositions most proper to effect a union, and to procure reciprocally the advantages which a sincere alliance can afford, and of which the two countries are susceptible. These are the sentiments which I can promise you, sir, on our part, and we flatter ourselves to find them likewise in America; nothing then can retard the conclusion of an arrangement, which I am happy to see so far advanced.

"Permit me to repeat to you, sir, again, the assurances of the perfect and distinguished consideration with which,

"I have the honor to be, &c."

"Bernstorff."

"*Copenhagen, April* 5, 1788.

"His Excellency M. le Comte DE BERNSTORFF, &c.

"SIR,

"I pray your excellency to inform me when I can have the honor to wait on you, to receive the letter you have been kind enough to promise to write me in answer to the act of Congress of the 25th of October last. As you have told me that my want of plenipotentiary powers to terminate, *ultimately*, the business now on the carpet between this court and the United States has determined you to authorize the Baron de Blome to negotiate and settle the same with Mr. Jefferson at Paris, and to conclude at the same time an advantageous treaty of commerce between Denmark and the United States; my business here will of course be at an end when I shall have received your letter, and paid you my thanks in person for the very polite attentions with which you have honored me.

"I am, with great respect, &c."

"*Copenhagen, April 8th*, 1788.

"His Excellency THOMAS JEFFERSON, Esq.

"SIR,

"By my letters to the Count de Bernstorff, and his excellency's answer, you see that my business here is at an end. If I have not finally concluded the object of my mission, it is neither your fault nor mine: the powers I received are found insufficient, and you could not act otherwise than was prescribed in your instructions. Thus it frequently happens, that good opportunities are lost when the supreme power does not place a sufficient confidence in the distant operations of public officers, whether civil or military. I have, however, the melancholy satisfaction to reflect that I have been received and treated here with a distinction far above the pretensions of my public mission; and I felicitate myself sincerely on being, at my own expense, (and even at the peril of my life, for my sufferings, from the inclemency of the weather, and my want of proper means to guard against it on the journey, were inexpressible; and I believe, from what I yet feel, will continue to affect my constitution,) the instrument to renew the negotiation between this country and the United States: the more so, as the honor is now reserved for you to display your great abilities and integrity by the completion and improvement of what Dr. Franklin had wisely begun. I have done, then, what perhaps no other person would have undertaken under the same circumstances; and while I have the consolation to hope that the United States will derive solid advantages from my journey and efforts here, I rest perfectly satisfied that the interests of the brave men I commanded will experience in you parental attention, and that the American flag can lose none of its lustre, but the contrary, while its honor is confided to you. America being a young nation, with an increasing commerce, which will naturally produce a navy, I please myself with the hope, that in the treaty you are about to conclude with Denmark, you will find it easy and highly advantageous to include certain articles for admitting America into the armed neutrality. I persuade myself beforehand, that this would afford pleasure to the Empress of Russia, who is at the head of that noble and humane combination; and as I shall now set out immediately for St. Petersburg, I will mention the idea to her Imperial Majesty, and let you know her answer.

"If Congress should think I deserve the promotion that was proposed, when I was last in America, and should condescend to confer on me the grade of rear-admiral, from the day I took the Serapis, (23d of September, 1779,) I am persuaded it would be very agreeable to the Empress, who now deigns to offer me an equal rank in her service, although I never yet had the honor to draw my sword in her cause, nor to do any other act that could directly merit her imperial benevolence. While I express, in the warm effusion of a grateful heart, the deep sense I feel of my eternal obligation to you, as the author of the honorable prospect that is now before me, I must rely on your friendship to justify to the United States the important step I now take, conformable to your advice. You know I had no idea of this new fortune when I found that you had put it in train, before my last return to Paris from America. I have not forsaken a country that has had many disinterested and difficult proofs of my steady affection; and I can never renounce the glorious title of *a citizen of the United States!*

"It is true, I have not the express permission of the sovereignty to accept the offer of Her Imperial Majesty: yet America is independent, is in perfect peace, has no public employment for my military talents; but why should I excuse a conduct which I should rather hope would meet with general approbation? In the latter part of the year 1782, Congress passed an act for my embarkation in the fleet of His Most Christian Majesty; and when, a few months ago, I left America to return to Europe, I was made the bearer of a letter to His Most Christian Majesty, requesting me to be permitted to embark in the fleets of evolution. Why did Congress pass those acts? To facilitate my improvement in the art of conducting fleets and military operations. I am, then, conforming myself to the views of Congress; but the roll allotted me is infinitely more high and difficult than Congress intended. Instead of receiving lessons from able masters, in the theory of war, I am called to immediate practice; where I must command in chief, conduct the most difficult operations, be my own preceptor, and instruct others. Congress will allow me some merit in daring to encounter such multiplied difficulties. The mark I mentioned of the approbation of that honorable body, would be extremely flattering to me in the career I am now to pursue, and would stimulate all my ambition to acquire the necessary talents to merit that, and even greater favors, at a future day. I pray you, sir, to explain the circumstances of my situation, and be the interpreter of my sentiments to the United States in Congress. I ask for nothing; and beg leave to be understood only as having hinted, what is natural to conceive, that the mark of approbation I mentioned could not fail to be infinitely serviceable to my views and success in the country where I am going.

"The Prince Royal sent me a messenger, requesting me to come to his apartment. His Royal Highness said a great many civil things to me, told me the King thanked me for my attention and civil behaviour to the Danish flag, while I commanded in the European seas; and that His Majesty wished for occasions to testify to me his personal esteem, &c. I was alone with the Prince half an hour.

"I am, with perfect esteem, &c."

In 1788 the Russians were at war with the Turks, and wanting naval talent, sought and procured it wherever it was to be found. Among others, it is not surprising that Jones should have attracted the notice of so enlightened a ruler as Catharine. He went to St. Petersburg, and no longer opposing the wishes of the Empress, attached himself to her service, under this single condition, "that he should never be condemned unheard." So expeditious was he in his movements, that we find him, in the month of June, 1788, writing a letter from on board a Russian man-of-war, on the Liman sea, to the Marquis de la Fayette. It contains an account of his passage through Sweden to St. Petersburg, and of his reception by the Empress:—

"*On board the Imperial ship Wolodimer, at anchor in the Liman, before Oczacoff, June* 15–26, 1788.

"Monsieur le Marquis de la Fayette, Major General et Chevalier des plusieurs Ordres, à son Hôtel, à Paris.

"My dear General and dear Friend,

"The kind letter you did me the honor to write me, the 20th of April, was delivered to me at St. Elizabeth, on my way here from St. Petersburg. It was very flattering to me to receive such a letter from a man whom I so much love and respect as I do, and have long done the Marquis de la Fayette. You will yourself do justice to my sensibility for all your good offices and good intentions, so I need only say, I shall always be ambitious to merit the flattering compliment with which you honor me by subscribing yourself my 'sincere friend.'

"I must tell you that Mr. Elliot (the same who filched Dr. Lee's papers at Berlin,) was furious when he found my business at Copenhagen; and that I was received with great distinction at court, and in all the best societies in Denmark. Every time I was invited to sup with the King, Elliot made an apology; he shut himself up for more than a month, and then left town. This occasioned much laughter; and as he had shunned society from the time of my arrival, people said he had gone off in a fright; I hope Mr. Jefferson is satisfied with the train in which I left the Danish business. It would have been impossible for me to have pushed it any farther as I had not full powers to conclude it finally.

"I went through Sweden to St. Petersburg. The advanced season did not permit my return to Paris, the distance would have been too long through Germany, and Elliot had influenced the English to put difficulties in the way of my passage to the Baltic. I found the Gulf de Botenea barred with ice, and after making several fruitless attempts to cross it in a small open boat (about 30 feet long), I compelled the Swedish peasants to steer as I directed them, for the Gulf of Finland; after about four or five hundred miles of navigation, I landed at Reval, and having paid the peasants to their satisfaction, I gave them a good pilot, with some provision, to reconduct them to their home. My voyage was looked upon as a kind of miracle, being what never had been attempted before, unless in large vessels.

"The Empress received me with a distinction the most flattering that perhaps any stranger can boast of. On entering into the Russian service, her Majesty conferred on me immediately the grade of Rear-Admiral. I was detained against my will a fortnight, and continually feasted at court and in the first society. This was a cruel grief to the English, and I own that their vexation, which, I believe, was general, in and about St. Petersburg, gave me no pain.

"I presented the Empress with a copy of the new American constitution. Her Majesty spoke to me often about the United States, and is persuaded that *the American revolution cannot fail to bring about others, and to influence every other government.* I mentioned the armed neutrality so honorably patronised by Her Majesty; and I am persuaded that no difficulty will be made about admitting the United States into that illustrious association, so soon as America shall have built some ships-of-war. I spoke of it to the Danish minister of foreign affairs, who seemed pleased with the idea.

"The United States have some commerce with Russia, which perhaps we may be able to increase. I should think whale oil, dried fish, spermaceti, and rice, may be articles to suit the Russia market; if the Mediterranean was not shut to the American flag, many articles might be supplied to the Russian fleet, now destined for the Archipelago. I certainly wish to be useful to a country I have so long served. I love the people and their cause, and shall always rejoice when I can be useful to promote their happiness.

"I am glad that the new constitution will be, as you tell me, adopted by more than nine states. I hope, however, they will alter some parts of it; and particularly that they will divest the President of all military rank and command; for though General Washington might be safely trusted with such tempting power as the chief command of the fleet and army, yet, depend on it, in some other hands it could not fail to overset the liberties of America. The President should be only the first civil Magistrate, let him command the military *with the pen;* but deprive him of the power to draw his sword and lead them, under some plausible pretext, or under any circumstances whatever, to cut the throats of a part of his fellow-citizens, and to make him the tyrant of the rest. These are not my apprehensions alone, for I have mentioned them to many men of sense and learning since I saw you, and I have found them all of the same sentiment.

"What are you about, my dear General? Are you so absorbed in politics as to be insensible to glory? That is impossible, quit then your divine Calypso, come here, and pay your court once more to Bellona, who, you are sure, will receive you as her favorite. You would be charmed with the Prince de Potemkin. He is a most amiable man, and none can be more noble-minded.

"For the Empress, fame has never yet done her justice. I am sure no stranger who has not known that illustrious character, ever conceived how much Her Majesty is made to reign over a great empire, to make the people happy, and to attach grateful and susceptible minds.

"Is not the present a happy moment for France to declare for Russia? Would it not be a means to retrieve her dignity, and to re-establish the affairs of Holland? What would England find to oppose to such an alliance? Denmark is with Russia, and Sweden ought surely to be with France. An alliance with Russia might be very advantageous, and can never be dangerous to France. In these circumstances the Isles of Candia and Cyprus appear among the objects which ought to attract her attention.

Perhaps they might be obtained and the affairs of Holland re-established without the expense of a war, for it is a question if England and Russia would venture to make opposition. One sure advantage would result to France, I mean the breaking of her destructive treaty of commerce with England. Since the time of the assembly of notables, I have always thought that the ministry ought to have seen the expediency of a war with England; to break the treaty of commerce, and to prevent the ruin of French manufactories; to obtain loans from Holland, and to render that republic for ever dependent on French protection; and, above all, to unite the nation, and prevent the broils that have since ensued, by exciting a brave patriotic people to support their national dignity.

"My motives are pure, and I am influenced only by the affection I feel for the two countries you love. Your known patriotism assures me that if you can make my ideas useful, you will not fail to do it.

"My kind respects await Madame la Marquise, and I hope her interesting family is well. It would afford me great happiness to see or hear from you, and if you cannot favor us with a visit, I beg the favor of any news that may be interesting.

"I am, my dear General, yours, &c.

"P. S.—Mr. Little Page has arrived at the army of the Prince de Potemkin, and I expect to see him here in a few days. The Captain Pasha has been beaten last week. This is a good beginning, and I hope we shall soon have greater success. The Count de Dumas was in the affair. To speak in our republican way he is a gallant fellow. I marked him well. He has my esteem, and his fair mistress owes him twenty *sweet* kisses for his first effort. He keeps his picture always at his heart."

"*On board the Wolodimer, before Oczacoff,* $\frac{29\ \textit{August,}}{9\ \textit{Sept.,}}$ 1788.

"His Excellency THOMAS JEFFERSON, Esq.

"SIR,

"Some of my friends in America did me the honor to ask for my bust; I enclose the names of eight gentlemen, to each of whom I promised to send one. You will oblige me much by desiring Mr. Houdan to have them prepared, and packed up two and two: and if Mr. Short, to whom I present my respects, will take the trouble to forward them by good opportunities, via Havre de Grace, writing at the same time a few words to each of the gentlemen, I shall esteem it a particular favor.

"Before I left Copenhagen I wrote to Mr. Amoureux, merchant at

L'Orient, to dispose of some articles of mine in his hands, and remit you the amount. I hope he has done it, and that his remittance may be sufficient to pay Mr. Houdan, and the expense of striking the medal with which I am honored by the United States. But lest this should not turn out as I expect, I have directed Dr. Bancroft to pay any draft of yours on him for my account, as far as four or five thousand livres. I shall want four gold medals as soon as the dies are finished. I must present one to the United States, another to the King of France, and I cannot do less than offer one to the empress. As you will keep the dies for me, it is my intention to have some more gold medals struck; therefore I beg you, in the mean time, not to permit the striking of a single silver or copper medal.

"I pray you to present me in the most respectful terms to Monsieur de Simolin. However my situation in Russia may terminate, I shall ever esteem myself under great obligation to him. I pray you to present my affectionate respects to the Count d'Estaing, and tell him I am infinitely flattered by the obliging things he has had the goodness to say of me in my absence. I admire him for his magnanimity, and it vexes me every time I reflect how little his bravery and patriotism have been rewarded by government. He is the only officer who served through the last war without promotion or honors. It is his honor to be beloved by his nation and to have deserved it.

"I send enclosed an extract of my journal on my expedition from France to Holland in the year 1779, for the information of the Academy of Inscriptions and Belles-Lettres. I trust at the same time more to your judgment than to theirs. There is a medallist who executed three medals for me in wax. One of them is the battle between the Bon homme Richard and the Serapis. The position of the two ships is not much amiss; but the accessory figures are much too near the principal objects; and he has placed them to windward, instead of being, as they really were, to leeward of the Bon homme Richard and Serapis. I do not at this moment recollect the medallist's name; but he lives on the 3d or 4th stage at a marble-cutter's, almost opposite, but a little higher than your former house, Cul-de-sac Rue Taitebout, and may be easily found. It would be of use to see the medal he has made, although it is by no means to be copied. I owe him a small sum, perhaps 200 livres. I wish to know how much, that I may take an arrangement for paying. I have not comprehended in the extract of my journal the extreme difficulties I met with in Holland, nor my departure from the Texel in the Alliance, when I was forced out by the Vice-Admiral Rhynst in the face of the enemy's fleet. The critical situation I was in in Holland needs no explanation, and I shall not say how much the honor of the American flag depended on my conduct, or how much it affected all the belligerent powers. I shall only say it was a principal cause of the resentment of England against Holland, and of the war that ensued. It is for you and the academy to determine, whether that part of my service ought to be the subject of one side of the medal?"

"*Before Oczacoff, Sept.* 15–26, 1788.

"Mr. Littlepage has postponed his departure. I expected him to remain with me till the end of the campaign, but he now sets out so suddenly that I cannot send by him the extract of my journal in 1779. I will send it in a week or two to my friend the Count de Segur at St. Petersburg, and he will forward it to you with his ministerial despatches. Your letters with which you honor me may also be forwarded to him. I persuade myself that Count de Montmorin will do it with pleasure. I trouble you with two enclosed letters, and am with perfect esteem, &c."

"List of gentlemen to whom busts are to be sent:

"General St. Clair, and Mr. Ross, of Philadelphia.—Mr. John Jay, General Irvine, Mr. Secretary Thompson, and Colonel Wadsworth, of New York.—Mr. J. Madison, and Colonel Carrington, of Virginia."

"Admiral Paul Jones presents his respectful compliments to Mr. Short, and begs the favor of him to forward the eight busts mentioned in the above list by the most direct opportunities, from Havre de Grace to America. Mr. Jefferson is wrote to on this subject; and Mr. Houdan, who prepares the busts, will also have them carefully packed up in four boxes. The admiral prays Mr. Short to be so obliging as to write a line or two to each of the gentlemen for whom the busts are destined."

Jones was now again in active employment, on the element most favorable to the display of his talents. That much reliance was placed on his skill and energy may be inferred from the annexed note of the Prince of Nassau:

"*May 30th*, 1788.

"To the VICE-ADMIRAL.

"I send you, my dear general, the two answers of M. de Suvorow, which he has transmitted, unsealed. I beg you to inform me what are your intentions, as I have decided, since I have the liberty, to march only when you can *protect me.*

"PRINCE NASSAU-SIEGEN."

From his flag ship, the Wolodimer, the Vice Admiral wrote to that Prince. His letter shows that some difference of opinion existed between them:

"*On board the frigate Wolodimer, June 1st*, 1788, *opposite the first village to the west of the River Bog.*

"The Vice Admiral to the PRINCE NASSAU-SIEREN.

"MY PRINCE,

"No person can desire more than myself to make a happy, and, at the same time, glorious campaign, for the arms of her imperial majesty. If you can show me a more advantageous position than the one I already have, I will change my plan with pleasure to adopt yours. If you are of opinion that my duty requires me to attack the Turkish fleet, under existing circumstances, I ask you if I ought not to wait until I can conquer it. Where is the man who will justify me, if following my own will, and without any necessity, knowing nothing certain of the position of the army of his highness the Marshal Prince Potemkin, I should expose the squadron under my command to be burnt or taken. Do you believe the enemy will dare make a descent on this side of Kimbourn, and thus place himself between two fires? The experience of the last year proves that nothing is risked on the other side, and that the garrison is strong enough, and the generals able enough, to repel an attack of ten thousand men. But if the squadron which I have the honor to command should be destroyed, it is not necessary for me to inform you that the *Bog*, the *Cherson*, &c. &c. would be open to the ravages of the enemy. I would desire from my heart that your highness would place one or two batteries under the walls of Kimbourn, to reinforce the place; but you must feel that it is impossible for me to escort you even under the guns of Kimbourn, without having first conquered the Turkish fleet. My intention is to protect Kimbourn, and I believe I do so at this moment. If I advance I shall find myself in a *position much less favorable*, without any perceptible advantage. The council of war of the squadron and of the flotilla, which I held the 4th of June, very inconsiderately determined to abandon the only good position in the Liman (without knowing the intentions of his highness the prince marshal) and to advance three versts to occupy another infinitely more exposed and less strong. It was compromitting our means for the remainder of the war, without placing Kimbourn the least more in safety —in fact, all was to the contrary. We have a stronger force in our barges than the Turks, in consequence we can always go to the assistance of Kimbourn, even against the wind.

"I have the honor to be, with the most distinguished consideration and attachment,

"MY PRINCE," &c.

Prince Potemkin, if the following letter may be considered as proof, highly approved of the behavior of Jones, and professed to be his friend:

"*Head quarters, on the Bog, near Nova Grigorersky, June 8th*, 1788.

"To the VICE ADMIRAL.

"The part you have taken in concert with the Prince of Nassau, in uniting your forces with his, and acting thus against the enemy, cannot, sir, but give me most particular pleasure. This junction is as necessary as useful for the service of her imperial majesty, and particularly at this time. I recommend it to you, therefore, sir, in the strongest manner possible, in assuring you that on every occasion it will do me the greatest pleasure to appreciate to the empress the services you may render the country. I would desire you could defer your operations until I may have approached nearer to you, excepting in case the enemy should give you a good opportunity to offer battle, or that the safety of Kimbourn should require it.

"I have the honor to be, with perfect consideration,

"Sir, your most obedient servant,

"PRINCE POTEMKIN-TAURICIEN."

Although there was not, in the whole fleet on the Liman, or on the Black Sea, an officer so well qualified to direct the naval operations against the Turks as Jones, yet, situated as he was, among rival commanders, he found it indispensable to defer his judgment to that of others. He appeared to be disposed to court the favor of Prince Potemkin.

On the 8th of June the Prince Potemkin had also written to the vice admiral a letter of thanks in the following terms:

"*June 8th*, 1788.

"To the VICE ADMIRAL.

"The zeal and intrepidity manifested by your excellency in the affair against the Turks, on the 7th of this month, in aiding the Prince of Nassau, merit a just distinction,* and I return you my thanks. I am persuaded that such undertakings will contribute much to the honor and glory of the Russian arms.

"PRINCE POTEMKIN-TAURICIEN."

The Vice Admiral replied to the Prince on the 10th and 11th:—

"*On board the Wolodimer, June 10th*, 1788.

"The Prince Marshal POTEMKIN-TAURICIEN.

"MY LORD,

"It is with the highest satisfaction that I find your Highness has been pleased with my conduct, and that by your letter which I have just received, dated the 8th instant, you have approved of the arrangements made by the Prince of Nassau and myself, to combine the forces which you have confided to us, to act in concert. For my own part, as it is my glory to serve under your orders, *I will sacrifice my own opinion, in every instance where the interests of Russia may render it necessary*, and I shall esteem myself most happy in doing all that honor may require, to prove how sensible, and how flattered I am at the goodness and kindness of the Empress, and how ambitious I am to merit the friendship of Your Highness, in contributing all in my power to advance the great views you entertain for the good of the country.

"I have the honor to be, &c."

"*Wolodimer, off Oczakoff, June 11th*, 1788.

"The Prince Marshal POTEMKIN.

"MY LORD,

"I am highly flattered by the letter which Your Highness done me the honor to write to me the 8th of this month, to inform me that you were satisfied with my conduct in the affair of the 7th inst. It is a new proof of your great and generous soul. I can assure you that I did not

* For this affair I received from his highness the order of St. Anne.

enter it to increase my own personal interests, but solely for the benefit of the Russian arms, as I saw the first division of the flotilla of Her Imperial Majesty in disorder, and in a most critical situation.

"I have the honor to be, &c."

On the 20th of June, 1788, in a letter to Prince Potemkin, the Vice Admiral adverts to an affair between the Russians and the Turks, in which he bore a part, and for which he received a second time the thanks of the Prince:

"*Wolodimer, off Oczakoff, June 20th,* 1788.

"His Highness the PRINCE MARSHAL.

"MY LORD,

"I could not have been more flattered than by the letter which it has pleased Your Highness to write to me the 19th inst., to mark your satisfaction for the victory gained over the enemy, and to do me the *particular honor of offering me your thanks.* This is a recompense grateful to a heart entirely devoted to you, and nothing can give me more pleasure than to find new opportunities to prove my devotion to the interests of Russia.

"My intention was to have attacked the Turkish fleet at the same instant I perceived the action commence between the fleet of Sevastopole and that of the Turks, outside of Kimbourn. I would have done it also, if Kimbourn had been attacked, and our position and our circumstances rendered it indispensable that we should remain firm in case of an attack. *We were to conquer or to die*, and my resolution was taken. But it is fortunate for us that we did not advance, for it was the intention of the Turks to attack and board us, and if we had been only three versts farther, the attempt would have been made on the 16th (before the vessel of the Captain Pasha ran aground, in advancing before the wind with all his forces to attack us), God only knows what would have been the result. The Turks had a very large force, and we have been informed by our prisoners that they were resolved to destroy us, even by burning themselves (in setting fire to their own vessels, after having grappled with ours).* It is certain we should have lost considerably, and it is at least

* Before their departure from Constantinople, they swore by the beard of the Sultan to execute this horrible plan; and if Providence had not caused its failure from two circumstances which no man could foresee, Cherson, being without a garrison, would have fallen into their power the next day, with all the provisions and military stores, as well for the army as for the navy.

to be presumed that our vessels would have been rendered unfit for service, so that, I repeat, Providence has highly favored us.

"Your Highness can now look upon the capture of Oczakoff as certain as the most superior means and arrangements can render military operations. We learn by our prisoners that there are eight thousand troops in that place, who are but badly disciplined. There remains only with Hassan Pacha four vessels of his fleet, to wit: One small frigate, one schooner, one sloop-of-war, and one chebec aground, but the flotilla is still with him. I would not have been surprised to have been attacked in the night; they are greatly enraged, and, in consequence, will commit some desperate acts. Each day some of their men are hung up to the yard arm.

"I have the honor to be, with the most perfect attachment, &c."

Being before Oczakoff, on the 29th of August, 1788, he wrote to Mr. Jefferson. In one part of his letter he speaks doubtingly of his situation:—

"*On board the Wolodimer, before Oczakoff,*
Aug. 29—9 *Sept.* 1788.

"His Excellency THOMAS JEFFERSON, Esq.

"DEAR SIR,

"Since I wrote you last from Copenhagen, the 8th of April, I have been very much hurried; but my greatest difficulty has not been want of time, but want of a private opportunity to write to you. Mr. Littlepage is now on the point of leaving the army of the Prince Marechal de Potemkin, and talks of being at Paris in the month of October; I avail myself, therefore, of the opportunity he offers to send you enclosed a copy of my last letter from Copenhagen, with a copy of the official letter I received from the Count de Bernstorff, and a copy of the letter I have just received on the subject of my public business there, from Monsieur Framery, Secretary to the Legation of France at the Court of Denmark, informing me he had received and forwarded to you the answer I expected from the Consul of France, at Bergen in Norway. This last must necessarily make you acquainted with all you wanted to know respecting our claim on the Court of Denmark.

"The within letter to the Marquis de la Fayette was intended for you as well as him, and I send you the copy because I am not sure if he received the original. The American constitution, I suppose, is adopted;

but I am still afraid of the danger that may result from entrusting the President with such tempting power as military rank and command must give him! I can in no situation, however remote I am, be easy, while the liberties of America seem to me to be in danger.

"I leave to Mr. Littlepage to inform you particularly of the military events that have taken place here this campaign. I can take no delight in telling over tales of blood. God knows there has been too much of it spilt! Scenes of horror have been acted under my eyes in which, however, I have the happiness to say, I had no part.

"I pray you to inform me, if you possibly can, what is become of Mrs. T——. I am astonished to have heard nothing from her since I left Paris. I had written to her frequently, before I left Copenhagen. If you cannot hear of and see her, you will oblige me much by writing a note to Monsieur Dubois, Commissaire du Regiment des Guardes Français, vis à vis la Rue de Vivienne, Rue neuve des petits Champs, desiring to speak with him. He will wait on you immediately. You must know, that besides my own purse, which was very considerable, I was good natured, or, if you please, foolish enough to borrow for her four thousand four hundred livres. Now Mr. Dubois knows that transaction, and as she received the money entire from me for the reimbursement, I wish to know if she has acquitted the debt? When that affair is cleared up, I shall be better able to judge of the rest.

"I am, with perfect esteem, dear Sir, &c."

"*Copenhagen, May 3d*, 1788.

"Commodore Paul Jones, St. Petersburg.

"Dear Commodore,

"The packet which M. Dechezlaux, Consul of France at Berghen in Norway, as you informed me at your departure, was about to forward you to Copenhagen, arrived on the 26th ult. to my address, accompanied by a letter from this Consul requesting me to transmit it to you. On the 29th I had the pleasure to expedite it, agreeably to your wishes, addressed to Mr. Jefferson, through the channel of the Department of Foreign Affairs, for greater safety. I have seized with eagerness this occasion, to offer my services to that minister, in every thing that could interest or please him in this country, without saying more, leaving the rest to your disposal. The advance which I made on account of the expenses of the packet which was very voluminous, amounting to 6rixd. 4m. 12s. or 30liv. 10s. Tour. I have requested of M. Jefferson to remit for my account to M. J. F. Frin, banker, rue de Carroussel, at Paris.

"It is to be believed you are yet at St. Petersburg. I will learn with increased gratification your arrival in this capital, as reports are in circulation here that you have perished in a storm in the Gulf of Finland, but as the relation of this pretended misfortune changes every day, I am still persuaded that it exists only in the mouths of evil disposed persons, who first forged and spread the account. My good wishes accompany you in every part of the world, animated by the remembrance of the friendship you expressed for me when at Copenhagen. The Baron de la Houze to whom I mentioned that I was about to write to you, has charged me renew to you the assurance of the sentiments of esteem and real attachment with which you have inspired him. He is so far from giving credence to the report which I have mentioned, that he awaits by the arrival of every courier, the letter which you promised to write him, as soon as you had reached your port of destination.

"Affairs are here in nearly the same situation as you left them, only that the Prince Charles of Hesse Cassel arrived in this capital a few days since, on account of the voyage which the Prince Royal of Denmark is about to make this summer to Norway, where the Prince Charles will precede him by a few weeks, in order to receive him; the voyage is fixed for the 17th of the next month. Everything appears very peaceable and tranquil in this country, even to the armament of 12 ships of the line and 8 frigates, which the King of Sweden has ordered to Carlscrone, since the Danish government confines itself, at least for the present, to 4 ships of the line and 2 or 3 frigates; but as we are not ignorant of the state of the finances of Gustavus III., it is asked, what power it is that furnishes him the necessary means of fitting out a squadron of such considerable force? If it is England, or rather the Porte? what is the intention of this monarch, as the armament is by far too large for a mere naval parade, and then, too small for any enterprise whatever? In fine, it is not known where his Swedish majesty will procure, in a season already so far advanced, a sufficient number of sailors to man his ships. These are, sir, the reflections which are made in Denmark, while you are gathering new laurels under the auspices of the immortal Catharine. I shall certainly not be the less happy to applaud your glorious successes; and the satisfaction I shall feel in seeing them public will equal the sincere devotion and profound respect with which I have the honor to be, &c.

"FRAMERY,

"Secretary of Legation of His Most Christian Majesty."

"P.S. The Count de Bernstorff informed the Baron de la Houze, in his last conference, that he was about to send plenipotentiary powers to the Baron de Blome, minister plenipotentiary to our court, to treat definitively with Mr. Jefferson, on the affair which was in agitation during your residence in Copenhagen.

On the 18th of October, 1788, from some cause or other, not fully explained, but in all probability from his having presumed to dispute the accuracy of the accounts which Prince Potemkin transmitted to the empress, of the military and naval operations under his direction, the command of the vice admiral was transferred from the Liman to the Northern Seas. The following extract from the preface of Eaton's Survey of the Turkish Empire, may serve to explain the principal motive of this change, which, in effect, was equivalent to a suspension from all present employment in the navy:—

W. Eaton's survey of the Turkish Empire.—2d Ed. London, 1799.— Preface to the 1st Edition.

"It is a difficult thing at all times to discover truth, amidst the misrepresentations of courts, of ministers, of commanders. Should any one write, for instance, the history of the last war between Russia and Turkey, he would take for his guide, in relating the first event, the siege of Oczacoff, the accounts published by the court of St. Petersburg, and the reports of the commanders. There he would find a brilliant victory gained by Prince Nassau over the Turkish fleet in the Liman; but if he could get the report made by Paul Jones to the admiralty of Cherson, signed by all the commanders of the fleet, he would find that no engagement took place (except a distant cannonade); that the Turkish ships ran aground by their ignorance and bad manœuvres; and that Nassau with his *flotilla*, instead of taking possession of them, set them on fire. This journal which I have read, and taken an extract from, was forbidden by Prince Potemkin to be sent to Petersburg, and the whole campaign, as it stands on record, is nearly a romance. The fortress might have been taken the 1st of July with more ease than on the 6th of December, 1788, and the commander-in-chief knew it. I was at the opening of the trenches, and at the storming of the place, and therefore can speak of facts to which I was an eye-witness."

It was on the 18th of October, 1788, that Prince Potemkin communicated to Vice Admiral Jones, an order to repair to St. Petersburg, in these terms:

"*October* 18*th*, 1788.

"*Order to the Vice Admiral.*

"According to the desire of her imperial majesty, your place of service is fixed in the Northern seas; and as this squadron, and the flotilla, are placed by me under the orders of the vice admiral and the Chevalier de Nordivinoff, your excellency will in consequence proceed on the said voyage; principally, as the squadron in the Liman, on account of the season being so far advanced, cannot be united with that of Sevastopole.

"PRINCE POTEMKIN-TAURICIEN."

The prince, however, was generous. He possessed an elevated soul; and, on the departure of the vice admiral, gave him the subjoined recommendatory certificate to the Empress Catharine:

From His Highness the PRINCE MARSHAL to Her IMPERIAL HIGHNESS of all the Russias.

"*At the camp before Oczacoff, Oct.* 31—11 *Nov.* 1788.

"MADAM,

"In placing before the august throne of your Imperial Majesty, his Excellency the Vice Admiral Paul Jones, I take, with submission, the liberty to certify the ardor and zeal which he has always shown for the service of your Imperial Majesty; endeavoring to render himself worthy of the august favor of your Imperial Majesty.

"The most faithful subject of your Imperial Majesty,

"PRINCE POTEMKIN, Tawritcheskoy."

Arrived at St. Petersburg, the vice admiral addressed a letter to Mr. Jefferson, in which it is plainly to be perceived, that he began to cast about him for new enterprises: but more particularly with a view to the promotion of the interests of the United States:

"*St. Petersburg, Jan.* 15—26, 1789.

"His Excellency THOMAS JEFFERSON, Esq.

"MY DEAR SIR,

"Having wrote you fully respecting the Denmark business by Mr.

Littlepage, with the papers necessary to finish it, I now have the honor to transmit you the extract of my journal that you wish to communicate to the Academy of Inscriptions and Belles-Lettres on the subject of the medal with which I am honored by Congress.—I have only at present to inform you that I returned here from the Black Sea a short time ago, by the special desire of her imperial majesty; but I know not yet my future destination.—I congratulate you on the establishment of the new American Constitution. Among other good effects, a marine force will naturally result from it. If there is still a disposition to send a force against the Algerines, would it not be a good thing to conclude a treaty with this country, and make the war a common cause in the Mediterranean. The Turks and Algerines are together, and acted in conjunction against us before Oczacoff. A treaty might now be concluded, permitting Her Imperial Majesty to enlist seamen in America, and assuring to America, after the peace, a free navigation to and from the Black Sea.—If you approve of this idea in general, various other things will necessarily be engrafted in the treaty, and I flatter myself I may obtain the command of the force destined to act in conjunction with that of the United States.

"I beg to hear from you as soon as possible, and I hope to be favored with your sentiments, as I have already had some conversation with this government on the subject.—Please to mention the situation of your arrangement with the Court of Denmark.

"Present my best respects to the Marquis and to Mr. Short. I congratulate you all on the happy acquisition of liberty in France. His present majesty has established a more glorious title than any of his predecessors, and posterity will bless his memory.

"I avail myself of an express that is just setting out from the office of foreign affairs, so that I have not time even to copy this.

"I am, dear sir, yours," &c.

"*St. Petersburg*, *January* 20*th*—31*st*, 1789.

"His Excellency THOMAS JEFFERSON, Esq.

"MY DEAR SIR,

"I had the honor to write you a line the 15th–26th from this place, where I am arrived a short time ago from the Black Sea. I send enclosed an extract of the journal of my campaign in 1779, as you desired; and I now enclose an extract of the letter I wrote you by Mr. Little Page. I have heard nothing from him since he left me. I know only that he arrived at Warsaw, but am quite uncertain about his return, as he proposed, to Paris. I can only inform you that I returned here by the special desire of the empress, but I know not as yet how or where I am to be employed for the next campaign. I mentioned in my last, as my opinion, that if the new government of America determines to chastise the Algerines, I think it now a favorable moment to conclude a treaty with Russia. The Turks and Algerines were combined against us on the Black Sea. The United States could grant leave for Russia to enlist American seamen; and making a common cause with Russia in the Mediterranean, America might, at the peace, obtain a free navigation to and from the Black Sea. If such a treaty were to take place, I believe I could obtain the command of the combined force; at least no objection would be made to it here. Such a connexion might lead to various mutual advantages in the commerce between the two nations. I beg to hear from you and to know the situation of our claim on the court of Denmark, for the only objection made by the Count Bernsdorff is now removed, by the establishment of the new American constitution.

"I am, with perfect esteem and attachment," &c.

The vice admiral remained a considerable time at Petersburg, enjoying the esteem of the empress, but obnoxious to the calumnies of the English party at that court. The annexed documents show that he had a fresh project in contemplation, and that he was, at least in some degree, countenanced in it by the Russian ministry:

Secret note addressed to the Minister at St. Petersburg by the Vice-Admiral.

"*June 6th*, 1789.

"The great object of a Russian fleet in the Mediterranean is to endeavor to cut off the communication between Egypt and the coast of Syria with Constantinople, from whence they procure their corn, rice, coffee, &c. This operation will oblige them to withdraw a very considerable part of their fleet from the Black Sea. To encompass this end, I ask a *carte-blanche*, and only, exclusive of small boats, five large vessels, like the East-Indiamen which are purchased in London after they have made three voyages, and which carry from forty to fifty guns. They are strong vessels and good sailers. They are sent from London to Naples under the English flag, under pretext of being engaged in mercantile enterprizes. No person can have anything to say against it. The crews of these vessels being arrived in Italy, would engage in the service of Russia. For the rest we would easily find good sailors at Malta and at Naples.

"I would employ two small French vessels between Malta and Naples trading to Smyrna to procure continual news from Constantinople, and of the force and position of the Turkish fleet. There are some very important blows to be made, but in order to succeed we must not speak of this matter beforehand.

"We are informed that the want of provisions at Constantinople has occasioned a rebellion, discouraged the people, and caused a great desertion of the troops. It is the policy of the Vizier to render himself popular by providing sufficiently for them.

"I have the honor to be, &c."

"To the Minister of State at St. Petersburg.

"*St. Petersburg, June 13th—24th*, 1789.

"The detachment of vessels of which your excellency has spoken to me, cannot but be very advantageous to the operations which I had projected: however, I regard the means mentioned in the private note which I addressed to you, as a thing most useful, and which will not cost so much in proportion. I would wish, since circumstances will permit of it, to unite the means, and then I think we will have reason to be content with the advantages which will be the result.

"I mentioned to your excellency that I am the *only officer* who has made the campaign of Liman without being *promoted*, but I beg you to believe that I did not enter into the service of Russia to create difficulties, and since the Empress has granted me her esteem and confidence, I desire nothing else, except occasions to prove my attachment by new services.

"I have the honor to be, &c."

That Jones was hated and slandered by the British party upon his first arrival at St. Petersburg, and when he returned to that city from before Oczakoff, is confirmed not only by his own letters to his friends, but by a passage in Tooke's Life of Catharine II. Tooke's work has long occupied a place in our libraries, both public and private; and an extract from it is inserted here for the purpose of demonstrating to the reader the little confidence that is to be placed in the narrative of his work, and upon what slender materials some authors venture to detail events. The Vice Admiral was disliked by the British officers in the Russian service because they envied his glory, at that time reviled the American name and character, and because he stood in their way to preferment. Tooke, imbibing the prejudices of his countrymen, and intermingling with them a bitterness of spirit of his own, declares him to have been "*a pirate and renegado.*" But in what instance did Jones fight or capture without a regular commission? In what respect was he "a pirate and renegado" more than the American people in general, who, before the revolutionary war, were all British subjects? Enjoying the friendship of Franklin, of Jefferson, of Adams, and of all the distinguished citizens of the United States of his day, honored by the King of France with a sword and the Order of Military Merit, by Congress with a gold medal, received by the Court of Denmark with personal distinctions, and invested by the Empress of Russia with the command of a Vice Admiral, and decorated for his brilliant achievements with the Order of St. Anne, was it for Mr. Tooke to brand a man so respected and honored with the name of "pirate and renegado?" Upon the evidence adduced in the present volume an impartial world will decide between the heroic Jones and his calumniators.

From W. Tooke's Life of Catharine II. of Russia, Vol. 2, p. 252, 1788.

"Another naval armament was prepared, with no less industry, for the service of the Euxine; but Russia not being able to cope with her enemy there, in the number or strength of line-of-battle ships which she could bring into action, intended to supply this defect by the construction of a numerous flotilla, composed of frigates, gallies, gun-boats, and various descriptions of light vessels, calculated to act near the shores, in a depth of water which would not admit the approach of capital ships. It was, however, principally intended for the security of Kimbourn, by rendering the entrance of the Dniepe inaccessible to the Turkish fleet. As these vessels were not, on this service, liable to be exposed to the dangers of the seas and storms, they were accordingly fortified with a tremendous artillery, composed of heavy battering cannon, and of large mortars; and besides excellently stored with able seamen and veteran soldiers; they were eminently fitted for the designed purpose. The prince of Nassau, who had been heard of in the late war, both in the French unfortunate attempt on the island of Jersey, and in the still more disastrous attack of the combined nations of France and Spain on the fortress of Gibraltar, and whose uncommon rage for adventure and eagerness to signalize himself, have led him almost to every part of the world where any service was to be performed, or danger encountered, was appointed to the command of the naval armament on the Euxine."

P. 259.—"It is well known that there is a want of native officers of sufficient ability and experience, to conduct the operations of the Russian navy with judgment and effect. It was not perhaps in the nature of things that this deficiency could be fully supplied by foreigners. It was, however, the only resource, and the conclusion of the American war afforded a considerable supply of young English officers, whose minds were too alert to live out of action, if it could any where be found. Few, if any of these, had risen to any higher rank in their own service than that of lieutenant, so that the command of single ships seemed the highest advancement to which they could yet be competent. They were, however, of the utmost importance to Russia in the present state of things; and Great Britain, notwithstanding the jealousies subsisting between the two courts, refrained from proceeding to the extremity of recalling them home.

"This known scarcity of commanders could not fail to attract the attention of foreign adventurers, who had acquired any experience and reputation in maritime affairs. Of this number was the English pirate and renegado Paul Jones, who had rendered himself so notorious in the American war, by the mischiefs which he did to the trade of his country, and whose desperate courage, which only served to render his atrociousness conspicuous, would, in a good cause, have entitled him to honor.

"This man could not but experience the common fate incident to his character; and, finding that he did not meet the consideration which he expected in America, he made a tender of his services to the court of St. Petersburg, where he was gladly received, and immediately appointed to a high command in the grand fleet which was under equipment at Cronstadt. The British officers, full of those national and professional ideas of honor, which they had imbibed in their own country and service, considered this appointment as the highest affront that could be offered to them, and a submission to it an act of such degradation that no time or circumstance could wipe away the dishonor. They accordingly went in a body, to the amount of near thirty, without a single dissentient lagging behind, or hesitating on the account of inconvenience or personal distress, to lay down their commissions; declaring at the same time that it was impossible for them to serve under, or to act in any manner or capacity whatever, with a pirate or a renegado.

"Nothing could have been more vexatious, or more embarrassing to the Court of St. Petersburg, at the present critical period, than the spirited conduct of the officers. Punctilios of honor operating in the face of command, was a thing unheard of in that service. No Russian, under the first rank or order, would dare to insinuate such an idea. As it was, it could not be considered as less than a direct insult to the court, and any submission to it as a grievous derogation from its dignity. It would, besides, establish a precedent which might be troublesome or dangerous with respect to her own subjects. It was well for the officers that they were not the members of a small state, and that this did not happen in a season of peace, when their services might be dispensed with. The necessity of the time however prevailed. The appointment of Paul Jones to a command in the Cronstadt fleet was recalled; and that adventurer (whose character of an impetuous courage had made an impression on the court far beyond its real value) was ordered to the armament in the Euxine, as second to the Prince of Nassau. In the meantime a report was raised of a scandalous adventure with a girl, which making a noise in the town, occasioned him to think it advisable to quit the country entirely."

The story of the "scandalous adventure with a girl," alluded to by Tooke, at first made an impression on the mind of Catharine unfavorable to the Admiral; but, on investigation, it was discovered to have been a base invention of his enemies. The following letter from the Count de Segur, which does equal credit to the head and the heart of that illustrious nobleman, is conclusive as to this particular:

Copies of the letter from Count de Segur, Minister Plenipotentiary from France to St. Petersburg, to the Count D'Esterns, Minister Plenipotentiary of His Most Christian Majesty, near His Majesty the King of Prussia, and the Chevalier Bourgoing, Minister Plenipotentiary from France to Hamburg.

"*St. Petersburg, August 26th*, 1789.

"Sir,

"The Vice Admiral Paul Jones, who will have the honor to deliver this letter, commanded during the last campaign, a Russian squadron stationed on the Liman. The empress has decorated him on this occasion with the order of St. Ann. He had a right by his actions to a promotion and to a recompense, but this celebrated sailor, knowing better how to conduct himself in the midst of his battles than in courts, has offended by his frankness some of the most powerful people, and amongst others the Prince Potemkin. His enemies and his rivals have profited by his momentary disgrace to hasten his destruction. Calumny has served their purposes, they have given credit to reports absolutely false—they have accused him of violating a girl. The empress being deceived has forbid him the court, and wished to bring him to trial. Every person has abandoned him, I alone have upheld and defended him. The country to which he belongs, the order of military merit which he bears, and which he has so nobly acquired, his brilliant reputation, and, above all, our long acquaintance, have made it a law to me: my cares have not been in vain, I have caused his innocence to be acknowledged. He has repaired to court, and has kissed the hand of the sovereign, but he will not remain in a country where he believes himself to have been treated with injustice. However, he has not given in his resignation. The empress still preserves for him his rank, his emoluments, and only grants him permission to absent himself for a limited time. The true motive of his departure is founded on his own discontent. But he has made use of, as a pretext, important affairs which call him to France, to Denmark, and which may, perhaps, require his presence in America. I beg you, sir, to render to this brave man, as interesting by the reverses of fortune which he has met with as by his past success, every service which may be in your power. It will lay me under a true obligation, and I shall share in a lively manner his gratitude.

"I have the honor to be, &c.

"LE COUNT SEGUR."

The vice admiral, it will have been observed, had himself solicited leave of absence, retaining his rank, and its emoluments. His enemies seized the opportunity to circulate a rumor that he was in disgrace. To counteract the effect of this report, his friend Count Segur wrote to Count Montmorin as follows:

"*St. Petersburg, July 21st*, 1789.

"The COUNT MONTMORIN.

"MONSIEUR,

"The enemies of the Vice Admiral Paul Jones, having caused to be circulated reports entirely destitute of foundation concerning the voyage which this general officer is about to undertake, I would wish the enclosed article, the authenticity I guaranty, should be inserted in the Gazette of France, and in the other public papers, which are submitted to the inspection of your department. This article will undeceive those who have believed the calumny, and will prove to the friends and to the compatriots of the vice admiral that he has sustained the reputation acquired by his bravery and his talents during the last war; that the empress desires to retain him in her service, and that if he absents himself at this moment it is with his own free-will, and for particular reasons which cannot leave any stain on his honor.

"The glorious marks of the satisfaction and bounty of the king towards Mr. Paul Jones, his attachment to France, which he has served so usefully in the common cause, his rights as a subject and as an admiral of the United States, the protection of the ministers of the king, and my personal friendship for this distinguished officer, with whom I made a campaign in America, are so many reasons which appear to me to justify the interest which I took in all that concerned him during his stay in Russia.

"I have the honor to be, &c.

"COUNT DE SEGUR."

Article to be inserted in the public prints, and particularly in the Gazette of France.

"*St. Petersburg, July* 21*st*, 1789.

"The Vice Admiral Paul Jones being on the point of returning to France, where private affairs require his presence, had the honor to take leave of the empress the 7th of this month, and to be admitted to kiss the hand of her imperial majesty. This general officer, so celebrated by his brilliant actions during the course of the American war, was called in 1787 to the service of her imperial majesty, who confided to him the command of her vessels of war stationed on the Liman, during the campaign of 1788. As a mark of favor for his conduct during this campaign, the empress has decorated him with the insignia of the order of St. Ann, and her imperial majesty, satisfied with his services, only grants him permission to absent himself for a limited time, and still preserves for him his emoluments and his rank.

"COUNT DE SEGUR."

The slander was finally put to rest. Among other letters of congratulation, the vice admiral received one from the Baron de la Houze, minister plenipotentiary of France at Copenhagen:

" *Copenhagen, February 9th,* 1790.

" The Vice Admiral J. Paul Jones.

" Sir,

" It is but a few days since I received with the letter with which you have honored me of the 29th of December, the copies of that of the Count de Segur, which you have been pleased to communicate to me, and which were accompanied by the article inserted on your account in the Gazette of France, and which I had read. This article, which has been repeated in many foreign gazettes, has entirely destroyed all the venomous effects which calumny had employed to tarnish the distinguished reputation which you have acquired by your talents and your valor. In consequence, public opinion still continues to render you justice, and the most noble revenge you can take on your enemies is to gather fresh laurels. The celebrated Athenian general Themistocles has said that he did not envy the situation of one who was not envied. As to the affair, concerning which you speak to me, and in which you have been witness to my zeal, as well for your compatriots as for my own, it remains still at the same point where you left it on your departure for St. Petersburg, the 15th April, 1788. A note in answer, which the Count de Bernstorff addressed to you on the 4th, keeps always in view the affair which you negotiated with him, but for the conclusion of which you are not clothed with the necessary plenipotentiary powers. You know, however, that according to the note of the Count de Bernstorff, Paris ought to have been the seat of the negotiation between the Baron de Blome, Envoy Extraordinary of His Danish Majesty, and Mr. Jefferson, Minister Plenipotentiary of the United States of North America near the king. You inform me that Mr. Jefferson is at present in America, where he has been appointed Secretary of State for foreign affairs. No person, then, can better instruct than him his successor to Paris, to take up the thread of this negotiation with the Baron de Blome. I spoke, three days since, to the Count de Bernstorff, who perseveres according to what he told me, in all that he mentioned to you in his note of the 4th of April, 1788, but this minister observed to me that the circumstances of the actual crisis of Europe did not permit him to follow at this time the negotiation, which it appeared to him best to keep back until the return of a calm.

" When I shall have the pleasure to see M. Broseronde, our consul at Elsineur, I shall take care to renew to him the assurance of your remembrance, to which he will most certainly be sensible, as likewise is M. Framery, Secretary of my Legation, who begs you to accept his compliments and his thanks.

" You will part, in all probability, about the commencement of the fine season to return to Russia. I wish that your voyage may procure me, as you have given me reason to expect, satisfaction to express personally to you the distinguished sentiments of attachment and consideration with which I have the honor to be, sir,

"Your obedient, &c.

"LE BARON DE LA HOUZE."

This letter of the Baron de la Houze looked forward to Jones's speedy return to the Russian service, and the subjoined address to Prince Potemkin evinces the desire of Jones to do so. At the same time that Jones, with the frankness of a man of courage, apologizes to the prince for what he supposed had offended him, he vindicates his own character with freedom and energy:

"*Paris, July 24th*, 1790.

"To His Highness the PRINCE MARSHAL.

"MY LORD,

"I do not think it becomes me to let pass the occasion of the return of your aid-de-camp, to congratulate you on the brilliant success of your operations since I had the honor to serve under your orders; and to express to you, in all the sincerity of my heart, the regret I feel in not being fortunate enough to contribute thereto.

"After the campaign of Liman, when I had leave, according to the special desire of Her Imperial Majesty, to return to the department of the northern seas, your Highness did me the favor to grant me a letter of recommendation to the Empress, and to tell me in these words, 'Rely upon my attachment. I am disposed to grant you the most solid proofs of my friendship, for the present and for the future.' Do you recollect them? This discourse was too flattering for me to forget it, and I hope you will permit me to remind you of it. Circumstances, and the high rank of my enemies, have deprived me of the benefits which I had dared to hope from the esteem which you had expressed for me, and which I had endeavored to merit by my services. You know the disagreeable situation in which I was placed, but if, as I dared to believe, I have preserved your good opinion, I may still hope to see it followed by advantages, which it will be my glory to owe to you. M. de Simolin can testify to you that my attachment to Russia, and to the great princess who is its sovereign, has always been constant and durable. I attended to my duties, and not to my fortune. I have been wrong, and I avow it with a frankness which carries with it its own excuse.—1. That I did not request of you a carte-blanche, and the absolute command of all the forces of the Liman.—2. To have written to your Highness under feelings highly excited, on the 14–25th October, 1788. These are my faults. If my enemies have wished to impute others to me, I swear before God, that they are a calumny. It only rests with me, my lord, to unmask the villainy of my enemies, by publishing my journal of the operations of the campaign of Liman, with the proofs clear as the day, and which I have in my hands. It only rests with me to prove that I directed, under your orders, all the useful operations against the Captain Pasha; that it was I who beat him on the 7th of June; that it was I, and the brave men I commanded, who conquered him on the 17th of June, and who chased into the sands two of his largest galleys, before our flotilla was ready to fire a single shot, and during the time a very considerable part of the force of the enemy remained at anchor immediately in the rear of my squadron; that it was I who gave to General Suwarrow, (he had the nobleness to declare it at court before me, to the most respectable witnesses,) the first project to establish the battery and breastworks on the Isthmus of Kinbourn, and which was of such great utility on the night of the 17–18th June; that it was I, in person, who towed, with my sloops and other vessels, the batteries which were the nearest to the place the 1st July, and who took the Turkish galleys by boarding, very much in advance of our line, whilst some gentlemen who have been too highly rewarded in consequence of it, were content to remain in the rear of the stragglers of our line, if I may be allowed to use the expression, sheltered from danger. You have seen yourself, my lord, that I never valued my person, on any occasion, where I had the good fortune to act under your eye. The whole of Europe acknowledges my veracity, and grants me some military talents, which it would give me pleasure to employ in the service of Russia, under your orders. The time will arrive, my lord, when you will know the exact truth of what I have told you. Time is a sovereign master. It will teach you to appreciate the man, who, loaded with your benefits, departed from the Court of Russia with a memorial prepared by other hands and the enemies of your glory, and of which memorial he made no use, because your brilliant success at the taking of Oczakoff, which he learned on his arrival in White-Russia, gave the lie to all the horrors which had been brought forward to enrage the Empress against you. You know it was the echo of another intriguer at the Court of Vienna. In fine, time will teach you, my lord, that I am neither a mountebank nor a swindler, but a man, true and loyal. I rely upon the attachment and friendship which you promised me: I rely on it, because I feel myself worthy of it: I reclaim your promise, because you are just, and I know you are a lover of truth.

"I commanded, and was the only responsible person in the campaign of Liman, the others being only of inferior rank, or simple volunteers: I am, however, the only one who has not been promoted or rewarded. I am extremely thankful for the order of St. Ann, which you procured for me, according to your letter of thanks *for my conduct in the affair of the 7th of June*, which was not decisive. The 17th June, I gained over the Captain Pasha a complete victory, which saved Cherson and Kinbourn, the terror of which caused the enemy to lose nine vessels of war, in their precipitate flight on the following night, under the cannon of the battery and breastwork which I had caused to be erected on the Isthmus of Kinbourn. On this occasion I had the honor again to receive a *letter of thanks;* but my enemies and my rivals have found means to abuse your confidence, since they have been exclusively rewarded. They merited rather to have been punished for having burnt nine armed prizes with their crews, which were absolutely in our power, having previously ran aground under our guns.

"I have been informed that, according to the institution of the order of St. George, I have the right to claim its decoration in the second class, for the victory of the seventeenth of June, but I rely upon your justice and generosity.

"I regret that a secret project which I addressed to the Count du Besborodska, the 6th of June of the last year, has not been adopted. I communicated this project to the Baron de Beihler, who has promised me to speak to you of it.

"I was detained in St. Petersburg until the end of August, in order to hinder me, as I have heard, from proceeding into the service of Sweden—my poor enemies, how I pity them! But for this circumstance, my intention was to have presented myself at your head-quarters, in the hope to be of some utility; and the Baron de Beihler, in departing from St. Petersburg in order to join you, promised me to assure you of my devotion for the service of your department, and that I held myself ready to return to you the instant I was called. My conduct has not since changed, although I hold in my hand a parole for two years, and I regard eighteen months of this parole, in a time of war, more as a punishment than as a favor.

"I hope that your Highness will succeed in concluding peace this year with the Turks; but in a contrary case, if it should please you to recall me to take command of the fleet in the ensuing campaign, I would ask permission to bring with me the French officer concerning whom I spoke to you, with one or two others, who are good tacticians, and who have some knowledge of war. On my return here, I received a gold medal, granted me by the *unanimous* voice of Congress, at the moment I received a parole from this honorable body. The United States have decreed me this honor, in order to perpetuate the remembrance of the services which I rendered to America eight years previous, and have ordered a copy to be presented to all the sovereigns and all the academies of Europe, with the exception of Great Britain. There is reason to believe that your Highness will be numbered among the sovereigns of Europe, in consequence of the treaty of peace which you are about to conclude with the Turks; but in any case, if a copy of my medal will be acceptable to you, as a mark of my attachment to your person, it will do me an honor to offer it to you.

"I have the honor to be, &c."

The following letter which the Vice Admiral wrote to the Empress Catharine, on the 25th of February, 1791, exhibits in unequivocal terms, the wound inflicted on his feelings and the pain which he endured from the unpleasant situation in which he was suffered to remain:—

"*Paris, Feb.* 25–8 *March*, 1791.

"Her Imperial Majesty of all the Russias.

"Madam,

"If I could imagine that the letter which I had the honor to write to Your Majesty from Warsaw, Sept. 25th–6th Oct. 1789, had come to hand, it would be without doubt indiscreet in me to beg you to cast your eyes on the documents enclosed which *accuse no person*, and the only intent of which is to let you see that in the important campaign of Liman, the part which I played was not either that of a *Zero* or of a *Harlequin* which required 'to be made a colonel at the *tail* of his regiment.' I have in my hands the means to prove incontestably that I directed all the useful operations against the Captain Pasha. The task which was given me at this critical conjuncture was very difficult. I was obliged to sacrifice my own opinion and risk my military reputation for the benefit of your Empire. But, I hope, you will be satisfied with the manner in which I conducted myself, and also of my subsequent arrangements of which I am persuaded you have not been acquainted until this moment. The gracious counsel which Your Majesty has often done me the honor to repeat to me before my departure for the Black Sea, and in a letter which you have deigned to write to me afterward, has since been the rule of my conduct; and the faithful attachment with which you have inspired me for your person, was the only reason which hindered me from requesting my dismissal when I wrote to you from Warsaw, for I confess that I was extremely afflicted and even offended at having received a parole for two years in time of war. A parole which it has never entered into my mind to wish for, and still less to ask, and of which I have not profited to go to America, or even to Denmark, where I had important business; for I had always hoped to have been usefully employed in your service before the expiration of this parole which has done me so much injury, and although in public I would not have failed to have spoken to you at the last audience which you granted me, but I unfortunately was led to believe the repeated promises made me, that I should have a private audience in order to lay before you my military projects, and to speak of them in detail.

"I hope that the brilliant success with which Providence has blessed your arms will enable you to grant peace to your enemies without shedding more of human blood, but in a contrary case Your Majesty can be well instructed from my project, No. 12, of last year.

"As I have my enemies, and as the term of my parole is about to expire, I await the orders of Your Majesty, and should be flattered, if it is your pleasure, to come and render you an account in person. Mr. —— who has the goodness to charge himself with this packet, which I have addressed to him, sealed with my arms, will also undertake to forward me your orders; I therefore pray you to withdraw me as soon as possible from the cruel uncertainty in which I am placed. Should you deign, Madam, to inform me that you are pleased with the services which I have had the happiness to render you, I will console myself for the misfortunes which I have suffered, as I drew my sword for you from personal attachment for you and ambition, but not for interest. My fortune, as you know, is not very considerable, but as I am philosopher enough to confine myself to my means, I shall always be rich.

"I have the honor to be, Madam, yours, &c."

Mr. Jefferson had now returned to America, and entered upon the duties of Secretary of State under the Presidency of Washington. Still smarting under the injuries he had received in Russia, Jones addressed the annexed letter to that old and steadfast friend :—

"*Paris, March 20th*, 1791.

"His Excellency THOMAS JEFFERSON, Esq.

"DEAR SIR,

"On my return from Russia to Amsterdam, in December, 1789, I wrote to several gentlemen in America, particularly to the *Vice President*, and to Mr. Secretary Thomson, enclosing some evidence of the treatment I met with in Russia. I wrote at the same time to the *President*, enclosing a letter from the Count de Segur. Messrs. Stuphorsts and Hubbard undertook to forward my packets by a ship, then ready to sail for Philadelphia, called the Pennsylvania Packet, John Earl, master; but though that ship arrived safe, I have not to this hour received a single line in answer.

"I need not express to you the pleasure I received from your acceptance of the honorable and high station of Secretary of State for domestic and foreign affairs. I felicitate our country on having wisely confided her interest to such worthy and able hands; but it gives me pain that so inadequate a provision has been made for doing the honors incumbent on the first minister of a nation of such resources as America, and I wish that matter may be soon changed to your satisfaction.

"As it has been, and still is, my first wish and highest ambition to show myself worthy of the flattering marks of esteem with which I have been honored by my country, I think it my duty to lay before you, both as my particular friend and as a public minister, the papers I now enclose relative to my connexion with Russia, viz.—Three pieces, dated at St. Petersburg, and signed by the Count de Segur; a letter from me, dated at Paris last summer, and sent to the Prince de Potemkin; and a letter from me to the Empress, dated a few days ago. I have selected these testimonials from a great variety of perhaps still stronger proofs in my hands; but though the Baron de Grimm has undertaken to transmit to her Imperial Majesty's own hands my last packet, I shall not be surprised, if I should find myself constrained to withdraw from the Russian service, and to publish my journal of the campaign I commanded: in that case, I hope to prove to the world, that *my operations* not only saved Cherson and Crimea, but decided the fate of the war.

"Chevalier Littlepage, now here on his way from Spain to the north, has promised me a letter to you on my subject, which I presume will show the meanness and absurdity of the intrigues that were practised for my persecution at St. Petersburg. I did not myself comprehend all the blackness of that business before he came here and related to me the information he received from a gentleman of high rank in the diplomatique, with whom he travelled in company from Madrid to Paris. That gentleman had long resided in a public character at the Court of St. Petersburg, and was there all the time of the pitiful complot against me; which was conducted by a little-great man, behind the curtain.

"The unequal reception with which I had, at first, been honored by the Empress had been extremely mortifying and painful to the English at St. Petersburg, and the courtier just mentioned, (finding that politics had taken a turn far more alarming than he had expected at the beginning of the war,) wishing to soothe the court of London into a pacific humor, found no first step so expedient as that of sacrificing me! But instead of producing the effect he wished, this base conduct, on which he pretended to ground a conciliation, rather widened the political breach, and made him to be despised by the English minister, by the English cabinet, and by the gentleman who related the secret to the Chevalier Littlepage.

"I must farther inform you, that a few days after my arrival from Denmark at St. Petersburg, I received from the Danish minister at that court, a letter under the seal of the Count de Bernstorff, which having opened, I found to be a patent from the King of Denmark, in the following terms:

"'Having reasons for wishing to give new proofs of our bounty to the Chevalier Paul Jones, Commander in Chief of the squadrons of the United States of America, and desiring, above all, to prove our esteem in consequence of the regard which he has shown for the Danish flag during the time of his command in the northern seas, we grant him from the present moment, and annually during his life, the sum of fifteen hundred crowns, Danish currency, to be paid at Copenhagen, without any retention whatsoever. Done at our Castle of Christianbourg, the 4th of April, 1788.'

"The day before I left the court of Copenhagen, the Prince Royal had desired to speak with me in his apartment. His Royal Highness was extremely polite, and after saying many civil things, remarked, he hoped I was satisfied with the attentions that had been shown to me since my arrival, and that the King would wish to give me some mark of his esteem. 'I have never had the happiness to render any service to His Majesty.' 'That is nothing; a man like you ought to be excepted from ordinary rules. You could not have shown yourself more delicate as regards our flag, and every person here loves you.'

"I took leave without farther explanation. I have felt myself in an embarrassing situation on account of the King's patent, and I have as yet made no use of it, though three years have nearly elapsed since I received it. I wished to consult you, but when I understood that you would not return to Europe, I consulted Mr. Short and Mr. G. Morris, who both gave me their opinion, that I may with propriety accept the advantage offered. I have in consequence determined to draw for the sum due, and I think you will not disapprove of this step, as it can by no means weaken the claim of the United States, but rather the contrary.

"You will observe that the Empress of Russia has decorated me with the great order of St. Ann; and as I have appeared with that order ever since, I must beg the favor of you to obtain and transmit to me, as soon as possible, the proper authority of the United States for my retaining that honor. You are sensible I did not accept the offer of Her Imperial Majesty with a view to detach myself from the service of America, but that I have done my utmost to fulfil the intention of Congress in sending me last to Europe, 'to acquire that degree of knowledge which may hereafter render me more extensively useful.' I have in some measure, by my experience and observation, effected the object of my pursuit: though I confess I have still much to learn, and I wish to embrace the first occasion to embark in the French fleet of evolution.

"I have not, since my return here, appeared at court; but the Marquis de la Fayette will shortly conduct me to the King, when I shall present my journal of the American war, with the letter of which I am bearer from the United States.

"I reserve for my return to America to produce to the United States full and unquestionable evidence, signed by the Grand Pensioner, that *my conduct*, in 1779, drew the United Netherlands into the war. This is saying enough to a man of your information; for it would be superfluous to enumerate the advantages that thence resulted to America particularly the great event which took place under your own eyes, and which could not have happened if Holland had remained a neutral power.

"I am much obliged by the trouble you took in forwarding, before you left Europe, the busts I had promised to different gentlemen in America. Having lately received a letter from Mr. Burton, a former member of Congress, with whom I had the honor of being acquainted at New York, requesting my bust in behalf of the State of North-Carolina, I have ordered Mr. Houdan to prepare and forward it by the first ship from Havre-de-Grace, for Philadelphia; and as that bust will be decorated with the order of St. Ann, on the American uniform, this is one reason why I wish to be authorized by the United States to wear that order. I shall take the liberty of addressing the bust to you, requesting you to deliver it to the North-Carolina delegates, who will be so good as to forward it to the Governor of that state.

"I continue to be sensibly affected by the situation of our poor countrymen at Algiers: the more so, as I learn indirectly from the pirate, now here, who took the greatest part of them, that if they are not very soon redeemed, they will be treated with no more lenity than is shown to other slaves. He told this to Mr. Littlepage, who repeated it to me.

"I have the honor to be, &c."

The letter promised by Mr. Littlepage, and adverted to by Jones, was as follows:—

"*Paris*, *March* 23, 1791.

"His Excellency THOMAS JEFFERSON, Esq.

"SIR,

"You will share my regret in reflecting that we were the principal means of engaging Admiral Sir John Paul Jones to accept the propositions made to him in 1788 by the Russian Court. Never were more brilliant prospects held forth to an individual, and never individual better calculated to attain them. The campaign upon the Liman of 1788, added lustre to the arms of Russia, and ought to have established for ever the reputation and fortune of the gallant officer to whose conduct those successes were owing: but unfortunately in Russia, more perhaps than elsewhere, everything is governed by intrigue. Some political motives, I have reason to think, concurred in depriving Admiral Paul Jones of the fruits of his services: he was thought to be particularly obnoxious to the English nation, and the idea of paying a servile compliment to a power whose enmity occasions all the present embarrassments of Russia, induced some leading persons to ruin him in the opinion of the Empress by an accusation too ridiculous.

"It would be needless to enter into details; you have too much confidence in Admiral Paul Jones to doubt the veracity of what he will personally communicate to you, and to which I refer you.

"I have the honor to be, &c.

"L. LITTLEPAGE."

Hitherto the reader has seen the Vice Admiral Paul Jones chiefly in his naval character. In another light, however, his life was not without interest. In his visits to Paris, and during his stay in the ports of France and Holland, his correspondence with several of the fair sex, and some of them of the highest distinction, demonstrates that he was not insensible to the charms of beauty and the delights of love. Judging him in this respect by the ardor of a few of those with whom he communicated by letter, he would seem to have been as successful in his amatory career as he was in that on the ocean. He triumphed as much in the affections of the ladies as he did in his contests with the enemy; and, amidst the gay scenes of Paris, the political intrigues of courts, and the bustle of nautical preparation, he found time to sacrifice to the graces, and win the attentions of the sex. It cannot be doubted that the fame of his actions contributed to render him popular wherever he appeared, and served as an introduction not only to the houses of the ordinary class of wealthy citizens, but to the hotels of nobles and to the palaces of princes. The French, always fond of glory, could not fail to receive with a cheering welcome the gallant Jones wherever he appeared, and the author of this work has before him the indubitable evidence, that, at Paris in particular, cards of courtesy, of invitation, and notes of congratulation poured in upon him in abundance. At his lodgings, on his visits to eminent personages, in the active pursuits of business, he was solicited, pressed, and fairly forced into parties, recreations, and amusements of all sorts. The nobility and gentry of Versailles were proud of his acquaintance, and the women of fashion did not think their assemblies complete unless Jones moved in the circle. From among many letters a number has been selected for publication to portray his influence with the fair :—

From a Lady who wrote under the Signature of Delia.

"Your letter of —— which I received on Sunday, the 20th, lacerates my heart, and increases my despair; I kissed with sad and concentred grief, the traces of thy precious tears, and shed a flood of the bitterest drops that ever flowed from a breaking heart. I am oppressed with the weight of my sorrows—and my mind is plunged in a chaos of doubts and fears. No! never, I feel, never did I love until that moment, at once so dear and so fatal to my repose, when fate presented you to my ravished sight; that moment fixed my destiny for ever. Yes! my tender and adorable friend! on you alone depends that destiny: you alone have the power to make my happiness or misery. Pardon this frank confession, oh! my dear Jones; and be persuaded that deeming thee incapable of a mean action, I love, esteem, and even respect thee; never otherwise would I have revealed thus freely all thy power over every faculty of my being. I adore thee, I again repeat; and never did any other mortal possess such sway over my heart—this, my dear and only friend, is my pledge of faith; I am thine—and thine only—during my whole life. Be, therefore, tranquil; console thyself; and let us hope that pitying heaven will reunite us, and watch over the lot of two beings, who love faithfully, and whose upright hearts deserve to be happy. Be careful of thy life, and remember that mine depends on it. I incessantly address myself to Heaven for your safe arrival in America; if you are satisfied with that government, you will continue in its service; if not resign, and rejoin your faithful friend; the whole world besides may forsake you, but her heart is eternally yours; I swear it by that sacred flame which will never be extinguished in my breast. You ask how you can render me happy;—take care of yourself love me—study the means of enabling us to pass our days together, and never forget that my life is bound up in yours,—and that the moment which deprives me of you, will put an end to all my miseries. Your health is dear—ten thousand times dearer to me than my own; if you love me, do not neglect it. I have received your letter of the 16th, which increases my solicitude on this point; in the name of all that is sacred, take care of your precious self. Rely on my heart; it is yours—and nothing can operate a change in its sentiments. I adore you for yourself alone, and it is thus that you should be loved. If I was capable of thinking otherwise, I would not suffer you to depart, and to expose your invaluable life. The thought of your danger brings back all the weakness of my sex; and I confess that my anxiety and frightful alarms for the object of all my wishes, will, without doubt, hasten my death. The terror and solicitude that I feel for my lover are indescribable. Dear Jones! adieu; I am forced to leave thee; I cannot go on. The Chevalier assures you of his respect and friendly sentiments; he sets out to-morrow evening; alas! happier than his unfortunate sister, he will soon see you. God! she would willingly be the lowest of your crew."

"Six posts have arrived, and still no tidings from you; my heart sinks at the thoughts of so cruel a neglect. Are you sick? or have you ceased to love me? Oh God! this idea chills my heart. No! I cannot believe you so barbarous; you cannot desire my death. Is it possible that absence has destroyed my happiness? Alas! if absence has deprived me of your heart, it is not thus with regard to my feelings towards you, since you are now a thousand times dearer to me than on that horrible day of our separation. Your letters, your assurances of attachment, the inclination of my heart, all have contributed to augment my affection. But perhaps I must renounce for ever all those fond hopes that have induced me to cherish life: but I may be wrong thus to despair. Yes! I am too sensitive and fearful; the amiable and tender Jones is as faithful a lover as he is a valiant warrior and a zealous patriot; all those rare qualities are united in the object of all my thoughts and affections; to doubt his constancy would be an injury—nay, a crime. Pardon, dear friend, my apprehensive terrors; I will compel my foolish heart to be more tranquil. Judge of the excess of my love by my agonizing dread of losing your esteem—your heart."

These letters from Delia, it will be admitted, are in rather an extravagant strain. They certainly discover a great excess of feeling, and if the effusions be not sincere, the writer must have had an uncommon faculty of giving reality to artificial expressions.

Jones wrote an affectionate letter to Delia after his arrival in America:

"*December* 25, 1781.

"I wrote, my most lovely Delia, various letters from Philadelphia, the last of which was dated the 20th of June. On the 26th of that month I was unanimously elected by Congress to command the America of 74 guns, on the stocks, at Portsmouth, New Hampshire. I superintended the building, which I found so much more backward than I expected, that a plan of operation I had in view is entirely defeated. I expected to have been at sea this winter, but the building does not go on with the vigor I could wish. Since I came here I have not found a single good opportunity to write to Europe. I have not since heard from your relation I left behind, but suppose he is with the army. This situation is doubly irksome to me, my lovely friend, as it stops my pursuit of honor as well as love! It is now more than twelve months since I left France; yet I have not received a single letter from thee in all that time, except the one written in answer to my letter at taking leave. That one is a tender letter indeed, and does honor to thy matchless heart! I read often and always with transport the many charming things that are so well expressed in thy letters; but especially the last. Thy adieu has in it all the finer feelings, blended with the noblest sentiments of the heart! Providence, all good and just, has given thee a soul worthy in all respects to animate nature's fairest work. I rest therefore sure that *absence* will not diminish, but *refine* the pure and spotless friendship that binds our souls together, and will ever impress each to merit the affection of the other. Remember and *believe* my letter at parting. It was but a faint picture of my heart. I will find opportunities to write, and be everything thou canst wish. My address is under cover to the Hon. Robert Morris, Esq., Minister of Finance, Philadelphia."

The men as well as the women were infatuated with the chevalier. The annexed letter affords proof of the flame which his reputation had kindled up, impelling individuals of good families and connexions to seek for celebrity under his command:

"*January*, 1780.

"SIR,

"Although I have not the honor of a personal acquaintance with you, the fame of your exploits, and the glory you acquired in your last engagement, induce me to ask a favor at your hands; it is to grant me an opportunity of being a witness of, and a partaker in your chivalrous adventures. Understanding that you are now at Dunkirk, where, without doubt, the desire of flying to achieve new conquests, will not suffer you to remain long; I hasten to offer you my services. I have the honor to request that you will receive me simply as a volunteer, in order that having no fixed post, I may be everywhere: I have farther only to stipulate that you will admit me to your own table, and place me under your immediate command, so that I may satiate my eyes with the pleasure of beholding your courage, and at least imitate, for it is impossible to equal it. If I should be fortunate enough to obtain this favor, rest assured that you will always find me in the path of honor. I have been long in the service of my country; but the reform which I have introduced in the corps to which I belong, leaves me at leisure to employ myself elsewhere. Having a passion for a sea-life, which I have already partially gratified by a voyage to the Indies, I am eager to make one or two campaigns. Since the moment when the fame of your glorious expedition spread through the world, I have wished to serve under your orders; and seize the present opportunity to assure you, that, if you accept my proffered services, you will never have cause to repent it: circumstances of a very peculiar nature render me very anxious to execute this intention. I will waive all mention of my family; chance has thrown me in an elevated situation; this is my only observation on this subject. If you design an expedition immediately, and will receive me in the number of those who are emulous to acquire glory under your command, have the goodness to write me, and I will immediately repair to the spot you may point out.

"I have the honor to be, &c.

"DE TOURNEVILLE."

On one occasion a lady declined his advances in the following delicate manner; although it would appear that she had induced them:

"Sir,

"I am grateful for the sentiments which you entertain for me, and it would give me pleasure to reply to them; but I could not do so without deceiving a gentleman with whom I live; and that is what I am incapable of doing. After this confession you must be aware of my way of thinking; and that what I said yesterday was only meant in jest.

"With all possible consideration, sir,

"I have the honor to be your affectionate servant."

The annexed note is rather more equivocal:

"Madame de H. begs Mr. Jones to pardon the liberty she takes in addressing him, without having the honor of his acquaintance; and requests a moment's conversation with him at her apartments in the royal palace, or at the hotel of the Duchess of ———. She asks a thousand pardons if she should be the means of giving him any trouble at the moment of his departure; but he must not be astonished that all are eager to profit by the present opportunity of seeing him."

In one of the preceding letters the enraptured Delia speaks of certain verses of the chevalier. Among his papers are those subjoined, which are, perhaps, the same that the lady alluded to:

I.

"When Jove from high Olympus goes
To Ida, and the fair below,
All heav'n laments—but Juno shows,
A jealous and superior wo:
In vain to her all pow'r is given,
To female weakness ever dear;
She scorns the sov'reignty of heav'n,
Her God, her Jove, seems all to her!

II.

"But when the Thunderer returns,
And seeks his skies (so Homer sings),
Soft flames th' impatient goddess burns!
She hastes to meet the King of kings:
Swift as the light her chariot flies,
Her swifter wishes fly before;
Still joyous in the middle-skies,
She meets the cloud-compelling pow'r.

III.

"Prolific nature feels th' embrace,
Superior blossoms, fruits and flow'rs,
Spring up,—heav'n wears a brighter face,
And fragrance in profusion show'rs.
Celestial raptures who can tell?
Ours all divine! are only *felt*,
What bold presumptuous strains shall swell,
With transports which the gods can melt!

IV.

"Thus when thy warrior, though no god,
Brings *Freedom's* standard o'er the main,
Long absent from thy blest abode,
Casts anchor in *dear France* again;
O! thou more heavenly!—far more kind
Than Juno, as thy swain than Jove,
With what heart's transport, raptur'd mind!
Shall *we* approach on wings of love!"

This is no unfavorable sample of Jones's poetical abilities. The sentiments are impressive, and in some degree sublime. The thoughts are comprehensive, and correspond with the vigor of his general character. It is apparent, from the original manuscript, that the chevalier, in making love, was a truant, adapting his rhymes to situation and circumstances. The fourth line of the fourth stanza is varied, so as to answer either for France or America: Thus,

"Cast anchor in *dear France* again,"

Is changed to,

"In *fair Columbia* moors again."

This may be denominated the economy of versification. It is a trick probably often practised by more persons than Jones.

Whatever may have been the devotion which Jones professed for the sex, it was obvious that ambition was the predominating passion in his breast, and that he even made his love affairs subservient to his desire of glory. The following letter to a lady at court, just before his departure for America, contains a mixture of respectful salutation, and a solicitation of female influence in his behalf:

"*L'Orient, August 6th*, 1780.

"To a Lady.

"Madam,

"I had the honor to write to you on the 14th ult., but have not yet had the satisfaction to receive any of your letters since that time. This makes me fear you are now determined to punish me for my former silence; yet I am frequently in doubt about this, as I hope you will show mercy when you know that I repent?—I send this by a certain conveyance; and will hope for the honor of having a letter from you in return. Present, if you please, my best respects to the duke and duchess; I shall ever entertain the most profound regard for that amiable princess, and be ambitious to merit the continuance of her friendship. I add my address at Philadelphia, and depend on frequent letters from you while I am in America. The court has a plan of mine respecting my future services to be asked of Congress by the court. I have the greatest desire to give the world farther proofs of my grateful zeal for the interests of the king, the government, and this generous-minded nation, by my actions against the common enemy of France and America. Will you, dear madam, honor me with your interest, that an application may be made by government to Congress, that I may henceforth, during the war, be employed in the most active and enterprising services.

"I am ever, with the highest sentiments of esteem and respect,

"Madam,

"Your most obliged and faithful servant."

A friend had written to the Chevalier, on the 30th of October, 1779, on the occasion of that friend's marriage:

"You have been reaping laurels, my friend, and I have been plucking roses; but your occupation is as much more glorious than mine, as the welfare of a community is more important than the happiness of an individual. I think, however, I have one advantage over you, for mine has not been the work of destruction, and I trust it will increase the species instead of diminishing them, and that you must allow is the '*cause of humanity!*' In short, I am a married man, and my wife will be happy to number you among her friends. I return to Nantes from St. Germain to-morrow morning, and as soon as I arrive I will write you on matters of business; at present I can think of nothing of that kind.

"Alas, poor Richard! We ought not, however, to regret so honorable an exit. Thank heaven you are preserved, and may another poor Dick shine gloriously under your command. All Europe are praising you except England."

The subjoined letter to the Duke de Chartres, afterward Duke of Orleans, is in good style:

"*Ariel, Groaix, September* 22*d*, 1780.

"His Royal Highness the Duc de Chartres,

"My Prince,

"Two days since, Monsieur de Roberdeau delivered me the letter you did me the honor to write me from Paris the 18th of last month. It will, my Prince, always afford me the truest pleasure, when in my power, to conform to your wishes by rendering my best services to any person whom you please to recommend to my attention; and Captain de Roberdeau will, I hope, be satisfied with my conduct towards him. No man, my Prince, can be more ambitious to merit your esteem and protection than myself; for no man can admire and venerate you more as a gallant and good officer, or esteem you with a more heartfelt affection than, my prince,

"Your most obliged, &c.'"

The following to Dr. John Read, of Virginia, is an excellent specimen of the expression of genuine friendship in an instance of pecuniary inability to comply with the request of a friend:—

"*L'Orient, November 9th*, 1780.

"Dr. Read.

"I have, my dear sir, to thank you for several favors lately received from you. I postponed my answer because I have been in daily expectation of returning to America, but cannot, however, omit the opportunity of your brother to acquaint you that for these five years past military affairs have engaged *my whole attention.* I am as much a stranger to trade as if I had never been concerned in it. I have served as a volunteer in the American Revolution, and to this moment have neither received pay nor subsistence from the public. My property in the many prizes I took before I left America went through the hands of agents who did great injustice to the captors; and it has since melted away by the depreciation of the Continental paper money. Gain has never been my object, and since I came to France hard blows and honor have been my sole income. Judge, therefore, my dear friend, if I am able to establish a loan for you—I could not do it for myself, because I want funds, and could not give the necessary security. If you are determined to enter into trade, I would advise you to buy bills of exchange on France from the Consul-General at Philadelphia. Send these bills to a good house here, with orders to ship the goods you propose in very small parcels by each of the fast-sailing vessels that come here from Philadelphia, Maryland, or Virginia. Thus you will divide your risk, and have more neat profit than by being concerned in shipping and cargoes from America. These opinions I take from the best merchants here, therefore you can the better depend upon them. Present my best respects to Mrs. Read; when I come to Virginia and have a moment to spare from my public duties, I will with great pleasure pay you a visit. Be assured it will ever give me happiness to be useful to you, when fortune puts in my power the means; for I truly am, my dear friend,

"Your most affectionate, &c."

To General Washington, in August, 1778, Jones wrote as follows:

"*Passy, Aug. 6th*, 1778.

"His Excellency General Washington, Commander-in-Chief of the American Army, at his head-quarters.

"Honored Sir,

"As the scene of war by sea is now changed from America to Europe, I have been induced to give up the command of the American ship of war Ranger, and to continue for some time in Europe, in compliance with the request of the minister of the French marine, in a letter to our ministers plenipotentiary at the Court of Versailles.

"I will not intrude on your excellency's time even by attempting to pay you the respect which you so justly command. The intention of this letter is only to beg your acceptance of two epaulettes, with which it is accompanied, and which my friend Mr. Williams, of Nantes, has undertaken to forward: I expected to have had the honor of delivering this little present into your own hands, but not having that satisfaction, if I can render you any acceptable services in France, I hope you will command me without reserve, being with sentiments of perfect esteem,

"Honored Sir, yours, &c."

The Chevalier's opinion of the qualifications requisite in a chaplain for his ship, is given in a letter to Mr. Grand:

Extract of a letter to H. Grand.

"*Passy, July* 12*th*, 1778.

"In the selection of a chaplain, the following qualifications are deemed requisite.

"I could wish him to be a man of reading and of letters, who understands, speaks, and writes, the French and English with elegance and propriety: for political reasons it would be well if he were a clergyman of the Protestant profession, whose sanctity of manners, and happy natural principles would diffuse unanimity and cheerfulness through the ship. And if to these essentials is added the talent of writing fast and in fair characters, such a man would necessarily be worthy the highest confidence, and might, therefore, assure himself of my esteem and friendship; he should always have a place at my table, the regulation whereof would be entirely under his direction."

One of his letters to Madame de la Fayette is in these terms:

"*L'Orient, July* 28*th*, 1780.

"Madame la Marquise DE LA FAYETTE, à Paris.

"MADAM,

"I am once more nearly ready for the sea. If I can in any respect render you acceptable services, you know I have so much esteem and respect for yourself, and so much affectionate friendship for your husband, that you will, I hope, command me freely. I expect to embrace the Marquis about the first of October, and it is not impossible—that we may return together to France.

"Believe me, I am, with great sincerity and regard,

"Madam, your most obedient, &c."

To Madam the President de Ormoy he wrote thus:

"*Ariel, Road of Groaix, Sept.* 13, 1780.

"Madame la Presidente de Ormoy, &c.

"Madam,

"I cannot leave France without expressing how much I feel myself honored and obliged by the generous attention that you have shown to my reputation in your Journal. I will ever have the most ardent desire to merit the spontaneous praise of beauty and her pen; and it is impossible to be more grateful than I am for the very polite attentions I lately received at Paris and Versailles. My particular thanks are due to you, Madam, for the personal proofs I have received of your esteem and friendship, and for the happiness you procured me in the society of the charming Countess, and other ladies and gentlemen of your circle. But I have a favor to ask of you, Madam, which I hope you will grant me. You tell me in your letter, that the inkstand I had the honor to present you as a small token of my esteem, shall be reserved for the purpose of writing what concerns me. Now I wish you to see my idea in a more expanded light, and would have you make use of that inkstand to instruct mankind, and support the dignity and rights of human nature.

"I shall be happy in every part of the world to hear from you, and I beg leave to assure you, my best wishes will always attend you and yours; being, with the highest esteem and respect,

"Madam, your most obliged friend, &c."

To the same lady he addressed another letter on the 16th of October, 1780.

"*L'Orient, October* 16, 1780.

"Madame la Presidente de Ormoy, &c.

"By the enclosed declaration of my officers you will see, my dear

Madam, that I was in a ticklish situation in the moment while you were employed in writing to me the 9th. It is impossible to be more sensible than I am of the obligation conferred on me by your attentions and kind remembrance, joined to that of the belle countess, your fair daughters, and the amiable ladies and gentlemen of your society. I have returned without laurels, and what is worse, without having been able to render service *to the glorious cause of liberty.* I know not why Neptune was in such anger, unless he thought it an affront in me to appear on his ocean with so insignificant a force. It is certain that till the night of the 8th I did not fully conceive the awful majesty of tempest and shipwreck. I can give you no just idea of the tremendous scene that nature then presented; which surpassed the reach even of poetic fancy and the pencil. I believe no ship was ever before saved from an equal danger off the point of the Penmark rocks. I am extremely sorry that the young English lady you mention should have imbibed the national hatred against me. I have had proofs that many of the first and fairest ladies of that nation are my friends. Indeed I cannot imagine why any fair lady should be my enemy, since upon the large scale of universal philanthropy, I *feel*, acknowledge, and bend before the sovereign power of beauty. The English nation may hate me, but *I will force them to esteem me too.* You have heard, no doubt, that Captain Landais and all the officers of the Alliance have been laid under an arrest by order of Congress, on their arrival in America, and the command of the Alliance was given to the brave Captain Barry. By tho latest advices, I have no enemies in that vast country. I shall be happy to hear from you, Madam, while I remain here, and I assure you I will embrace every occasion to prove my grateful attachment to this beloved nation, as well as to my friends in it.

"I am, with the highest esteem and respect," &c.

On the 12th of December following, he wrote again to the same lady:—

"*Ariel, L'Orient, Dec.* 12*th*, 1780.

"Madame la Presidente de ORMOY, &c.

"To merit, dear Madam, the praise so warmly and well expressed in the letter you did me the honor to write me the 22d ult. would be my supreme ambition. If I have any merit, it consists in good will and perseverance. My abilities are poor, and I want experience; but opposition shall never cause my ardor to abate in pursuit of the glorious cause I have undertaken to support. When I received your letter I was again ready for the sea, and have been waiting here with a fair wind ever since, expecting from hour to hour the arrival of Mr. Gourlade, who brings the public despatches from our minister for Congress. In this situation the boy you mentioned must have arrived here too late, otherwise I should, with great pleasure, have received him under my protection. Mr. Gourlade is, I hear, arrived at Nantes; to-morrow, if he appears here, I shall depart. I am much flattered by your having mentioned me to so great a man as the King of Prussia—the world will ever treat his opinion with the highest respect. It is impossible for me to express the happiness I derive from your good opinion, and how proud I shall ever be to be found worthy of your affectionate friendship. With these sentiments and the most profound respect,

"I am, Madam, yours, &c."

To the Countess of Bourbon, on the 21st of September, 1780, he addressed himself in the following manner, in reply to one of her letters to him:—

"*Ariel, Road of Groaix, Sept.* 21, 1780.

"Madame la Comtesse de Bourbon, &c.

"Madam,

"I was honored with the very polite letter that your Ladyship condescended to write me the 5th of last month. I am sorry that you have found it necessary to refuse me the honor of accepting the deposit mentioned in my last; but am now determined to follow your advice and be myself its guardian. A day or two before I wrote to you last I had received a challenge from Sir James Wallace, who in the Nonesuch, a ship of the line, copper bottomed and of superior swiftness, declared he waited in sight for my departure. Had I commanded an equal force I hope you will believe I would have employed my time otherwise than in writing you any proposition for the safety of a weapon that I should have hoped to use immediately with success. I have been detained in this open road by contrary and stormy winds since the 4th of this month. There is this moment an appearance of a fair opportunity, and I will eagerly embrace it. I have received a letter from the first minister very favorable to the project I mentioned to you; and you may depend on my utmost interest with Congress to bring the matter to issue. I am sure that assembly will with pleasure say all yourself or the court could wish respecting the count, if my scheme is adopted. I have the satisfaction to inform you that by the testimony of all the persons just arrived in four ships at L'Orient from Philadelphia, the Congress and all America appeared to be warmly my friends; and my heart, conscious of its own uprightness, tells me I shall be well received. Deeply and gratefully impressed with a sense of the obligation I owe to you and your husband's attentions and good wishes, and ardently desiring to merit your friendship, and the love of this nation, by my whole conduct through life,

"I remain, Madam, your most obliged, &c.

"N. B.—I will not fail to write whenever I have anything worth your reading, at the same time may I hope to be honored now and then with a letter from you, directed to Philadelphia? I was selfish in begging you to write me in French, because your letters would serve me as an exercise. Your English is correct and even elegant."

To a Lady, whose letters he had neglected to answer, he wrote as an apology thus:—

"*L'Orient*, *July* 14*th*, 1780.

"Madam,

"When one is conscious of having been in fault I believe it is the best way to confess it, and to promise amendment. This being my case with respect to you, Madam, I am too honest to attempt to excuse myself; and therefore cast myself at your feet, and beg your forgiveness on condition that I behave better hereafter. For shame, Paul Jones, how could you let the fairest lady in the world, after writing you two letters, wait so long for an answer! Are you so much devoted to war, as to neglect wit and beauty? I make myself a thousand such reproaches, and believe I punish myself as severely as you would do, Madam, were you present here.

"The truth is, I have been willing that the extraordinary events that have taken place here with respect to the frigate Alliance should be communicated to you rather by others, than by myself; for though, God knows, I have not been to blame for these events, yet I have felt rather ashamed that they should have happened: the more so as the cause has been rather of a delicate nature. I will mention it however to you. M. de Chaumont has, to this moment, unjustly retained from these poor people every sol, both of their wages and shares of prizes. And some envious persons found means to persuade them that I had concurred with him in these measures. Nothing can be more false, I despise his base conduct, and have not even spoken nor written to him on account of it: on the contrary, to procure for the men who had so bravely served under my command their just rights, was the only business that brought me to court in the month of May. If I had not at last been sent back here without the means of paying them, no difficulty would have happened. As it is I have the satisfaction to know that none of them have complained of any ill treatment from me.

"I will write you often, and do everything in my power to convince you how much I wish to merit your friendship, and with how much respect, and how profound regard, I have the honor to be,

"Yours, &c."

The subjoined convivial and gallant Letter was written to the Marquis de Nieuil:—

"*Dauphine Royale, Brest, June 9th*, 1778.

"The Marquis de Nieuil,

"Were I disposed to be affronted with you, Marquis, you have given me a fair opportunity; but, fortunately for you, being at present under a cloud, I am not mounted on Pegasus, nor shall I be satirical in prose.

"Since you have endeavored to prove by great force of reason and argument that you have made a bad bargain, I am determined to realize your 'dream,' as a punishment for your breach of friendship, for you know there is no friendship in trade. I intend to dine with you every day if possible, and I will bring with me too father John, if I can, so that, as you will not save your wine, you have made a bad bargain indeed.

"I thank you for your friendly caution to use the wine you have sent me with moderation. As I am to drink so much on board the Dauphine, and as I do not incline to drink in the morning, your advice shall have its due effect. Some of your champaign will, perhaps, be reserved to make glad the hearts of our American fair; and I hope, on such occasions, to have so much 'remembrance' left, as to propose the health of the giver.

"I am, &c."

In the following lines another metrical effusion of Jones is presented for perusal:—

Verses written on board the Alliance off Ushant, the 1*st day of January,* 1780, *immediately after escaping out of the Texel, from the Blockade of the British fleets; being in answer to a piece written and sent to the Texel by a young Lady at the Hague.*

I.

"Were I, Paul Jones, dear maid, 'the King of sea,
 I find such merit in thy virgin song,
A coral crown with bays I'd give to thee,
 A car which on the waves should smoothly glide along:
The Nereides all about thy side should wait,
And gladly sing in triumph of thy state
'Vivat, vivat, the happy virgin muse!
Of liberty the friend, who tyrant power pursues!'

II.

"Or, happier lot! were fair Columbia free
 From British tyranny,—and youth still mine,
I'd tell a tender tale to one like thee
 With looks and breast as pure as hers—or thine;
If she approved my flame, distrust apart,
Like faithful turtles, we'd have but one heart:
Together then we'd tune the silver lyre,
As love or sacred freedom should our lays inspire.

III.

"But since, alas! the rage of war prevails,
 And cruel Britons desolate our land,
For Freedom still I spread my willing sails,
 My unsheath'd sword my country shall command.
Go on, bright maid! the muses all attend
Genius like thine, and wish to be its friend.
Trust me, although conveyed through this poor shift,
My New-Year's thoughts are grateful for thy gift."

A letter from a Captain O'Connelly to the Chevalier will divert the reader. It proves at once the popularity of Jones, and the embarrassment of the Captain, a worthy Irishman, it is presumed, who was mistaken for him:

"*Rotterdam, December* 17*th*, 1779.

"My Dear Commodore,

"I am sincerely sorry I could not have the happiness of seeing you before setting off from the Helder. Having but little money to perform a long journey, obliged me to benefit of an occasion that offered in the cheap way to Amsterdam. You'll easily conceive my reason for quitting, although I take nothing from the merit of Mr. Chamillard, yet, I thought myself too much advanced in years to be under his orders, besides, I perceived proceedings that were not agreeable to me: and hope you don't take the step that I have taken amiss. Believe me, sir, that if I had the honor of being embarked with you, I would not quit you before the campaign was decided one way or the other.

"If I have no other advantage by the cruise I have made, I am amply recompensed by being conducted by crowds of all ranks, through the streets in every town I come to in this country; and can't dissuade them but I am the brave Paul Jones, but they will absolutely persist in their opinion, notwithstanding all the proofs I can allege to the contrary. When I show them my passport, they tell me I make use of a fictitious name, so that I suppose they will make me believe at last I am you.

"If in case you should come into France to arm for the next year, and that you should have occasion for one in my way, I beg you may let me know, and you may depend I will join you on sight. You'll be sure of finding me by writing to Marquis de Braneas, Lieutenant General et Cordon blue in rue Tourneau, F. S. G. Paris. As I have some demands to make of the minister, and as Dr. Franklin could be of use to me on the occasion, you will greatly oblige me if you will be so kind as to solicit him in my favor, if you think you can do it without putting yourself under any obligations to him; for I would be very sorry to think that on my account you should hurt your delicacy in the least. If otherwise, and that you should think me worthy your remembrance, I will always esteem it as the greatest favor as long as I have the honor of being your most devoted, humble, and obedient servant,

"O'Connelly.

"P.S. If you should honor me with a few lines, my address is au Caffée Conty, F. S. G. Paris. My sincere compliments, if you please, to your gentlemen in general."

In the course of his correspondence with one of the most distinguished citizens of America, who was at Paris in 1787, the chevalier unveiled a court secret. He was, at that time, in New York, and wrote under date of the 4th of September of that year:

(*Private.*) "*New York, Sept. 4th,* 1787.

"His Excellency THOMAS JEFFERSON, Esq.

"SIR,

"I am much obliged to you for the letter from Madam T——, which you forwarded by the June packet. I now take the liberty to enclose a letter for that worthy lady; and as I had not the happiness to introduce you to her (because I wished her fortune to have been previously established), I shall now tell you, *in confidence*, that she is the daughter of the late K*** and of a lady of quality, on whom his M****** bestowed a very large fortune on her daughter's account. Unfortunately the father died while the daughter (his great favorite) was very young; and the mother has never since shown her either justice or natural affection. She was long the silent victim of that injustice; but I had the pleasure to be instrumental in putting her in a fair way to obtain redress. His present M****** received her last year with great kindness: he gave her afterward several particular audiences, and said he charged himself with her fortune. Some things were, as I have understood, fixed on, that depended solely on the K***; and he said he would dictate the justice to be rendered by the mother. But the letter you sent me left the feeling author all in tears! Her friend—her protectress—her introductress to the K***, was suddenly dead! She was in despair! She lost more than a mother! A loss, indeed, that nothing can repair; for fortune and favor are never to be compared to tried friendship. I hope, however, she has gone to visit the K*** in July, agreeable to his appointment given her in the month of March. I am persuaded that he would receive her with additional kindness, and that her loss would, in his mind, be a new claim to his protection; especially as he well knows and has acknowledged her superior merit and just pretensions. As I feel the greatest concern for the situation of this worthy lady, you will render me a great favor by writing a note, requesting her to call on you, as you have something to communicate from me. When she comes, be so good as to deliver her the within letter, and show her this; that she may see both my confidence in you and my advice to her.

"I am, with the highest esteem, sir, yours," &c.

The latter part of the life of the Chevalier Jones was spent partly in Holland and partly in France. He died at Paris, of water in the chest, on the 12th of September, 1792, and although a Calvinist, his funeral was attended by a deputation of the National Assembly, and an eloquent oration pronounced over his tomb by M. Marron.

The following is the last Will and Testament of the chevalier, accompanied with schedules of the property which belonged to him at the time of his death:—

[TRANSLATION.]

EXEMPLIFICATION.

TESTAMENT OF

PAUL JONES.

July 18th, 1792.

"Before the underwritten Notaries at Paris, personally appeared Mr. JOHN PAUL JONES, citizen of the United States of America, now residing at Paris, and lodging in Tourmon Street, at the house of M. D'Arbergue, tipstaff to the Tribunal of the Third Precinct, whom we found in a parlor on the first story above the entry, lighted by two windows looking on the said street, sitting in an easy chair, sick in body, but of sound mind, memory, judgment, and understanding, as appeared to us, the underwritten Notaries, by his discourse and conversation,—who, with a view to death, did make, speak, and dictate to the said underwritten Notaries his Testament, as follows, to wit:—

"I give and bequeath all the property, moveable and immoveable, and other property generally whatsoever, which shall belong to me on the day of my decease, in whatever countries the same may be situate, to my two sisters, Jane, wife of William Taylor, and Mary, wife of Mr. Loudon, and to the children of my said sisters, to be divided into as many shares as my said sisters and their children shall form individual persons, and the same to be enjoyed by them in the following manner, viz:—My sisters, and such of their children as shall have attained the age of twenty-one years, shall enjoy their respective shares in full and property from the day of my decease: As to such of my said nephews and nieces as, on the day of my decease, shall not have attained the age of twenty-one years, their mothers shall enjoy their respective shares until they shall have attained the said age, charged with the board, maintenance, and education of the said children; and as my said nephews and nieces shall respectively attain the age of twenty-one years, they shall enjoy their respective shares in full and absolute property. If one or more of my said nephews and nieces shall happen to die without issue, and before attaining the age of twenty-one years, the share of such of them as shall so have died, shall be divided between my said sisters and my other nephews and nieces, by equal portions.

"I appoint the Honorable Robert Morris, Esq., of Philadelphia, my sole testamentary Executor. I revoke all other testaments and codicils which I may have made anterior to the present, in which alone I persist, as containing my last will."

"It was thus done, spoken, and dictated by the said Testator to the said underwritten Notaries, and afterward to him by one of them, the other being present, read, and read again, which he declared well to understand and persist therein, at Paris, the eighteenth day of July, in the year one thousand seven hundred and ninety-two, at five o'clock in the afternoon, in the apartment above described; and the Testator has signed on the minute of these presents remaining with M. Pottier, one of the underwritten Notaries, in the margin of which is written, Recorded at Paris, the twenty-fifth day of September, 1792, the first year of the Republic, in the sixth Office. Received one hundred livres, provisionally, the duty to be hereafter finally settled, on the declaration of the revenue of the Testator.

"De France,
"Barmier Pottier."

"*Philadelphia City and County, ss.*

"These are to certify, that the foregoing is a true copy from a translation of a certain instrument of writing, written in the French language, filed and remaining in the Register's Office at Philadelphia.

[Seal.] Given under the seal of office this tenth day of November, in the year of our Lord one thousand seven hundred and ninety-seven.

"I. Wampole, *D. Register.*

"*Schedule of the Property of Admiral John Paul Jones, as stated by him to me, this* 18*th day of July*, 1792.

"1. Bank Stock in the Bank of North America, at Philadelphia, six thousand dollars, with sundry dividends.

"2. Loan Office Certificate, left with my friend John Ross, of Philadelphia, for two thousand dollars, at par, with great arrearages of interest, being for 10 or 12 years.

"3. Such balance as may be in the hands of my said friend John Ross, belonging to me, and sundry effects left in his care.

"4. My lands in the State of Vermont.

"5. Shares in the Ohio Company.

"6. Shares in the Indiana Company.

"7. About £1800 sterling due to me from Edward Bancroft, unless paid by him to Sir Robert Herries, and is then in his hands.

"8. Upwards of four years of my pension due from Denmark, to be asked from the Count de Bernstorff.

"9. Arrearages of my pay from the Empress of Russia, and all my prize-money.

"10. The balance due to me by the United States of America, of sundry claims in Europe, which will appear from my papers.

"This is taken from his mouth.

"Governeur Morris.

"This is to certify those whom it may concern, that the following papers and vouchers belonging to the estate of the late Commodore John Paul Jones, are left in my hands, when any of the property is recovered, or payment obtained, to be accounted for to his heirs, according to his last Will and Testament, agreeably to the copy left with me:

"Major William Trent's deed for three hundred shares in the Indiana Company.

"Robert Morris's note, at 12 months, for $3332 18, with interest at 6 per cent., dated the 18th of July, 1797.

"Robert Morris's note, at 2 years, for $3332 18, with interest at 6 per cent., dated the 18th of July, 1797.

"Also, a certificate for 67 shares in the Pennsylvania Property Company, deposited as a collateral security for the payment of the two notes above mentioned.

"Ten certificates, No. 2311 *a* 2320, for $300 each, dated the 10th of July, 1777, at 4 per cent. interest. Interest paid till 1781.

"Two certificates, No. 598 and 599, for $400 each, at 6 per cent. interest, dated the 25th of June, 1779.

"Two certificates, No. 685 and 686, for $400 each, at 6 per cent. int., dated the 18th of August, 1779.

"One hundred and forty-seven old Continental dollars and lawful money.

"Richard Platt's receipt for five shares in the Ohio Company, for $5000 in certificates, and $50 in specie.

"Also, a number of letters, accounts, journals, log-books, &c., with various other papers, are supposed to be of no value.

"ROBERT HYSLOP.

"New-York, August 10th, 1797."

"P. S. Likewise received at the same time, John G. Frazier's bill on William Frazier, Virginia, dated Bordeaux, the 29th of March, 1779, for £100, Virginia currency, at 10 days sight, to be paid in Loan Office certificates, bearing interest from the 1st of November, 1777, which bill was presented the 30th of August, 1781, and refused.

"ROBERT HYSLOP."

As every thing relating to the Revolutionary period must be interesting to the American public, and there being a mass of correspondence between the Chevalier Jones and a number of the most distinguished men of that day, not included in the preceding life and character, we have thought that it would be historically useful to publish a part of them, in connexion with his life, by way of Appendix.

APPENDIX.

"*Marine Office, Philadelphia, September* 30*th*, 1784.

"The Chevalier PAUL JONES, Paris.

"SIR,

"I am to acknowledge the receipt of your several favors of 26th of December, 13th of April, and 18th of June last. I have to reproach myself for not making an early reply to the first, but I was so much harassed when I received it, that I could not find an opportunity. Afterward I lived in the daily expectation of making my personal acknowledgment, but since your stay in Europe has been delayed beyond either your expectation or mine, I now take the last opportunity which I shall ever have of expressing my sentiments *officially* upon the *zeal, activity, fortitude, and intelligence*, which you have exhibited on so many occasions in the service of the United States. Accept, I pray you, sir, this last feeble testimony which I can give, and which, however unequal to your deserts, is at least expressive of that respect and sincere esteem with which,

"I have the honor to be, &c.

"R. MORRIS."

"*Paris, February* 27*th*, 1786.

"Mr. PAUL JONES, Commodore in the Navy of the United States.

"SIR,

"I have received with much gratitude the mark of confidence which you have given me, and I have read with great eagerness and pleasure that interesting relation.

"My first impression was to desire you to have it published, but after having read it, I perceive that you had not written it with a view to publication, because there are things in it which are written to the King, for whom alone that work was intended. However, actions memorable as yours are, ought to be made known to the world by an authentic journal published in your own name.

"I earnestly entreat you to work at it as soon as your affairs will allow you; and in the meantime, *I hope that the King will read this work with that attention which he owes to the relation of the services which have been rendered to him by a person so celebrated.*

"I beg you to be persuaded of the sincere attachment with which

"I have the honor to be, &c.

"MALESHERBES."

"*Paris, January* 1*st*, 1786.

"His Most Christian Majesty LOUIS, King of France, &c.

"SIRE,

"History gives the world no example of such generosity as that of your Majesty towards the young republic of America; and I believe there never was a more flattering compliment shown by a sovereign to his allies, than when your Majesty determined to arm and support a squadron under the flag of the United States.

"Words cannot express my sense of the preference I obtained when your Majesty deigned to make choice of me to command that squadron.

"Your Majesty has as much reputation for knowledge and the desire of information, as you have for wisdom and justice; but besides that consideration, I conceived it to be my duty to lay before your Majesty an account of my conduct as an officer, particularly from the date of the alliance between your Majesty and the United States. As your Majesty understands English, I have perhaps judged ill by presenting extracts of my journal in French; my motive was to give your Majesty as little trouble as possible.

"Accept, Sire, with indulgence, this confidential offering of my gratitude, which is an original written for your particular information.

"It has been and will be the ambition of my life to merit the singular honor conferred on me by your Majesty's Brevet, dated at Versailles, on the 28th of June, 1780, which says, 'Sa Majesté voulant marquer au J. Paul Jones, Commodore de la marine des Etats Unis de l'America, l'estime particulière qu'elle fait de sa personne, pour les preuves de bravoure et d'intrepidité qu'il à données et qui sont connues de sa Majesté, elle a jugé à propos de l'associer à l'institution du Mérite militaire,' &c.

"The Congress of the United States has, with great justice, styled your Majesty 'The protector of the rights of human nature.'

"With the order of military merit your Majesty conferred on me a gold sword—an honor which I presume no other officer has received; and 'the protector of the rights of human nature' will always find me ready to draw that sword and expose my life for his service.

"I am, Sire, with the truest gratitude,

"Your Majesty's most obliged and devoted servant,

"PAUL JONES."

"Protector of fair freedom's rights,
Louis, thy virtues please thy God!
The good man in thy praise delights,
And tyrants tremble at thy nod.
Thy people's father, loved so well,
May time respect! When thou art gone
May each new year of history tell,
Thy sons with lustre fill thy throne.

For the purpose of perpetuating the names and rank of the American naval heroes of the Revolutionary War, the following authentic list of the commission officers is inserted in this work:

CAPTAINS AND COMMANDERS.

WHEN APPOINTED.		NAMES.	TO WHAT VESSEL.	GUNS.
December 22,	1775.	Ezekiel Hopkins,	Alfred,	30
" "	"	Dudley Saltonstall,	Trumbull,	28
" "	"	Abraham Whipple,	Columbus,	28
" "	"	Nicholas Biddle,	Andrew Doria,	16
" "	"	John B. Hopkins,	Sebastian Cabot,	14
April 17,	1776.	William Manley,	Hancock,	32
" "	"	Isaac Cozneau,		
June 6,	"	Thomas Thompson,	Raleigh,	32
" "	"	Samuel Tompkins,		
" "	"	Christopher Miller,		
" "	"	John Barry,	Effingham,	28
" "	"	Thomas Read,	Washington,	32
" "	"	Charles Alexander,	Delaware,	24
" "	"	James Nicholson,	Virginia,	28
" 15	"	Hector M'Niel,	Boston,	24
" "	"	Thomas Grennall,	Congress,	28
August 13,	"	Elisha Hinman,	Alfred,	30

WHEN APPOINTED.			NAMES.	TO WHAT VESSEL.	GUNS.
August 22,		1776.	John Hodge,	Montgomery,	24
"	"	"	John Manley,		
October 10,		"	Lambert Wickes,	Reprisal,	16
"	"	"	William Hallock,		
"	"	"	Hoysted Hacker,		
"	"	"	Isaiah Robinson,		
"	"	"	John Paul Jones,	Providence,	12
"	"	"	James Josiah,		
"	"	"	Joseph Olney,	Cabot,	14
"	"	"	James Robertson,	Sachem,	10
"	"	"	John Young,	Independence,	10
"	"	"	Elisha Warner,		
"	"	"	Lieut. Com. I. Baldwin,		
"	"	"	Thomas Albertson,	Musquito,	4
February 5,		1777.	Henry Johnson,		
March 15,		"	Daniel Waters,		
"		"	Samuel Tucker,		
May 1,		1778.	William Burke,		
June 18,		"	Peter Landais,		
September 25,		"	Seth Harding,		
"	17,	1779.	Silas Talbot,		
"	"	"	Samuel Nicholson,		
"	"	"	John Nicholson,		
"	"	"	Henry Skinner,		
"	"	"	Benjamin Dunn,		
"	"	"	Samuel Chew.		

LIEUTENANTS.

December 22,		1775.	John Paul Jones,	First,
"	"	"	Rhodes Arnold,	"
"	"	"	——— Stansbury,	"
"	"	"	Hoysted Hacker,	"
"	"	"	Jonathan Pitcher,	"
"	"	"	Benjamin Seabury,	Second,
"	"	"	Joseph Olney,	"
"	"	"	Elisha Warner,	"
"	"	"	Thomas Weaver,	"
"	"	"	——— M'Dougall,	"
"	"	"	John Fanning,	Third,

December 22,	1775.	Ezekiel Burroughs,	Third,
" "	"	Daniel Vaughan,	"
June 6,	1776.	Israel Turner,	First,
" "	"	Joseph Doble,	Second,
" "	"	Mark Dennett,	Third,
July 22,	"	Peter Shores,	"
" "	"	John Wheelright,	"
" "	"	Josiah Shackford,	"
August 17,	"	William Barnes,	First,
" "	"	Thomas Vaughan,	Third,
" 22,	"	Jonathan Maltby,	First,
" "	"	David Phipps,	Second,
" "	"	——— Wilson,	First,
" "	"	John Nicholson,	Second,
February 5,	1777.	Elijah Bowen,	First,
August 6,	"	John Rodeg,	Second,
" 12,	"	William Molleston,	Third,
July 20,	"	Richard Dale,	"
" "	"	Alexander Murray,	"
" "	"	——— Plunkett,	"
" "	"	Joshua Barney,	"
" "	"	Isaac Buck,	"
" "	"	John Stephens,	"
" "	"	Aquilla Johns.	"

CHARACTER

OF

COMMODORE JOHN PAUL JONES.

THE incidents in the life of the Chevalier John Paul Jones, as far as the papers in the possession of the author, and information from respectable sources will explain and establish them, have been faithfully recited in the preceding pages. It only remains to draw from them the features of his character.

It appears to the writer of this volume that there is a prevalent mistake in estimating the merits of singular or extraordinary men. They are measured by a standard somewhat like that of Procrustes, to correspond with which, those who were too long were cut shorter, and those who were too short were stretched to a greater length. If an individual who has distinguished himself in literature, in science, in the arts, in the affairs of state, or in arms, does not exhibit all the virtues of which human nature in its varieties is capable, he is pronounced defective, and condemned accordingly. On the contrary, where the partiality of friendship or admiration would *make a character*, and the materials are inadequate to the structure, the individual is raised beyond his level by praises for frivolous qualifications, which, as they relate to human actions, are utterly insignificant.

The memory of the Chevalier John Paul Jones does not require any thing more, to ensure its perpetuation, than a just representation of his achievements. There was nothing artificial about him: everything was natural; and whether he was addressing himself to Congress, to kings, nobles, or citizens, he uniformly manifested the same frankness of disposition and resolution of purpose. We do not expect to find absolute perfection in him or in any other man. The temperament which belonged to him, the spirit of adventure by which he was impelled, his careless indifference to the accumulation of wealth, precisely in the proportion that they existed in him, were indispensable to form JOHN PAUL JONES. Every being acts agreeably to the constitution of its nature; and it would be just as absurd to look for a contemplative philosopher in the bustle of business, or a daring naval commander in the ordinary pursuits of civil life, as to seek for a gently purling stream in the crater of a volcano.

Of the birth, parentage, education, first associations, and early avocations of Jones, but little is known. That his rise in the world, whatever of fortune he had acquired, and knowledge he had obtained, were principally owing to his own personal application and exertions, is apparent. That he was no novice when he entered the American service, is equally manifest. That he understood the method of advancing his own interests, is also evident. But there is this distinguishing trait in his character, which at once places him in the class of great men—his schemes for preferment were always founded upon considerations of accruing national benefits. Thus, when he insisted on his seniority of rank in the United States from the date of his original commission, he claimed it as well from his efficiency as an officer as from that circumstance. When, in France, he requested an independent command, he urged it upon the ground of his capacity for rendering more essential services than others to the common cause, and appealed to facts which no one could deny. And in Russia, where his nautical skill was so conspicuous, and his gallant behavior against the Turks so beneficial to the empress, he merely sought for the reward to which his conduct entitled him.

Although not peculiarly trained to the usages of courts, he was obviously a courtier in no small degree; for at Paris and Versailles he commonly carried his points against the intrigues of disciplined intriguers. He baffled the petty artifices of his rivals more by his energy, and the utility of his plans, than by finesse and cunning. He had, nevertheless, a native shrewdness which was not easily foiled. The vivacity of his temper did not qualify him for prolonged negotiations; for, in his correspondence, as well as in combat, he was eager to grapple with his adversary, and to bring the question at issue to a termination as speedily as possible. He was impatient when out of employment; and notwithstanding that he was, in his moments of leisure, disposed to be convivial, and occasionally indulged in the pleasures of society, it was more to relieve himself from the uneasiness of lassitude than from any positive inclination to prodigality or dissipation. The same activity of mind that incessantly urged him to seek for new enterprises, made him restless in port, led him to the social board, or the society of the fair sex. Fruitful in expedients, he was never at a loss for a fresh project in which his talents might shine. Returning from the Bahamas, he wrote to his friends in Congress, pressing them to confide to him some new expedition; when in France, his various propositions to the Minister of the Marine, showed the fertility of his genius; at the close of the war of the American revolution, he soon found occupation in the fleet of Catharine; and when that scene closed upon him, he had his eye fixed on an adventure against the Algerines. He was, emphatically, a man of *action;* and, fond of writing, he was indefatigable in recording not only his deeds but his sentiments. He seemed to abhor indolence; and every hour that was not strictly devoted to the acquisition of glory, appeared to make him unhappy.

There is reason to believe, from the frequent altercations in which Jones was engaged, that he was fond of supreme command, and that he did not bear with the best grace the dictates of a superior, or even the advice of an equal. His weakness was that of selfishness in all that relates to personal fame. But who, in this respect, is not selfish? Sincere in friendship and intense in animosity, his feelings were expressed in strong and unequivocal terms. These, gaining currency, were seized upon to his disadvantage; and his enemies, who could not dispute his bravery, continually thwarted his purposes, by representing him as a person better qualified for the command of single ships than of squadrons—better suited to execute than to direct an enterprise. The difficulties which he had to encounter with regard to prize-money, embroiled him with M. le Ray de Chaumont, who had been his friend and patron, and with whom he had been upon the most intimate terms. This unhappy difference arose chiefly from the different views which the parties took of the same transactions, and was probably precipitated and continued by the impetuosity of Jones. The chevalier was hurt at the *equality* which the "*Concordat*" prescribed between himself and the other captains in the squadron whose cruize terminated in the capture of the Serapis. That equality wounded the sensibility of Jones, and interfered with his predominating passion for renown. It is known to the author, from a letter dictated by Dr. Franklin from a bed of sickness, dated at Philadelphia, in November, 1789, to the elder M. le Ray de Chaumont, that he did not regard the latter in the same unfavorable light that Jones did. In that letter, after the close of the revolutionary war, Dr. Franklin speaks to his old acquaintance as the friend of America; a language which he undoubtedly would not have held had M. le Ray de Chaumont been guilty of any thing improper concerning the prize-money alluded to, or of anything dishonest touching the American cause. It has been verified to the author in a manner which leaves no room for doubt, that M. le Ray de Chaumont, until the time of his death, entertained for the Chevalier John Paul Jones the most sincere esteem, duly valuing his great faculties, but perceiving likewise the imperfections of his temper, and his unbounded thirst for glory, which sometimes misled his judgment.

Had Jones been born within the limits of the United American Colonies, or been a native of France, he would perhaps have risen to a greater height of authority than he did in either country. He would not have arrived at greater honors; and the command of the America, 74, which was assigned to him by the unanimous vote of Congress, was probably as high a distinction as any that an American naval officer could at that time have aspired to: Indeed, it is one of the highest naval trusts in the gift of the government of the United States at this time.

Jones displayed his ruling passion in other instances than those of a warlike character. He had his bust taken, and distributed casts of it to a number of American gentlemen of high standing; and especially to

General Washington, John Jay, General Irvine, General St. Clair, Mr. Ross, Mr. Thomson, Secretary of Congress, Colonel Wadsworth, James Madison, and Colonel Carrington. The busts were made by M. Houdan, of Paris. In the medal voted to him by the Congress he was also very particular. In giving directions for its execution he declared that he would have none struck but in gold.

The influence of Jones's achievements in Europe was very considerable. His firmness whilst lying in the Texel, the ability with which he conducted himself in that critical situation, and the impression which his capture of the Serapis had made, had an effect on the deliberation of the States General of Holland, and hastened their resolutions in favor of the independence of the United States of America.

Whilst in the command of a squadron in Europe, Jones had treated the Danish flag with much respect. When he visited Copenhagen this courtesy was recollected; and the court of Denmark subsequently granted him a yearly pension of fifteen hundred rix-dollars. At first he did not touch this stipend, but his affairs falling into some embarrassment, he accepted it; not, however, without the privity, and, it is presumed, the assent of his own government. Had his affairs been in a more prosperous train, he would in all probability never have applied for it.

In his letters to Lady Selkirk will be perceived the generous delicacy of a noble mind. He could not restrain the cupidity of his men; but he did what it remained in his power to do: he restored the plundered plate at the expense of his private purse. Alexander the Great himself never performed a more liberal action.

On the whole, the Chevalier John Paul Jones was a man of strong natural faculties; of a good English education; of an ardent temperament; of a quick penetration; of a firm and daring courage; with an inclination to literature, an extraordinary ambition, a restless activity of soul, an indifference for money, a heart that felt for the distress of his fellow creatures, a spirit that would neither give nor brook an insult, and a philanthropy co-extensive with the globe. He delighted in being considered an American citizen, but was still more pleased with being known as the friend of the human race, and as the enemy of its oppressors.

> "Glory! Immortal glory, was his goal,
> On which he fix'd his fond unerring eye;—
> It nerv'd his arm; it warm'd his inmost soul;
> It taught him how to live, and how to die."

BIOGRAPHICAL SKETCH

OF

COMMODORE RICHARD DALE.

Commodore Dale having been mentioned in the course of the foregoing life of the Chevalier Paul Jones, a brief biographical sketch of that respectable officer may be satisfactory to the reader.

He was born on the Western Branch, four or five miles from Norfolk, Virginia. He went to sea when he was between twelve and thirteen years of age, and served his time in the employment of Thomas Newton, a respectable merchant of Norfolk. In the autumn of 1775 he was the mate of a brig belonging to Col. Newton, and arrived at Norfolk, where a British ship of war was lying, and things very unsettled. He proceeded with the brig up James River, to City Point. In March, 1776, Captain Barrett, the commander of the brig, was engaged in the Virginia state service, and Commodore Dale was sent down the river by him to Sandy Point, in a small schooner, for some guns, and was captured by a British tender and taken to Norfolk. In July he entered as a midshipman on board the United States brig Lexington, Captain Barry. In October he sailed in that brig as master's mate, from Philadelphia to Cape Francois. On his return, towards the end of December, Commodore Dale was captured by the British frigate Liverpool, off the Capes of Virginia. The wind was strong and the sea high at the time, so that the enemy could take only seven of the officers out. The remaining officers and crew retook the brig the following night, and carried her to Baltimore. On the 1st of January, 1777, he was landed on Cape Henlopen, made the best of his way to Philadelphia, and was ordered by the Navy Department at Baltimore. From thence he sailed in March for Bordeaux, in the brig Lexington, Henry Johnston commander, and from Bordeaux to Nantes, to join Captain Wicks in the ship Reprisal, and Captain Samuel Nicholson in a cutter. He sailed on a cruise from that place in May or June to the Bay of Biscay, the English and Irish channels, and was chased into Morlaix, where he remained for some time. He sailed from that port about the 17th or 18th of September, bound for the United States, and the next morning fell in with a British cutter. After an action of four hours, the ammunition having all been expended, the vessel struck, and Commodore Dale was carried into Mill prison. He made his escape in February following, arrived at London, was retaken, and sent back to prison. In February, 1779, he made his escape a second time, went up to London, thence to Dover, to Calais, to Paris, to Nantes, and to L'Orient, where he joined Commodore Jones, in the Bon homme Richard, as master's mate. Before the sailing of that ship, Jones made him his first lieutenant. Commodore Dale's account of the battle with the Serapis will be found in the preceding narrative. He returned, about the age of 22 years and 6 months, with Jones in the Ariel to Philadelphia, where he entered on board the Trumbull of 28 guns, Captain James Nicholson, and was taken off the Capes of Delaware by two British ships of war, and carried into New York, in August, 1781. He was exchanged in the succeeding November.

When, under the present Constitution of the United States, the naval establishment was commenced, Commodore Dale was honorably remembered. He was appointed a captain on the 11th of May, 1798, to take rank from the 4th of June, 1794. In May, 1798, the command of the sloop of war Ganges, of 24 guns, was given to him, with orders to cruise between the Capes of Virginia and Long Island, so as to afford the best protection in his power to our jurisdictional rights, and to all vessels of the United States coming in or going off the coast, against French cruisers. On the 1st of February, 1779, he went to the East Indies on furlough.— On the 28th of April, 1801, he was appointed to the command of the

American squadron in the Mediterranean, to protect our commerce from the attacks of the Regencies of Algiers, Tunis, and Tripoli. He resigned his commission on the 17th of December, 1802, and now resides in Philadelphia, in the bosom of an amiable family, respected and beloved by a numerous circle of relations, friends, and acquaintances, enjoying the fruits of his manly and patriotic exertions in the cause of American Independence. The following attestation of character, by the Chevalier John Paul Jones, speaks impressively in favor of the gallant, intrepid, and worthy veteran, Dale:

Commodore J. Paul Jones's letter of recommendation and certificate of merit for Lieutenant Richard Dale, dated July 18*th*, 1781.

"The bearer hereof, Mr. Richard Dale, having served as a master's mate in the continental brigantine Lexington, and escaped from an English prison long after that brigantine was taken in the European seas, was employed by me in France in the spring of 1779, on board the continental ship of war Bon homme Richard, as a master's mate. In the summer of that year I promoted him to the station of lieutenant, and gave him a commission. He was with me as lieutenant in that ship on a cruise in the Bay of Biscay, and on the expedition from France round the west of Ireland, by the north, to the Texel. He afterward was with me as a lieutenant in the Alliance from the Texel to Spain and back to France, and from France he came with me as lieutenant in the Ariel to this city. In the action between the Bon homme Richard and the Serapis, he commanded the fore part of the battery of 12-pounders, and did his utmost till it was silenced by the fire of the Serapis, the Countess of Scarborough, and the Alliance. He afterward did his best to assist at the pumps and other places, showing a firmness and military spirit which does him the highest honor, and for which he has my particular thanks. When the Ariel was dismounted he showed no less firmness, and in the action between the Ariel and Triumph, did his duty with great spirit. Mr. Dale is included in the vote of thanks with which I have been honored by the United States in Congress assembled, since my return from Europe, and will, I am sure, always approve himself a good man and deserving officer. Given under my hand and seal at Philadelphia this 18th day of July, 1781."

BIOGRAPHICAL SKETCH

OF

LIEUTENANT ELIJAH HALL.

HAVING given a brief outline of the character of Commodore Dale, it would be injustice to omit a due notice of another brave and meritorious officer, who served with the Chevalier John Paul Jones. We allude to Elijah Hall, who was a lieutenant under the Chevalier in the Ranger.

Lieut. Hall had entered on board this vessel at Portsmouth, New Hampshire, before her departure for France, and was in her with Jones in his cruise on the coasts of Scotland and Ireland, in the descent on Whitehaven, and in the battle with the Drake. When Simpson behaved so badly as to disobey orders, it was Hall that was selected to arrest him, and to command the Drake in his stead. The prominent traits of Lieut. Hall's character were promptitude and energy; of which he gave a remarkable instance in repairing the Drake in the course of one night with the assistance of forty men, after Simpson had pronounced it impossible in her then shattered condition.

Lieutenant Hall went to Brest with Jones; and when, through the benevolence of the latter, Simpson was put in command of the Ranger for the purpose of returning to America, Hall occupied the post of first lieutenant. After his return to the United States, he was engaged in several expeditions against the enemy, on board the same ship with Commodore Whipple, and was very successful in making captures, most of which arrived safely in port. When the America, 74, was assigned to

Jones, he offered Lieut. Hall a very honorable and efficient station in her; but the gift of that vessel to France frustrated his good intentions. Lieut. Hall eventually proceeded in the Ranger, with other ships-of-war, to assist in the defence of Charleston, South Carolina, where he fell into the hands of the enemy, in common with the garrison, by capitulation. He returned to New Hampshire, but was not exchanged until a general surrender of prisoners. He never resigned his commission, and was always ready for active service. At the close of the war of the revolution he engaged in commercial pursuits, by which he enriched himself; but suffered considerably by the British orders in council and the French Berlin and Milan decrees. Although offered a pension by government, he would not receive it; but accepted the appointment of naval officer for Portsmouth, a situation which he still retains at the advanced age of 83. With the snow of so many winters upon his head, he discharged his duty, it is understood, with the greatest satisfaction to the merchants and others, affording proof of an uncommon vigor of constitution and strength of intellect. Faithful to his country and true to his duty in every situation, there can be no doubt that a consciousness of probity has ensured for him that intellectual tranquillity, which is so favorable to human life.

In closing the foregoing sketch of the Life of Mr. Hall, the author will remark, to show the true patriotism that ever filled the inmost soul of this late gallant naval officer, that after the passage of the act of Congress, placing the officers of the revolution on the pension list, Mr. Hall politely refused to have his name entered as a pensioner: observing that, in defending his country, and assisting in giving her independence, he was doing but his duty as an American officer, feeling content in having the approbation of his heroic commander Paul Jones, endorsed by his country, which would be left as a legacy to his children, and far more valuable than a pension certificate.

PAUL JONES TO COL. SHERBURNE.

The following letter from Paul Jones to his friend, Colonel Sherburne, late Judge of the Admiralty Court of New Hampshire (the father of the author), shows that Jones was schooled in the fashionable circles of etiquette as well as in the well known school of discipline in the navy, so highly necessary on board a man-of-war, and to which may be attributed the many signal triumphs in battling with the British commanders on the ocean, and carrying in triumph the flag of independence which he was never known to strike, while, like a meteor, he dashed over the seas in quest of new victories over a proud and cruel enemy.

The letter will also do away the false impression that Jones was distressed in his pecuniary means after the peace with England in 1783. The Mrs. Langdon mentioned was the aunt of the author and wife of the late Governor John Langdon, of Portsmouth, New Hampshire, who was the Navy Agent during the Revolutionary war at Portsmouth, where was built and fitted for a cruize the sloop-of-war Ranger, of 20 guns, commanded by Paul Jones,—which ship captured in the Irish Channel, off Carrickfergus, the British ship-of-war Drake, of 22 guns, and sent her as a prize into Brest under command of Lieut. Elijah Hall (father-in-law of the author), a biographical sketch of whose life is published in this work

"*Bernam, Penn'a, August* 21*st*, 1783.

"Dear Colonel,

"You did me the honor to write me a very handsome letter after your arrival in France, which claims my thanks both as a mark of your attention, and on account of the polite compliments it pays my endeavours as an officer. *My wishes* would have impelled me to far greater exertions, but my projects were constantly cramped for want of *means*. It is now peace, and, I hope, I may have occasion to learn war no more. I was in hopes you would have brought me some letters. I persuade myself, that if some of my Parisian friends had known of the opportunity, they would have embraced it. I shall be glad to hear from you at Philadelphia, where I expect to find myself about the latter end of this month. I am here for the recovery of my health, which has been in a bad state ever since my return from South America.

"You will oblige me with the history of your travels *in the great world* at Paris, as well as in the *agreeable world* at Portsmouth. You will please to make my respectful compliments to your sister, Mrs. Langdon, and to any other of the fair ladies to whom you have reason to think they will be acceptable; *of which, dear Colonel, you are to render an account.*

"I am, dear Sir,

"Your most obedient and most humble sevant,

"JOHN PAUL JONES."

COL. JOHN S. SHERBURNE,
Portsmouth,
New Hampshire.

"P. S.—Perhaps I may visit Portsmouth this fall. In the mean time, do you know of any advantageous scheme where three or four thousand pounds sterling might be employed?"

PAUL JONES'S PILLAGE OF SELKIRK CASTLE,

ST. MARY'S ISLE, IN 1778;

For which he was branded a Pirate by England.

THE author will refer the reader to page 50 in this work, to an unanswerable, polite, and most feeling letter from Commodore Paul Jones, commanding the U. S. sloop of war Ranger of 20 guns, dated May 8th, 1778, on board his victorious ship, the day following his capture of the British ship of war Drake, after a long and bloody engagement, yard-arm and yard-arm, off Carrickfergus, Ireland, in which is fully and most feelingly explained the reason of his visit to St. Mary's Isle, the taking of the *plate*, &c., and its intended restitution on his arrival at Brest; all of which will be seen in the correspondence on the subject;—Jones most strictly complied with his promise to the very letter. For this, this gallant naval officer was branded a "*freebooter*," "*pirate*," &c., by England, echoed by Europe, and re-echoed by his enemies in America. This vile censorious stigma rested on the hero's name until he had lain quietly in his grave for thirty-three years, not even his own relations would own him as a relation in Scotland, or in South Carolina, until the author published an authentic history of the life and character of Paul Jones, under the supervisement of the late Samuel L. Southard, Secretary of the Navy, assisted by the late ex-presidents Thomas Jefferson, Mr. Madison, and John Quincy

Adams, also the Marquis La Fayette, as will be seen in this work from their correspondence with the author. And notwithstanding the copyright was purchased for publication in London, from the Author, by John Murray, of Albemarle street, through his bankers, Baring, Brothers, & Co., thus placing the character of Paul Jones on an equal, if not a superior footing with many of the British admirals, yet still his name was stigmatized in England whenever it happened to be named, and for the sole cause Britain never can forgive Jones for bearding the "*lion*" in his lair, capturing their *crack* frigates single handed, dashing through her proud, hitherto invincible fleets, taking their most valuable merchant ships in sight of their harbors, landing and spiking the guns in their forts, carrying off prisoners to exchange for American seamen who were dying in British prisons, and causing alarm throughout the coasts of England, Ireland, and Scotland, which cost millions of gold to defend against the small American squadron of Paul Jones, whom they stigmatized the *pirate*, although under the protection of the American flag which he first hoisted, but never disgraced by striking it to a foe. The whole history of the landing at St. Mary's Isle, the taking of the *plate* from Selkirk Castle, was given verbally to the author by the late Elijah Hall, of Portsmouth, New Hampshire (father-in-law to the author), and one of the lieutenants who landed at the Isle, and superintended the packing of the plate to convey on board the Ranger, every article of which (as will be seen in the correspondence page 50) was returned in the same good order a few months subsequent to its being carried from the castle, and duly, politely acknowledged by the Earl of Selkirk, with many thanks to *Captain John Paul Jones, of the American Navy,—not Paul Jones the Pirate.*

Commodore John Paul Jones on the ocean, during the American revolution, was, as General Washington on the land, never known to be defeated in battle, and neither ever receiving a wound, seemingly under the protection of Providence in America's struggle for independence.

The following is a copy of letters of administration taken out by the author for the purpose of examining the accounts of Paul Jones at the Treasury of the United States, to see if his heirs had any demand on the government; the result was, that no demand could be made, as the books and accounts at the treasury show conclusive evidence, that previous to

Paul Jones's departure for Europe, after the peace of 1783, he had, in person, settled his accounts at the Treasury, and received in full all and every just demand for pay, rations, &c., since he entered the navy in 1776, likewise all *prize-money* due, as he paid himself while in France, as will be seen by page 276 in this work. The prizes sent into Bergen, in Norway, in 1799, as per insurance in London, to £50,000 sterling, is still due from Denmark, as will be seen by the joint resolution of Congress in appendix of this work, passed and approved July, 1848, in which all the officers, seamen, and marines who served under Paul Jones, in 1779, are entitled to a share of this money according to their relative rank, or their heirs and assigns when it shall be received from Denmark, except the sole heir of Paul Jones and heirs of Captain Landais, who have received their full share of the above amount from the U. S. Treasury, per acts of Congress, as will be seen in this work. Paul Jones's heirs are all dead but one,—Miss Lowden, a grand-niece, and daughter of the late John Lowden, merchant of Charleston, S. C., who was a nephew of Paul Jones. The author, to be positive as regards the heirs, made full enquiry on his late tour in Scotland, and issued a public notice through the press in Scotland, notifying all concerned to send or call on the author at Tate's Royal Hotel, Prince Street, Edinburgh, or the Star Hotel, James's Square, Glasgow, but no response to the notice to this date.

The splendid sword presented in person to Paul Jones by Louis XVI. of France, for his heroic achievements during the American Revolutionary war against the British, is now in possession of Captain Dale, U. S. Navy, Philadelphia, son of the late Commodore Richard Dale, first lieutenant under Jones. This splendid sword, the only relic left of value as belonging to Paul Jones, should be demanded by Miss Lowden, only heir, as the author has no evidence or knowledge how this sword came into the possession of Commodore Dale, and by what right it is still held from the heir of so distinguished and heroic naval commander of the revolution;—an explanation should be demanded.

"District of Columbia.
"County of Washington, to wit:
"United States of America.

"To all persons to whom these presents shall come, greeting:

"Know ye, that whereas John Paul Jones, late of the United States Navy, deceased, hath died intestate, as it is said, leaving certain goods, chattels, and personal estate to be administered: *Now, know ye*, That administration of all and singular the goods, chattels, rights and credits of the said John Paul Jones, deceased, is hereby granted and committed unto Col. John Henry Sherburne, of the County and District aforesaid.

"*Witness*, Nathaniel P. Caurin, Esquire, Judge of the Orphans' Court of Washington County aforesaid, this 18th day of February, in the year of our Lord one thousand eight hundred and thirty-nine, and of the Independence of the United States the sixty-second.

"*Test.*, Edward N. Roach, *Register of Wills.*

"Oath administered to the above named administrator, and sworn before me on the day above mentioned, and public notice in the papers duly given.

"EDWARD N. ROACH, *Register of Wills.*"

OFFICIAL LETTERS TO THE AUTHOR,

RELATIVE TO THE ORIGINAL MUSTER ROLLS OF THE UNITED STATES FRIGATES BON HOMME RICHARD, ALLIANCE, AND SLOOP OF WAR PALLAS, IN THE DISTRIBUTION OF THE PRIZE-MONEY DEPOSITED IN THE TREASURY IN 1800.

From the First Auditor of the U. S. Treasury.

"*Treasury Department, Washington, May 7th,* 1827.

"SIR,

"Will you have the goodness to inform this Department, where an *official list* of the crew of the United States frigate Alliance, when commanded by Commodore John Paul Jones in the Revolutionary War, exhibiting a distribution of *prize-money*, can be procured? It is not to be found in either of the State or Treasury Departments.

"Very respectfully, sir,
"Your obedient servant,
"JESSE MILLER, 1st Auditor.

"Col. JOHN H. SHERBURNE, Author Life of Paul Jones,
Washington City."

From the Register of the Treasury of the United States.

"*Treasury Department, Register's Office, August* 2*d.*

"SIR,

"After a careful examination of the files of this office, the only paper found in relation to the *prize-money* ($50,000) due to the officers and crews under command of the late Commodore John Paul Jones, is a copy of a certified copy of the crew of the *Bon homme Richard and Alliance.* No original muster or pay roll appears to have been filed with any of the accounts for prize-money mentioned in the list made out for you by Mr. Underwood, herewith returned. I also enclose a memorandum of Mr. Underwood on the subject of the lists.

"I am, very respectfully, yours, &c.,

"DANIEL GRAHAM, Register.

"Col. JOHN H. SHERBURNE, Present."

From J. W. Underwood, Chief Clerk of First Auditor's Office, as mentioned in Mr. Graham's letter, of August 2d, to the author.

"SIR,

"I have no recollection of ever having seen the *original rolls* of which Colonel Sherburne speaks in 1837. I was not Chief Clerk then, and had nothing to do with the distribution of the *prize-money*, but after the resignation of Mr. Mahan, Chief Clerk, I had to adjust one or two of the accounts, and in doing so, referred to lists filed with one of the early settlements, perhaps the first, under the third section of act of Congress, 3d March, 1837, (Naval Appropriation,) but the lists, I am persuaded, of the Bon homme Richard and Alliance were *not originals*, but copies: they are to be found, I presume, now filed with said settlement. I think that about a year since Major T. L. Smith (late Register) made inquiry for them.

"Yours truly, &c.,

"J. W. UNDERWOOD.

"Hon. DANIEL GRAHAM, Register of the Treasury."

From the Secretary of State to the author.

"*Department of State, April* 18*th.*

"SIR,

"In answer to your letter of the 14th instant, I have to inform you that there are no muster rolls of the frigate Alliance, in 1782, among the papers of Commodore John Paul Jones in this Department.

"I am, sir, your obedient servant,

"JAMES BUCHANAN, Secretary of State.

"Col. JOHN H. SHERBURNE, Present."

PRIZE MONEY

DUE TO THE OFFICERS, SEAMEN, AND MARINES OF THE U. S. FRIGATES BON HOMME RICHARD AND ALLIANCE, UNDER COMMAND OF COMMODORE JOHN PAUL JONES IN 1779, AND NOT PAID UNTIL MARCH, 1837, AND THEN *thirty-seven years' interest refused* TO THE HEIRS OF THE GALLANT TARS, SO JUSTLY DUE.

WHILE the author was examining the documents and papers which Ex-President Thomas Jefferson had sent him a year previous to the patriot's death, all relative to his friend, the late Paul Jones, a discovery was made of great importance which had been secreted since 1800, viz.: That Paul Jones had paid into the hands of Mr. Jefferson then Minister to France, and on the eve of returning to the United States, $50,000 to be by him deposited in the U. S. Treasury for the benefit as prize money due to all those officers and men who served in the American squadron in Europe, and to be paid them by the government pro rata immediately after the amount was deposited by Mr. Jefferson. It was the last day of February, 1837, when it was by accident discovered by the author, who at once called at the Treasury to ascertain why and wherefore this large amount of money had been so long withheld from the brave tars of the revolution who had fought and bled under their heroic commander, while carrying in triumph the flag of liberty over every sea, seeking and capturing the foe, to independence. On examination there it was found correct, but the money could not be withdrawn without an act of Congress, which body was then in session, and but three days remained before adjournment. The author called on the Revolutionary Committee, stated the case which was satisfactory, when they agreed to report it to the House that morning, and endeavor to have it attached as a rider to the Navy Bill, then before the Senate for amendment, on its return to the House, which proved successful by a unanimous vote. The author, by authority, advertised through the press for all concerned to forward their claims to the first Auditor of the Treasury for payment according to their rank, and the following is an official statement transmitted to the author in 1842, giving the names, rank, and prize money paid to claimants, &c., viz. :—

Paid in 1838.

Lawrence Brooks,	Surgeon,	Bon homme Richard,	$141 41
Cutting Lunt,	Lieutenant,	" " "	739 74
Jonathan Wells,	Gunner,	" " "	79 58
Gilbert Wall,	Seaman,	" " "	36 88
Richard Wall,	"	" " "	36 88
Aaron Goodwin,	"	" " "	29 84
Benjamin Balch,	Chaplain,	Frigate Alliance,	47 74
John Green,	Carpenter's Mate,	" "	79 58
Thomas Balch,	Seaman,	" "	39 79
Thomas Case,	"	" "	39 79
Joseph Ferdinand,	"	" "	39 79
Ephraim Clark,	"	" "	39 79
John Gunnerson,	"	Bon homme Richard,	120 11
			$1470 92

Paid in 1839.

Richard Dale,	First Lieut.,	Bon homme Richard,	$756 58
Samuel Stacy,	Sail. Master,	" " "	756 58
Samuel Guild,	Surg. Mate,	Frigate Alliance,	79 58
Amos Windship,	Surgeon,	" "	189 14
Benjamin Balch,	Chaplain,	" "	15 90
Andrew Withan,	Seaman,	" "	39 79
Samuel Gray,	"	" "	39 79
			$1877 36

Paid in 1840.

Jacob Nutter,	Qu'r Master,	Frigate Alliance,	$79 58
John Stickney,	Seaman,	" "	19 90
			$99 48

Paid in 1841 *and* 1842.

Nathaniel Fanning,	Midshipman,	Bon homme Richard,	$ 66 42
Henry Lunt,	Lieutenant,	" " "	387 40
			$3899 58

XXIXth Congress, First Session. } *H. R.* 200.—*Report No.* 206.

February 10*th*, 1846.

Read and committed to a Committee of the Whole House to-morrow.

Mr. Maclay, from the Committee on Naval Affairs, reported the following Bill :—

"A BILL

"*For the Relief of the Heirs of John Paul Jones.*

"Be it enacted by the Senate and House of Representatives of the United States of America in Congress assembled, That the accounts of the late Commodore John Paul Jones with the United States be referred to the Secretary of the Treasury, to adjust and pay upon the principles of justice and equity, according to acts in similar cases, and applicable thereto.

"*Section 2d.—And be it further enacted*, That the Secretary of the Treasury is hereby instructed to pay to the legal representatives of the said John Paul Jones, out of any moneys in the Treasury not otherwise appropriated, his proportion of the value, as estimated by Benjamin Franklin with interest, of three prizes captured by the squadron under the command of the said Jones, and delivered up to Great Britain by Denmark in 1779; to be apportioned on the basis of the distribution of a settlement made with, for prizes captured by the said squadron, and received from the Court of France, and confirmed by Congress in 1787; the said proportion to be deducted from the indemnity to be received from Denmark, in satisfaction of the loss sustained in the three prizes aforesaid."

Passed, and approved by the President of the United States, July 6, 1848, granting $50,000 to the heirs of the gallant hero, leaving $150,000 of the Danish Claim to be distributed among the officers and crews in the Squadron of 1779, when demanded.

OFFICIAL CORRESPONDENCE,

RELATIVE TO THE REMOVAL OF PAUL JONES'S REMAINS FROM PARIS TO THE UNITED STATES FOR INTERMENT, IN THE UNITED STATES FRIGATE ST. LAWRENCE, COMMANDER JOSHUA R. SANDS, BY ORDERS FROM THE HON. WILLIAM A. GRAHAM, SECRETARY OF THE NAVY.

The author had made a request of Mr. Bancroft, in writing, in 1845, when at the head of the Navy Department, asking that the remains might be brought home, in one of the return ships in the Mediterranean, but received no reply.

"*Navy Department, January* 30*th*, 1851.

"SIR,

"Agreeably to the request contained in your letter of the 27th instant, an order has this day been issued to the commander of the frigate St. Lawrence, directing him to receive on board at Southampton, the remains of the late John Paul Jones, to be transported to New York.

"I am, respectfully, your obedient servant,

"WILLIAM A. GRAHAM, Secretary of the Navy.

"Col. JOHN H. SHERBURNE, New York."

As there were no instructions in the above letter to receive the author on board the frigate St. Lawrence, with the remains of the late Commodore Paul Jones, at Southampton, (England,) to be taken to New York, the author addressed a note to the Secretary, to inquire if it were necessary for a specific order to the commander of the St. Lawrence to that effect, and the following letter from the Secretary wishes it to be so understood, both by the Department and the commander of the frigate, Captain Sands, that the author should accompany the remains to New York, in the frigate.

"*Navy Department, February* 21*st*, 1851.

"SIR,

"Your letter of the 20th instant, requesting that directions may be given to Commander Sands to receive you on board the frigate St. Lawrence, on your arrival at Southampton from Paris, with the remains of the

24

late John Paul Jones, has been received. The Department does not deem it necessary to issue the order asked for, as it presumes there will be no difficulty in the case.

"I am, respectfully, your obedient servant,

"William A. Graham, Secretary of the Navy.

"Col. John H. Sherburne, New York."

Extract of a letter from a distinguished author in Philadelphia, relative to the removal of the remains of the late Commodore Paul Jones from France to the United States, to the author.

"My Dear Colonel,

"I regret exceedingly that I was not able to see you previous to your departure for New York. So fearful was I that you would not decide as I desired as regards the disposition of the remains of Paul Jones, that I concluded to send this letter after you.

"I repeat to you, that in no event must the remains of the Chevalier Jones repose anywhere save in this country. America, which is the legatee of his fame, should be the guardian of his ashes. I guarantee to you a most glorious reception, an honorable and public interment for them. This I give you on my own personal responsibility. But that were needless; for so soon as we learn that you are about to start with them, so soon will we prepare for a public demonstration, which will be enthusiastic.

"On no account must the remains of *Paul Jones* repose in other than *American soil.*

"With sentiments of the highest respect, I am, dear Colonel,

"Yours very truly, &c."

Letter from the Hon. Richard Rush, Minister to the Court of St. Cloud, to the author, in relation to the removal of the remains of Commodore John Paul Jones to the United States, for interment at Washington City.

"*Legation of the United States, Paris, January 3d,* 1848.
3, *Rue de Matignon.*

"My Dear Sir,

"In reply to your letter of the 28th ult., I beg to say, that on your arrival at Paris I will gladly aid you in any suggestions or steps that may be proper and practicable, on my part, towards the interesting object you propose to yourself, of removing to our country, for interment in the Congress cemetery at Washington, the remains of Paul Jones, from their present entombment in this capital. But, uninstructed by the Secretary of State on this subject, and uninformed if Congress has passed any resolution in regard to it, I must wait your arrival for information on these and other points, preliminary to any steps of mine, official or otherwise, with this government or the public authorities of Paris on the occasion. I have no knowledge of the place of his interment, of which, perhaps, you may know something. I am happy to see, by our papers, that the Senate has already, at the present session of Congress, passed a bill for the relief of the heirs of this gallant patriot and warrior of our Revolution.

"I remain, dear sir, very respectfully,
"Your obedient servant,
"RICHARD RUSH.

"Col. JOHN H. SHERBURNE, 96 Strand, London."

NAVY AND REVENUE SERVICE.

THE author professes to have had some experience in naval as well as military matters, during the last quarter of a century, and the pleasure of corresponding with officers of high rank in both departments, while holding responsible confidential appointments under the several administrations; consequently his feelings naturally became enlisted in their behalf, more especially when neglect, or injustice, seemed their only reward for long service and sacrifice in the cause of our model republic, the *pole-star*, on which all nations now gaze with astonishment at its power, magnanimity, and greatness.

While casting a glance over the printed naval register for the current year (which was politely inclosed to the author from the department, a copy of which is added in the appendix to this work), and seeing so many officers marked "*off duty*," or "*waiting orders*," the idea suggested itself, why the revenue cutters on the several stations should not be officered from the *navy* instead of taking *civilians* from their trade or profession to command *cutters*, being wholly ignorant of navigation, or the discipline required on board ship, &c.

Therefore, would it not, under such circumstances, be advisable for the Secretary of the Navy (who is ever alive to all that concerns the welfare of the department over which he presides with so much credit to the Republic) to suggest the expediency, at the next session of Congress, of placing the revenue cutters under the command of lieutenants in the navy, and ordering passed midshipmen to them as acting lieutenants, with two or three midshipmen to learn practical navigation *coastwise*, until other duties can be given them. If this were done, *active* employment would be given to a goodly number of the grade of officers named, who are anxious for active service and a chance for a more thorough knowledge of their profession, which the present limited nnmber of our vessels of war, and the yearly increase of officers of these grades, *now* prevent. In fact revenue cutters would prove good schools for the officers, inasmuch as they would, in time, become efficient *pilots* on our widely extended coast, which would not only be useful to *them*, but of great importance to the whole country in time of *war*, more particularly as these officers, on being transferred to large ships of war, could, on any emergency, act as skilful practical pilots on approaching the coast, or entering harbors, in war or peace, in calms or tempests, without waiting for a harbor pilot.

If *economy* be the foundation of a Republican form of government, as it would seem to be, a regulation as suggested would prove an immense saving on the calls of the Treasury; for the grade of officers alluded to, who are from year to year doing *no* active service, and drawing regularly their *full monthly pay and rations*, if ordered to the cutters, would not increase the appropriation for the navy but a mere trifle, while an immense saving would unquestionably be made to the nation by substituting the navy officers for the present revenue officers, who, near half of their time, are, with their beautiful craft, at anchor in harbors, or engaged on fishing and other excursions during the summer months, and, in winter, most frequently, are seen frozen up in the ice, and helpless as a birch canoe.

It will be easily conceived that the minds of navy officers must necessarily become uneasy when they are continued *too long* in any one grade, and become *rusty*, which must be the case while the present law exists regulating the *number* in the service, and consequently slow promotions; for it must be conceded by all who are anywise acquainted with naval tactics, that it is the work of many years' study and experience to acquire the high degree of science necessary to a great sea officer, and the plan suggested of having the revenue cutters officered by lieutenants and midshipmen, would be *one step* towards allowing these officers some chance of acquiring a knowledge of their profession before they become *grey*, as some already are, and also to learn that there is as much difference between a battle between two ships, and an engagement between two fleets, as there is between a duel and a ranged battle between two armies; that the mere holding a *commission* and wearing a *button* for twenty years on shore, is no evidence of an officer being a thorough seaman, or fit to command a man-of-war in case of sudden emergency. A navy may be *officered*, but it is not so sure that officers are always *equal* to their *commissions*. Let them have experience. There are about thirty vessels in the revenue service, officered by civilians, to the number of over a hundred, while streets and hotels are thronged with supplemental naval officers, drawing pay and soliciting service in vain.

FRIGATE PAUL JONES.

THE author has repeatedly been asked the question, both in Europe and his own country, why the government omitted naming a ship of war in honor to the memory of *Paul Jones*, who so distinguished himself in the American Revolution, and so triumphantly disputed with England the supremacy of the sea, by conquering her *crack* frigates, single handed, whenever an opportunity offered, and sending them as prizes into port.

In answer to this question, the author has invariably screened the government from any reproach for the want of any neglect on their part in the desire that a frigate of the first class should expressly be built, to be named the *Paul Jones*, in memory of the late naval chieftain, and the following act was passed *unanimously* by Congress, and approved by the President, *June* 30*th*, 1834.—See volume 9, page 121, section 1st, chapter 125, Laws of the United States.

"*An Act authorizing the Purchase of Live-oak Frames for a Frigate and Sloop of War, and for other Naval Purposes:*

"*Section First.* Be it enacted by the Senate and House of Representatives of the United States of America in Congress assembled: That the Secretary of the Navy be and he is hereby authorized to direct the procurement, in the usual mode, of a live-oak frame for a frigate, to be called the PAUL JONES; and of a live-oak frame for a sloop of war, to be called the LEVANT; and the sum of $50,000 is hereby appropriated, out of any money in the Treasury not otherwise appropriated, for that purpose.—*Approved June* 30*th*, 1834."

It is for the late Navy Board of Commissioners to answer the inquiry, why they neglected, in the face of the above act of Congress, approved by the President *seventeen years* ago, and who were then authorized by law to name the public ships as they were ordered to be built, to obey the law in purchasing the live-oak for the building of the frigate to be called the PAUL JONES, or say what became of the *fifty thousand dollars specially appropriated for the object named.* The ships Bainbridge, Decatur, Warren, Dale, Somers, et al., were built and so named by the then Navy Board, but it would seem that the name of *Paul Jones*, the hero who first proclaimed to the astonished world that the cross of Britain had been humbled by the modest bunting of America in single combat, was *intentionally forgotten* by the Honorable Navy Commissioners in 1834.

It is hoped by the author, (as the humble biographer of the late Commodore Paul Jones,) that the present energetic Secretary of the Navy, whose patriotic feelings have never been known to wane under any circumstances, will, at a convenient season, see proper to make the inquiry relative to the foregoing act of Congress, and why it was not carried into effect; as the $50,000 could not be transferred to any other use without act of Congress, it is to be presumed the amount yet remains in the Treasury, subject to draft for the purpose contemplated.

To have a first class frigate named the *Paul Jones*, would be an endorsement by the American Republic to the world, that he was not a *pirate*, (so named by the English press,) but an American naval officer, holding a commission from the Congress of 1776, and entrusted with its national banner, which was never disgraced while under the hero's protection, at home or abroad.

On the arrival of Commodore Paul Jones in the Texel, (Holland,) with his prize, the *crack* British frigate Serapis, 50, Commodore Pearson, captured after a most bloody and desperate engagement, off Flamborough Head, by moonlight, (in which the Bon homme Richard went down the next day,) the French consul, General M. le Chevalier de Linoncourt, was so elated at so splendid a victory, that he wrote the following hasty note to Jones, (which the author copied from the original and translated,) urging him to say that he captured the Serapis, holding a commission from the *French* court, which was lost in the sinking of his ship, the Bon homme Richard, thereby uttering a falsehood. So gross was this insult to the American commission, so dear to him, who with it had performed such glorious, valorous conquests on sea and land, under freedom's stripes, that he the same day addressed a letter on the subject (so insulting to himself and America, his adopted country,) to the French ambassador, Monsieur le Duc de la Vauguyon, which patriotic epistle alone places the name of *Paul Jones* among the first patriots of the Revolution in 1776, and should cause the hero's name to be remembered and revered by every American heart.

Note from M. le Chevalier de Linoncourt, French Consul-General at the Hague, to Commodore John Paul Jones.

"M. le Commodore Paul Jones anoncera à M. le Vice Amiral Reyan, que quoiqu'en qualité d'Americain il n'ait fait usage que de la commission des Etats Unis, il n'en etait pas moins vrai qu'il avait une *francaise* qui a été perdue, dans du desastre du Bon homme Richard, et dont l'acte qui lui a été adressé est la *copie.* M. le Commodore Paul Jones fera même cette declaration pour ecrit, et la signera, si par hazard M. le Vice Amiral venait à l'exiger."

[TRANSLATION.]

"Commodore Paul Jones will state to Vice Admiral Reyan, that, although as an American he has only used the commission of the United States, it is not the less true that he had a *French* commission, which was lost at the time of the disaster to the Bon homme Richard, and that the *document* which has been sent to him is the copy. Commodore Paul Jones will even make this declaration in writing, and sign it, if by chance the Vice Admiral should demand it."

NOTE.—The following lines are in the handwriting of Paul Jones, written under the above, on the note from the French Consul-General at the Hague, in which he thinks himself most grossly insulted.

"N. B. The above is the proposition that was given me in writing, the 13th December, 1779, on board the frigate Alliance, at the Texel, by M. le Chevalier de Linoncourt, to induce me to *say and sign a falsehood.*

"JOHN PAUL JONES."

From Paul Jones to the French Ambassador at the Hague.

"*On board the American frigate Alliance, in the Texel, December* 13*th*, 1779.

"My Lord,

"Perhaps there are many men in the world, who would esteem as an honor the *commission* that I have this day *refused*. My rank from the beginning knew no superior in the marine of America; how, then, must I be *humbled*, were I to accept of a letter of marque! I should, my lord, esteem myself inexcusable, were I to accept of even a commission of equal or superior denomination with that I bear, unless I were previously authorized, either by Congress or some other competent authority in Europe; and I must tell you, that on my arrival at Brest from my expedition in the Irish Channel, Count d'Orvilliers offered to procure for me from the Court at Versailles, a commission of *Capitaine des Vesseaux*, which I did not then accept for the same reason, although the war between England and France was not then begun, and of course the commission of France would have protected me from an enemy of superior force.

"It is a matter of the highest astonishment to me, after so many compliments and fair professions, the French Court should offer the *present insult* to my understanding, and suppose me capable of disgracing my present commission! I confess that I have not merited all the praise that has been bestowed on my past conduct; but I also feel that I have far less merited such a *reward!* Where profession and practice are so opposite, I am no longer weak enough to form a wrong conclusion. They may think as they please of me; for where I cannot continue my esteem, praise or censure from any man is to me matter of indifference. I am much obliged to them, however, for having at last fairly opened my eyes, and enabled me to discover *truth* from *falsehood*. The prisoners shall be delivered agreeably to the orders which you have done me the honor to send me from his excellency the American ambassador in France.

"I will also, with great pleasure, not only permit a part of my seamen to go on board the ship under your excellency's orders, but I will also do my utmost to prevail with them to embark *freely;* and if I can now, or hereafter, by any other honorable means facilitate the success or the honor of his Majesty's arms, I pledge myself to you, as his ambassador, that none of his own subjects would *bleed* in his cause with greater freedom than myself, an *American.*

"It gives me the more pain, my lord, to write this letter, because the *court* has enjoined you to propose what would destroy my peace of mind, and my future veracity in the opinion of the world. When, *with the consent of the court*, and by orders of the American ambassador, I gave *Ame-*

rican commissions to *French* officers, I did not fill up these commissions to command privateers! nor even for a rank *equal* to that of their commissions in the marine of France. They were promoted to a rank far *superior*. And why? Not from personal friendship, nor from my knowledge of their services or abilities, (the men and their characters being entire strangers to me,) but from the respect which I believed *America* would wish to show for the service of France. While I remained, (eight months,) *seemingly forgot* by the French Court, at Brest, many commissions, such as that in question, were offered me; and I believe (when I am in pursuit of plunder,) I can still obtain such an one, *without application to the French Court.*

"I hope, my lord, that my behavior through life will ever entitle me to the continuance of your good wishes and opinion, and that you will take occasion to make mention of the warm and personal affection with which my heart is impressed towards his Majesty.

"I am unalterably, my lord,

"Your excellency's obedient and humble servant,

"JOHN PAUL JONES.

"Son Excellence,

"Monsieur le duc de la VAUGUYON, Paris,

"And Ambassadeur de France, &c., &c."

Among the voluminous correspondence, public documents, private papers, &c., amounting to many hundreds, all connected with naval matters during the American Revolution, left by the late Commodore Paul Jones, was a complete tabular list, in his own handwriting, of every vessel, large and small, in the English navy during the Revolution, and under each proper head were the names of the vessels of war, rates, dimensions, men, guns, depth, width, tons, where built, when rebuilt, by whom, and draught of water; also, the number of pinnaces, yawls, and long boats, attached to each vessel of war.

The author presumes that Jones must have had a friend of influence attached to the English Admiralty Office, from whom such highly important information was received, giving the possessor of such a document the great advantage in war, in knowing the strength of an adversary. This may account, in some measure, that whenever Paul Jones engaged his enemy at sea, even if a superior force, he always was victorious. Strange as it may appear, Jones never received a wound in all his severe engagements.

ABOLITION OF THE "CAT" IN THE NAVY.

Every Member and Senator in the XXXIst Congress of the United States who voted for the abolition of the *Cat* as a punishment in the American Navy deserve to have their names enrolled among the philanthropists of the Nineteenth Century. The use of the *Cat* for the punishment of men on board the public ships for the most trivial offence, was a disgrace to the *Stars* and *Stripes*, that floated proudly overhead of the victim lashed to the gratings, to receive blow after blow on his naked back from the *Cat* in the hands of the boatswain's mate. The gallant Paul Jones, the *Washington* on the ocean during the American Revolution, never disgraced his name, or the ship or squadron he had the honor to command, by cruelty to those under his command; hence it was no rendezvous was required to drum up the *old salts* to enlist on board the ship-of-war that had for her commander *Paul Jones*, and it was the confidence he had in all under his command that was the great secret why he never turned his heel, or show his stern ports to an enemy on the ocean, even if of superior force; knowing that all would sooner *sink* than *strike* the American banner to a proud foe who claimed the mastery of every sea. Paul Jones was, as will be seen in this work, always victorious.

Haines, the sailor philanthropist, overleaped every obstacle to sponge from the American escutcheon the punishment of the *Cat* in the Navy, which will be most deeply remembered with gratitude by the American sailor.

Previous, however, to Mr. Haines's coming forward with his philanthropic views for abolishing the *Cat*, the U. S. ship Vandalia, Capt. Levy, returned to Norfolk from a long cruise in the Gulf of Mexico (1838, '39), without punishment by the *Cat* to the crew of that ship, her commander, on his own responsibility, substituting fatigue duty, badges of disgrace, &c., touching the pride of the sailor, which had the happy effect of doing away with the use of the *Cat* during the cruize of the Vandalia.

ODE

To the Memory of the late JOHN PAUL JONES, *U. S. Navy, on the occasion of his hoisting, with his own hands, the first American Naval Flag on board the American Frigate "Alfred," 44, under a Salute of 13 guns off Chestnut Street Wharf, Philadelphia, October 10th, 1776. By* MISS G. H. SHERBURNE (*Daughter of the Author*), *now* MRS. A. HULL, *New York, and Granddaughter of Elijah Hall, First Lieutenant under Paul Jones in the Revolutionary War.*

'TWAS Jones, Paul Jones, who first o'er Delaware's tide
From "*Alfred's*" main displayed Columbia's pride;
The *Stripes** of Freedom proudly waved on high,
While shouts of freemen rang for liberty.

All hail! Paul Jones, Columbia's friend in need,
In humbling Britons, thou first took the lead;
Sailing in triumph over every sea,
Proclaiming to all, Columbia should be free.

Old *Neptune* hailed thee as his favorite son,
With corals crowned thee for thy victories won;
Sea-Nymphs chimed thy praise in merry glee,
While meteor-like thou ploughed the foamy sea.

Through England's fleets thou dashed in bold array,
On Albion's coast spread terror and dismay;
Thy cannon's thunder shook her rockbound shore,
Her *Lion* trembled amid his boastful roar.

* The Flag was 13 Stripes (without the field of stars), with the rattlesnake, and motto, "*Don't tread upon me!*"

At thy dread name were tyrants made to quake,
    And offer *Gold** for the head they could not take;
Till lowly humbled, owned Columbia free,
    Home of the oppressed, blest land of liberty.

Thy triumphs, Jones, the magic muse shall trace,
    Thy matchless deeds shall fire a future race;
Thy name shall live in song till times no more,
    Till ocean's mountain wave shall cease to roar.

* Ten thousand guineas, reward was offered for the capture of Paul Jones during the Revolutionary War by the British Government.

ORGANIZATION

OF THE

NAVY DEPARTMENT,

1851.

OFFICE OF THE SECRETARY OF THE NAVY.

Name.	Duty.	Salary.
William A. Graham,	Secretary,	$6,000
John Etheridge,	Chief Clerk,	2,000
Samuel L. Harris,	Principal Corresponding Clerk,	1,500
Lauriston B. Hardin,	Register,	1,400
Henry L. Harvey,	Warrant Clerk,	1,200
George S. Watkins,	Assistant Corresponding Clerk,	1,200
William W. Morrison,	Assistant Corresponding Clerk,	1,200
Charles W. Welsh,	Additional Clerk,	1,200
W. Brenton Boggs,	Additional Clerk,	1,200
Abel B. Upshur,	Recording Clerk,	1,000
John J. Berret,	Recording Clerk,	1,000
S. Bulow Erwin,	Recording Clerk,	1,000
William King,	Miscellaneous Clerk,	1,000
Samuel Mickum,	Messenger,	650
Lindsay Muse,	Assistant Messenger,	400

BUREAU OF CONSTRUCTION, EQUIPMENT, AND REPAIR.

Name	Duty	Salary
Charles W. Skinner,	Chief of Bureau,	$3,500
P. C. Johnson,	Chief Clerk,	1,400
John H. Reily,	Clerk,	1,200
E. M. Cunningham,	Clerk,	1,200

Name.	Duty.	Salary.
Lauriston Ward,	Clerk,	1,000
James Selden,	Clerk,	1,000
Edward Chapman,	Clerk,	1,000
John W. Bronough,	Clerk,	1,000
William Robinson,	Clerk,	800
Richard Powell,	Draughtsman,	800
William A. Elliott,	Messenger,	700

ATTACHED TO THE BUREAU OF CONSTRUCTION, EQUIPMENT, AND REPAIR.

John Lenthall,	Naval Constructor,	$3,000
Charles B. Stuart,	Engineer in Chief,	3,000
Benjamin F. Isherwood,	Chief Engineer,	1,500
Edmund S. De Luce,	3d Assistant Engineer,	600
Harman Newell,	3d Assistant Engineer,	600

BUREAU OF ORDNANCE AND HYDROGRAPHY.

Lewis Warrington,	Chief of Bureau,	$3,500
Joseph P. McCorkle,	Clerk,	1,200
Charles K. King,	Clerk,	1,000
Edward M. Tidball,	Clerk,	1,000
Israel Robinson,	Clerk,	1,000
Charles K. Stellwagen,	Draughtsman,	1,000
Azariah H. Gatton,	Messenger,	700

BUREAU OF NAVY YARDS AND DOCKS.

Joseph Smith,	Chief of Bureau,	$3,500
William G. Ridgely,	Chief Clerk,	1,400
Stephen Gough,	Clerk,	1,000
William P. Moran,	Clerk,	1,000
James M. Young,	Clerk,	800
William P. S. Sanger,	Civil Engineer,	2,000
George F. de la Roche,	Draughtsman,	1,000
Charles Hunt,	Messenger,	700

ATTACHED TO THE BUREAU OF NAVY YARDS AND DOCKS.

Albert G. Southall,	Sup. of Timber Agencies,	$1,500

BUREAU OF PROVISIONS AND CLOTHING.

William Sinclair,	Chief of Bureau,	$3,500

Name.	Duty.	Salary.
William S. Parrott,	Chief Clerk,	1,400
Thomas Fillebrown,	Clerk,	1,200
Henry J. Schreiner,	Clerk,	1,200
J. S. Williams,	Clerk,	1,000
Lucius B. Allyn,	Clerk,	800
Ignatius Lucas,	Messenger,	700

BUREAU OF MEDICINE AND SURGERY.

Name.	Duty.	Salary.
Thomas Harris,	Chief of Bureau,	$3,000
S. Ridout Addison,	Assistant Surgeon (passed),	1,400
Moses Poor,	Clerk,	1,200
William Plater,	Clerk,	1,000
Marsh B. Clark,	Messenger,	700

REGISTER

OF THE

NAVY OF THE UNITED STATES,

FOR 1851.

CAPTAINS. (68)

Name, and Date of Entry.	Name, and Date of Entry.
James Barron, 9 Mar. 1798.	Lawrence Rousseau, 16 Jan. 1809.
Charles Stewart, 9 Mar. 1798.	George W. Storer, "
Charles Morris, 1 July 1799.	Francis H. Gregory, "
Lewis Warrington, 6 Jan. 1800.	Philip F. Voorhees, 15 Nov. 1809.
John Downes, 1 June 1802.	David Geisinger, "
Stephen Cassin, 21 Feb. 1800.	Isaac McKeever, 1 Feb. 1809.
A. S. Wadsworth, 2 April 1804.	J. P. Zantzinger, 15 Nov. 1809.
George C. Read, "	William D. Salter, "
Henry E. Ballard, "	C. S. McCauley, 16 Jan. 1809.
Jesse Wilkinson, 10 July 1805.	Thomas M. Newell, 11 Sep. 1813.
T. Ap Catesby Jones, 22 Nov. 1805.	Elie A. F. Lavallette, 25 June 1812.
Wm. B. Shubrick, 20 June 1806.	Thomas T. Webb, 1 Jan. 1808.
Charles W. Morgan, 1 Jan. 1808.	John Percival, 6 March 1809.
Lawrence Kearny, 24 July 1807.	John H. Aulick, 15 Nov. 1809.
Foxhall A. Parker, 1 Jan. 1808.	W. V. Taylor, 28 April 1813.
Edward R. McCall, "	Bladen Dulany, 18 May 1809.
David Conner, 16 Jan. 1809.	Silas H. Stringham, 15 Nov. 1809.
John D. Sloat, 12 Feb. 1800.	Isaac Mayo, "
Mathew C. Perry, 1 March 1809.	William Mervine, 16 Jan. 1809.
C. W. Skinner, 16 Jan. 1809.	Thomas Crabbe, 15 Nov. 1809.
John T. Newton, "	Thomas Paine, 10 Oct. 1812.
Joseph Smith, "	James Armstrong, 15 Nov. 1809.

Name, and Date of Entry.

Joseph Smoot, 1 Dec. 1809.
Samuel L. Breese, 17 Dec. 1810.
Benjamin Page, "
Thomas W. Wyman, "
W. K. Latimer, 15 Nov. 1809.
Hiram Paulding, 1 Sept. 1811.
Uriah P. Levy, 21 Oct. 1812.
Charles Boarman, 9 June 1811.
French Forrest, "
William Jamesson, 1 Sept. 1811.
Charles Gauntt, "
William Ramsay, "

Name, and Date of Entry.

Henry Henry, 1 July 1812.
Samuel W. Downing, 1 Sep. 1811.
Henry W. Ogden, "
Thomas A. Conover, 1 Jan. 1812.
John C. Long, 18 June, 1812.
John H. Graham, "
James Mc. McIntosh, 1 Sept. 1811.
Josiah Tattnall, 1 Jan. 1812.
Hugh N. Page, 1 Sept. 1811.
William Inman, 1 Jan. 1812.
Stephen Champlin, 22 May 1812.
Joel Abbot, 18 June 1812.

COMMANDERS. (97)

Lewis E. Simonds, 1 Jan. 1812.
John M. Dale, 18 June 1812.
Harrison H. Cocke, "
W. J. McCluney, 1 Jan. 1812.
J. B. Montgomery, 4 June 1812.
Horace B. Sawyer, "
C. B. Stribling, 18 June 1812.
Joshua R. Sands, "
John J. Young, 1 Jan. 1812.
Charles H. Bell, 18 June 1812.
Abraham Bigelow, "
Frederick Varnum, "
Joseph R. Jarvis, "
S. W. LeCompte, 4 June 1812.
Charles T. Platt, 18 June 1812.
W. M. Armstrong, 30 Nov. 1814.
William F. Shields, 2 Feb. 1814.
G. J. Pendergrast, 1 Jan. 1812.
W. C. Nicholson, 18 June 1812.
James B. Cooper, 9 July 1812.
E. W. Carpender, 10 July 1813.
John L. Saunders, 15 Nov. 1809.
Joseph B. Hull, 9 Nov. 1813.
John Stone Paine, "
Joseph Morehead, "
Thomas Petigru, 1 Jan. 1812.
John S. Chauncey, "

John Kelly, 1 Feb. 1814.
William H. Gardner, 6 Dec. 1814.
David G. Farragut, 17 Dec. 1810.
R. S. Pinckney, 3 Aug. 1814.
Stephen B. Wilson, 1 Jan. 1812.
T. Aloysius Dornin, 2 May 1815.
R. B. Cunningham, 30 Nov. 1814.
James Glynn, 4 March 1815.
Joseph Myers, 6 Dec. 1814.
Thomas R. Gedney, 4 Mar. 1815.
V. M. Randolph, 11 June 1814.
Frederick Engle, 6 Dec. 1814.
John Rudd, 30 Nov. 1814.
Robert Ritchie, 1 Feb. 1814.
W. W. McKean, 30 Nov. 1814.
F. Buchanan, 28 June 1815.
Samuel Mercer, 4 March 1815.
Charles Lowndes, 28 March 1815.
L. M. Goldsborough, 18 June 1812.
George N. Hollins, 1 Feb. 1814.
D. N. Ingraham, 18 June, 1812.
John Marston, 15 April 1813.
Henry Bruce, 9 Nov. 1813.
Henry A. Adams, 14 Mar. 1814.
James D. Knight, 30 Nov. 1814.
Joseph Mattison, "
William S. Walker, "

Name, and Date of Entry.

George F. Pearson, 11 Mar. 1815.
James T. Gerry, 20 Dec. 1815.
John S. Nicholas, 6 June 1815.
Samuel F. Dupont, 16 Dec. 1815.
William L. Hudson, 1 Jan. 1816.
George A. Magruder, 1 Jan. 1817.
John Pope, 30 May 1816.
Levin M. Powell, 1 March 1817.
Charles Wilkes, 1 Jan. 1818.
Elisha Peck, 4 March 1817.
Thomas J. Manning, 1 Jan. 1817.
William Pearson, 1 Jan. 1818.
W. L. Howard, 10 Jan. 1815.
Thomas J. Leib, 1 Sept. 1811.
T. O. Selfridge, 1 Jan. 1818.
Henry Eagle, "
Andrew K. Long, 1 Nov. 1818.
G. J. Van Brunt, 3 Nov. 1818.
W. M. Glendy, 1 Jan. 1818.
G. P. Upshur, 23 April, 1818.
George S. Blake, "
Z. F. Johnston, "

Name, and Date of Entry.

William Green, 1 Jan. 1818.
Samuel Barron, 1 Jan. 1812.
T. G. Benham, 30 Nov. 1814.
A. G. Slaughter, 3 Nov. 1818.
Oscar Bullus, 1 Nov. 1817.
C. H. Jackson, 4 March 1818.
Andrew A. Harwood, 1 Jan. 1818.
Theodorus Bailey, "
H. Y. Purviance, 3 Nov. 1818.
George Adams, 1 Jan. 1818.
C. Ringgold, 4 March, 1819.
William F. Lynch, 26 Jan. 1819.
Henry W. Morris, 21 Aug. 1819.
Isaac S. Sterrett, 24 March 1819.
Francis B. Ellison, 28 May 1819.
Edward B. Boutwell, 3 Mar. 1819.
Sydney Smith Lee, 30 Dec. 1820.
W. C. Whittle, 10 May 1820.
Thompson D. Shaw, "
R. D. Thornburn, 30 March 1820.
Samuel Lockwood, 12 July 1820.

LIEUTENANTS. (327)

W. A. C. Farragut, 16 Jan. 1809.
Frank Ellery, 1 Jan. 1812.
Arthur Lewis, 1 Jan. 1817.
John H. Little, 1 Jan. 1818.
Lloyd B. Newell, 10 May 1820.
Hillary H. Rhodes, "
William S. Ogden, 26 July 1820.
Frederick A. Neville, 10 May 1820.
Charles C. Turner, "
John Manning, "
James L. Lardner, "
Robert G. Robb, 6 Sept. 1821.
John Colhoun, 25 Jan. 1821.
Law. Pennington, 22 Nov. 1822.
Thomas T. Craven, 1 May 1822.
Andrew H. Foote, 4 Dec. 1822.
William W. Hunter, 1 May 1822.

Amasa Paine, 1 May 1822.
Nathaniel W. Duke, "
Edward G. Tilton, "
James H. Ward, 4 Mar. 1823.
Henry K. Hoff, 28 Oct. 1823.
Murray Mason, 14 Nov. 1823.
Charles H. Davis, 12 Aug. 1823.
Jonathan W. Swift, 24 Aug. 1823.
Ebenezer Farrand, 4 Mar. 1823.
Henry H. Bell, 4 Aug. 1823.
William Smith, 4 Mar. 1823.
Charles H. McBlair, "
James M. Watson, 1 Feb. 1823.
John W. Livingston, 4 Mar. 1823.
Junius J. Boyle, 27 Aug. 1823.
William E. Hunt, 28 Oct. 1828.
Jonathan D. Ferris, 28 Feb. 1809.

Name, and Date of Entry.

Archibald B. Fairfax, 4 Aug. 1823.
Peter Turner, 4 Mar. 1823.
John A. Davis, "
Henry K. Thatcher, "
James H. Rowan, 19 Aug. 1823.
Samuel E. Munn, 27 Aug. 1823.
William H. Noland, 31 Dec. 1823.
William D. Porter, 1 Jan. 1823.
William McBlair, 16 Nov. 1824.
John S. Missroon, 27 June, 1824.
James Noble, 27 May 1824.
Richard L. Page, 1 Mar. 1824.
Frederick Chatard, 16 Nov. 1824.
G. G. Williamson, 2 June 1824.
Benjamin J. Totten, 4 Mar. 1823.
C. G. Hunter, 16 Nov. 1824.
Arthur Sinclair, 4 Mar. 1823.
R. B. Hitchcock, 1 Jan. 1825.
C. H. A. H. Kennedy, 10 Feb. 1819.
Thomas W. Brent, 1 Mar. 1825.
Joseph Lanman, 1 Jan. 1825.
John K. Mitchell, 1 Feb. 1825.
Thomas Turner, 21 April 1825.
Henry Moor, 1 Mar. 1825.
Charles H. Poor, "
J. Findlay Schenck, "
Mathew F. Maury, 1 Feb. 1825.
Timothy A. Hunt, 1 Mar. 1825.
S. Wm. Godon, 1 Mar. 1819.
James S. Palmer, 1 Jan. 1825.
William Radford, 1 Mar. 1825.
Samuel F. Hazard, 1 Jan. 1823.
John M. Berrien, 1 Mar. 1825.
George A. Prentice, "
John C. Carter, 1 Jan. 1825.
George Hurst, "
Alfred Taylor, "
Samuel P. Lee, 22 Nov. 1825.
John P. Gillis, 12 Dec. 1825.
Simon B. Bissell, 1 Mar. 1825.
Samuel Swartwout, 10 May 1820.

Name, and Date of Entry.

John J. Glasson, 1 Feb. 1823.
Raphael Semmes, 1 April 1826.
James F. Miller, 1 Nov. 1826.
J. P. McKinstry, 1 Feb. 1826.
Henry A. Steele, 1 Nov. 1826.
Charles Heywood, "
Oliver S. Glisson, "
John A. Dahlgren, 1 Feb. 1826.
Stephen C. Rowan, "
Edward R. Thomson, 1 Dec. 1826.
J. T. McDonough, 1 April 1826.
Guert Gansevoort, 4 Mar. 1823.
Robert Handy, 1 Feb. 1826.
Henry Darcantel, 1 April 1826.
Charles Green, 1 May 1826.
Edward L. Handy, 1 June 1826.
Melancton Smith, 1 Mar. 1826.
William C. Chaplin, 1 Nov. 1826.
Cicero Price, 1 Feb. 1826.
J. R. Goldsborough, 6 Nov. 1824.
Charles S. Boggs, 1 Nov. 1826.
A. H. Kilty, 4 July 1821.
William Chandler, 1 Aug. 1826.
Theodore P. Green, 1 Nov. 1826.
John R. Tucker, 1 June 1826.
Richard W. Meade, 1 April 1826.
Thomas J. Page, 1 Oct. 1827.
George Minor, 1 April 1827.
Percival Drayton, 1 Dec. 1827.
William P. Griffin, 1 Oct. 1827.
Robert F. Pinckney, 1 Dec. 1827.
Thomas R. Rootes, 1 Mar. 1827.
Edward M. Yard, 1 Nov. 1827.
James M. Gilliss, 1 Mar. 1827.
Alexander Gibson, 1 July 1822.
William S. Young, 1 Mar. 1827.
Wm. W. Bleecker, 1 May 1827.
Joseph F. Green, 1 Nov. 1827.
John De Camp, 1 Oct. 1827.
Bushrod W. Hunter, 1 Nov. 1827.
C. W. Pickering, 1 May 1822.

Name, and Date of Entry.

Overton Carr, 1 Mar. 1827.
Luther Stoddard, 1 April 1827.
Wm. M. Walker, 1 Nov. 1827.
George R. Gray, 1 Nov. 1826.
Robert E. Johnson, 1 Oct. 1827.
John A. Winslow, 1 Feb. 1827.
Ben. More Dove, 1 Dec. 1826.
Bernard J. Moeller, 1 April 1827.
Henry Walke, 1 Feb. 1827.
Thornton A. Jenkins, 1 Nov. 1828.
Joseph C. Walsh, "
John Rodgers, 18 April 1828.
John B. Marchand, 1 May 1828.
Wm. Rogers Taylor, 1 April 1828.
Henry J. Hartstene, "
Benjamin F. Sands, "
Henry French, 1 Jan. 1828.
William Leigh, 1 Nov. 1828.
Samuel Larkin, 1 April 1828.
Henry S. Stellwagen, "
James L. Henderson, 1 June 1828.
Daniel B. Ridgely, 1 April 1828.
John L. Ring, "
William T. Muse, 1 June 1828.
William H. Brown, 1 Jan. 1828.
Charles Steedman, 1 April 1828.
Wm. Lewis Herndon, 1 Nov. 1828.
John P. Parker, 1 April 1828.
James Alden, "
Augustus L. Case, "
Roger Perry, 1 July 1828.
Alex. M. Pennock, 1 April 1828.
George F. Emmons, "
Edward Middleton, 1 July 1828.
Montgomery Lewis, 1 Nov. 1828.
George M. White, "
Thomas T. Hunter, 1 July 1828.
Albert A. Holcomb, 1 April 1828.
Gustavus H. Scott, 1 Aug. 1828.
Richard Forrest, 1 Nov. 1828.
David McDougal, 1 April 1828.

Name, and Date of Entry.

Charles F. McIntosh, 1 Nov. 1828.
James W. Cooke, 1 April 1828.
C. F. M. Spotswood, 1 Nov. 1828.
Henry C. Flagg, 1 April 1828.
Daniel F. Dulany, "
George L. Selden, "
William H. Ball, "
Charles C. Barton, 1 Dec. 1824.
John J. B. Walbach, 1 Dec. 1827.
Joshua Humphreys, 2 Feb. 1829.
Stephen Decatur, 17 Mar. 1829.
William L. Maury, 2 Feb. 1829.
David D. Porter, "
John J. Almy, "
Edward C. Bowers, "
O. H. Berryman, "
Thomas A. Budd, "
A. F. V. Gray, 15 Oct. 1829.
Tunis A. M. Craven, 2 Oct. 1829.
Dominick Lynch, "
F. B. Renshaw, 1 Nov. 1828.
H. N. Harrison, 1 April 1828.
James H. North, 29 May, 1829.
Robert E. Pegram, 2 Feb. 1829.
Edward C. Ward, "
Edwin J. DeHaven, 2 Oct. 1829.
Charles Thomas, 2 Feb. 1829.
R. L. Tilghman, 27 Oct. 1830.
James H. Strong, 2 Feb. 1829.
J. M. Frailey, 1 May 1828.
C. P. Patterson, 2 Sept. 1830.
A. S. Baldwin, 2 Feb. 1829.
E. T. Shubrick, 22 June 1829.
W. B. Whiting, 2 Feb. 1829.
Charles Hunter, 25 April 1831.
B. F. Shattuck, 25 June 1831.
Thomas M. Brasher, 6 June 1831.
George T. Sinclair, 23 April 1831.
John Mooney, 13 Dec. 1831.
Samuel R. Knox, 1 April 1828.
Enoch G. Parrott, 10 Dec. 1831.

Name, and Date of Entry.

R. Wainwright, 11 May 1831.
G. M. Totten, 5 May 1831.
W. Decatur Hurst, 2 Feb. 1829.
W. Ross Gardner, 29 Dec. 1831.
W. B. Renshaw, 22 Dec. 1831.
C. B. Poindexter, 16 Nov. 1831.
H. T. Wingate, 13 Dec. 1831.
Alonzo B. Davis, 25 April, 1831.
Richard L. Love, 17 Sept. 1830.
William Reynolds, 17 Nov. 1831.
Lewis C. Sartori, 2 Feb. 1829.
Edmund Lanier, 9 July 1831.
Fabius Stanly, 20 Dec. 1831.
Latham B. Avery, 19 Dec. 1831.
James B. Lewis, 31 March 1831.
G. W. Chapman, 20 Sept. 1832.
W. P. McArthur, 11 Feb. 1832.
W. S. Drayton, 16 July 1832.
Simon F. Blunt, 7 Sept. 1831.
W. Taylor Smith, 17 July 1832.
William May, 2 May 1831.
Henry H. Lewis, 1 May 1828.
Joseph P. Sanford, 11 Feb. 1832.
G. W. Harrison, 20 Jan. 1832.
J. F. Armstrong, 7 March, 1832.
Montgomery Hunt, 17 Jan. 1832.
John Contee, 27 Oct. 1832.
Joseph H. Adams, 8 Dec. 1831.
William A. Parker, 3 July 1832.
James D. Johnson, 30 June 1832.
John N. Maffit, 25 Feb. 1832.
W. Gwathmey, 21 July 1832.
W. Rockendorff, 17 Feb. 1832.
John Hall, 11 Jan. 1832.
Francis Lowry, 3 Aug. 1831.
W. E. Leroy, 11 Jan. 1832.
Maxwell Woodhull, 4 June, 1832.
Lafayette Maynard, 4 Feb. 1832.
Roger M. Stembel, 27 Mar. 1832.
G. Colvocoressis, 21 Feb. 1832.
F. S. Haggerty, 17 Feb. 1832.
Thomas Brownell, 30 Oct. 1840.

Name, and Date of Entry.

J. R. M. Mullany, 8 Jan. 1832.
James A. Doyle, 4 Jan. 1832.
Mathias C. Marin, 3 Jan. 1832.
W. A. Wayne, 27 April 1833.
James S. Biddle, 18 Oct. 1833.
C. R. P. Rodgers, 5 Oct. 1833.
W. A. Bartlett, 22 Jan. 1833.
Francis Winslow, 8 July, 1833.
J. C. Williamson, 7 Jan. 1832.
C. Vanalstine, 27 Feb. 1833.
Albert G. Clary, 8 May 1832.
George W. Doty, 4 Jan. 1833.
George Wells, 18 Dec. 1833.
Peter U. Murphey, 12 May 1831.
John B. Randolph, 11 June, 1833.
J. B. Carter, 31 Dec. 1833.
H. P. Robertson, 28 June 1832.
Isaac N. Brown, 15 March, 1834.
Napoleon Collins, 12 Jan. 1834.
John L. Worden, 10 Jan. 1834.
W. L. Blanton, 2 Jan. 1834.
Benjamin S. Gantt, 16 June, 1834.
Henry A. Wise, 8 Feb. 1834.
C. St. G. Noland, 16 June 1834.
Reed Werden, 9 Jan. 1834.
W. H. Macomb, 10 April 1834.
S. D. Trenchard, 23 Oct. 1834.
W. R. McKinney, 20 March 1834.
A. Davis Harrell, 4 Jan. 1834.
S. J. Shipley, 14 Jan. 1834.
John J. Guthrie, 26 Feb. 1834.
Mayo C. Watkins, 8 May 1834.
M. B. Woolsey, 24 Sept. 1832.
J. N. Barney, 30 June 1825.
A. Murray, 22 Aug. 1835.
E. Donaldson, 21 July 1835.
S. Chase Barney, 28 June 1835.
G. H. Preble, 10 Oct. 1835.
T. B. Huger, 5 March 1835.
Robert B. Riell, 2 Sept. 1835.
M. C. Perry, 1 July 1825.
C. S. McDonough, 8 April 1835.

Name, and Date of Entry.	Name, and Date of Entry.
J. D. Todd, 26 June 1835.	John S. Taylor, 14 Dec. 1836.
Wilmer Shields, 19 Oct. 1835.	J. H. Brown, 1 July 1836.
C. E Fleming, 15 Jan. 1835.	E. F. Beale, 14 Dec. 1836.
John Rutledge, 9 April 1835.	E. T. Nichols, "
John Q. Adams, 3 July 1825.	J. P. Decatur, 31 Aug. 1836.
Charles Deas, 15 Oct. 1835.	E. L. Winder, 29 April 1836.
W. C. B. S. Porter, 29 June 1835.	John K. Duer, 28 Dec. 1836.
T. M. Crossan, 1 July 1836.	Israel C. Wait, "
T. H. Stevens, 14 Dec. 1836.	J. H. Parker, 30 Dec. 1836.
C. Ap R. Jones, 18 June 1836.	W. B. Muse, 1 July 1836.
James Blair, 8 Jan. 1836.	G. W. Rodgers, 30 April 1836.
T. H. Patterson, 5 April 1836.	A. McRae, 26 Jan. 1837.
F. K. Murray, 29 April 1836.	R. H. Wyman, 11 March 1837.
Silas Bent, 1 July 1836.	E. A. Barnett, 24 June 1837.
John C. Howell, 9 June 1836.	N. C. Bryant, 23 Dec. 1837.
Edward Higgins, 23 Jan. 1836.	G. B. Balch, 30 Dec. 1837.
W. E. Boudinot, 1 Feb. 1836.	J. M. Wainwright, 13 June 1837.
Van R. Morgan, 8 Dec. 1836.	F. A. Parker, 11 March 1837.
Madison Rush, 16 Oct. 1836.	I. G. Strain, 11 Dec. 1837.
Daniel Ammen, 7 July 1836.	E. Thompson, 13 March 1837.
Henry Rolando, 28 Dec. 1836.	R. Townsend, 4 Aug. 1837.
Andrew Weir, 6 July 1836.	J. S. Kennard, 10 March 1837.

SURGEONS. (68)

J. Cowdery, 1 Jan. 1800.	Benjamin F. Bache, 9 July 1824.
W. P. C. Barton, 10 April 1809.	Thomas Dillard, 15 Nov. 1824.
T. Harris, 6 July 1812.	Stephen Rapalje, 30 June 1823.
William Turk, 15 May 1800.	James M. Greene, 29 April 1825.
B. Washington, 9 May 1810.	Benjamin R. Tinslar, 1 Feb. 1823.
William Swift, 14 May 1813.	George W. Codwise, 14 May 1825.
Peter Christie, 8 July 1812.	G. R. B. Horner, 26 May 1826.
S. Jackson, 10 July 1812.	W. S. W. Ruschenberger, 10 Aug. 1826.
T. Williamson, 13 May 1813.	Wm. Johnson, 16 Aug. 1826.
B. Ticknor, 10 Dec. 1814.	Samuel Moseley, 17 Aug. 1826.
J. Cornick, 11 Sept. 1819.	Robert J. Dodd, 29 May 1826.
Charles Chase, 10 Dec. 1814.	Wm. Fairlie Patton, 17 Aug. 1826.
D. S. Edwards, 30 July 1818.	William Whelan, 3 Jan. 1828.
Isaac Hulse, 12 May 1823.	Samuel Barrington, "
John S. Wily, 20 Dec. 1815.	Thomas L. Smith, "
George Terrill, 28 Mar. 1820.	George Blacknall, "
E. L. DuBarry, 30 June 1823.	

Name, and Date of Entry.

Lewis B. Hunter, 3 Jan. 1828.
George Clymer, 1 July 1829.
Isaac Brinkerhoff, "
W. Maxwell Wood, 16 May 1829.
Jones W. Plummer, 20 June 1829.
G. B. McKnight, 16 May 1829.
Solomon Sharp, 15 Sept. 1829.
Daniel Egbert, 22 Aug. 1829.
Amos G. Gambrill, 20 June 1829.
W. A. W. Spotswood, 2 Dec. 1828.
Jonathan M. Foltz, 4 April 1831.
Edward Gilchrist, 26 Jan. 1832.
John A. Lockwood, 8 Feb. 1832.
Daniel C. McLeod, "
Lewis W. Minor, "
N. C. Barrabino, 28 Feb. 1833.
Henry S. Rennolds, "
M. G. Delaney, "

Name, and Date of Entry.

W. F. McClenahan, 28 Feb. 1833.
Wm. L. Van Horn, 4 April 1831.
Daniel S. Green, 18 Oct. 1833.
James C. Palmer, 26 Mar. 1834.
Ninian Pinkney, "
Robert T. Barry, "
David Harlan, 23 Feb. 1835.
Robert Woodworth, "
J. Dickinson Miller, 5 Dec. 1836.
John L. Fox, 9 Feb. 1837.
Chas. F. B. Guillou, "
Augustus J. Bowie, "
Joseph Beale, 6 Sept. 1837.
S. Wilson Kellogg, "
John T. Mason, "
Charles D. Maxwell, "
Edward J. Rutter, "
John J. Abernethy, 9 Feb. 1837.

PASSED ASSISTANT SURGEONS. (34)

John B. Elliot, 20 May 1829.
George Maulsby, 7 March 1838.
William Grier, "
J. Winthrop Taylor, "
Wm. B. Sinclair, 20 June, 1838.
Samuel Jackson, "
J. Jeffray Brownlee, "
S. A. McCreery, "
J. McClelland, "
J. S. Messersmith, 9 Feb. 1837.
J. O'Conner Barclay, 17 Oct. 1839.
James B. Gould, "
C. H. Wheelwright, "
Richard W. Jeffery, "
Thomas M. Potter, "
S. Ridout Addison, 20 June 1838.
William A. Nelson, 9 Dec. 1839.
John H. Wright, 9 Dec. 1839.
John Thornley, 13 Oct. 1840.
Daniel L. Bryan, "
Joseph Hopkinson, "
A. A. Henderson, 8 Sept. 1841.
R. T. Maxwell, "
J. F. Tuckerman, 25 Jan. 1842.
Morris B. Beck, 2 Dec. 1841.
Lewis J. Williams, 25 Jan. 1842.
Marius Duvall, "
William S. Bishop, 11 April 1843.
Joseph Wilson, jr., 13 May 1843.
Charles Eversfield, 29 May 1843.
Elisha K. Kane, 21 July 1843.
Edward Hudson, 11 Sept. 1843.
Richard McSherry, 22 Nov. 1843.
Robert E. Wall, 27 Nov. 1844.

ASSISTANT SURGEONS. (44)

E. H. Van Wyck, 20 June 1838.
John L. Burtt, 30 May 1844.

Name, and Date of Entry.

James Hamilton, 22 July 1844.
Charles H. Oakley, 2 Oct. 1844.
Robert T. Maccoun, "
William A. Harris, "
W. Sherman, 25 April 1845.
Henry O. Mayo, 24 Feb. 1846.
John Rudenstein, "
R. F. Mason, 29 Aug. 1846.
Philip Lansdale, 5 March 1847.
Alexander J. Rice, "
John A. Pettit, "
Thomas B. Steele, "
James F. Harrison, "
A. Nelson Bell, "
J. W. B. Greenhow, 24 April 1847.
R. Farquharson, "
E. R. Squibb, 26 April 1847.
Benj. Rush Mitchell, "
James S. Gilliam, "
William Lowber, 8 Nov. 1847.
George H. Howell, "

Name, and Date of Entry.

Dinwiddie B. Phillips, 8 Nov. 1847.
Ashton Miles, "
Phineas J. Horwitz, "
Alonzo A. F. Hill, 6 March 1848.
Owen Jones Wister, "
Wm. D. Harrison, 25 April 1848.
John Ward, 28 April 1848.
Wm. F. Carrington, 17 June 1848.
Charles Martin, 5 Sept. 1848.
F. M. Gunnell, 22 March 1849.
James Suddards, 17 May 1849.
Robert Carter, 2 June 1849.
S. Allen Engles, 24 July 1849.
Edward Shippen, 7 Aug. 1849.
Gerard Alexander, 1 May 1850.
Benj. Vreeland, 9 May 1850.
Walter Hore, 23 July 1850.
Richard B. Tunstall, 28 Aug. 1850.
C. H. Williamson, 24 Sept. 1850.
James F. Heustis, 30 Sept. 1850.
Arthur M. Lynah, 12 Oct. 1850.

PURSERS. (63)

F. A. Thornton, 29 Jan. 1811.
Edward Fitzgerald, 22 Mar. 1811.
Samuel P. Todd, 20 July 1812.
Joseph Wilson, 24 July 1813.
Wm. Sinclair, 15 Nov. 1809.
Joseph Terry, 6 June 1813.
John de Bree, 29 Dec. 1817.
J. N. Hambleton, 26 Oct. 1819.
G. R. Barry, 15 Jan. 1824.
D. Walker, 4 March 1819.
Henry Etting, 1 Jan. 1818.
F. B. Stockton, 11 March 1829.
F. G. McCauley, 27 May 1829.
B. J. Cahoone, 12 Nov. 1830.
Sterrett Ramsey, 18 Nov. 1830.
E. T. Dunn, 21 Feb. 1831.
J. A. Bates, 2 March 1831.
A. J. Watson, 1 May 1831.

W. A. Bloodgood, 2 March 1821.
D. Fauntleroy, 7 July 1834.
T. M. Taylor, 3 Nov. 1834.
A. E. Watson, 31 Aug. 1836.
Joseph Bryan, 1 Sept. 1836.
S. Forrest, 8 Oct. 1836.
Robert Pettit, 6 April 1837.
W. Speiden, 30 Aug. 1837.
Horatio Bridge, 16 Feb. 1838.
G. F. Sawyer, 20 March 1838.
H. W. Greene, 28 Feb. 1839.
T. B. Nalle, 17 Oct. 1839.
P. T. McBlair, 11 Nov. 1839.
J. D. Gibson, 8 June 1840.
J. B. Rittenhouse, 21 July 1840.
L. Warrington, jr., 13 Sept. 1841.
G. H. White, "
H. M. Hieskell, "

Name, and Date of Entry.	Name, and Date of Entry.
W. A. Christian, 13 Sept. 1841.	E. C. Doran, 15 Sept. 1845.
L. T. Waller, "	Aristides Welch, 27 June 1846.
J. C. Douglass, 25 Sept. 1841.	E. R. Reynolds, 16 Oct. 1846.
C. Murray, 31 March 1843.	L. D. Slamm, 30 Nov. 1846.
T. R. Ware, 28 June 1843.	J. Van B. Bleecker, 16 Jan. 1847.
G. F. Cutter, 5 June 1844.	J. C. Eldredge, 2 Feb. 1847.
J. A. Semple, 12 Oct. 1844.	C. Anderson, 29 Feb. 1848.
J. H. Watmough, 12 Dec. 1844.	R. T. Allison, 30 Oct. 1849.
J. O. Bradford, 14 March, 1845.	Nixon White, 13 Nov. 1849.
J. Y. Mason, jr., 18 April 1845.	J. J. Jones, 21 Nov. 1849.
J. G. Harris, 19 Aug. 1845.	J. Tattnall, jr., 28 June, 1850.
J. F. Steele, 29 Aug. 1845.	J. Johnston, 28 Aug. 1850.

CHAPLAINS. (23)

John W. Grier, 3 March, 1825.	T. B. Bartow, 8 Sept. 1841.
C. S. Stewart, 1 Nov. 1828.	J. Stockbridge, "
T. J. Harrison, 2 Oct. 1829.	W. McKenney, "
Walter Colton, 6 Nov. 1830.	Photius Fisk, 14 March 1842.
George Jones, 20 April 1833.	J. W. Newton, 30 May 1844.
T. R. Lambert, 31 Dec. 1833.	Nathaniel Frost, 5 Oct. 1844.
Peter G. Clark, 3 Oct. 1838.	T. C. Stanley, 27 Feb. 1847.
Rodman Lewis, 13 March 1839.	Edwin Eaton, "
F. W. Taylor, 23 April 1841.	J. L. Lenhart, "
M. R. Talbot, 8 Sept. 1841.	John Blake, "
Moses B. Chase, "	E. C. Bittinger, 30 Sept. 1850.
Chester Newell, "	

PROFESSORS OF MATHEMATICS. (12)

J. H. C. Coffin, August 14, 1848.	William Flye, August 14, 1848.
A. G. Pendleton, "	W. Chauvenet, "
Mordecai Yarnall, "	James Major, "
W. B. Benedict, "	J. S. Hubbard, "
M. H. Beecher, "	Ruel Keith, "
H. H. Lockwood, "	Arsene N. Girault, "

MASTERS IN THE LINE OF PROMOTION. (11)

J. Wilkinson, 25 June 1850.	J. M. B. Clitz, 16 Aug. 1850.
John Guest, 16 July 1850.	John D. Read, 17 Sept. 1850.
D. McN. Fairfax, 4 Aug. 1850.	C. Benham, 21 Sept. 1850.
Henry Rodgers, 7 Aug. 1850.	W. H. Thompson, 27 Sept. 1850.

Name, and Date of Entry.	Name, and Date of Entry.
John F. Abbott, 3 Oct. 1850.	B. N. Westcott, 18 Oct. 1850.
G. H. Cooper, 11 Oct. 1850.	

PASSED MIDSHIPMEN (233).

Samuel Pearce, 30 March 1833.	A. K. Hughes, 20 Oct. 1838.
W. W. Pollock, 30 June 1837.	E. R. Calhoun, 1 April 1839.
J. F. Stenson, 15 Dec. 1837.	J. D. Bulloch, 21 June 1839.
Andrew Bryson, 1 Dec. 1837.	C. H. Baldwin, 24 April 1839.
J. Downes, jr., 4 Sept. 1837.	R. W. Shufeldt, 11 May 1839.
C. M. Morris, 15 Dec. 1837.	H. K. Stevens, 2 March 1839.
A. J. Drake, 5 Dec. 1837.	Abner Read, "
J. H. Spotts, 2 Aug. 1837.	A. C. Rhind, 3 Sept. 1838.
J. M. Duncan, 8 Dec. 1837.	Richard M. Cuyler, 28 Nov. 1839.
L. Gibbon, 22 Dec. 1837.	G. M. Ransom, 25 July 1839.
S. Marcy, 16 March 1838.	W. F. Spicer, 21 June 1839.
J. P. Bankhead, 10 Aug. 1838.	W. W. Roberts, 2 March 1839.
J. W. A. Nicholson, 10 Feb. 1838.	R. Fairfax, 28 May 1839.
T. G. Corbin, 15 May 1838.	S. Nicholson, 21 June, 1839.
G. V. Fox, 12 Jan. 1838.	W. A. Webb, 26 Jan. 1838.
J. Matthews, 22 Feb. 1838.	John Stuart, 21 June 1839.
J. C. Beaumont, 1 March 1838.	Joseph S. Day, 16 March, 1839.
C. H. B. Caldwell, 27 Feb. 1838.	M. Simons, 10 Dec. 1839.
C. M. Fauntleroy, 3 March 1838.	W. E. Hopkins, 13 Nov. 1839.
W. B. Fitzgerald, 30 Jan. 1838.	Paul Shirley, 25 July 1839.
M. K. Warrington, "	C. C. Simms, 9 Oct. 1839.
H. K. Davenport, 19 Feb. 1828.	R. C. Rogers, 14 Oct. 1839.
N. B. Harrison, 27 Feb. 1838.	H. T. N. Arnold, 13 March 1839.
J. H. Moore, 10 Feb. 1838.	T. Pattison, 2 March 1839.
S. Edwards, 9 March 1838.	W. W. Bassett, 9 March 1838.
C. W. Place, 10 Feb. 1838.	Julian Myers, 2 March 1839.
Alphonse Barbot, 26 Feb. 1838.	J. Higgins, 13 March 1839.
Albert N. Smith, 26 Oct. 1838.	J. S. Bohrer, 31 Dec. 1839.
W. H. Hudson, 16 July 1838.	R. Aulick, 19 Oct. 1840.
J. C. Febiger, 4 Sept. 1838.	R. A. Marr, 29 April 1840.
D. R. Lambert, 16 Feb. 1838.	W. N. Jeffers, jr., 25 Sept. 1840.
H. S. Newcomb, 21 July 1838.	W. D. Austin, 3 Nov. 1840.
J. S. Maury, 10 Feb. 1838.	E. Brinley, jr., 14 Sept. 1840.
P. Crosby, 5 June 1838.	E. Simpson, 11 Feb. 1840.
R. T. Renshaw, 26 Feb. 1838.	W. G. Temple, 18 April 1840.
C. W. Hays, 12 March 1838.	G. P. Welsh, 14 Sept. 1840.
J. B. Creighton, 10 Feb. 1838.	S. P. Carter, 14 Feb. 1840.

Name, and Date of Entry.

W. Nelson, 28 Jan. 1840.
W. H. Smith, 31 July 1840.
R. M. McArann, 12 May 1840.
Charles W. Aby, 8 Feb. 1840.
E. C. Stout, 18 Feb. 1840.
R. Harris, 25 Jan. 1840.
John Walcutt, 2 March 1840.
J. B. McCauley, 8 Feb. 1840.
T. S. Phelps, 17 Jan. 1840.
J. Madigan, jr., 19 Feb. 1840.
A. F. Warley, 17 Feb. 1840.
G. V. Denniston, 10 March 1840.
L. Paulding, 19 Dec. 1840.
G. A. Stevens, 13 May 1840.
F. S. Conover, 11 May 1840.
S. B. Elliott, 20 Aug. 1838.
F. Gregory, 23 May 1840.
E. Barrett, 3 Nov. 1840.
C. Terrett, 3 Jan. 1840.
J. W. Bennett, 10 Feb. 1840.
P. Wager, jr., 12 Feb. 1840.
J. P. Hall, 29 Dec. 1840.
H. C. Blake, 2 March 1840.
C. H. Wells, 25 Sept. 1840.
S. P. Quackenbush, 15 Feb. 1840.
Earl English, 25 Feb. 1840.
D. Ochiltree, 21 June, 1839.
J. M. Bradford, 10 Jan. 1840.
R. B. Lowry, 31 Jan. 1840.
J. H. Carter, 12 March 1840.
J. Wilkes, jr., 9 Sept. 1841.
W. H. Parker, 19 Oct. 1841.
A. C. Jackson, 23 Feb. 1841.
W. De Koven, 9 Sept. 1841.
J. P. Jones, 19 Oct. 1841.
W. P. Buckner, 9 Sept. 1841.
G. E. Morgan, 18 Feb. 1841.
W. W. Low, 3 March 1841.
W. K. Bridge, 14 Jan. 1841.
S. P. Griffin, 9 Sept. 1841.
R. L. Law, 17 Feb. 1841.

Name, and Date of Entry.

W. H. Wilcox, 30 Jan. 1841.
E. D. Denny, 17 Sept. 1841.
J. T. Barraud, 20 Sept. 1841.
T. Roney, 3 March 1841.
J. H. Upshur, 4 Nov. 1841.
J. Van N. Philip, 25 Nov. 1841.
S. R. Franklin, 18 Feb. 1841.
M. J. Smith, 9 Oct. 1841.
J. J. Hanson, 21 Sept. 1841.
F. G. Clark, 19 Oct. 1841.
R. J. D. Price, 9 Sept. 1841.
W. V. Gilliss, 27 Oct. 1841.
W. D. Whiting, 1 March 1841.
W. L. Powell, 20 Sept. 1841.
S. L. Phelps, 10 Oct. 1841.
E. Y. McCauley, 9 Sept. 1841.
T. L. Walker, 10 Sept. 1841.
W. Mitchell, 24 Sept. 1841.
F. A. Roe, 19 Oct. 1841.
J. B. Smith, 19 Oct. 1841.
W. H. Murdaugh, 9 Sept. 1841.
J. M. Brooke, 3 March 1841.
W. Gibson, 11 Feb. 1841.
J. J. Cook, 19 Oct. 1841.
J. Armstrong, 9 Sept. 1842.
E. Renshaw, 4 Nov. 1841.
J. D. Danels, 19 Oct. 1841.
C. Latimer, 9 Sept. 1841.
J. T. Walker, 18 Feb. 1841.
J. C. P. De Krafft, 19 Oct. 1841.
J. Van McCollum, 26 Feb. 1841.
John E. Hart, 23 Feb. 1841.
Oscar C. Badger, 9 Sept. 1841.
T. C. Harris, "
John Kell, "
J. L. Davis, 9 Jan. 1841.
J. H. March, 19 Oct. 1841.
W. H. Weaver, "
A. A. Semmes, 17 Oct. 1841.
J. B. Stewart, 9 Sept. 1841.
M. P. Jones, "

Name, and Date of Entry.	Name, and Date of Entry.
Watson Smith, 19 Oct. 1841.	J. E. Jouell, 10 Sept. 1841.
A. M. De Bree, "	T. L. Fillebrown, 19 Oct. 1841.
J. E. De Haven, "	J. Fry, 15 Sept. 1841.
E. A. Selden, "	L. H. Lyne, 10 Sept. 1841.
A. W. Habersham, 3 March 1841.	E. C. Grafton, 5 Oct. 1841.
W. G. Hoffman, 19 Oct. 1841.	M. Haxtun, 19 Oct. 1841.
J. McL. Murphy, 18 Feb. 1841.	R. Selden, 9 Sept. 1841.
W. T. Truxtun, 9 Feb. 1841.	W. W. Wilkinson, 4 Nov. 1841.
S. K. Wilson, 3 March 1841.	A. Allmand, 10 Sept. 1841.
J. L. Friend, 27 Oct. 1841.	Robert Stuart, 19 Oct. 1841.
Greenleaf Cilley, 26 Feb. 1841.	E. Shepherd, "
H. N. Crabb, 19 Oct. 1841.	T. Lee, 9 Sept. 1841.
S. Magaw, 23 Nov. 1841.	G. H. Bier, 19 Oct. 1841.
J. H. Rochelle, 9 Sept. 1841.	P. G. Watmough, 20 Sept. 1841.
R. D. Minor, 26 Feb. 1841.	G. W. Young, 19 Oct. 1841.
W. C. West, 30 Jan. 1841.	W. Van Wyck, "
N. H. Van Zandt, 19 Oct. 1841.	J. H. Russell, 10 Sept. 1841.
C. W. Woolley, 30 Nov. 1841.	E. E. Stone, 9 Oct. 1841.
S. S. Basset, 10 Sept. 1841.	T. C. Eaton, 9 Sept. 1841.
A. F. Monroe, 3 March 1841.	W. R. Mercer, 8 Dec. 1841.
N. T. West, 18 Feb. 1841.	D. Phenix, 30 Sept. 1841.
R. C. Duvall, 19 Oct. 1841.	R. F. R. Lewis, 19 Oct. 1841.
D. P. McCorkle, 21 Sept. 1841.	C. P. McGary, "
W. Reily, 9 Feb. 1841.	H. St. G. Hunter, 19 Nov. 1841.
C. F. Hopkins, 19 Oct. 1841.	H. Davidson, 29 Oct. 1841.
G. H. Hare, 10 Oct. 1841.	A. W. Johnson, 10 Oct. 1841.
W. F. Jones, 20 Sept. 1841.	S. B. Luce, 19 Oct. 1841.
H. C. Hunter, 10 Sept. 1841.	G. T. Simes, "
S. J. Bliss, 19 Oct. 1841.	Jefferson Maury, 9 Sept. 1841.
W. W. Holmes, 21 Sept. 1841.	Dulany A. Forrest, 3 March 1841.
W. Sharp, 9 Sept. 1841.	C. Gray, 19 Oct. 1841.
J. I. Waddle, 10 Sept. 1841.	G. Harrison, 27 Oct. 1841.
W. M. Gamble, 1 March, 1841.	R. W. Scott, 9 Sept. 1841.
J. Young, 19 Oct. 1841.	R. R. Carter, 30 March 1842.
T. W. Brodhead, 3 March 1841.	A. McLane, 24 May, 1842.
W. K. Mayo, 18 Oct. 1841.	E. W. Henry, 7 April 1842.
T. Young, 27 Oct. 1841.	J. D. Langhorne, 6 July 1842.
W. O. Crain, "	J. A. Seawell, 2 July, 1842.
A. T. Byrens, 26 Feb. 1841.	

MIDSHIPMEN. (171)

Name, and Date of Entry.

Adams, John, 5 Sept. 1845.
Allen, Oliver P., 28 Sept. 1846.
Abbot, Trevett, 13 Oct. 1848.
Abbott, William A., "
Armstrong, W. McN., 20 Nov. 1848.
*Adams, jr., H. A., 16 Oct. 1849.
*Armstrong, Æneas, 2 Oct. 1850.
*Arnold, Thomas, 11 Nov. 1850.
Breese, J. Lewis, 14 May 1846.
Braine, Daniel L., 30 May 1846.
Brodhead, Edgar, 9 July 1846.
Breese, K. R., 6 Nov. 1846.
Baker, John P., 11 Feb. 1847.
Brosè, Fred. F., 9 Sept. 1847.
Blake, J. D., "
Belknap, G. E., 7 Oct. 1847.
Benham, A. E. K., 24 Nov. 1847.
Bowen, R. T., 24 Dec. 1847.
Bruce, J., 12 Oct. 1848.
Baker, F. H., "
Brintnall, J. P., 21 Dec. 1848.
Brown, G., 5 Feb. 1849.
*Boardman, F. A., 20 Oct. 1849.
*Boyd, jr., R., 14 Jan. 1850.
*Beardslee, L. A., 5 March 1850.
*Babcock, C. A., 8 April 1850.
*Baber, G. F. B., 24 April 1850.
*Bacon, G., 1 Oct. 1850.
*Bradford, W. L., "
*Bowen, R. J., 20 Nov. 1850.
Chandler, R., 27 Sept. 1845.
Carnes, E. O., 24 June, 1846.
Cornwell, J. J., 1 Feb. 1847.
*Cannon, C. C., 7 April, 1847.
Chapman, R. T., "
Cummings, A. B., "

Name, and Date of Entry.

Caldwell, R. M., 9 Sept. 1847.
Chapman, G. H., "
Campbell, W. P. A., 14 Dec. 1847.
Carter, C., 12 Oct. 1848.
Coddington, E. F., "
*Cushman, C. H., 24 March 1849.
*Cheever, W. H., 19 Oct. 1849.
*Campbell, M. C., 4 Feb. 1850.
*Carpenter, C. C., 1 Oct. 1850.
*Carroll, F., 4 Oct. 1850.
*Chaplin, J. C., "
*Cooper, R. F., 25 Oct. 1850.
Dallas, A. J., 24 March 1845.
Davis, A. McF., 16 March 1849.
Dunnington, J. W., 10 April 1849.
*Dozier, W. G., 1 April, 1850.
*Dawson, L. W., 27 April 1850.
*Dana, W. H., 1 May 1850.
*Dodge, G. P. 1 Oct. 1850.
Eggleston, J. R., 2 Aug. 1847.
Erben, jr., H., 17 June 1848.
Foster, J. P., 14 May 1846.
Flusser, C. W., 19 July, 1847.
Fyffe, J. P., 9 Sept. 1847.
Fitzhugh, W. E., 20 Nov. 1848.
*Foster, R. C., 1 Oct. 1850.
Grundy, F., 21 Oct. 1845.
Gray, E. F., 8 April 1846.
Gherardi, B., 29 June 1846.
Gwin, W., 7 April 1847.
Greer, J. A., 10 Jan. 1848.
Glassell, W. T., 15 March 1848.
Greene, C. H., 13 May 1848.
Gillis, J. H., 12 Oct. 1848.
Gayle, R. H., 13 Oct. 1848.
Garland, H. M., 20 Nov. 1848.

* Those Midshipmen whose names are marked with an asterisk [*] have not yet received their warrants.

Name, and Date of Entry.

Houston, T. T., 26 Aug. 1845.
Hamilton, J. R., 8 Sept. 1845.
Harmony, D. B., 7 April, 1847.
Hand, B. E., "
Hand, G. D., 9 Sept. 1847.
Haralson, C. L., 10 Sept. 1847.
Hammond, C. L. O., 8 Nov. 1847.
Heileman, J. G., 10 March 1848.
Hester, I. W., 12 Oct. 1848.
Hodges, J. B., 13 Oct. 1848.
*Hawley, C. E., 3 Dec. 1849.
*Harrison, G. R., 2 Oct. 1850.
Irwin, John, 9 Sept. 1847.
*Izard, A. C., 2 Oct. 1850.
Johnston, O. F., 14 Aug. 1846.
Johnson, jr., P. C., 31 Aug. 1846.
Johnston, J. E., 9 Aug. 1848.
Kennon, B., 22 Aug. 1846.
Kimberly, L. A., 8 Dec. 1846.
*Kirkland, W. A., 2 July 1850.
Law, L. R., 5 Feb. 1838.
Lynch, D. H., 6 Nov. 1846.
Looker, T. H., "
Laughlin, J. J., 1 May 1847.
Lovell, W. S., 8 Nov. 1847.
Livingston, De G., 7 March 1848.
Lagow, J. K., 31 March 1848.
Legaré, J. D., 26 Dec. 1848.
Loyall, B. P., 5 March 1849.
*Little, W. A., 8 April 1850.
McGunnegle, W., 10 Dec. 1845.
Maffitt, W. H., 30 May 1846.
Morris, G. U., 14 Aug. 1846.
Mygatt, J. P. K., 24 Sept. 1847.
Maxwell, J. G., 15 Dec. 1847.
McThorne, H., 18 April 1848.
Means, E. J., 12 Oct. 1848.
McCann, W. P., 1 Nov. 1848.
Mish, S. C., 8 Jan. 1849.
*McCrea, E. P., 16 Oct. 1849.
*May, R. L., 7 Nov. 1847.

Name, and Date of Entry.

*McLanahan, J. W., 2 Oct. 1850.
*Mitchell, J. G., "
*Meade, jr., R. W., "
*McCartney, A. J., 3 Oct. 1850.
*McEntee, 4 Oct. 1850.
*Mathis, G. M., 7 Oct. 1850.
Newman, L. H., 24 Sept. 1847.
Oakley, E. H., 2 Aug. 1847.
Owen, E. K., 7 Dec. 1848.
*Offley, R. H., 19 Oct. 1850.
Parker, jr., J., 14 Nov. 1846.
Palmer, M. E., 23 March, 1848.
Pendergrast, A., 14 Oct. 1848.
Pelot, T. P., 2 June 1849.
*Potter, E. C., 5 Feb. 1850.
*Pearce, W., 1 Oct. 1850.
*Peck, C. F., 3 Oct. 1850.
Quackenbush, J. N., 24 Sep. 1847.
Rainey, J. D., 19 March 1846.
Rowan, jr., J. H., 8 Nov. 1847.
*Roche, J. R. 30 May 1850.
*Ramsay, F. M., 5 Oct. 1850.
*Riley, B. J., 27 Dec. 1850.
Smith, W. H., 16 Oct. 1845.
Sproston, J. G., 15 July 1846.
Smith, C. B., 30 Nov. 1846.
Stillwell, J., 9 Sept. 1847.
Spaulding, R., 12 Oct. 1848.
Skerrett, J. S., "
Sullivan, S. C., "
Spedden, E. T., 20 Nov. 1848.
Shubrick, E. R., 9 Feb. 1849.
Shirk, J. W., 26 March 1849.
*Stockton, E. C., 16 Oct. 1849.
*Shepperd, F. E., "
*Stanton, O. F., 29 Dec. 1849.
*Sparks, C. D., 18 April 1850.
*Stephens, D. H., 1 Oct. 1850.
*Shields, W. B., 2 Oct. 1850.
*Sumner, E. E., "
*Smith, W. H., 3 Oct. 1850.

Name, and Date of Entry.	Name, and Date of Entry.
Thorburn, C. E., 9 Sept. 1847.	Williams, E. P., 9 Sept. 1847.
Totten, W., 9 Nov. 1847.	Wilson, H., 22 Oct. 1847.
Toon, W. H., 21 April 1848.	Weaver, A. W., 10 May 1848.
Taylor, B. B., 3 April 1849.	Walker, J. C., 12 Feb. 1849.
*Thomas, C. F., 16 Oct. 1849.	Ward, W. H., 17 Feb. 1849.
*Taylor, jr., J., 6 Dec. 1849.	*Wishart, A., 2 Oct. 1850.
Watters, J., 12 Feb. 1846.	*Williams, W., 4 Oct. 1850.
Wood, J. T., 7 April 1847.	*Walker, J. G., 5 Oct. 1850.
Ward, W. H., "	

MASTERS. (19)

A. Ford, 28 March 1810.
A. B. Bloodgood, 25 June 1812.
R. Knox, 20 July 1812.
W. Vaughan, 22 Aug. 1812.
F. Mallaby, 22 Sept. 1812.
J. Ferguson, 22 May 1800.
A. Cunningham, 15 Nov. 1815.
J. Robinson, 27 Nov. 1815.
John Quin, 1 Nov. 1816.
N. A. Prentiss, 18 June 1812.
F. W. Moores, 19 May 1827.
H. A. F. Young, 16 May 1829.
M. Clear, 28 Dec. 1839.
C. V. Morris, 1 Jan. 1818.
W. Brady, 7 Sept. 1836.
S. C. Reid, 3 July 1843.
R. C. Jones, 4 March, 1823.
J. Pearson, 7 June, 1844.
J. W. West, 3 Nov. 1818.

SECOND MASTERS. (3)

W. H. Morse, 1 July 1839.
W. H. Burns, 11 May 1842.
E. F. Olmstead, 28 June, 1843.

MASTER'S MATES. (3)

Adam Young, 29 Sept. 1840.
J. T. Power, 1 Nov. 1840.
J. W. W. Dyes, 18 March 1843.

BOATSWAINS. (43)

E. Crocker, 16 June 1828.
John Morris, 28 Oct. 1828.
L. Gallagher, 15 Nov. 1828.
W. Hart, 2 Dec. 1831.
W. Black, 20 March 1835.
W. Waters, 8 Dec. 1835.
Van R. Hall, 15 Nov. 1847.
John Mills, 16 Jan. 1838.
*W. Whitehead, 5 May 1838.
T. G. Bell, 18 June 1838.
W. Smith, 2 Aug. 1838.
C. Johnson, 21 May 1839.
S. Drew, 26 July, 1839.
J. Lewis, 6 Sept. 1839.
J. Munro, 14 Jan. 1850.
E. Cavendy, 8 April 1840.
R. Simpson, 8 Dec. 1840.
G. Wilmuth, 16 Sept. 1841.

Name, and Date of Entry.	Name, and Date of Entry.
John Dunderdale, 5 May 1838.	J. Crosby, 8 Feb. 1848.
John Featherson, 7 Dec. 1841.	W. Whiting, 19 Feb. 1848.
A. Hingerty, 27 Jan. 1842.	*C. Woodland, 27 June 1848.
R. Dixon, 5 Feb. 1842.	Z. Whitmarsh, jr., 3 Feb. 1849.
R. Whitaker, 27 Dec. 1834.	J. Burrows, 4 Dec. 1849.
M. Hall, 18 April 1842.	*W. Burditt, 7 Jan. 1850.
G. Williams, 11 July 1842.	*F. A. Oliver, 28 May 1850.
John Bates, 20 Oct. 1845.	*John Stout, 24 July 1850.
G. Smith, "	*C. Smith, "
A. Colson, 26 March 1842.	*S. Fosdick, 6 Sept. 1850.
J. J. Young, 5 April 1847.	*R. Follins, 15 Nov. 1850.
H. Brooks, 20 May 1847.	*T. S. Buxton, 19 Nov. 2850.
*M. Hall, 11 June 1847.	

GUNNERS. (46)

G. Marshall, 15 July 1809.	S. M. Beckwith, 14 March 1843.
John Blight, 3 May 1821.	A. A. Randall, 29 Aug. 1843.
Asa Curtis, 1 March 1825.	D. Rankin, 19 March 1844.
W. H. Brown, 9 Dec. 1825.	T. M. Crooker, 3 March 1841.
A. S. Lewis, 27 Sept. 1834.	W. Arnold, 21 April 1845.
S. G. City, 19 May 1832.	D. Douglass,26 May 1845.
T. Robinson, 18 Nov. 1835.	*E. Haskell, 13 Sept. 1845.
J. Myrick, 13 June 1836.	J, C. Ritter, 18 Sept. 1845.
G. Newman, 6 Sept. 1836.	C. B. Oliver, 3 May 1843.
A. A. Peterson, 25 Oct. 1836.	*T. P. Venable, 19 March 1847.
D. James, 10 June 1837.	J. M. Ballard, 14 June 1842.
J. M. Cooper, 20 June 1837.	*W. Burniece, 20 Dec. 1847.
W. Burton, 26 July 1837.	J. C. Davis, "
R. F. Dunn, 1 Nov. 1837.	*F. Dawson, 20 March 1848.
J. Clapham, 15 Nov. 1837.	*W. W. Fisher, 16 Nov. 1848.
W. Craig, 20 Jan. 1838.	A. F. Thompson, 3 March 1849.
John Martin, 31 March 1832.	*J. D. Brandt, 7 July 1849.
E. Whiton, 13 April 1838.	E. Mack, 10 Sept. 1849.
B. Bunker, 21 Nov. 1838.	*R. M. Stocking, 22 Dec. 1849.
G. Sirian, 17 June 1841.	*W. H. Hamilton, 15 June 1850.
John Caulk, 2 Sept. 1841.	*E. C. Hine, 3 Aug. 1850.
S. Allen, 3 Dec. 1841.	*J. Hutchinson, 19 Sept. 1850.
John Owins, 7 March 1842.	*H. Robinson, 11 Nov. 1850.

CARPENTERS. (45)

J. Southwick, 21 Dec. 1826.	W. E. Sheffield, 8 April 1820.

Name, and Date of Entry.

F. Sagee, 13 April 1831.
P. Dee, 9 May 1832.
J. Green, 23 Jan. 1833.
J. Cox, 29 May 1834.
W. M. Laighton, 29 Sept. 1836.
H. P. Leslie, 15 Oct. 1833.
J. Rainbow, 10 June 1837.
J. Cahill, 8 July 1837.
F. M. Cecil, 19 Feb. 1838.
C. Jordan, 24 April 1838.
J. Dibble, 16 June 1838.
A. Chick, 14 July 1838.
W. Knight, 17 July 1839.
J. Meads, 27 Jan. 1840.
W. D. Jenkins, 24 March 1840.
J. McDonnell, 21 Oct. 1840.
H. Lindsay, 4 Nov. 1840.
William Lee, 31 May 1841.
J. O. Butler, 18 Sept. 1835.
E. W. Barnicoat, 17 Dec. 1841.
G. Wisner, 30 Dec. 1841.
C. Bordman, 23 Aug. 1833.

Name, and Date of Entry.

L. Manson, 9 May 1842.
H. G. Thomas, 10 Feb. 1844.
M. M. Dodd, 18 June 1845.
J. G. Thomas, 16 March 1847.
H. M. Lowry, 26 March 1847.
*C. W. Babbit, 2 July 1847.
N. Mager, 9 July 1847.
Daniel Jones, 9 Dec. 1847.
A. Poinsett, 11 Dec. 1847.
*D. James, 8 Feb. 1848.
G. W. Elliott, 15 Aug. 1848.
J. Linn, 31 Oct. 1848.
*L. Holmes, 14 Dec. 1848.
W. F. Laighton, 7 April 1849.
*R. M. Bain, 3 July 1849.
E. Thompson, 16 Nov. 1849.
*J. T. Rustic, 8 Nov. 1849.
*T. C. Ferrall, 31 May 1850.
*L. Moses, 6 July 1850.
*R. Leach, 22 Oct. 1850.
*J. Jarvis, 21 Nov. 1850.

SAILMAKERS. (37)

J. R. Childs, 8 June 1822.
W. Ryan, 18 Sept. 1827.
J. G. Gallagher, 27 Nov. 1829.
R. Van Voorhis, 8 Feb. 1834.
M. Weeden, 19 Aug. 1834.
G. Thomas, 19 Dec. 1834.
J. Ferguson, 24 Feb. 1835.
John Joins, 26 Sept. 1837.
B. B. Burchsted, 28 April 1838.
I. D. Freeman, 9 July 1838.
W. Bennett, 23 Aug. 1833.
John Peed, 8 April 1840.
R. C. Rodman, 28 April 1840.
G. T. Lozier, 30 Oct. 1840.
G. Parker, 17 Oct. 1840.
E. Middleton, 15 July 1841.
J. Frazer, 11 Dec. 1841.
G. T. Blackford, 19 Feb. 1838.
J. Stephens, 30 Sept. 1844.
D. Bruce, 25 Oct. 1844.
*R. Hunter, 12 July 1845.
S. Seaman, 22 April 1846.
T. J. Griffin, 13 May 1846.
J. C. Bradford, 21 July 1846.
W. B. Fugitt, 29 Jan. 1848.
J. A. Birdsall, 7 March 1848.
*S. Tatem, 30 March 1848.
L. Rogers, 12 June 1848.
*C. T. Frost, 10 Aug. 1848.
H. W. Frankland, 2 Nov. 1848.
J. J. Stanford, 4 Nov. 1848.
*W. N. Maull, 18 Jan. 1849.
*J. W. North, 3 July 1849.
*T. Tatem, 10 Sept. 1849.

Name, and Date of Entry.

*H. T. Stocker, 1 July 1850.
*W. H. Mahoney, 15 Nov. 1850.

Name, and Date of Entry.

*T. C. Herbert, 15 June 1842.

MARINE CORPS.

Colonel Commandant.

A. Henderson, 4 June 1806.

General Staff.

P. G. Howle, *Adj't and Inspector*, with the rank of Major, 1 March 1815.
G. W. Walker, *Paymaster*, with the rank of Major, 10 June 1817.
A. A. Nicholson, *Quarter Master*, with the rank of Major, 28 Mar. 1820.
G. F. Lindsay, *Assistant Quarter Master*, with the rank of Captain, 1 April 1823.

Lieutenant Colonel.

S. Miller, 1 June 1808.

Majors. (4)

J. Harris, 13 April 1814.
T. A. Linton, 28 Feb. 1813.
J. Edelin, 1 Mar. 1815.
W. Dulany, 10 June 1817.

Captains. (16)

T. S. English, 10 June 1817.
W. Marston, 3 March 1819.
B. Macomber, 28 March 1820.
A. N. Brevoort, "
R. Douglas, 7 May 1822.
J. G. Williams, "
H. B. Tyler, 3 March 1823.
J. L. C. Hardy, "
J. G. Reynolds, 26 May 1824.
F. C. Hall, 5 July 1825.
G. H. Terrett, 1 April 1830.
W. E. Stark, 8 July 1831.
N. S. Waldron, 23 Sept. 1831.
J. Zeilin, 1 Oct. 1831.
D. D. Baker, 20 Oct. 1832.
A. H. Gillespie, "

First Lieutenants. (23)

B. E. Brooke, 8 July 1833.
J. C. Rich, 12 June 1834.
A. Garland, 17 Oct. 1834.
F. B. McNeill, "
E. L. West, "
R. C. Caldwell, "
W. L. Young, 23 Feb. 1835.
J. Watson, 21 July 1835.
H. B. Watson, 5 Oct. 1836.
I. T. Doughty, 26 Sept. 1837.
W. A. T. Maddox, 14 Oct. 1837
W. B. Slack, 28 Jan. 1839.
J. S. Devlin, 21 Feb. 1839.
A. S. Taylor, "
W. L. Shuttleworth, 28 Feb. 183
J. W. Curtis, 4 May 1840.
R. Tansill, 3 Nov. 1840.

* Those Boatswains, Gunners, Carpenters, and Sailmakers, to whose name an * prefixed, have not been warranted, and are only acting.

Name, and Date of Entry.

J. C. Grayson, 4 May 1841.
M. R. Kintzing, 8 Sept. 1841.
J. D. Simms, 7 Oct. 1841.
H. W. Queen, 14 March 1842.
D. J. Sutherland, 29 March 1842.
W. W. Russell, *Aide-de-Camp* to the Bv't Brig. Gen. Comd't, 5 April 1843.

Second Lieutenants. (21)

John C. Cash, 14 March 1845.
G. Adams, 19 March 1845.
James H. Jones, 3 March 1847.
E. McD. Reynolds, "
W. Butterfield, "

Name, and Date of Entry.

T. Y. Field, 3 March 1847.
C. G. McCawley, "
I. Green, "
F. Norvell, "
J. Read, "
C. A. Henderson, 16 March 1847.
A. S. Nicholson, "
G. F. Lindsay, jr., "
James Wiley, 9 June 1847.
G. R. Graham, 27 July 1847.
J. R. F. Tattnall, 3 Nov. 1847.
A. J. Hays, 4 Dec. 1847.
J. L. Broome, 12 Jan. 1848.
W. S. Boyd, "
J. H. Strickland, 22 March 1848.
George Holmes, 3 March 1849.

* NAVY AGENTS. (14)

C. W. Cutter, Portsmouth, N. H.
I. H. Wright, Boston.
W. H. Le Roy, New York.
W. Sloanaker, Philadelphia.
W. Hindman, Baltimore.
J. H. Lathrop, Washington, D. C.
F. Mallory, Norfolk, Va.
B. D. Heriot, Charleston, S. C.
B. D. Wright, Pensacola, Fa.
E. O. Perrin, Memphis, Tenn.
J. Wilson, San Francisco, Cal.

Temporary.

Baring, Brothers & Co., London.
E. McCall & Co., Lima, Peru.

NAVAL STOREKEEPERS.

J. Rice, Portsmouth, N. H.
N. W. Coffin, Boston.
H. Fuller, New York.
A. Diller, Philadelphia.
T. Woodward, Washington, D. C.
J. G. Hatton, Norfolk, Va.
R. Joyner, Pensacola, Fa.
J. C. Allen, Memphis, Tenn.
B. S. Hines, San Francisco, Cal.
R. P. Desilver, Macao, E. I.
W. L. Long, Spezzia, Sardinia.

* Navy Agents receive *one per cent.* on their expenditures, and not to exceed two thousand dollars per annum.

SHIPS OF THE LINE.

Name.	Rate.	Name.	Rate.	Name.	Rate.
Pennsylvania,	120	Delaware,	74	New Orleans,	74
Franklin,	74	Alabama,	74		
Columbus,	74	Vermont,	74	Independence,	54
Ohio,	74	Virginia,	74	(Razee.)	
North Carolina,	74	New York,	74		

FRIGATES, 1*st Class.*

United States,	44	Columbia,	44	Raritan,	44
Constitution,	44	Congress,	44	Santee,	44
Potomac,	44	Cumberland,	44	Sabine,	44
Brandywine,	44	Savannah,	44	St. Lawrence,	44

FRIGATES, 2*d Class.*

Constellation,	36	Macedonian,	36

SLOOPS OF WAR.

Saratoga,	20	St. Louis,	20	Albany,	20
John Adams,	20	Cyane,	20	Germantown,	20
Vincennes,	20	Levant,	20	Ontario,	18
Warren,	20	Portsmouth,	20	Decatur,	16
Falmouth,	20	Plymouth,	20	Preble,	16
Fairfield,	20	St. Mary's,	20	Marion,	16
Vandalia,	20	Jamestown,	20	Dale,	16

BRIGS.

Dolphin,	10	Porpoise,	10	Bainbridge,	10
Perry,	10				

SCHOONERS.

Wave,	1	Phenix,	2	Petrel,	1

STEAMERS.

Steam Frigates.

Mississippi,	10	Susquehanna,	9	Powhatan,	9
San Jacinto,	6	Saranac,	6		

Name.	Rate.	Name.	Rate.	Name.	Rate.
		1st Class.			
Fulton,		Michigan,	1	Alleghany,	2
		Less than 1st Class.			
Union,		Water Witch,	2	General Taylor,	
Vixen,	3	Massachusetts,		Engineer,	
		John Hancock.			
		STORE SHIPS AND BRIGS.			
Relief,	6	Southampton,	4	Fredonia,	4
Lexington,	6	Supply,	4		

AN ACT

To Regulate the Pay of the Navy of the United States.

SEC. 1. *Be it enacted by the Senate and House of Representatives of the United States of America in Congress assembled*, That from and after the passage of this act the annual pay of the officers of the Navy of the United States shall be as follows:

TO SENIOR CAPTAINS.

At all times when in service, four thousand five hundred dollars.

When on leave of absence, or waiting orders, three thousand five hundred dollars.

ALL OTHER CAPTAINS.

When in command of stations or foreign squadrons, four thousand dollars.

When on other duty, three thousand five hundred dollars.

When off duty, two thousand five hundred dollars.

COMMANDERS, OR MASTERS COMMANDANT.

When attached to vessels for sea service, two thousand five hundred dollars.

When attached to navy yards, or on other duty, two thousand one hundred dollars.

When on leave of absence, or waiting orders, one thousand eight hundred dollars.

LIEUTENANTS.

Commanding, one thousand eight hundred dollars.

On other duty, one thousand five hundred dollars.

Waiting orders, one thousand two hundred dollars.

ASSISTANT SURGEONS.

Waiting orders, six hundred and fifty dollars.

At sea, nine hundred and fifty dollars.

After passing and found qualified for promotion to surgeon, eight hundred and fifty dollars.

At sea, one thousand two hundred dollars.

When stationed at navy yards, hospitals, rendezvous, and receiving ships, nine hundred and fifty dollars.

After being passed and stationed as above, one thousand one hundred and fifty dollars.

SURGEONS.

For the first five years after the date of his commission, one thousand dollars.

For the second five years, one thousand two hundred dollars.

For the third five years, one thousand four hundred dollars.

For the fourth five years, one thousand six hundred dollars.

After he shall have been commissioned as a surgeon twenty years and upwards, one thousand eight hundred dollars.

All surgeons of the navy under orders for duty, at navy yards, receiving vessels, rendezvous, or naval hospitals, shall have an increase of one fourth of the foregoing amount of their respective annual pay, from the date of their acceptance of such orders.

All surgeons of the navy ordered to any of the ships or vessels of the United States commissioned for sea service, shall have an increase of one third of the foregoing amount of their respective annual pay, from the date of their acceptance of such orders.

All surgeons of the navy, ordered as fleet surgeons, shall have an increase of one half of their respective annual pay, from the date of their acceptance of such orders.

CHAPLAINS.

When attached to vessels for sea service, or at navy yards, one thousand two hundred dollars.

When on leave of absence, or waiting orders, eight hundred dollars.

PROFESSORS OF MATHEMATICS.

When attached to vessels for sea service, or in a yard, one thousand two hundred dollars.

SECRETARIES.

To commanders of squadrons, when commanding in chief, one thousand dollars.

To commanders of squadrons, when not commanding in chief, nine hundred dollars.

SAILING MASTERS.

Of a ship of the line, for sea service, one thousand one hundred dollars.

When on other duty, one thousand dollars.

When on leave of absence, or waiting orders, seven hundred and fifty dollars.

SECOND MASTERS.

When attached to vessels for sea service, seven hundred and fifty dollars.

When on other duty, five hundred dollars.

When on leave of absence, or waiting orders, four hundred dollars.

PASSED MIDSHIPMEN.

On duty, seven hundred and fifty dollars.

Waiting orders, six hundred dollars.

WARRANTED MASTER'S MATES.

When attached to vessels for sea service, or at navy yards, four hundred and fifty dollars.

When on leave of absence, or waiting orders, three hundred dollars.

MIDSHIPMEN.

When attached to vessels for sea service, four hundred dollars.

When on other duty, three hundred and fifty dollars.

When on leave of absence, or waiting orders, three hundred dollars.

CLERKS.

Of a yard, nine hundred dollars.

First clerk to a commandant of a navy yard, nine hundred dollars.

Second clerk to a commandant of a navy yard, seven hundred and fifty dollars.

To commanders of squadrons, captains of fleets, and commanders of vessels, five hundred dollars.

FINIS.

www.ingramcontent.com/pod-product-compliance
Lightning Source LLC
LaVergne TN
LVHW011158110826
845150LV00006B/1250

* 9 7 8 1 4 2 5 5 4 5 7 2 7 *